THE

MARCUS GARVEY

AND

UNIVERSAL NEGRO
IMPROVEMENT ASSOCIATION

PAPERS

SUPPORTED BY
The National Endowment for the Humanities
The National Historical Publications and Records Commission
The Ford Foundation
The Rockefeller Foundation
The New York African American Institute

SPONSORED BY
The University of California, Los Angeles

EDITORIAL ADVISORY BOARD

MARCUS GARVEY

LIFE AND LESSONS

A Centennial Companion to
THE MARCUS GARVEY AND
UNIVERSAL NEGRO IMPROVEMENT
ASSOCIATION PAPERS

ROBERT A. HILL, *Editor*
BARBARA BAIR, *Associate Editor*

UNIVERSITY OF CALIFORNIA PRESS
Berkeley   Los Angeles   London

University of California Press
Berkeley and Los Angeles, California

University of California Press, Ltd.
London, England

This volume has been funded in part by the National Endowment
for the Humanities, an independent federal agency. The volume has
also been supported by the National Historical Publications and
Records Commission, the Ford Foundation, the Rockefeller Foundation, the New York African American Institute, and the University of California, Los Angeles.

Designed by Linda M. Robertson and set in Galliard type.
This volume has been typeset by Stephen Gil de Montes of the
Garvey Papers project using the TYXSET software system (ver-
sion 2.1) supplied by TYX Corp., Reston, Virginia.

Library of Congress Cataloging in Publication Data

Main entry under title:

Marcus Garvey: Life and Lessons, a centennial companion to the
    Marcus Garvey and Universal Negro Improvement Association
    papers.

    1. Garvey, Marcus, 1887–1940. 2. Universal Negro Improvement
Association—History—Sources. 3. Black power—
United States— History—Sources. 4. Afro-Americans—Race
identity—History— Sources. 5. Afro-Americans—Civil rights—
History—Sources.   I. Hill, Robert A., 1943–   .
II. Bair, Barbara, 1955–   . III. Garvey, Marcus, 1887–1940.
IV. Universal Negro Improvement Association.

E185-97.G3M36   1987   305.8 96073   82-13379
ISBN 0–520–06214–0

Printed in the United States of America

1 2 3 4 5 6 7 8 9

To

James Kubeck and Fred Shelley

in appreciation

I am a public lecturer, but I am President-General of the Universal Negro Improvement Association. As a public lecturer I endeavour to help to educate the public, particularly of the race, as I meet that public . . . if the public is thoughtful it will be benefited by the things I say. I do not speak carelessly or recklessly but with a definite object of helping the people, especially those of my race, to know, to understand, to realise themselves.

MARCUS GARVEY
Halifax, Nova Scotia
Fall 1937

CONTENTS

INTRODUCTION

What's in a name—to be precise, in the name Marcus Garvey? A century after his birth, what should we know about him and the extraordinary movement that bears his name?

The name Garvey has come to define both a discrete social phenomenon, organized under the banner of the Universal Negro Improvement Association (UNIA) and African Communities League (ACL), and an era of black renaissance, in which Garveyism and the concept of black racial pride became synonymous. Before white America fell enraptured before the spell of what Claude McKay termed "the hot syncopated fascination of Harlem" in the Jazz Age, black America had already traversed the age of Garvey and the New Negro.[1] Garveyism as an ideological movement began in black Harlem's thirty or so square blocks in the spring of 1918, and then burgeoned throughout the black world— nearly a thousand UNIA divisions were formed, and tens of thousands of members enrolled within the brief span of seven years. The reign of the Garvey movement, as Rev. Adam Clayton Powell, Sr., wrote, "awakened a race consciousness that made Harlem felt around the world."[2]

POPULAR HERO

Borne along on the tide of black popular culture, Garvey's memory has attained the status of a folk myth. While the

1. Claude McKay, *A Long Way from Home* (1937; reprint New York: Lee Furman, 1970), p. 150.

2. Adam Clayton Powell, Sr., *Against the Tide: An Autobiography* (New York: Richard R. Smith, 1938), p. 71.

1987 centennial of Garvey's birth will be marked by formal ceremonies honoring his memory, on a more dynamic plane, Garvey is daily celebrated and re-created as a hero through the storytelling faculty of the black oral tradition.

As the embodiment of that oral tradition transmuted into musical performance, Jamaica's reggae music exhibits an amazing fixation with the memory of Garvey. Re-evoking spiritual exile and the historic experience of black dispossession, the music presents a Garvey who *speaks* from the past directly to the present:

> Marcus say, Marcus say, red for the blood
>   that flowed like a river
> Marcus say, Marcus say, green for the land,
>   Africa
> Marcus say, Marcus say, yellow for the gold
>   that they stole
> Marcus say, Marcus say, black for the people
>   they looted from . . .

> —"Rally Round," Steel Pulse

In extending the legend of Garvey, the downtrodden have succeeded in rescuing his image from years of official neglect. In addition to carrying out this process of vindication, the music has succeeded in merging his name into an anthem of dispossession:

> Marcus Garvey words come to pass
> Marcus Garvey words come to pass
> Can' get no food to eat
> Can' get no money to spend

> —"Marcus Garvey," Burning Spear

In the transfiguration of Garvey in popular memory, historical time has been replaced with mythical timelessness. "Garvey soul yet young / Older than Garvey / Younger than Garvey," lyrically muses Burning Spear, the Jamaican reggae songwriter and performer, venerating the ongoing importance of Garvey.

In the course of this musical apotheosis, the mythic Garvey becomes the black race's prophet, as we hear in the exhortation calling people to account:

> Marcus Garvey prophesy say, Oh yeah
> Man a' go find him back against the wall, yeah
> It a' go bitter . . .
> 'Dis 'yah a' prophecy,
> Hold 'dem, Marcus.
>
> —"Right Time," Mighty Diamonds

If there is a moral in the music, it is that the memory of Garvey is a vital force—daily oral-musical performance has transformed the historic Garvey into a symbolic image that lives on in the popular imagination. Like the sacred African trickster-hero, who interprets the hidden to humans, the name Garvey serves to remind:

> I'll never forget, no way
> They sold Marcus Garvey for rice . . .
> So don't you forget, no way
> Who you are and where you stand
> in the struggle
>
> —"So Much Things to Say,"
> Bob Marley

These lyrics are testimony to that fact that in the struggle for the ultimate regeneration of Africa, Garvey has continued to inspire succeeding generations. "While Mr. Garvey might not live to see his dream come true," prophesied one of his followers in 1924, "what he has said from the platform of Liberty Hall will be repeated in the years to come by unborn generations, and some day in the dark remote corners of

Africa the Red, the Black and the Green will float."[3] This statement, with its figurative depiction of the liberation of Africa and the international influence of Garveyism in the struggle for its attainment, has proved to be an accurate prognosis of political transformation in Africa. "The question may start in America," Garvey had promised, speaking in Washington, D.C., "but [it] will not end there."[4]

THE MAN AND THE MOVEMENT

While Garvey's name has achieved legendary proportions, and his movement has had an ongoing international impact, Garvey as a mortal being was a man who embodied the contradictions of his age. He was seen by his own contemporaries in a plethora of ways, both positive and negative. "A little sawed-off and hammered down Black Man, with *determination* written all over his face, and an engaging smile that caught you and compelled you to listen to his story" was how the veteran black journalist John E. Bruce ("Bruce Grit") recalled his initial encounter with the young Jamaican in the spring of 1916. Encouraged by Booker T. Washington, Garvey had come to America hoping to gather support for a proposed school, to be built in Jamaica, patterned on the model of the famed Tuskegee Institute. By the time Garvey could get to the United States, however, Washington was dead. Garvey started with a nucleus of thirteen in a dingy Harlem lodge room. Within a few short years, he was catapulted to the front rank of black leadership, at the head of a social movement unprecedented in black history for its sheer size and scope. Writing in 1927, six months before Garvey was to be deported from America, Kelly Miller, the Afro-American educator and author, reflected upon the phenomenon:

> Marcus Garvey came to the U.S. less than ten years ago, unheralded, unfriended, without acquaintance, relation-

3. *Negro World* (hereafter *NW*), 23 November 1924.
4. *NW,* 26 January 1924.

ship, or means of livelihood. This Jamaican immigrant was thirty years old, partially educated, and 100 per cent black. He possessed neither comeliness of appearance nor attractive physical personality. Judged by external appraisement, there was nothing to distinguish him from thousands of West Indian blacks who flock to our seaport cities. And yet this ungainly youth by sheer indomitability of will projected a propaganda and commanded a following, within the brief space of a decade, which made the whole nation mark him and write his speeches in their books. [5]

– In the world of the twenties, personalities quickly became notable and were fastened upon by admirers, detractors, and the merely curious. But even by the standards of the day, Garvey's rise from obscurity was spectacular. Speaking to an audience at Colón, Panama, in 1921, Garvey himself noted that "two years ago in New York nobody paid any attention to us. When I used to speak, even the policeman on the beat never noticed me." [6]

Garvey voiced the marvelous nature of his own rise when he asked an audience in 1921 "how comes this New Negro? How comes this stunned awakening?" [7] The ground had been prepared for him by such outspoken voices as those of Hubert H. Harrison, A. Philip Randolph, Chandler Owen, and W. A. Domingo. These and other stepladder orators—who began speaking along Lenox Avenue with the arrival of warm weather in 1916 and whose number rapidly grew with each succeeding summer—were the persons who, along with Garvey, converted the black community of Harlem into a parliament of the people during the years of the Great War and after. The World War I era was the time of the

5. Kelly Miller, "After Marcus Garvey—What?" *Contemporary Review* 131 (April 1927):492.

6. *NW,* 30 July 1921.

7. *NW,* 18 June 1921.

rise of "the ebony sages," as William H. Ferris termed the New Negro intelligentsia, who laid the foundation in those years for what would eventually come to be known as the Harlem Renaissance. Garveyism was fed in an environment where "in barber shops and basements, tea shops and railroad flats," Ferris revealed, "art and education, literature and the race question were discussed with an abandon that was truly Bohemian."[8] By the middle of the decade, Ferris would go so far as to claim that "The New Negro is Garvey's own Child, whose mother is the UNIA."[9]

When the UNIA was organized in Harlem in February 1918, its Jamaican leader merged not only with representatives of the New Negro, but with another minority: from the perspective of America's polyglot of ethnic groups, Garvey was simply one more immigrant voice. The Garvey phenomenon began amidst the multiple migrations of America, and it was not unusual to find Garvey issuing pronouncements of confraternity with the causes of various immigrant groups.[10] "Just at that time," recalled Garvey, speaking in Liberty Hall in early 1920 about his start as a street orator in Harlem, "other races were engaged in seeing their cause through—the Jews through their Zionist movement and the Irish through their Irish movement—and I decided that, cost what it might, I would make this a favorable time to see the Negro's interest through."[11]

A notable feature of Garveyism as a political phenomenon was the staunch manner in which it accentuated the identity of interests among blacks all over the world. For Hodge Kirnon, this quality of internationalism essentially defined the New Negro mood. He observed:

> The Old Negro press was nationalistic to the extreme, even at times manifesting antipathy and scorn for foreign

---

8. William H. Ferris, "The Negro Intellectual," *NW*, 10 June 1922.

9. *Spokesman* 1, no. 4 (March 1925): 4.

10. *New York Globe and Advertiser*, 3 August 1920.

11. *NW*, 6 March 1920.

born Negroes. One widely circulated paper went as far as to cast sarcasm and slur upon the dress, dialect, etc., of the West Indian Negro, and even advised their migration and deportation back to their native lands— a people who are in every way law abiding, thrifty and industrious. The new publications have eliminated all of this narrow national sentimental stupidity. They have advanced above this. They have recognized the oneness of interests and the kindredship between all Negro peoples the world over.[12]

A special feature by Michael Gold in the 22 August 1920 Sunday supplement of the *New York World* reported upon Garvey's meteoric ascent, and registered as well his immigrant status and the international nature of his message. The headlines accompanying the story made the following announcement:

The Moses of the Negro Race Has Come to New York
and Heads a Universal Organization
Already Numbering 2,000,000
Which is About to Elect a High Potentate
and Dreams of Reviving the Glories of Ancient Ethiopia

Gold captured a defining characteristic of the Garvey phenomenon, namely, its rapid spread throughout the world, including sub-Saharan and southern Africa. Writing from Johannesburg, South Africa, a number of years later, Enock Mazilinko echoed the messianic vision of Garvey held by many in America when he wrote that "after all is said and done, Africans have the same confidence in Marcus Garvey which the Israelites had in Moses."[13] "Marcus Garvey is now admitted as a great African leader" concurred James Stehazu, a Cape Town Garveyite; indeed, Garvey was the embodiment

---

12. Hodge Kirnon, "The New Negro and His Will to Manhood and Achievement," *Promoter,* 1 (August 1920): 7.

13. *NW,* 9 February 1929.

for tens of thousands of black South Africans in the postwar years of the myth of an Afro-American liberator.[14] "Already his name is legend, from Harlem to Zanzibar," allowed the venerable *Guardian* of Boston when it appraised the significance of his life in 1940.[15]

But not everyone shared this concept of Garvey. Detractors labeled him a madman or the greatest confidence man of the age. "We may seriously ask, is not Marcus Garvey a paranoiac?" enquired the NAACP's Robert Bagnall in his 1923 article "The Madness of Marcus Garvey."[16] An earlier psychological assessment by W. E. B. Du Bois diagnosed Garvey as suffering from "very serious defects of temperament and training," and described him as "dictatorial, domineering, inordinately vain and very suspicious."[17] In the view of the organ of South Africa's African Political Organization, "the newly-created position of Provisional President of Africa [was] an empty honour which no man in the history of the world has ever held, and no sane man is likely to aspire after."[18]

➤ It was mainly as an embarrassment to his race, however, that Garvey was dismissed. "The Garvey Movement," reported Kelly Miller in 1927, "seemed to be absurd, grotesque, and bizarre."[19] "If Gilbert and Sullivan were still collaborating," commented one African editorial writer, "what a splendid theme for a musical comic opera Garvey's pipe-dream would be."[20] W. E. B. Du Bois echoed this

14. *NW,* 16 July 1932.

15. *Boston Guardian,* 18 May 1940.

16. Robert Bagnall, "The Madness of Marcus Garvey," *Messenger* 5 (March 1923): 638.

17. W. E. B. Du Bois, "Marcus Garvey," *Crisis* 11 (December 1920): 58–60.

18. *NW,* 28 January 1922 (The African Political Organization was later renamed the African People's Organization).

19. Kelly Miller, "After Marcus Garvey—What?" *Spokesman,* May 1927, p. 11.

20. *Nigerian Pioneer,* 17 December 1920.

opinion when he described UNIA pageantry as like a "dress-rehearsal of a new comic opera."[21] A West Indian resident in Panama, writing in the April 1920 issue of the *Crusader,* offered an ironic commentary on what he took to have been Garvey's assumption of the grand title of African potentate: "Pardon me," the gentleman interposed, "but this sounds like the story of 'The Count of Monte Cristo' or the 'dream of Labaudy,' or worse still, 'Carnival,' as obtains in the city of Panama, where annually they elect 'Her Gracious Majesty, Queen of the Carnival,' and other high officials."[22] White commentators were not excluded from this game of describing Garvey's conduct through the metaphor of entertainment. Borrowing from Eugene O'Neill's surrealistic play about the dramatic downfall of a self-styled black leader, Robert Morse Lovett referred to Garvey as "an Emperor Jones of Finance" to convey Garvey's financial ineptitude to highbrow readers of the *New Republic.*[23]

The wide variety of contemporary opinion about Garvey serves as a backdrop for his own eclectic descriptions of himself. He once announced that: "My garb is Scotch, my name is Irish, my blood is African, and my training is half American and half English, and I think that with that tradition I can take care of myself."[24] While Garvey told his audiences that his mind was "a complete machine," one "that thinks absolutely in the original," and, on another occasion, that his mind was "purely Negro," he also lamented that "the average Negro doesn't know much about the thought of the serious white man."[25] His own ideology encompassed these two contradictory conceptions. For him, the thought

21. W. E. B. Du Bois, "Back to Africa," *Century Magazine* 105, no. 4 (February 1923): 539.

22. Letter to the Editor, *Crusader,* April 1920, p. 28.

23. Robert Morse Lovett, "An Emperor Jones of Finance," *New Republic,* 11 July 1923.

24. *Daily Gleaner,* 19 January 1935.

25. *Black Man* (London) (hereafter *BM*) 3 (November 1938): 13; 4 (February 1939): 12; 3 (March 1938): 3.

of the New Negro had to be a new thought, for it was incumbent upon the race to develop intellectual (as well as economic and political) independence as a precondition of survival in a world ruled by Darwinian ideas of the survival of the fittest. Nevertheless, the New Negro had to build this original thought on a strong foundation in the mainstream intellectual tradition, borrowing from that tradition while creating new racial imperatives. The present collection is a testimony to the diverse origins of Garvey's thought and to the ways in which he consciously embraced many of the dominant intellectual traditions of his age, reshaping them to the cause of pan-African regeneration.

THE ERA

Garvey's career spanned the years of the climax of the Victorian era of empire and its denouement in the period of revolution and counterrevolution. Born in 1887, just after Queen Victoria's Golden Jubilee, Garvey grew up as a black colonial during the Edwardian era. He arrived at political maturity in the era of the nationalist revolution in Ireland and the October Revolution in Russia. He died on 10 June 1940, the day that Fascist Italy declared war on the Allies and a month after Nazi Germany invaded France. He had predicted in 1937 that "the Negro's chance will come when the smoke from the fire and ashes of twentieth-century civilization has blown off."[26] His thought was of a piece with the dominant ideas of his tumultuous age, while at the same time offering a new response for blacks to the paradigm of white supremacy.

LIFE AND LESSONS

The present volume, *Marcus Garvey: Life and Lessons,* is a compendium of Garvey's eclectic philosophy. It is arranged in six sections. The first section, entitled "African Fundamentalism," contains the 1925 creed by that name—

26. *BM* 2 (December 1937): 3.

Garvey's attempt at a modern race catechism. The second section contains his abstract vision of the ideal state. Garvey's little-known serialized autobiography supplies the third section, and the fourth features Garvey's epic poem, *The Tragedy of White Injustice*. A series of dramatic dialogues from the *Black Man* makes up the fifth section. The sixth, and final, section consists of the lessons in leadership from Garvey's School of African Philosophy. The whole—garnered from materials created in the last fifteen years of Garvey's life—constitutes vintage Garvey and makes possible an enriched understanding of the popular allegiance that his ideas inspired.

THE DOCTRINE OF SUCCESS

Garvey's strong belief in the success ethic, a theme that forms a constant thread throughout his speeches and writings, is reflective of the popular culture of his times. Speaking in Halifax, Nova Scotia, in 1937, Garvey summed up for his audience the principle that he claimed life had taught him. "At my age I have learnt no better lesson than that which I am going to impart to you to make a man what he ought to be—a success in life. There are two classes of men in the world, those who succeed and those who do not succeed."[27] Rejecting the class analysis being embraced by some of his black contemporaries, Garvey regularly illustrated his speeches with rags-to-riches stories, and offered examples from the fields of business and industry to his followers as models to emulate. In 1927 Joseph Lloyd, a Garveyite in Cuba, won a UNIA-sponsored "Why I am a Garveyite" contest with an essay on Garvey-inspired aspirations to become a black captain of industry or political leader. Garvey "has taught me," Lloyd wrote in the 6 January 1927 issue of the *Negro World*, "that I can be a Rockefeller, a Carnegie, a Henry Ford, a Lloyd George, or a Calvin Coolidge." Garvey himself had earlier asked readers of the *Negro World* in a 6 November 1926 editorial, "Why should not Africa give to the world its

27. *BM* 3 (March 1938): 8.

black Rockefeller, Carnegie, Schwab, and Henry Ford?" In the following year he spelled out the connection between such economic achievement and political power, informing his audience that

> there is no force like success, and that is why the individual makes all efforts to surround himself throughout life with the evidence of it. As of the individual, so should it be of the race and nation. The glittering success of Rockefeller makes him a power in the American nation; the success of Henry Ford suggests him as an object of universal respect, but no one knows and cares about the bum or hobo who is Rockefeller's or Ford's neighbor. So, also, is the world attracted by the glittering success of races and nations, and pays absolutely no attention to the bum or hobo race that lingers by the wayside. [28]

~ Garvey's gospel of success was distinguished from more traditional versions of the doctrine because he merged personal success with racial uplift and established a link between these twin ideals and an overarching vision of African regeneration. In Garvey's perspective, success of the individual should serve the ends of race, and vice versa. "There are people who would not think of their success," Garvey insisted, "but for the inspiration they receive from the UNIA."[29] Speaking in New York in 1924, Garvey claimed to have "already demonstrated our worth in helping others to climb the ladder of success."[30] Reciprocally, the UNIA relied for its own success on the organized support of individuals. "Help a Real Race Movement: The Way to Success Is Through Our Own Efforts" was the entreaty printed on the UNIA's contribution card in the early 1920s.

28. *NW,* 29 January 1927.

29. *BM* 3 (July 1938): 8.

30. *NW,* 14 June 1924.

Garvey offered a doctrine of collective self-help and racial independence through competitive economic development. "As a race we want the higher success that is within humanity's grasp," Garvey was quoted in the 21 February 1931 "Garvey's Weekly Digest" column of the *Negro World:* "We must therefore reach out and get it. Don't expect others to pave the way for us towards it with a pathway of roses, go at what we want with a will and then we will be able to successfully out-do our rivals, because we will be expecting none to help us." Garvey also told his followers that the achievement of a higher class status among black people was the most direct route to obtaining opportunities and individual rights. "Be not deceived," he wrote, in the spirit of Andrew Carnegie, "wealth is strength, wealth is power, wealth is influence, wealth is justice, is liberty, is real human rights."[31]

This imperative of success was tied to what a 21 March 1922 *Negro World* article termed "a universal business consciousness" among blacks in all parts of the world. By featuring the slogan "Africa, the Land of Opportunity," emblazoned on a banner draped across a picture of the African continent, the official stationery of Garvey's Black Star Line graphically illustrated this philosophy of racial vindication and uplift through capital investment and development.

SELF-MADE MAN

Garvey himself was frequently cited in the pages of the *Negro World* as a prime example of a self-made man, one of those "who worked their way to the top of the ladder by the long, steady climb."[32] Garvey's interest in conduct-of-life literature and the persistent echoes of it heard in his speeches and writings reflect the impact that such classic success treatises as Booker T. Washington's *Up from Slavery* and Andrew Carnegie's *Gospel of Wealth* made upon

31. *BM* 1 (July 1935): 5.

32. *NW,* 23 August 1924.

him. These works were in turn part of an older genre dating back to Emersonian treatises on self-reliance, slave narratives of personal endurance and triumph such as Frederick Douglass's *My Bondage and My Freedom,* and Benjamin Franklin's colonial guide to practical behavior and economic success. Garvey's racial ideal was built upon the concept of success, and he saw himself as a black version of the Horatio Alger myth.

New Thought

Garvey's pragmatic philosophy, with its emphasis on self-mastery, determination, and willpower, also contained elements of New Thought, which emerged during the Gilded Age out of the allied branches of the mental healing phenomenon. With its emphasis on mind mastery, New Thought offered a set of metaphysical theories that proffered to its millions of adherents a system of mental hygiene to equip them for the journey along the road to success. In 1920 Hodge Kirnon commented on the pervasiveness of ideas from the teachings of Christian Science and the New Thought movements in the black community. "The Negro has been seized by this spirit," Kirnon declared, "he has taken a real change of attitude and conduct. So great has been the change," he continued, "that he has designated himself under the name of The New Negro."[33] Another member of the New Negro phalanx, William Bridges, also alluded to the subsistence of a link between the "spirit of radicalism and new thought."[34] Garvey was assessed by one of his closest colleagues in the leadership of the UNIA, Robert L. Poston, as "the man who is truly the apostle of new thought among Negroes."[35] Indeed, what was deemed a new racial philosophy was in fact Garvey's wholesale application of the dynamics of

33. "The New Negro and His Will to Manhood and Achievement," *Promoter* 1 (August 1920): 4.

34. *Challenge* 2, no. 5 (1919): 140.

35. *NW,* 8 September 1923.

New Thought to the black condition. "I have come to you in Jamaica," Garvey announced on his tour of the Caribbean in spring 1921, "to give new thoughts to the eight hundred thousand black people in this land."[36] Speaking before the UNIA's fourth international convention, he declared: "The Universal Negro Improvement Association is advancing a new theory and a new thought . . .;" and in 1937 he stated that "to rise out of this racial chaos new thought must be injected into the race and it is this thought that the Universal Negro Improvement Association has been promulgating for more than twenty years."[37]

Metaphysics and politics were explicitly linked in Garvey's mind. Turning to New Thought to explain the "African vision of nationalism and imperialism," Garvey advised that "the African at home must gather a new thought. He must not only be satisfied to be a worker but he must primarily be a figure."[38] This New Thought philosophy permeated many UNIA functions and was a strong influence in the literature surrounding the movement. In 1930 the Black Cross Nurses of the Garvey Club of New York City held a medical demonstration at the facilities of the New York branch of the Field of New Thought on 94th Street.[39] The *Negro World* regularly advertised books that showed New Thought influences, including I. E. Guinn's *Twelve of the Leading Outlines of New Thought*.[40] Alonzo Potter Holly's popular book on blacks in sacred history, *God and the Negro*, was, according to Holly, inspired by Ella Wheeler Wilcox. Wilcox, whom Holly described as "an impassioned apostle of 'the New Thought,'" was in turn one of Garvey's favorite poets.[41]

36. *Daily Gleaner,* 4 April 1921.

37. *NW,* 9 August 1924; *BM* 2 (August 1937): 3.

38. *BM* 3 (July 1938): 5.

39. *NW,* 4 October 1930.

40. *NW,* 27 September 1930.

41. Alonzo Potter Holly, *God and the Negro* (Nashville: National Baptist Publishing Board, 1937), p. 14.

BOOSTERISM

Besides its affinity with the gospel of success and the New Thought movement, Garveyism shared the strong emphasis on boosterism that pervaded the popular culture of the Progressive period. On 28 April 1921 Garvey informed an audience in Colón, Panama, that he admired "the white man's spirit for he boosts for race and nation."[42] A few months earlier he had written that "no sensible person objects to any man boasting, booming, and advertising the work or cause that he represents. The old adage still applies: 'He who in this world would rise/ Must fill his bills and advertise.'"[43] One of the *Negro World's* own advertisements read "If it is Success You Need in Business, Advertise in the Negro World"[44] and advertisements heralding various pathways to success and self-promotion regularly appeared in its pages under such titles as "Develop Your Power of Achievement," "How to Get Rich," "Key to Progress, Success, and How Attained," "Knowledge is Power: Make Your Life Yield its Greatest Good," and "Read This Book for Wealth and Health."

VICTORIAN SENSIBILITY

While Garvey's speeches and writings display the influence of popular success ideologies and a racial interpretation of international politics, they also reflect an adherence to a Victorian historical sensibility and literary taste. An admirer of the great and forceful men of history—statesmen, emperors, and conquerors (e.g., Alexander, Charlemagne, Hannibal, Napoleon, Genghis Khan)—Garvey called blacks to rise to a similar vision of political patriarchy and racial leadership. Likewise, while urging his readers and audiences to know and respect the works of black writers and artists, he consistently held up to blacks the work of minor

42. National Archives, RG 165, file 10218-418-18.

43. *NW,* 5 February 1921.

44. *NW,* 7 February 1925.

and major white authors—Elbert Hubbard, William Ernest Henley, Robert Browning, Cervantes, Shakespeare—for inspiration and reference. By doing so, he upheld the tradition of schooling in "great works" common to the artisan class in the Victorian era. Indeed, Garvey's motto for the UNIA was quite likely a paraphrase of a line found in the poem of Alfred, Lord Tennyson, written for the occasion of Queen Victoria's opening of the Indian and Colonial Exhibition.

> Britain's myriad voices call,
> 'Sons, be welded each and all,
> Into one imperial whole,
> One with Britain, heart and soul!
> One life, one flag, one fleet, one Throne!

In Garvey's hands, the triumphal exhortation of the final line is paraphrased in the well-known UNIA motto, "One God, One Aim, One Destiny." Likewise, the name given by Garvey to the general assembly hall of the UNIA in Harlem, Liberty Hall, which became the cradle of the movement, is reminiscent of Oliver Goldsmith's ever-popular *She Stoops to Conquer* (1773). In the second act of the play, the residence Liberty Hall is defined as a haven from the outer world, a place of freedom of thought and action—"pray be under no constraint in this house," Mr. Hardcastle assures his guests; "this is Liberty Hall, gentlemen. You may do just as you please here."

VANITY FAIR

More deliberatively, Garvey's choice of the title for his epic poem, "The White Man's Game, His Vanity Fair" (later reprinted in pamphlet form under the title *The Tragedy of White Injustice*) reflects a similar penchant for alluding to great works of English literature. But just as he endowed the gospel of success with new racial meanings, so he converted common literary allusion to his own purposes, making it a medium of a new racial politics. The incorporation of "Vanity

Fair" in the poem's title alludes to the infamous marketplace by that name in John Bunyan's *Pilgrim's Progress* (1678). While William Makepeace Thackeray used the name of Bunyan's town as a metaphor for the decadence of bourgeois society in London in his 1848 novel *Vanity Fair,* Garvey employed the name of the town in his 1927 poem to encapsulate its theme of white oppression and decadence. Just as Bunyan's work is a kind of sacred picaresque in which evil is pitted against good, so Garvey's poem is a chronicle of the atrocities committed against native peoples by white colonizers. In Bunyan's allegory, Christian, the protagonist, and Faithful, his traveling companion, are waylaid on their journey toward the Celestial City at Vanity Fair, a market town ruled by Beelzebub. In this hellish town, the streets are named after Britain, France, Italy, Spain, and Germany. "Knaves and rogues" and "thefts, murders, adulteries, false swearers" are met with on these thoroughfares, and vanities bought and sold. The two travelers are taken prisoner, tortured, and ridiculed. Faithful is tried in a court presided over by Judge Hategood—with a jury made up of Mr. Blind-man, Mr. Malice, Mr. Cruelty, and others—and sentenced to death. He is whipped, stoned, and finally burned at the stake, whereupon his spiritual body is released from his ashes and carried up into the heavens by a horse-drawn chariot—a metaphor of deliverance popularly preserved in Negro spirituals.

In referring to Vanity Fair in *The Tragedy of White Injustice,* Garvey sought an analogy between the persecution experienced by Bunyan's travelers at the hands of the immoral townspeople and that experienced by Africans, Native Americans, and aboriginal Australians at the hands of Europeans during imperial expansion.

THE PLACE NEXT TO HELL

Bunyan's work was popular in the nineteenth century as a moral guide for children, and Garvey would undoubtedly have been familiar with it since his youth. Bunyan's 1678 classic was laden with social and political criticism, as was

Garvey's own epic poem of the 1920s. Bunyan wrote *Pilgrim's Progress* while imprisoned for religious dissent in the county jail at Bedford, England, and gave it an autobiographical premise by having the dreamer who narrates the story sleeping in "the gaol." A vocal Nonconformist who opposed the teachings of the Church of England, he was arrested while preaching and served two six-year sentences, from 1660 to 1672, and another six-month sentence, in 1676 and 1677. Garvey wrote *The Tragedy of White Injustice* while imprisoned in Atlanta, where he was incarcerated in large measure for his militant racial stand, which diverged sharply from prevailing norms. In writing the poem, he translated, as Bunyan did, his excellent oratorical skills into written form and created a text intended to convert a popular audience to a new philosophy and new conduct.

Garvey's references to Bunyan's classic continued after his release from prison and his deportation to Jamaica in 1927. While campaigning for a seat in Jamaica's colonial legislature in October 1929, he was convicted of contempt of court for criticizing the judicial system on the island. He declared that many judges were influenced by bribes and suggested that some be impeached and imprisoned. The Jamaican Supreme Court did not look kindly upon such contumacy and sentenced him, as a result, to three months' imprisonment in the Spanish Town prison. The episode— a major setback in Garvey's efforts to establish a political career—contributed to his subsequent decision to make a permanent move to England in the mid-1930s. Garvey referred to Jamaica in this period as "the place next to hell."[45] In a *New Jamaican* editorial he created a Bunyanesque dialogue between two Jamaicans who referred to the country as a "Land of Agony and Tears," which was "small, small in size and small in character," and where people who spoke their minds would be imprisoned. In Bunyan's work, the City of Destruction, where Christian was born, is described as "a populous place, but possessed with a very ill conditioned, and idle sort of People." Just as Bunyan's Christian leaves the City of Destruction to its brimstone, so Garvey's two imaginary Jamaicans recommend that the only way to remedy the evils they had witnessed was "by leaving the place and make it perish by itself."[46] Garvey echoed these themes in a May 1934 speech in which he denounced the hypocrisy of the country and announced his intention to publish a book about his journey through life, called, significantly, *The Town Next to Hell*. He told his audience that he had experienced a vision of "a night in hell" in a dream and that what he had seen was an authentic reflection of life under colonial rule in the Depression.

Garvey's promise to write an allegory on the subject of Jamaica was to some extent fulfilled; in July 1934 a poem written by him and entitled "A Night in Hell," was performed at a musical and poetic program at the Ward Theater in Kingston. Unfortunately, however, the text of the poem has not been preserved.

Poetry and Oral Tradition

Garvey's penchant for literary allusion and persuasion reflect his own belief that literature, particularly poetry, could be a powerful agent of personal uplift and a tool for teaching success. In the first lesson of the School of African Philosophy course for prospective UNIA leaders, he told his students to "always select the best poets for your inspirational urge." Writing a review of a poetry reading for the *New Jamaican,* he reminded his readers that "many a man has gotten the inspiration of his career from Poetry."[47] He went on to describe the beneficial effects of poetry readings, stating that the listener "is able to enter into the spirit of the Poets who write the language of their souls," while the poets themselves, in creating poetry, are forced to contemplate their

46. *New Jamaican,* 4 September 1933.

47. *New Jamaican,* 26 January 1933.

lives deeply, "and when they start to think poetic they may realize that after all life is not only an 'empty dream.'" In this perspective, poetry grants those receptive to it inspiration, and inspiration leads to ideation and action.

Garvey's writings and speeches also show the powerful legacy of his schooling in Victorian moral exhortation through elocution, as well as his genius in integrating the practice of declamation with West Indian and Afro-American traditions of verbal performance. In the dialogues created for the *Black Man* in the mid-1930s, Garvey adapted the Platonic form of didactic conversation between teacher and student, with its progression of statement, discussion, and debate, leading to the transfer and growth of knowledge. The dialogues also demonstrate his special sensitivity to communicating with an audience steeped in an oral tradition. By translating the written word into a script of two voices that was to be read as if it were spoken, Garvey created a kind of call-and-response conversational pattern designed both to uplift and to instruct. In any event, Garvey loved an argument.

DIALOGUES

Garvey's experimentation with the dialogue form occurred during the period of its revival following the publication of Goldsworthy Lowes Dickinson's *After Two Thousand Years: A Dialogue between Plato and a Modern Young Man* (1930). Dickinson had earlier received wide scholarly acclaim for his brilliant series of dialogues in the Socratic tradition, the most famous of which was *A Modern Symposium* (1905), a treatise that was in some ways a manual of modern politics. In 1931, while Garvey was visiting England, Dickinson broadcast a series of popular radio courses on the dialogues of Plato which were expanded for publication in *Plato and His Dialogues* (1931).

During the period of Dickinson's success, the prominent black journalist Joel A. Rogers also popularized the dialogue form as a medium for the discussion of the race question.

His *From "Superman" to Man* (1919) contained debates on race issues presented under the guise of a series of conversations between the erudite Dixon, a black porter, and various passengers who traveled aboard his train, particularly a southern Senator with well-entrenched beliefs in white supremacy. What emerged was a scathing critique of the doctrine of white racial superiority. Rogers's work was widely read and acclaimed, both for its content and for what a reviewer for the *Boston Transcript* called its "fascinating style and convincing logic."[48]

RELIGIOUS INFLUENCES

It might be said that Garvey's greatest achievement was his ability to change the consciousness of black people. Upon his return to New York following a month-long speaking tour of the Midwest in 1920, he likened his movement's impact upon popular consciousness to a religious conversion: "The masses of the race absorb the doctrines of the UNIA with the same eagerness with which the masses in the days of the supremacy of imperial Rome accepted Christianity. The people seem to regard the movement in the light of a new religion."[49] Garvey aimed to organize the instruction of black children according to the new "religion." He stated in a 27 June 1931 *Negro World* editorial that "the white race has a system, a method, a code of ethics laid down for the white child to go by, a philosophy, a set creed to guide its life," and that black children needed a similar code.

AFRICAN FUNDAMENTALISM

"African Fundamentalism" was Garvey's quasi-religious manifesto of black racial pride and unity. It attained canonical status within a short time after it was first published as

48. Joel A. Rogers, *From "Superman" to Man* 5th ed., 1968; reprint, Helga M. Rogers, 1982.

49. *NW,* 16 October 1920.

a front-page editorial in the *Negro World* of 6 June 1925. Written, like *The Tragedy of White Injustice,* while Garvey was confined in the Atlanta penitentiary, the essay proclaims ideological independence from white theories of history, makes concomitant claims of racial superiority, and articulates major themes that recur throughout Garvey's other writings and speeches. Chief among these are the ideas of racial self-confidence, self-development, and success; international black allegiance and solidarity; and the importance of acquiring a knowledge of ancient black history.

Garvey's use of the term *fundamentalism* in the title reflects this stress on the need for regaining a proud sense of selfhood by setting aside modern racist labels of inferiority and reviving the basic, fundamental beliefs in black aptitude and greatness that he saw exemplified in ancient African civilization. At the same time, the term resonated with Garvey's long-standing preoccupation with development of an original "Negro idealism." This notion was essentially grounded in religion. "I don't think that anyone who gets up to attack religion will get the sympathy of this house," Garvey declared in a speech in 1929, "for the Universal Negro Improvement Association is fundamentally a religious institution."[50]

"African Fundamentalism" was written at the peak of the fundamentalist revival that swept American following World War I. The revival was expressed both as a theological doctrine and as a conservative neopolitical movement. While the concerns of Christian fundamentalists focused on a sociocultural return to a set of principles untainted by modern rationalism and secularism, and while Populist fundamentalists called for the maintenance of an older agrarian order that would belie the impact of industrialization and urbanization—so Garvey's call heralded a recognition of the achievements of Africans in the past and a return to the principles of black dignity and self-rule, principles that had been denigrated under the impact of modern racial oppression,

50. *Blackman* (Kingston), 31 August 1929.

slavery, and imperial colonization.

As in his sardonic use of the phrase "Vanity Fair," Garvey's choice of the word *fundamentalism* reflects an intuitive understanding of the types of associations people would apply to his use of the term. He employs these associations in the context of the essay itself, wherein his references to monkeys, caves, and the process of evolution inevitably call to mind the opposing ideas of social Darwinism and the fundamentalist movement. The conflict between these two philosophies peaked symbolically in the Scopes trial, which got under way during the same summer "African Fundamentalism" was written. The trial, which was held in Dayton, Tennessee, in July 1925, pitted prominent attorneys William Jennings Bryan and Clarence Darrow against one another in a much-publicized courtroom battle. At issue was the acceptance of the theory of evolution and its place in the American school curriculum. Bryan argued for the creationist viewpoint (a fundamentalist perspective associated with the agrarian and southern sections of the United States and with the lower classes), while Darrow represented the modern, humanist viewpoint (a secular perspective associated with the urban and industrial areas of the North, with the growth of the social sciences, and with the educated middle classes). Bryan's side in the conflict prevailed, and teacher John T. Scopes was found guilty of breaking a law, passed by the Tennessee legislature in March 1925, prohibiting the teaching of any doctrine denying the divine creation of mankind as taught from a literal interpretation of the Bible.

In his essay, Garvey played on the social Darwinist issues that were publicly highlighted by the Scopes trial and gave them an ironic twist. He adopted elements of the evolutionary theory of the secularists and of the strong nativist strain of the fundamentalists and utilized them both as premises to support his own counterargument. He presented blacks in northern Africa as representatives of a higher form of life and culture than their white counterparts in Europe. He thus reversed the popular contemporary claims of white eugenicists, who applied evolutionary theory to the social milieu, associating people of African heritage with the slow development of the apes and offering their results as "proof" of white racial superiority.

Similar reversals of white-dictated beliefs and standards were reflected in Garvey's fervent praise for the compelling beauty of black skin and African features; in his championing of the worship of black images of the Virgin Mary, God, and Jesus Christ in the place of white conceptions of the deity; and in his call for a recognition of the heroic accomplishments of black people, such as Crispus Attucks and Sojourner Truth, whose martyrdom, selflessness, and rebelliousness qualified them for respect equal to that accorded white saints like Joan of Arc.

CLASSICAL INFLUENCES AND THE IDEAL STATE

Much of Garvey's theory of education—with its emphasis on self-mastery and self-culture as precursors to good race leadership—can be traced to the classical model of education, where the training of the child is the basis of virtue, and virtue in turn is the necessary requirement of statesmanship. "Governing the Ideal State," written by Garvey in Atlanta Federal Penitentiary in 1925, manifests the influence of classical philosophy on Garvey's thought and on his view of contemporary political events. The essay stands also as a propagandistic exercise in self-vindication in the wake of Garvey's recent conviction on fraud charges. It offers an indictment of the behavior of UNIA leaders and staff members whose misconduct Garvey felt had led to his imprisonment. It is also a scathing comment on the American political system at large and on the widespread corruption among government officials and leaders in the era of the Teapot Dome scandal.

Garvey enjoyed using classical allusions to convey to his audiences the concept of greatness and nobility. In his 1914 pamphlet *A Talk with Afro-West Indians,* he urged his readers to "arise, take on the toga of race pride, and throw off the brand of ignominy which has kept you back for so many centuries." Nearly two decades later he told readers that "the mind of Cicero" was not "purely Roman, neither were the minds of Socrates and Plato purely Greek." He went on to characterize these classical figures as members of an elite company of noble characters, "the Empire of whose minds extended around the world."[51] The title of his 1927 *Poetic Meditations of Marcus Garvey* parallels the title of the work of the "philosopher-emperor" of Rome, *The Meditations* of the Emperor Marcus Aurelius Antoninus (121–180). Like the work of Marcus Aurelius, Garvey's meditations included a fascination with the themes of conduct and the moral tenets of Stoicism and Platonism.

In fact, Garvey subsequently described his "Governing the Ideal State" as an abstract exercise to be likened to "Plato's *Republic* and *Utopia*."[52] And like Plato and the Greeks, Garvey shared a strong belief, though he applied it to Africa of antiquity, in the notion of historical decline from a golden age. Garvey believed civilizations were subject to an inevitable cyclical process of degeneration and regeneration. In one of his earliest essays, entitled "The British West Indies in the Mirror of Civilization" published in the October 1913 issue of the *African Times and Orient Review,* he held up the prospect of a future historical role for West Indian blacks in relation to Africa on the premise of this cyclical view. "I would point my critical friends to history and its lessons," he advised, then proceeded to draw what was to be one of his favorite historical parallels: "Would Caesar have believed that the country he was invading in 55 B.C. would be the seat of the greatest Empire of the World? Had it been suggested to him would he not have laughed at it as a huge joke? Yet it has come true."[53] The essay is important as an early example of the equation, in Garvey's mind, of history with empire building and decline.

In "Governing the Ideal State," he announced the failure

---

51. "An Apostrophe to Miss Nancy Cunard," handbill, 28 July 1932.

52. *Daily Gleaner,* 21 January 1933.

53. Marcus Garvey, "The British West Indies in the Mirror of Civilization," *African Times and Orient Review* (October 1913): 160.

of modern systems of government and called for a return to the concept of the archaic state, ruled over by an "absolute authority," or what Aristotle termed an absolute kingship. The fact that Garvey was well versed in Aristotle is highlighted by his request to his wife, shortly after the beginning of his imprisonment, to send him a copy of A. E. Taylor's *Aristotle* (1919), a standard commentary. In his essay, Garvey rejected democracy in favor of a system of monarchy or oligarchy similar to the one presented in Aristotle's *Politics,* the rule of "one best man," along with an administrative aristocracy of virtuous citizens. As was the case in Aristotle's utopia— where those individuals with a disproportionate number of friends would be ostracized from society, while an individual demonstrating disproportionate virtue should be embraced and given supreme authority—in Garvey's ideal state the virtuous ruler would have no close associations other than with his family and, free from the corrupting influences that companionship might bring, would devote full attention to the responsibilities of state.

Plato's *Laws*

Garvey borrowed the concept that the key function of law is the maintenance of authority not only from Aristotle, but from Plato, whose *Republic* and *Laws* presented a vision of an ideal state in which virtuous behavior is encouraged through education, while conduct deemed corrupt is punished according to a harsh system of penalties. Plato's penal code was in turn partially derived from the Hammurabic code that preceded it. The crimes of embezzlement and treason to the state through political factionalization, which Garvey suggested should be punishable by death, were also crimes meriting capital punishment in Plato's ideal state (*Laws,* 9.856) (however, Garvey's call for stoning as the means of administering the death penalty is more likely derived from biblical descriptions than from Plato). Plato recommended that all public officials be subject to an audit and, should the audit reveal unjust self-aggrandizement, "be branded with public disgrace for their yielding to corruption" (*Laws*, 6.761–762). Similarly, Plato wrote that "the servants of the nation are to render their services without any taking of presents" and, if they should disobey, be convicted and "die without ceremony" (*Laws*, 12.955). If, however, leaders passed the state audit and were shown to have discharged their offices honorably, they should, as Garvey's virtuous leader would, be pronounced worthy of distinction and respect throughout the rest of their lives and be given an elaborate public funeral at their deaths (*Laws*, 12.946–947). Just as Garvey suggested that a child who identified a father's crime should be spared the penalty of death, so Plato suggested that children who "forsake their father's corrupt ways, shall have an honourable name and good report, as those that have done well and manfully in leaving evil for good" (*Laws*, 9.855).

Garvey's inclusion of kinship and property relations in consideration of the organization of his ideal state also mirrored the teachings of the Greek philosophers. He borrowed from Plato, who saw the state evolving from the family into a more communal relation and who granted free women some role in public life, in "universal education," and in the administration of the state. Garvey also borrowed from Aristotle, who, more than Plato, preserved the notion of the private household and the subordination of women as an integral part of his ideal state. Garvey centered the private life of his ideal ruler in a nuclear family and made the wife of the ruler a kind of chamberlain accountable for her husband's financial dealings. Both Aristotle and Plato based their ideal states on monogamous marriage and patriarchy, in which the household of a citizen was compared to the larger hierarchy of the state, with a wife subject to her husband as a subject is subordinate to a ruler. Garvey echoed this model in his essay, wherein the wives of leaders are deemed "responsible for their domestic households," regulated by law in the keeping of their husbands' private and public accounts, and subject to capital punishment along with their husbands for financial crimes committed during their husbands' tenure in office. Garvey's recommendation that both the wife and husband should be disgraced and put to death in cases of corruption in office mirrors not only the family relations of the Greek state but archaic Mesopotamian codes governing debt slavery, in which the wives or children of a male debtor could be enslaved or put to death in payment for his financial failures.

THE IDEAL STATE AND THE UNIA

"Governing the Ideal State" emerges as an essay in self-vindication and wish fulfillment and draws thinly disguised parallels between Garvey's vision of the ideal state and his desires for the correct operation of the UNIA. Just as the philosopher-ruler is the central theme of Plato's *Republic*, so is Garvey the focus of the essay. Garvey's character might also be adduced from the authoritarian type of society he proposes—an exercise that would be consistent with Plato's attempt to sketch the four types of character corresponding to the four types of society depicted in book 8 of the *Republic*.

Written from prison, at a period in his life that called for reflection about the course of his career and the factionalization and corruption that had overtaken the movement, Garvey's essay takes on an autobiographical quality, with significant psychohistorical connotations. Garvey clearly identified with the extreme authoritarianism of the supreme leader who appoints subordinate officials and exercises absolute authority over them. Just as Garvey impeached or expelled UNIA officers who disagreed with his policies or digressed from his vision of the organization's goals (often publicly disgracing them in the process), so Garvey's Spartan utopia would ensure strict accountability, as well as define the boundaries of conduct for subordinates. The role of the president's wife as his personal accountant in the ideal state closely parallels that of Amy Jacques Garvey as business manager at the UNIA headquarters as well as overseer of her husband's—the president general's—personal accounts.

Garvey suggests, through his philosophical musing on the austerity of the ideal state, his own, as well as his wife's, exculpation by sketching draconian consequences for fraud and mismanagement. At the same time, Garvey's call for the disgrace of public officials who do not correctly perform their duties reflects a desire for retribution and revenge against fellow UNIA officers and staff members, many of whom he felt had deceived him and whom he charged with graft. Similarly, the call for clemency toward a family member who defied and reported corruption acknowledged Garvey's feelings toward those who remained loyal to him and who had testified in his defense during the mail fraud trial, offering evidence against the "disloyal" actions of others. The recommendations that the president of the ideal state be freed from pecuniary obligations are natural wishes from a man whose struggles to gain world renown as the head of a movement were always compromised by debt and material need. In addition, Garvey's description of the absolute leader as a man without friends is also a poignant reflection of his own, perhaps deliberate, isolation from close companionship, a theme that reappears in his advice to prospective UNIA leaders in his lessons for the School of African Philosophy.

POLITICAL CORRUPTION

On a more overt level, "Governing the Ideal State" is a critique of the widespread corruption evidenced on the local, state, and federal levels of government in the 1920s. Garvey was fond of noting that prison mates in Atlanta included former politicians, including Gov. Warren McCray of Indiana, who was convicted of embezzlement, forgery, and mail fraud in 1924; and Mayor Roswell Johnson of Gary, Indiana, who was imprisoned in Atlanta in April 1925 for participation in a liquor conspiracy ring during Prohibition. On a federal level, the nation was rocked in the early 1920s by Senate investigations into irregularities committed by officials associated with the Harding administration, including the Teapot Dome oil reserve scandal of 1922–1923, which led to the eventual prosecution and conviction of government officials on bribery and conspiracy charges and to the investigation and prosecution of former attorney general Harry M. Daugherty in 1924–1927, which revealed his close alliance with organized crime and frequent abuse of civil liberties through the power of his office. The irony of such malfeasance arising from within the institution of government that condemned him was not lost upon Garvey.

RACIAL EDUCATION

Ethical and cultural instruction—the basis of virtue in Aristotle's ideal state—was one of the basic goals of the UNIA from its inception. Garvey believed in offering instruction both popularly and institutionally, with the dual goals of reaching a wide audience and of establishing educational facilities. The soapbox oratory, mass meetings, and large conventions that characterized the Garvey movement were all directed at instructing and organizing a large mass of people. Similarly, the dramatic performances, elocution contests, debates, and concerts that UNIA members participated in were forms not only of fund-raising and socializing, but of racial education as well. When Garvey purchased Edelweiss Park in Kingston, Jamaica, as a meeting center for the black community in the early 1930s, he continued the practices established in New York and throughout the local UNIA divisions—practices based on the nineteenth-century tradition of the Chautauqua circuit, where people would gather locally for popular education and enrichment combined with entertainment, often outdoors or beneath a tent. He advertised Edelweiss Park as a "great educational centre" and a "centre of people of intellect" in the pages of the *New Jamaican*.[54]

Garvey's interest in founding educational facilities was also a lifelong one. He attended courses at Birkbeck College in England before he founded the UNIA in 1914, and one of the new organization's earliest goals was the creation of an industrial training institute for blacks in Jamaica based on the Tuskegee model. Well before the turn of the century,

54. *New Jamaican,* 9 July and 23 July 1932.

the practical education in skilled crafts that industrial training offered had become one of the popular paths for artisans in their quest for self-culture. The 26 March 1915 Jamaican *Daily Chronicle* reported that Garvey listed the establishment of "educational and industrial colleges for the further education and culture of our boys and girls" as among the several benevolent goals of the UNIA. Garvey received support in this goal from Booker T. Washington, who, on 17 September 1914, wrote to invite the UNIA leader to "come to Tuskegee and see for yourself what we are striving to do," and promised again in April 1915 to help Garvey achieve his local aims.

Garvey's interest in education based on the principles of self-culture persisted after Washington's death in November 1915 and the relocation of the headquarters of the movement in the United States in 1916. UNIA meetings and programs continued to foster the ideal of self-improvement, and as the association grew, auxiliaries were created with their own educational standards for membership. These standards included examinations in the geography of Africa, mathematics, reading, writing, and other subjects for commissioned officers in the uniformed Universal African Legion; first aid and nutrition classes for the members of the Black Cross Nurses; automobile repair and operation instruction for the Universal African Motor Corps; and a curriculum of elementary courses, including instruction in black history, economics, and etiquette, for members of the Juvenile Divisions. In some areas, local Black Cross Nurse auxiliaries also contracted with community hospitals and clinics to provide members with more advanced practical training in nursing and maternity care.

In February 1918 Garvey invited Columbia University president Nicholas Murray Butler to address the members of the UNIA on the topic of "Education and What It Means," and in April of the same year he and the other officers appealed to Butler to contribute toward the purchase of a $200,000 building in Harlem for an organization headquarters, which they hoped would "be the source from which we will train and educate our people to those essentials that will make them a more cultured and better race."[55]

BOOKER T. WASHINGTON UNIVERSITY

At the 1922 UNIA convention, Garvey announced the proposed opening of the Booker T. Washington University, which would be used to train leaders of the UNIA from around the world. The university, located on the same site as the UNIA-operated Phyllis Wheatley Hotel (3–13 West 136th Street, New York, a building rented by the UNIA), was designed to train officers for UNIA civil service positions in accordance with article 31 of the 1922 *UNIA Constitution and Book of Laws*. A convention committee on labor and industry offered a resolution that a course in agriculture and commerce also be provided at the university, enabling the UNIA to send experts on the subject into the field as advisers.

LIBERTY UNIVERSITY

While the operation of Booker T. Washington University was short-lived, in September 1926 the UNIA celebrated the opening of the newly acquired Smallwood-Corey Industrial Institute. Located in Claremont, Virginia, the school property included several buildings and sixty-six acres of land along the St. James River. A coeducational school, it was operated by a Hampton Institute graduate with a faculty of nine when it was purchased by the UNIA and renamed Liberty University. Amy Jacques Garvey referred to Liberty University in her memoirs as "a practical High School,"[56] and young UNIA members became students there beginning with the fall session in 1926. Advertisements for the university appeared in the *Negro World*, informing readers that the school had opened for the fall term on September 15 and that "every division or chapter should grant a scholarship to a deserving

55. *Garvey Papers*, 1: 238.

56. Amy Jacques Garvey, *Garvey and Garveyism* (Kingston, 1963), p. 164.

boy or girl and enable them to secure a liberal education."[57] Optimistic officers announced the establishment of the school as the first in a chain of academies to be founded by the association. The school experienced great financial difficulties and, after struggling through three years of poverty, was closed in October 1929.[58]

Garvey was imprisoned in Atlanta when the UNIA acquired Liberty University, and he was never able to see the school in operation. During his incarceration he continued his personal dedication to self-education, ordering books and newspapers, and in October 1927 he contacted representatives of the Columbia University Home Study Department for information about their mail-order courses in philosophy and poetry. After his release and return to Jamaica, he used the editorial pages of the *Blackman* and *New Jamaican* for instruction in racial uplift. He began publishing the *Black Man* magazine in Kingston in 1933, and when he relocated the headquarters of the movement to London in 1935, he also transferred the publication of the monthly magazine. In March 1936 he described the London journal as "a kind of universal University to educate those who want to be educated in our school of thought."[59]

SCHOOL OF AFRICAN PHILOSOPHY

Garvey's long-standing interest in establishing a school to train individuals in his racial philosophy was realized a decade after his deportation from the United States, when he launched the School of African Philosophy in Toronto. Garvey reported to the readers of the December 1937 *Black Man*:

> The School of African Philosophy has come into existence after twenty-three years of the Association's life for

57. *NW,* 28 August 1926 and 26 November 1927.

58. *NW,* 12 October 1929.

59. *BM* 1 (March 1936): 3.

the purpose of preparing and directing the leaders who are to create and maintain the great institution that has been founded and carried on during a time of intensified propaganda work. The philosophy of the school embodies the most exhaustive outlines of the manner in which the Negro should be trained to project a civilization of his own and to maintain it.[60]

The first session of the school was held in September 1937, following the second regional conference of the American and Canadian branches of the UNIA in August. Garvey served as principal of the school and led the classes, which met daily, in day and evening sessions, from 1 to 23 September. Entrance was restricted to individuals with a high school education. Eleven students enrolled in the session, including four women and seven men, all from the northern or eastern United States or Canada. Ten of them passed the final examination and received appointments as UNIA regional commissioners.

Garvey described the course in African philosophy as including "a range of over forty-two subjects" and announced that an extensive correspondence course had been drawn up, open "only to Negroes." The course was available through mail order from UNIA headquarters at 2 Beaumont Crescent, West Kensington, London, for a fee of twenty-five dollars. According to a press release issued by Garvey from his London headquarters, the course "guarantees to prepare each man and woman for a useful career and sure success and prosperity."[61]

THE LESSONS AND THE GOSPEL OF SUCCESS

Garvey's course in African philosophy displays a strong affinity with the how-to lessons of New Thought therapeutics,

60. *BM* 2 (December 1937): 4.

61. "Garvey Opens New School of African Ideals," *Richmond Planet*, 5 March 1938.

exemplified in the titles of such well-known New Thought treatises as W. W. Atkinson's *The Secret of Success: A Course in Nine Lessons* (1908), Elizabeth Towne's *Lessons in Living* (1910), Fenwicke L. Holmes's *Being and Becoming: Lessons in Science of Mind* (1920), Nona L. Brooks's *Short Lessons in Divine Science* (1928), and Brown Landone's *The ABC of Truth: Fifty-five Lessons for Beginnings in New Thought Study* (1926). Garvey's course in racial leadership could be justly described as a black version of New Thought, offering a similar system of practical metaphysics geared to achieving mental emancipation and personal success.

Garvey may also have been influenced by the phenomenal success of Dale Carnegie's *How to Win Friends and Influence People,* which was first published in November 1936. By the time that Garvey started the course in African philosophy, over half a million copies of Carnegie's treatise had been sold, making it the national best-seller for the preceding five months. The Carnegie Institute in New York, where Carnegie conducted courses for people who hoped to become leaders in the business and professional world, may well have served as a model for Garvey's own school for UNIA leaders. Garvey and Carnegie both emphasized the need to arouse enthusiasm in order to assume leadership and earn power and recognition. Both preached a gospel of self-improvement and practical study of a set of success-oriented principles. Both used examples of great leaders and businessmen, citing how many of the same favorites— Theodore Roosevelt, Thomas Edison, John Wanamaker, John D. Rockefeller, Benjamin Disraeli, Edward VIII, and P. T. Barnum—had succeeded, stressing the principle of hard work. Both shared the common phraseology of success, including a penchant for the terms *fundamental, self-improvement,* and *self-education.* Both taught their lessons in order to change behavior, practicing the dictum of Herbert Spencer that Carnegie quoted in his 1936 introduction: "The great aim of education, is not knowledge but action."[62] Carnegie told his readers that

62. Dale Carnegie, *How to Win Friends and Influence People* (1936; reprint, New York: Simon and Schuster, 1964), p. 17.

he was "talking about a new way of life"[63] while Garvey
termed his lessons in African philosophy a "New Way to
Education."[64] Both included tricksterlike advice on how to
manipulate and persuade others. While Carnegie saw human
relations as a kind of game of disarming potential enemies, in
which an appearance of sincerity was key, Garvey gave lessons
in what he called "diplomacy," or the artful deception of
opponents. While Carnegie noted the power of a "captivating
smile"[65] in swaying people, Garvey advised his students to
"win the world to you with a smile."[66] He echoed the title
of Carnegie's book when he told his students to "Never
approach anybody that you want to get anything out of
or any good results from, in an offensive manner; to the
contrary, win them with the perfect smile . . . the idea is to
make friends and to get results."[67] Both men were interested in
the organizing power of what Carnegie called showmanship
and style; and Carnegie illustrated the concept by the example
of Garvey's hero, Napoleon, who stimulated a feeling of
importance among his followers by awarding them exalted
titles he had himself created. Each of the graduates of the
first class of Garvey's School of African Philosophy received
a new title and appointment as a regional commissioner for
the UNIA.

ETHIOPIANISM

Some of the ideas Garvey presents in the lessons from
the School of African Philosophy are also similar to thought
current in the Ethiopianist movement in Jamaica of the same
period and to his own "African Fundamentalism." The idea
of finding antecedents of Egyptian civilization in ancient
Ethiopian culture—including the view that Ethiopians were

63. Carnegie, *How to Win Friends,* p. 37.

64. *BM* 4 (February 1939): 6.

65. Carnegie, *How to Win Friends,* p. 67.

66. lesson 18.

67. lesson 9.

the architects of the pyramids and of the Sphinx—is one such common link. The "leprosy" theory of Caucasian racial origin that Garvey presents in lesson 12 was also an ideological strain of Ethiopianism. By 1937, when Garvey taught the first course in African philosophy, the identification of the white man as a leper had become a part of emergent Rastafarian doctrine in Jamaica, which drew upon the older Ethiopianist reference to Numbers 12:10, wherin Miriam becomes leprous—"white as snow." Garvey taught that Adam and Eve and their progeny were black and that Cain was the first leper, stricken white as a punishment by God for the murder of his brother, Abel. Garvey differed from Ethiopianist teachings when he claimed that Tutankhamen and other Egyptians were blacks who enslaved the Hebrews. For many adherents of Ethiopianism, people of African descent—enslaved and subjected to dispersion from their ancestral African homeland—were strongly identified with the Jews; indeed, some believed that black people were actual descendants of the Jews who had experienced slavery. "The Negro must be [the] original Children of the Sun, of Is-Ra-El," declared the *Norfolk Journal and Guide* in 1924, "as the Lord appears to make an opening for them where none appeared to exist."[68]

AFRICAN ZIONISM

Garvey's philosophy of racial loyalty expressed in the School of African Philosophy as well as in his other speeches and writings, was earlier influenced by the Zionist movement. At the Fourth UNIA International Convention in New York in August 1924, for example, a reporter for a Hebrew Zionist newspaper was heard to exclaim across the press table, "This is Negro Zionism."[69] The Dahomean protonationalist Kojo Tovalou-Houénou declared at the same convention that "your

68. quoted in *NW*, 5 July 1924.

69. *Daily Worker*, 18 August 1924.

association, Mr. President . . . is the Zionism of the Black Race."[70]

Identification of Garveyism with Zionism is a theme that runs throughout commentaries on the Garvey phenomenon. In a November 1922 interview Claude McKay stated that the Garvey "movement has all the characteristic features of the Jewish Zionists."[71] The same ideological identification persisted after World War II. In the classic statement of the theory and practice of postwar pan-African liberation, *Pan-Africanism or Communism*, George Padmore addresses the prehistory of the movement and describes the phenomenon of what he defines as "Black Zionism or Garveyism."[72] Amy Jacques Garvey also described Garveyism in her 1963 memoir as "Black Zionism."[73]

The political parallels between Garveyism and Zionism were remarkable. As irredentist phenomena, the twin movements were spawned in significant ways by territorial and diplomatic developments during World War I and by the perfervid debate surrounding the settlement of the nationalities question and the issue of national self-determination, matters that were important parts of the protracted peace negotiations. The ground swell of feeling on the part of blacks toward Africa and of Jews toward Palestine occurred within the same twelve months following the Armistice, the period that many historians believe registered the greatest change in attitudes of Jews and persons of African descent toward the question of national independence.

When interviewed by Michael Gold in August 1920, Garvey informed Gold, "Many white men have tried to uplift them [the Negroes], but the only way is for the [N]egroes to have a nation of their own, like the Jews, that will command the respect of the world with its achieve-

70. *Les Continents,* 15 October 1924.

71. "The Race Question in America," *Izvestia,* 18 November 1922.

72. George Padmore, *Pan-Africanism or Communism* (1955; reprint, Garden City, N.Y.: Doubleday-Anchor, 1972), pp. 65–82.

73. *Garvey and Garveyism,* pp. 252, 267.

ments."[74] The men of the American volunteer Jewish Legion—the first contingent of which was raised in New York in February 1918—became identified as a kind of Jewish national guard for Palestine, while the men of Garvey's uniformed Universal African Legion (UAL), organized the following year, symbolized the armed detachment of African liberation. At Garvey's mail-fraud trial the former UAL head Emmett L. Gaines was asked by the government prosecutor whether the UNIA had a military branch. He answered, "It has a uniform rank . . . like the Masons and Odd Fellows and any other organization." To elucidate the character of his African legion, Garvey then interjected the simple declaration—"Zionists."[75]

In the case of both the Garvey and the Zionist movements, the center of political organization was the United States, specifically New York. Garvey launched a series of construction loans in 1920 that were analogous to the Palestine Restoration Fund promoted by the Zionist Organization of America for the avowed of purpose developing the "Jewish commonwealth of Palestine."[76] The various reconstruction funds that formed so intrinsic a feature of the organizing efforts of both movements were a reflection of their shared concepts of exodus and preparation. The *Negro World* of 8 August 1922, in providing a summary of one of Garvey's speeches, reported that Garvey asked his audience "if the Jews could have Palestine, why not the Negroes another Palestine in Africa?" The hoped-for African Palestine, as conceived by Garvey, was to have been Liberia. "We are asking the world for a fair chance to assist the people of Liberia in developing that country," he announced, "as the world is giving the Jew a fair chance to develop Palestine."[77] Similarly, a

74. Michael Gold, "When Africa Awakes," *New York World,* 22 August 1920.

75. *Marcus Garvey* v. *United States,* no. 8317, Ct. App., 2d Cir., 2 February 1925, p. 1,699.

76. *New York Times,* 19 September 1919.

77. *NW,* 14 June 1924.

proposal presented at the September 1919 Chicago convention
of the Zionist Organization of America to transfer "all central
Zionist Administrative Institutions and activities" to Palestine
was mirrored by Garvey's announcement, in a Liberty Hall
speech on 14 December 1919, that "after the [UNIA] convention to be held next August the headquarters of the association must be transferred to Monrovia, Liberia."[78]

JEWISH PATRONAGE

During the peak years of the UNIA in the early twenties,
a number of Jewish figures endorsed and contributed funds
to Garvey's various schemes of African colonization. The
Hungarian-born banker and philanthropist William C. Ritter
of Brooklyn made a financial contribution to the UNIA's
1924 Liberian colonization program.[79] Two Jewish physicians,
Dr. L. A. Goldfine of Chicago and Dr. J. Gordon of New
York, also gave warm endorsements to the movement.
Gordon addressed the Third UNIA International Convention
in August 1921 from the platform of Liberty Hall.[80] Garvey's
Jamaican patrons included Abraham Judah, the city engineer
of Kingston, and Lewis Ashenheim, a leading luminary of
the Jamaican bar. Whereas the former helped make possible
Garvey's first English visit in 1913 and 1914—an undertaking
that proved of immeasurable importance to Garvey's political
and ideological orientation—the latter provided Garvey with
critical legal defenses in Jamaica's courts after he was deported
to the island from the United States. Garvey reciprocated by
taking to the hustings in support of Ashenheim's candidacy
in the 1935 election, the final election held in Jamaica under
the old restricted franchise of crown colony rule. Garvey's
support for Ashenheim proved unpopular with the electorate

78. Meyer W. Weisgal, "The Zionist Convention in Chicago,"
Maccabean, December 1919, p. 345; *New York Times,* 17 September 1919;
National Archives, RG 165, file 10218-364-18-190X.

79. *NW,* 7 June 1924.

80. *NW,* 3 July and 16 September 1922.

and occasioned a number of violent disturbances at meetings addressed by Garvey in Kingston. It also marked the
end of twenty-five years of close political allegiance between
Garvey and the opposing candidate and mayor of the city of
Kingston, H. A. L. Simpson.

RACIAL SUCCESS

Garvey made frequent calls for blacks to emulate the
economic successes and national ambition of Jews. "The Jew
has something the Negro hasn't got," Garvey averred, "he
has racial stamina."[81] "We want to work out a plan like the
Zionist so as to recover ourselves," Garvey advised readers
of the December 1937 *Black Man*.[82] In an editorial penned in
mid-1936, at the outbreak of civil war between Arabs and Jews
in Palestine, Garvey drew out the following moral for blacks:

> The Negro, primarily, like the Jew, needs money, but
> he also needs simultaneously a strong nationalism. Let
> the Negro couple the urge for money with that of
> nationalism, so that in another hundred years when
> he arrives he will not have the difficulty the Jew is
> now having in Palestine, but he will have a formidable
> and well-established nation to protect him anywhere he
> happens to find himself with his wealth. There is no
> better place than Africa, his original home. The Negroes
> of the world, therefore, should concentrate on making
> money and in using a part of it for helping to establish
> an independent nationalism in Africa. [83]

ANTI-SEMITISM

Yet even while Garvey supported Jews as positive
socioeconomic and political role models, he was by no means

81. *BM* 1, no. 9 (August–September 1935): 10.

82. *BM* 2, no. 9 (December 1937): 13.

83. *BM* 2, no. 2 (July–August 1936): 3.

free from the anti-Semitism of his times. He became increasingly anti-Semitic in his rhetoric following conviction on mail
fraud charges in 1923, when he became convinced that Jewish
and Catholic jurors and Judge Julian Mack, a leading Zionist
and former head of the Zionist Organization of America, had
been biased in the hearing of the case because of their political objections to his meeting with the acting imperial wizard
of the Ku Klux Klan—an avowedly anti-Semitic and anti-
Catholic organization—in 1922. "When they wanted to get
me," Garvey informed the Afro-American journalist Joel A.
Rogers in 1928, "they had a Jewish judge try me, and a Jewish
prosecutor. I would have been freed but two Jews on the
jury held out against me ten hours and succeeded in convict-
ing me, whereupon the Jewish judge gave me the maximum
penalty."[84]

This bitterness continued to pervade his thinking, and
tainted the positive view of Jews he upheld earlier in his
career. By the mid-1930s racist suspicion of the motivation of
Jews was mixed with a more positive identification with Jews
as an oppressed minority, so that Garvey frequently made
statements about Jewish solidarity that were contradictory.

Garvey was a propagator of the anti-Semitic rhetoric
common in the political era epitomized by the formation of
the Rome-Berlin Axis in October 1936. He identified with
the rise of both Hitler and Mussolini from lower-class status,
and admired the power manifested in their nationalistic brand
of leadership. He praised both men in the early thirties as
self-made leaders who had restored their nations' pride, and
used the resurgence of Italy and Germany as an example to
blacks for the possible regeneration of Africa. He admired in
particular the remarkable ideological stamp the fascist leaders
had succeeded in imprinting on the world. "In politics as in
everything else," he declared, "movements of any kind [once]
established, when centralized by leading characters generally
leave their impression, and so Hitler, Mussolini, Stalin and

84. *Philadelphia Tribune,* 27 September 1928.

the Japanese political leaders are leaving on humanity at large an indelible mark of their political disposition."[85] This admiration was tinged with jealousy over the spectacular impact of the fascist movement. In 1937 he went so far as to claim in a London interview with Joel A. Rogers that, as Rogers reported,

> . . . his Fascism preceded that of Mussolini and Hitler. "We were the first Fascists," [Garvey] said, "when we had 100,000 disciplined men, and were training children, Mussolini was still an unknown. Mussolini copied our Fascism." [86]

Later the same year he declared that the "UNIA was before Mussolini and Hitler ever were heard of. Mussolini and Hitler copied the programme of the UNIA—aggressive nationalism for the black man in Africa."[87]

His naive identification with fascism in the mid-thirties merged readily with the unfortunate anti-Semitic beliefs he had been voicing since the mid-twenties. In his lessons for the School of African Philosophy—which were first delivered when the events of the past few years had brought Nazi policies of racial discrimination and oppression to the attention of the world—Garvey cautioned against relying on Jews, stating that the very racial solidarity he admired made Jews loyal only to themselves and not to other racial groups. These distasteful comments mark the development of anti-Semitism within the black community in the United States, reflecting the tension that had developed in urban areas, in the course of the previous twenty years, between blacks who had migrated from the South or the Caribbean in the World

85. *BM* 3, no. 10 (July 1938): 3; see also *BM* 1, no. 1 (December 1933): 2–3; and *BM* 2, no. 3 (September–October 1936): 2.

86. Joel A. Rogers, "Marcus Garvey," in Negroes of New York series, New York Writers Program, 1939, Schomburg Center for Research in Black Culture, New York.

87. *BM* 2, no. 8 (December 1937): 12.

War I era and Jewish immigrants already established in the cities. Black perceptions of Jews were influenced by personal resentment of Jewish landlords and shopkeepers, on whom many blacks depended for housing and consumer goods. Jews, in turn, were influenced by the larger atmosphere of racial prejudice against blacks and prevailing patterns of residential segregation. This economic tension and cultural dissonance between Jews and blacks in areas where the UNIA was strong made blacks receptive toward anti-Semitic theories of international financial conspiracy.

These racist theories, popular in the early twenties, were propagated by such widely distributed organs as Henry Ford's *Dearborn Independent* and *The International Jew*. Garvey admired Ford as a self-made captain of industry, and was undoubtedly familiar with the anti-Semitic leanings of the Ford publications. Garvey also subscribed to the notorious *Protocols of the Elders of Zion,* which went through six editions in the United States between 1920 and 1922. He told Joel A. Rogers in the course of a 1928 interview in England that "the Elders of Zion teach that a harm done by a Jew to a Gentile is no harm at all, and the Negro is a Gentile."[88] Garvey apparently accepted the theory—widely popular in the twenties and propagated by Ford's *Dearborn Independent* reporters and the *Protocols*—about the existence of a Jewish-capitalist-Bolshevik conspiracy. Garvey details the same conspiracy theory in his otherwise sympathetic editorials criticizing Nazi persecution of Jews. "Hitler is only making a fool of himself," Garvey argued in publicly denouncing Hitler's attacks upon Jews, declaring further:

> Sooner or later the Jews will destroy Germany as they destroyed Russia. They did not so much destroy Russia from within as from without, and Hitler is driving the Jews to a more perfect organization from without Germany. Jewish finance is a powerful world factor. It

88. *Philadelphia Tribune,* 27 September 1928.

can destroy men, organizations and nations. When the Jewish capitalists get together they will strike back at Germany and the fire of Communism will be lighted and Hitler and his gang will disappear as they have disappeared in Russia . . . If Hitler will not act sensibly then Germany must pay the price as Russia did.[89]

Two years before, when Hitler rose to power in Germany, Garvey wrote of the ability of the Jews to ruin Germany financially. "The Jews are a powerful minority group," assayed Garvey, "and although they may be at a disadvantage in Germany, they can so react upon things German as to make the Germans, and particularly Hitler and the Nazis, rue the day they ever started the persecution."[90]

While Garvey promulgated prejudicial theories about Jewish culture in the lessons from the School of African Philosophy and elsewhere, he also expressed contrary views, at times harshly criticizing racial discrimination against Jews. In 1933 he directly linked the Jewish reputation for business acumen with German anti-Semitism. He strongly denounced discrimination against Jews as a minority group and ascribed anti-Jewish prejudice to racism motivated by jealousy of Jewish economic success. "The Jewish race is a noble one," he wrote in a 28 March 1933 *New Jamaican* editorial, and "the Jew is only persecuted because he has certain qualities of progress that other people have not learnt." He then drew a direct analogy between the persecution of Jews and the prejudice directed against blacks in the United States, and strongly denounced Nazi racial intolerance.[91] He specifically denounced Hitler's and Mussolini's designs on African colonies, and linked Nazi prejudice against blacks with the persecution of Jews, describing both as racist policies that presented dangerous ramifications for world affairs.[92]

89. "Hitler and the Jews," *BM* 1, no. 8 (July 1935): 9.

90. *New Jamaican,* 1 April 1933.

91. see also *New Jamaican,* 1 April 1933.

92. *BM* 1, no. 7 (June 1935): 8; 1, no. 12 (March 1936): 1–3; 3, no. 9 (March 1938): 1–2; 3, no. 11 (November 1938): 1–2; 4, no. 1 (February 1939): 1–2.

DISSEMINATION OF THE LESSONS

Garvey's School of African Philosophy was advertised in the *Black Man* throughout 1938, and in February 1939 Garvey announced that several more students had completed the lessons. In May 1939 a second session of the school was taught by Garvey at the Beaumont Crescent headquarters in London, and in June he released a new list of graduates, most of whom were from the United States. African graduates included Mr. J. O. Nwanolue, Onitsha, Nigeria; Mr. D. S. Musoke, Kampala, Uganda; and Mr. H. Illitintro, Cape Province, South Africa. African interest in the school did not go unnoticed by colonial authorities. On 22 June 1939 an intelligence report was sent to the chief secretary in Nairobi, Kenya, by the provincial commissioner of Nyanza province, reporting that collections were being taken up in North Kavirondo, Kenya, to pay for Garvey's correspondence course.[93]

In the years immediately following Garvey's death the correspondence lessons from the School of African Philosophy continued to be circulated. Charles James of Philadelphia and James Stewart of Cleveland, both graduates of the original 1937 session in Toronto, continued to offer the course to applicants by mail. Later, William Sherrill offered the course to students through advertisements in the Philadelphia *Garvey's Voice* in the 1950s, and Clifford Barnes, commissioner of Louisiana, served as examiner for those students who subscribed to the correspondence course through Stewart's wing of the movement in the late 1940s.

THE LEGACY

The circumstances of Garvey's life and the lessons he taught his followers reflect the popular intellectual and political currents of his times, revised to the service of the revival of black consciousness. His life remains a testimony to his

93. Kenya National Archives, "Nyanza Province Intelligence Reports, 1939–1942," PC/NZA 4/5/3.

spectacular ability to capture the popular imagination and move people to a new outlook. "After all discount is made," declared a contemporary, "after all the tinsel is brushed away, the fact remains that the grandiose schemes of Marcus Garvey gave to the race a consciousness such as it had never possessed before."[94]

Marcus Garvey: Life and Lessons is a record, one hundred years after the birth of Garvey, of the travail of self-education among blacks. It was out of this tradition that the ideal of Africa's regeneration evolved. Garvey's positive contribution was to enrich its continuing legacy of race pride, self-mastery, and hope.

In her memoirs Amy Jacques Garvey wrote of a May 1928 symposium on Garvey at Howard University, where students debated the difference "between 'The Man' and 'The Movement'" that shared his name. The debaters agreed that Garveyism, as a philosophy of black pride and pan-Africanism, was the solution to "the international problem of the Negro." They also agreed that "Garvey's philosophy was distinguished from the man Garvey" and stressed the timelessness and universality of his legacy. "Garvey was temporal," they noted, "but Garveyism was eternal."[95]

What's in a name? As anyone familiar with the Afro-American folktale tradition knows, the answer to the question comes in the telling of the tale.

The Editors

94. Benjamin Brawley, "The Negro Literary Renaissance," *Southern Workman,* 56 (April 1927): 177.

95. *Garvey and Garveyism,* pp. 190–191.

CHRONOLOGY

The Life of Marcus Garvey

1887	Malcus Mosiah ("Marcus") Garvey, Jr., born at St. Ann's Bay, parish of St. Ann, Jamaica, son of Malcus Mosiah Garvey, Sr., and Sarah Jane Richards.
1901–1903	Leaves Church of England school after completing sixth standard; begins work as printer's apprentice in St. Ann's Bay.
1904	Moves to Port Maria, St. Mary's Parish, to work as journeyman printer.
ca. 1906	Moves to Kingston; employed in printing department of P. A. Benjamin Manufacturing Co.
1907	Elected vice president of compositors' branch of printers' union.
1908	Mother dies; printers' strike begins.
1909	Printers' strike collapses and union disintegrates.
1910	Garvey elected assistant secretary of National Club of Jamaica; publishes pamphlet *The Struggling Mass;* travels to Central America; visits Costa Rica, Guatemala, Panama.
1911	Returns to Jamaica.
1913	Leaves Jamaica for England; attends classes at Birkbeck College, London; publishes "The British West Indies in the Mirror of Civilization: History Making by Colonial Negroes" in Duse Mohamed Ali's *African Times and Orient Review;* travels to European continent.
1914	Returns to Jamaica; founds Universal Negro Improvement Association (UNIA) and African Com-

munities League (ACL), 20 July; publishes pamphlet, *A Talk with Afro–West Indians: The Negro Race and Its Problems;* writes to Booker T. Washington and receives invitation to visit Tuskegee Institute.

1915   Father committed to St. Ann Poor House; Booker T. Washington dies.

1916   Garvey leaves Jamaica for U.S.; arrives in New York City in March and holds his first public lecture in St. Mark's Church Hall; embarks on yearlong speaking tour of thirty-eight states.

1918   New York branch of UNIA formed in January with thirteen members; UNIA and ACL incorporated separately in New York State; *Negro World* begins publication; UNIA's *Constitution and Book of Laws* written.

1919   Black Star Line (BSL) incorporated in state of Delaware; UNIA establishes Liberty Hall in Harlem; U.S. attorney general requests commissioner general of immigration to investigate Garvey in regard to institution of deportation proceedings; Bureau of Investigation of Department of Justice places Garvey under surveillance; *Negro World* banned in areas of Caribbean and Central America; BSL purchases S.S. *Yarmouth;* UNIA and BSL offices opened at 54–56 West 135th St. in Harlem; assassination attempt against Garvey by George Tyler fails; Garvey marries Amy Ashwood.

1920   Negro Factories Corp. incorporated in New York State; Garvey's father dies in Jamaica; Garvey sues for annulment of marriage; S.S. *Shadyside* and S.S. *Kanawha* purchased by BSL; First UNIA International Convention opens at Madison Square Garden; UNIA Declaration of Rights adopted; Garvey elected provisional president of Africa; Liberian Construction Loan and colonization plan launched.

1921   Liberian president C.D.B. King meets with UNIA representatives in New York; UNIA delegation arrives in Monrovia, Liberia; Garvey makes organizational tour of the Caribbean and Central America; State Department instructs American consuls to deny Garvey visa to reenter the U.S.; later reverses stance and permits entry; Garvey returns to New York in July; Second UNIA International Convention held in August.

1922 Garvey arrested on mail fraud charges, 12 January, and indicted by federal grand jury, 15 February; free on bail, undertakes nationwide speaking tour to raise funds for UNIA; obtains divorce from Amy Ashwood in June; marries Amy Jacques in July; meets with Ku Klux Klan Acting Imperial Wizard Edward Young Clarke in Atlanta; UNIA delegation delivers petition to League of Nations; Rev. J.W.H. Eason impeached by UNIA and forms rival Universal Negro Alliance; UNIA publishes *Daily Negro Times,* ca. August–October; Third UNIA International Convention held in August.

1923 Eason assassinated in New Orleans; Chandler Owen and seven other black leaders urge Garvey's deportation in letter to Attorney General Harry M. Daugherty; mail fraud trial begins 18 May; Garvey sentenced to five years' imprisonment, 21 June; incarcerated for three months in Tombs Prison, New York, then released on bail; visits Tuskegee Institute; UNIA delegation to Liberia leaves for Monrovia; Amy Jacques Garvey publishes first volume of *Philosophy and Opinions of Marcus Garvey.*

1924 Amy Jacques Garvey becomes associate editor of *Negro World*—Spanish, French, and women's sections added; Black Cross Navigation and Trading Co. founded; Fourth UNIA International Convention held in New York; Liberian government forms pact with Firestone Rubber Co.; UNIA's Universal Negro Political Union endorses presidential candidacy of Calvin Coolidge.

1925 S.S. *General Goethals* makes maiden voyage for BSL; mail fraud conviction reaffirmed by U.S. Court of Appeals, 3 February; Garvey imprisoned in Atlanta Federal Penitentiary, 8 February; Amy

Jacques Garvey becomes Garvey's unofficial representative in UNIA affairs; Garvey corresponds with Earnest Sevier Cox, president of White America Society; writes "African Fundamentalism"; application for pardon denied; endorses John Powell, president of Anglo-Saxon Clubs, to speak at Liberty Hall; Liberty Hall mortgaged; Amy Jacques Garvey publishes second volume of *Philosophy and Opinions of Marcus Garvey.*

1926   Special UNIA convention held in Detroit in March; officers loyal to Garvey elected, including Fred A. Toote as acting president general; rival UNIA, Inc., elects its own officers in convention in New York; Smallwood-Corey Industrial Institute, Claremont, Va., purchased by UNIA, renamed Liberty University.

1927   Toote resigns and E. B. Knox becomes Garvey's personal representative; President Coolidge commutes Garvey's sentence, 18 November; Garvey deported; arrives in Jamaica, 10 December; speaks to overflow crowd at Ward Theater in Kingston; Liberty Hall sold at auction in New York.

1928   Garvey and Amy Jacques Garvey travel to Europe; Garvey speaks at Royal Albert Hall; continues speaking tour of Britain, France, Belgium, and Germany; addresses audience at Century Theatre, London; travels to Geneva to renew UNIA petition to League of Nations; sails to Canada; detained in Montreal; returns to Jamaica; presides over meeting of newly formed People's Political party.

1929   Purchases Edelweiss Park as Jamaican headquarters; establishes Blackman Printing and Publishing Co.; commences publication of daily newspaper, *Blackman;* international UNIA convention held in Kingston; reincorporates organization as UNIA and ACL (August 1929) of the World, resulting in an official split between Jamaica-based and U.S.-based wings of movement; convicted of contempt of court and sentenced to three months in prison; elected to Kingston and St. Andrew Corp.

1930   Defeated in general election for seat in Jamaica's colonial legislative council; first son, Marcus Garvey, Jr., born, 17 September; M.L.T. De Mena becomes U.S. representative; *Blackman* becomes a weekly.

1931   *Blackman* ceases publication; Garvey sails for England and Geneva; again elected member of Kingston and St. Andrew Corp.; returns to Jamaica; organizes Edelweiss Amusement Co., hosts shows, plays, and concerts.

1932   Rival Parent Body of UNIA, Inc., headed by Lionel Francis, holds convention in New York; Garvey begins publication of evening newspaper, *New Jamaican*.

1933   Garvey's second son, Julius Winston Garvey, born 16 August; machinery of Blackman Printing and Publishing Co. seized for debts; publication of *New Jamaican* ends; publication of monthly magazine, *Black Man*, begins; regular publication of *Negro World* ceases in New York.

1934   International UNIA convention held at Edelweiss Park; Garvey announces plans to move UNIA headquarters to London; Edelweiss Park placed under foreclosure and sold at public auction.

1935   Garvey relocates to London; publishes new edition of *The Tragedy of White Injustice*; denounces Italian invasion of Ethiopia; opposes involvement of UNIA members in New York–based Provisional Committee for the Defense of Ethiopia because of coalition's ties with members of Communist party.

1936   Begins publication of series of negative editorials on Haile Selassie and his policies; presides over UNIA regional conference held in Toronto; criticizes depiction of blacks in films; protests Church of England's declaration of opposition to Edward VIII's affair with divorced Wallis Simpson.

1937   Amy Jacques Garvey joins Garvey in London with sons; Garvey accuses Haile Selassie of lack of identification with fellow blacks and of being "visionless and disloyal to his country"; presides over UNIA regional conference in Toronto; organizes School of African Philosophy with eleven students; travels to eastern Caribbean; returns to England; heckled at Speakers' Corner in Hyde Park for his views on the Italo-Ethiopian conflict.

1938   UNIA, Inc., of New York wins judgment in Isaiah Morter case, denying UNIA (August 1929) of the World rights to lucrative bequest; UNIA convention held in Toronto; convention passes resolution of support for Greater Liberia bill sponsored by Sen. Theodore Bilbo of Mississippi; Garvey announces availability of lessons from School of African Philosophy as correspondence course; Amy Jacques Garvey returns to Jamaica with sons while Garvey absent in Canada; Amy Jacques Garvey and Garvey cease direct communication.

1939   Garvey endorses the Greater Liberia bill in *Black Man;* Garvey's lawyer, George Gordon Battle, files application for presidential pardon for Garvey.

1940   Garvey suffers cerebral hemorrhage in January and is partially paralyzed; erroneous report of his death circulated in May leads to printing of obituaries in newspapers around the world; Garvey suffers second cerebral hemorrhage and/or cardiac arrest; dies in London, 10 June; buried in St. Mary's Roman Catholic cemetery, Bethnal Green, London.

1964   Garvey declared Jamaica's first national hero; his remains reinterred at Marcus Garvey Memorial, Kingston.

Textual Devices

[roman] Conjectural reading for missing, mutilated, or illegible text, with a question mark inside the square brackets when the conjectural reading is doubtful. Also used in editorial correction of typographical errors in original printed or typed document and in identification of unnamed individuals alluded to in text, such as [Edward Smith-Green].

[*italic*] Editorial comment on original text, such as [*line missing*], [*illegible*], or [*torn*].

/　/ Text inside slashes indicates autograph insertions in typewritten original.

[. . .] Redundant portion of original text deleted.

AFRICAN
FUNDAMENTALISM

African Fundamentalism

Editorial by Marcus Garvey

Fellow Men of the Negro Race, Greeting:

The time has come for the Negro to forget and cast behind him his hero worship and adoration of other races, and to start out immediately, to create and emulate heroes of his own.

We must canonize our own saints, create our own martyrs, and elevate to positions of fame and honor black men and women who have made their distinct contributions to our racial history. Sojourner Truth is worthy of the place of sainthood alongside of Joan of Arc; Crispus Attucks and George William Gordon are entitled to the halo of martyrdom with no less glory than that of the martyrs of any other race. Toussaint L'Ouverture's brilliancy as a soldier and statesman outshone that of a Cromwell, Napoleon and Washington; hence, he is entitled to the highest place as a hero among men. Africa has produced countless numbers of men and women, in war and in peace, whose lustre and bravery outshine that of any other people. Then why not see good and perfection in ourselves?

Ours the Right to Our Doctrine

We must inspire a literature and promulgate a doctrine of our own without any apologies to the powers that be. The right is ours and God's. Let contrary sentiment and cross opinions go to the winds. Opposition to race independence is the weapon of the enemy to defeat the hopes of an unfortunate people. We are entitled to our own opinions and not obligated to or bound by the opinions of others.

A Peep at the Past

If others laugh at you, return the laughter to them; if they mimic you, return the compliment with equal force. They have no more right to dishonor, disrespect and disregard your feeling and manhood than you have in dealing with them. Honor them when they honor you; disrespect and disregard them when they vilely treat you. Their arrogance is but skin deep and an assumption that has no foundation in morals or in law. They have sprung from the same family tree of obscurity as we have; their history is as rude in its primitiveness as ours; their ancestors ran wild and naked, lived in caves and in the branches of trees, like monkeys, as ours; they made human sacrifices, ate the flesh of their own dead and the raw meat of the wild beast for centuries even as they accuse us of doing; their cannibalism was more prolonged than ours; when we were embracing the arts and sciences on the banks of the Nile their ancestors were still drinking human blood and eating out of the skulls of their conquered dead; when our civilization had reached the noonday of progress they were still running naked and sleeping in holes and caves with rats, bats and other insects and animals. After we had already unfathomed the mysteries of the stars and reduced the heavenly constellations to minute and regular calculus they were still backwoodsmen, living in ignorance and blatant darkness.

Why Be Discouraged?

The world today is indebted to us for the benefits of civilization. They stole our arts and sciences from Africa. Then why should we be ashamed of ourselves? Their MODERN IMPROVEMENTS are but DUPLICATES of a grander civilization that we reflected thousands of years ago, without the advantage of what is buried and still hidden, to be resurrected and reintroduced by the intelligence of our generation and our prosperity. Why should we be discouraged because somebody laughs at us today? Who to tell what tomorrow will bring forth? Did they not laugh at Moses, Christ and Mohammed? Was there not a Carthage, Greece and Rome? We see and have changes every day, so pray, work, be steadfast and be not dismayed.

NOTHING MUST KILL THE EMPIRE URGE

As the Jew is held together by his RELIGION, the white races by the assumption and the unwritten law of SUPERIORITY, and the Mongolian by the precious tie of BLOOD, so likewise the Negro must be united in one GRAND RACIAL HIERARCHY. Our UNION MUST KNOW NO CLIME, BOUNDARY, or NATIONALITY. Like the great Church of Rome, Negroes the world over MUST PRACTICE ONE FAITH, that of Confidence in themselves, with One God! One Aim! One Destiny! Let no religious scruples, no political machination divide us, but let us hold together under all climes and in every country, making among ourselves a Racial Empire upon which "the sun shall never set."

ALLEGIANCE TO SELF FIRST

Let no voice but your own speak to you from the depths. Let no influence but your own raise you in time of peace and time of war. Hear all, but attend only that which concerns you.

Your first allegiance shall be to your God, then to your family, race and country. Remember always that the Jew in his political and economic urge is always first a Jew; the white man is first a white man under all circumstances, and you can do no less than being first and always a Negro, and then all else will take care of itself. Let no one inoculate you for their own conveniences. There is no humanity before that which starts with yourself. "Charity begins at home." First to thyself be true, and "thou canst not then be false to any man."

WE ARE ARBITERS OF OUR OWN DESTINY

God and Nature first made us what we are, and then out of our own creative genius we make ourselves what we want to be. Follow always that great law.

Let the sky and God be our limit, and Eternity our measurement. There is no height to which we cannot climb by using the active intelligence of our own minds. Mind creates, and as much as we desire in Nature we can have through the creation of our own minds. Being at present the scientifically weaker race, you shall treat others only as they treat you; but in your homes and everywhere possible you must teach the higher development of science to your children; and be sure to develop a race of scientists par excellence, for in science and religion lies our only hope to withstand the evil designs of modern materialism. Never forget your God. Remember, we live, work and pray for the establishing of a great and binding RACIAL HIERARCHY, the founding of a RACIAL EMPIRE whose only natural, spiritual and political limits shall be God and "Africa, at home and abroad."

MARCUS GARVEY

SOURCE NOTES

Printed in the *Negro World,* 6 June 1925, as a front-page editorial; written in Atlanta Federal Penitentiary. Original headlines omitted. Creed reprinted in slightly revised form, under the title "African Fundamentalism," as a UNIA poster, sold by mail order through the *Negro World* by Amy Jacques Garvey, 1925.

AFRICAN FUNDAMENTALISM: FOUNT OF INSPIRATION

Speeches by Marcus Garvey

HON. MARCUS GARVEY SPEAKS

For the next few Sunday nights, I am going to speak to you from the thoughts contained in "AFRICAN FUNDAMENTALISM," so that they may be advised, I expected every Negro home at this time to secure a copy of this Creed for the guidance of the Race. Tonight I will speak from the first sentence of "AFRICAN FUNDAMENTALISM"—"THE TIME HAS COME FOR THE NEGRO TO FORGET AND CAST BEHIND HIM HIS HERO WORSHIP AND ADORATION OF OTHER RACES, AND TO START OUT IMMEDIATELY TO CREATE AND EMULATE HEROES OF HIS OWN."

HAVE YOUR OWN OPINION

Any race that accepts the thoughts of another race, automatical[l]y, becomes the slave race of that other race. As men think, so they do react above the things around them. When men are taught to think in a certain groove they act similarly. It is no wonder that the Negro acts so peculiarly within our present civilization, because he has been trained and taught to accept the thoughts of a race that has made itself by assumption superior. The Negro during the time of slavery accepted his thoughts and opinions from the white race, by so doing he admitted into his system the idea of the superiority of a master in relationship to a slave. In one instance he was freed, that is, from chattel slav[e]ry; but up to the time of the Universal Negro Improvement Association, he was not free in mind. "African Fundamentalism" seeks to emancipate the Negro from the thoughts of others who are encouraging him to act on [their?] opinions and thoughts. Any [race?] that has succeeded in the world—speaking of the ancient world up to the present world, will tell you that they succeeded by thinking and acting for themselves. Whether they be the Meads [Medes] or the Persians, the Greeks or the Romans, the English or the Americans, each and everyone, ancient and modern, will tell you that their ability to rise above others and to establish themselves in the world was only made possible through the fact that they thought and acted for themselves. And we who have studied the trend of world events, seriously recommend to the Negro that he can only do this when he starts to think and act for himself. He must create around him his own philosophy—the semblance of everything that he desires for himself. That is what "AFRICAN FUNDAMENTALISM" seeks to do,—establish a creed, as a guide, so that you will make few mistakes, if any, in the world. Because if you act on the thoughts of others, so long will they remain your superiors; for no man is so just, because of the sins of the world, to treat his brother as he would that others treat him. Man will not treat his brother with equity. We have one race pulling against the other, so that it has almost become an axiom. "That no man will think equally for his brother," and so those who have imposed their thoughts upon you, will give you only that thought to let you serve them as slaves.

ACCEPT SOMETHING ORIGINAL

To emancipate yourselves from that you must accept something original, something racially your own, and that is what we want you the Negroes, not only of Edelweis Park, to do—accept a Philosophy entirely your own, serviceable to your actions and cease imitating the thoughts of others. I have often spoken of the heroes of [*line missing*?] other races have made their heroes, we have had few names to warrant my calling them, but not because we have not made many heroes in the past, we cannot start out now. The other races [h]ave made their heroes, we also can create our own heroes and point our people to them as examples because of their noble deeds. The Universal Negro Improvement Association is seeking to put the Negro in his right position. Whatever the criticisms of the Universal Negro Improvement Association may be, above all that has been said about the Organization, it stands for the loftiest and noblest ideals pertaining to the work of man. There is nothing that the black man has done that the Universal Negro Improvement Association has not inspired him to do through its creed that he should stand on his own.

There is nothing that man cannot do if he applies himself rigorously to do it. We are therefore inspiring you to apply yourselves consistent[l]y, in season and out of se[a]son to what you have decided to do. The Creed of "African Fundamentalism" must be maintained and protected every day. It is a Philosophy that is to serve as a guide to the Negro Peoples of the world. The other peoples do not live their lives by chance, they have a Creed to guide them. Our race is the only one that has not done that, and so long as we continue the slack methods, so long will we be the slaves of the world. God intended that you should rise to every occasion; He gave you the same mental reserve as any other race. He blessed you with the same intelligence as others; but your intelligence has been so warped, so abused as to [m]ake you almost the slave of those who have thought more of life and know how to husband it, so as to get the best out of it.

━ A SPLENDID RECOMMENDATION

The Universal Negro Improvement Association makes the recommendation and I honestly support this recommendation, that there is such glory and honour for the Negro to attain in the world, as have been achieved and attained by any other race before. There is nothing in nature's law so limited as to prevent the Negro enjoying what the other people are enjoying, which they obtained through method. I tell you, whether it is the thought of Socrates, Plato, or Napoleon; the white race has a system, a method, a code of ethics laid down for the white child to go by, a philosophy, a set Creed to guide its life. When the child comes into the world, this Creed is set out for him to follow and he is trained thereby, so you will not wonder that the white race has reached such a height in civilisation. They will not tell you what is to be found in that Creed, you must find that out for yourselves. We go to the same school that they go to, we study out of the same text books that they study from, yet there are things, many things that the white child knows that you have never seen or heard of. The white child is given private tuition in the knowledge of life. There is no man in the world of one race who will impart to the members of another race the things that would enable that race to launch out successfully in life to compare itself with his race. The Negro must understand that he is

STANDING BY HIMSELF.

If he is to enjoy the best out of life, he must create for himself, and he can only create for himself when he has given to the world his philosophy and code to guide him. And I can recommend to you nothing more enhancing than the Creed we have laid down in "African Fundamentalism." If you will absorb it you will get inspiration to guide you and your children. Take the Jews for example, they have a set philosophy of life; as the Jewish child is born into the world that philosophy is laid before him; he grows in that philosophy, lives and dies in that philosophy. As of the Jews so of the other people. They have set philosophies, that have not been thought out-doors, but within themselves. You, the Negro, bring children into the world without any policy to guide them, when they should have inherited from their fathers a Creed, a policy to advance the race. You will make excuse that you have been in slavery for three hundred years. We excuse you for that; but you have been emancipated now one hundred years, and it is time that you were able to stand upon the same level as the other peoples, understanding nature and nature's laws. When you get to understand that, you will no longer be the cringing creatures as others would have you be; but a master. The opportunity is yours, you can lift your selves any height, as others have done; it is only for you to summon the courage and absorb these things, which are at your doors, and so merit the blessing of God. The Universal Negro Improvement Association is opening the door of intelligence to the Four Hundred Million Negroes of the world—the door of inspiration. Go to the fount and drink, and when you do so you will see all honour in your own race, create your own heroes so that in another generation, I will not have to refer to the heroes of another race, but the teachers will recommend to you the heroes of your own race even though they may have passed this way three thousand years ago. The opportunity is yours to play your part as an Alexander did, as a Constantine did, as a Cortez did, as a C[ae]sar did, as a Napoleon did, as a William the Conqueror did, as the great white men are now playing their part in the world.

LORD BIRKENHEAD

Just a couple of days ago a great white man passed away in England—Lord Birkenhead—a man who felt the responsibility of Empire, who at every turn stood firm to not only the inspiration of the Empire: but its solidarity; a man who was regarded and respected by the Empire and the entire world; a man who was honoured by his king; a man who contributed to the Empire to make it more solid and firm than he found it. We therefore point you to "African Fundamentalism" a fount of inspiration; so that you too may enjoy the inspiration that made Lord Birkenhead the power that he was. We point you to the inspiration so that you may be a replica of Napoleon and climb your Alps; not of Europe, but of Africa, so that you too may be as able a Statesman as Pitt, as able a man as any that has passed this way, from

C[ae]sar up to the present time. When God Almighty made you, He did not make you with less mentality than the white man; when God Almighty made you, He fashioned you out of the same mould as the other races: He gave you an equality of gray matter: He gave you an equality of superior reserve as He gave the great white men; as He gave the great warriors; as He gave to the great champions; as He gave to the great captains, but the great difference is they found themselves, and you have not yet found yourselves.

AN APPEAL TO THE
FOUR HUNDRED MILLION NEGROES

Tonight we want you to find yourselves, like Constantine found himself, like Darwin found himself, like Napoleon found himself, like George Washington found himself, and left behind them great deeds by which men will remember them and bless them. Get your inspiration right, and it can come to you in no better way than by the common Creed, the common Guide of "African Fundamentalism." Get a copy tonight, hang it up on your wall, point your children to it; let them study it; let them follow it; let it be an inspiration to greater things. That is my message to you tonight. Take to it kindly, understand it properly, and let it be an inspiration to guide you to the level of men, so that you can look men in the face, not as slaves and serfs, but as masters. God made you to be masters, when He placed you in this world above all things visible and invisible.—(Applause).

———————

On Sunday night last the Hon. Marcus Garvey, President-General of the Universal Negro Improvement Association, at "Edelweis Park," continued a discourse on the subject of "African Fundamentalism[."] The week before he promised that he would speak for several Sundays on this topic explaining the real meaning of the Creed of the Negro race.

There was a tremendous crowd that listened to him most attentively; and from all indications were generally edified through the masterly manner in which Mr. Garvey expressed himself. Among other things, he said that there is no reason why the Negro should select the martyrs, heroes and saints of other races as their pattern when in their own race they have characters equally as eminent who could be put alongside the greatest of the white race. He said that Sojourner Truth, the greatest American Negro woman, occupied a similar place in history as Saint Joan of Arc, as a pattern, they should look up to St. Sojourne[r] Truth as their pattern.

HEROISM OF CRISPUS ATTUCKS

Mr. Garvey said in continuation that all of us know about the history of the American Revolution; and nearly everybody has heard of the great deeds of George Washington; but there is one American who stood out in the early stage of the American Revolution even more prominent than George Washington and he was a black man by the name of Crispus Attucks, who on Boston Commons shed the first drop of blood for American Independence. As Washington has a place in history to be admired by white men then Crispus Attucks has one equally as great to be admired by Negroes. He said in the Military Field that Toussaint L'Ouverture acquitted himself and demonstrated that he was more brilliant and able a soldier than Napoleon; therefore, while the white man thinks of Napoleon, we should think of the great Negro General who in the plains of Santo Domingo defeated the combined armies of France, England and Spain and made his country free and independent.

Mr. Garvey impressed upon his auditors that it was the duty of every Negro in the world to take a copy of "African Fundamentalism" which is the

CREED OF THE RACE;

and that it should be framed and placed in the home as a

source of inspiration to the members of the family and friends. Every race, he said, has some kind of source of inspiration; and the Negro cannot afford to live without his and it was for [t]hat reason that the Creed of "African Fundamentalism" was given to the world.

The time had come, he said, when the Negro, each and every one, should feel proud of his race and no less so than others feel about themselves. We must treat our heroes, saints and martyrs and great men and women just the same as other races treat theirs; we must elevate them to the same loftiness as others have done. While the Church has given us their Saint Jerome, their Saint Benedict, their Saint Catherine, we of the black race can also give to the world our Saints, men and women who by their pious usefulness and courageous deeds have left behind them such blessings as to make their race thankful for their existence. Then why not honour them equally as the white race honour their benefactors. This is the age when all races should think feelingly of their own and the Negro is now inspired to do so.

HON. MARCUS GARVEY SPEAKS

I am continuing my discourse from the Subject in keeping with what I started to explain thoroughly to each and everyone—the meaning of this Creed of our Race. I am pleased to learn that nearly everybody is securing a copy of "AFRICAN FUNDAMENTALISM." This Creed should be in the home of every Negro all over the world, and we in Jamaica should not be any different to the other members of the race.

The part of the Creed that I am going to speak from to-night says: "AFRICA HAS PRODUCED C[OUNT]LESS NUMBERS OF MEN AND WOMEN IN WAR AND IN PEACE WHOSE LUSTRE AND BRAVERY OUTSHINE THAT OF ANY OTHER PEOPLE. THEN WHY NOT SEE GOOD AND PERFECT IN OURSELVES? WE MUST INSPIRE A LITERATURE AND PROMULGATE A DOCTRINE OF OUR OWN WITHOUT ANY APOLOGIES TO THE POWERS THAT BE. THE

RIGHT IS OURS AND GOD'S."

To repeat: "Africa has produced countless numbers of men and women in war and in peace whose lustre and bravery outshine that of any other people." In my many discourses recently here and elsewhere, I have, as it was my duty, spoken in a vein or strain to suggest that at the present time as a race, we have not been doing much nor accomplished much to warrant our present existence. Some of you may have taken it to heart, become discouraged and taken it to mean that well, we have not amounted to anything. But again I have tried to encourage you not to ignore your past, but to think that although you have not accomplished and achieved anything in our modern civilization[,] the race has a history, the proudest history of the world. The Negro has a history which enables him to compare himself with any other race. He stands topmost among other men because he was the father of our civilization. This however is no credit to us because we have not lived up to the glories of our fathers. But we ought to feel proud when we remember that our fathers gave the first civilization to the world.

AFRICA THE CRADLE OF CIVILIZATION

Africa, the Scribes tell us today and history has told us, has been the cradle of civilization. When all Europe was in darkness: was only a settlement of cannibals and barbarians. Africa held up the torch of civilization, the Negro was the teacher of the ages, the blessed man of the Continents. Of the many Continents of the world, Africa stands out most prominently as the leader. All other Continents copied their civilization from Africa. And so if not in modern days, in ancient days Africa produced heroes and martyrs that we in any age should be proud of. As I suggested last week we should not accept any exemplary characters from any race because they are only borrowed from Africa when it was great. And if they could have borrowed from our civilization and produced heroes and saints for us to imitate, there is no reason why the Negro should not lean upon his own shoulders, accepting his leaders from his own men and women who have led the path of civilization for centuries.

GREAT AFRICAN LEADERS

We have heard of great leaders, but in all times no leaders have stood out as the African leaders. The greatest leaders of ancient days who brought Rome to tears were not white men, they were the father Hamilcar and the son, Hannibal—two great leaders who made the Romans so fearful that at one period of Roman History no Roman could sleep comfortably because he was afraid that he would wake up a slave of Carthage. These are only two examples that have come out of Africa in war; but in Science and in Art, Africa claims a position Par excellence. Whatsoever the German, the Englishman, the Italian boast of they will tell you, if they wish to be truthful, that they take credit for thes[e] things only because they were able [t]o copy them from the Africans. Up to now they are excavating to discover the mysteries that once stood out in Africa in the time of the Pharoahs. During that time Africa occupied a unique position in history. They will try to tell you that the Pharoahs were white, but the mummified characteristics of the Pharoahs were black men. In later years the Pharoahs became somewhat coloured. In all ages, (those who are students of sociology will bear this out that) wheresoever you find a conquering race you will find them impressing their features and their morals upon the particular people conquered, or subdued. And so it is only a question of time when the strong people of any age will reduce the conquered or weaker people of any age and bring about different kinds and colours that were never produced before. As a proof of this I am now speaking to differently coloured people it is because the conquering whiteman has been able to impress his type upon the weaker people. When the white man held the black man in slavery he was able to reduce his women to his will, thereby impressing his features upon the black race. In the same way when Africa was strong; when Carthage was strong; when the black man held the reigns of the world in his hands he went conquering in Asia, reducing the morality of the Asiatics; he went conquering in Spain: he went conquering in Northern France reducing their morality, and that is the result of the vast coloured population in the world, proving the blackman's greatness in ages past. Originally there was no coloured race. There were only white and black. The exist[e]nce therefore of a mixed race proves that the blackman was once the conqueror of the world. That is why the black man stands consoled to-day because he knows that he was once great and that he will again come back into his own.

AFRICA'S POWER WIDE SPREAD

Those of you who have travelled must of noticed that the people of Mediterranean Europe are darker than the people of Northern Europe. This is because they have come in closer contact with the people of Africa. The people of Italy are dark; the people of Southern Spain are darker than those of Northern Spain; the people of southern France are darker than those of Northern France; it is bec[au]se when Africa was in her power it was easier for her to cross over to the southern parts of Europe conquering the people of Italy, of Spain and of France. The Spaniard, if he wants to tell you the tru[t]h, will tell you that up to to-day, he respects the black man. And when they talk of Saints, the patron saints of the Spaniard is a black man, for up to that time they had to look up to a black man. Prior to that day Homer tells us that when the Greek[s] were getting out of their swaddling clothes the Africans were the only companions they would keep because they were superior to them in intelligence, and they could gain knowledge from them. And it is said that when a god was missing from Greece he was gone over to Africa to spend time with the Ethiopians. So whatsoever might have been the development in civilization you hold the credit that it was borrowed from your fathers, and if you are a true descendant of Africa you will be able to duplicate the deeds of your fathers. We of the Universal Negro Improvement Association are inspiring you to go forth into the world as others have done in the ages past and are doing now, and if you are courageous and bold you will take kindly to the deeds of your fathers.

A few days after the destruction of the air-ship R-101 a gentleman remarked to me that if I did not think that God had a hand in this disaster. He said that the airship being on its way to India and Africa for the sole purpose of bluffing the Indians, God, in his opinion, did not want this bluff to take place, so He destroyed the airship. I can not see my way to accept this interpretation because I do not believe that God interferes with things like that; but I do believe, as another party said, that it was a mechanical defect in the ship. I do not believe that God puts any handicap upon any people for the exercising of their intelligence and the use of their brains. It was complimentary to the white man to have done what he did, exercising prowess in the law of monopoly over creation and Nature constituting himself so ably to do what he did. The white man has been able to raise his intelligence far above any creature in the world, you are as capable of using your intelligence as any other white man that came here because at one time you were the fathers of civilisation and intelligence, and if you were able to do it once you are able to do it again: but while the white man is thinking in terms of greatness, the Negro is sleeping on his intelligence. The Universal Negro Improvement Association in inspiring you to imitate not the deeds of the white man, but to accomplish over again the deeds of your fathers. You have accomplished them once already, you can do it again, and I do hope that this will be an inspiration to some black man or woman to some black boy or girl to go through the world accomplishing something grand and great as the white man is now doing. Can I repeat: "Africa has produced countless numbers of men and women in war and in peace whose lustre and bravery outshine that of any other peoples." Therefore look to the colours of the Race; look to the colours of the Negro for your inspirations; look to the colours of that great Empire of Ethiopia that is now scattered all over the world; select our leaders from out of our own race; and not from the other races because others look down upon us contemptuously and scornfully when we have to follow them.

STIR YOURSELVES

We must give up that silly idea of folding our hands and waiting upon God to do everything for us. If God intended that, He would not have given us a mind; He would not have given us intelligence; He would not have given us His soul; He would not have placed us here in the midst of creation, and surrounded us with all the beautiful things of nature. Whatsoever you want in life you must make up your mind to do it for yourself and accomplish it for yourself; whether it is rearing a home, expanding an Empire, if you want to do it, you must do it for yourself and then God will bless the effort because He will realise that you are using your intelligence for the best. That is my message to you tonight and I do hope you have absorbed it because it is only by absorbing it you will be able to mentally and physically rise above the things that environ you. So tonight I am inspiring you to experiment in your own sphere placing in the airships, placing on the sea Titanics. Africa calls you to service; Africa calls you to Empire—a universal Empire. Africa calls you to a universal freedom and until we answer, Africa will never rise from the dust, because we have lost the inspiration of our fathers. (Applause).

HON. MARCUS GARVEY'S SPEECH

I shall again speak on the subject of "AFRICAN FUNDAMENTALISM." For the benefit of those who have not heard me on this before I will explain, that "AFRICAN FUNDAMENTALISM" is a written Creed of the Negro race which is now being circulated all over the world, a copy of which is to be placed in every home as an inspiration to the members of the

[fa]mily, because it is only by this accepted Creed—a universal acceptance—that we will be able to unitedly go forward to the great object that we have in view. I am going to speak to you on the second paragraph.

"A Peep in the Past"

If others laugh at you, return the laughter to them; if they mimic you, return the compliment with equal force. They have no more right to dishonour, disrespect and disregard your feeling and manhood than you have in dealing with them. Honour them when they honour you; disrespect and disregard them when they vilely treat you. Their arrogance is but skin deep and a[n] assumption that has no foundation in morals or in law. They have sprung from the same family tree of obscurity as we have. Their history is as rude in its primitiveness as ours; their ancestors ran wild and naked, lived in caves and in branches of trees, like monkeys, as ours; they made human sacrifices, ate the flesh of their own dead and the raw meat of the wild beast for centuries even as they accuse us of doing; their cannibalism was more prolonged than ours; when we were embracing the arts and sciences on the banks of the Nile their ancestors were still drinking human blood and eating out of the skulls of their conquered dead[.] When our civilization had reached the noonday of progress they were still running naked and sleeping in holes and caves with rats, bats, and other insects and animals. After we had already unfathomed the mystery of the stars and reduced the heavenly constellations to minute and regular calculus they were still backwoodsmen living in ignorance and blatant darkness.

The Turning Point in Man's History

This is really the turning point in the history of man in which the Negro plays a prominent part. Men or Man came into this world under the same circumstances. When creation opened, man was a creature of creation, and in his rude and crude nativity he knew not where to turn in nature for the enjoyment of the best. His mind was young, his thoughts had not then reached the zenith, and so like a child, man crept along with the other creatures of the world, became the companion of the animals around and drank in the crudity of that which he saw. His growth, his development was not sudden. It was gradual. Among the first of men to have gotten the new thought of the higher life was the black man. Out of nature's rudeness, out of nature's virginity, he, the black man in thought, was the first to lift himself to a position of superiority among the other creatures that came with the dawn of creation. (Hear Hear). So while Europe and Asia lagged behind, remained ignorant of the higher thoughts of man, remained ignorant of the higher calling of man; Africa steadily took her growth upwards, and on the banks of the Nile, black men founded Institutions of learning; black men built a civilization on the banks of the Congo that became wonder, not only to men, but to the gods. The black man started to build, and succeeded in building the first civilization the world ever saw, and by contact and by natural prowess and conquest he came in contact with the peoples of the other countries, and imposed their morality upon them, so that they found it a grand and glorious opportunity to be in companionship with the Ethiopians. Even the Greeks who looked towards their gods for counsel and guidance could find no better companionship than that of the Ethiopians. So from the caves of Europe and Asia, they wended their way over to Africa to

SUP WITH THE GODS
OF ETHIOPIA

and learn from the sciences and the arts of the civilization of the black man. They took that civilization back with them to Europe and to Asia, and as the years rolled by, they kept that civilization, built on it and brought it up to the civilization of the 20th century. So whatsoever man has succeeded in creating from the dawn of civilization up to the 20th century must be traced back to the black man. (Hear Hear). When black men were giving philosophies, literature, and sciences to the world, the other people were living in caves and dens, they were wild men; kept company with the wild animals around, because they had not started to think. We have no cause to hang our heads in shame, because our fathers reached the highest pinnacle of glory first, and so

AFRICAN FUNDAMENTALISM SUGGESTS

if others laugh at you, return the laughter to them, if they mimic you, return the compliment with equal force; for they have nothing over you, because they have come out of no finer mould than you have come out of. You came out of the same mould as they, and you gave light and learning to the white man. (Applause). If they mimic you return it, because you are men. They have no more right to dishonour, disrespect and disregard your feelings and manhood than you have in dealing with them. That is the position that the black man must take up throughout the world. He can be as proud as any other man of any other race. We are not desirous of insulting any one, but if anyone insult us we shall return him the insult.

WHAT MAKES A MAN A MAN

What makes a man a man? The thoughts of man, the soul of man make him a man, and so tonight we want to inspire the Four Hundred Million of black humanity, by the kindling of their souls to rise to the highest in man. Man is a great genius; man is a g[re]at creature, and as your fathers created on the banks of the Nile, so can we too create and so show that we are the offsprings of a worthy ancestry from which we have sprung. The Universal Negro Improvement Association is endeavouring to instill in you the thoughts and the sentiments that make up the principles of the Association—the principles that will one day give us the promise of Africa redeemed and a race emancipated throughout the world, so that the black race, like the other races of the world will not only stand socially equal, but politically equal to the other races of the world. We have reached a time when the Negro can take no less a position than the other peoples. Everybody is looking towards Empire to insure protection—a protection for their own. "African Fundamentalism" points to Imperialism. Imperialism means that whether we are in Africa or abroad, we are united with one tie of life blood, with one tie of race, and as Four Hundred Million we must stand together, willing to fall together or die together. That is the thought we are echoing throughout the world, and when men realize that you are responsible for such a thought, they will respect you as they respect others. What the white man has done are but copies, replicas, are but duplicates, facsimiles of what the black man originated and endowed civilization with. Who to tell that I am not now talking to a direct descendant of the Pharoahs. We are all related, we have sprung from the same family tree. It is only an accident that has torn us from Africa, but there is a tie of blood in all men black, that we cannot ignore, but think kindly of, and be willing to sacrifice for. They, the other people of the world, their history is as rude in its primitiveness as ours: their Ancestors ran wild and naked. When man first saw in the light of day, they were not garbed as you are, but a naked animal running wild. If it were not for the advanced fashion of civilization, you would be down under the trees with the hogs, you would be basking with the cats, because at the early stage of civilization you had not begun to think, and men were wild; but it was a black man who got up from among the snakes, by deeds and actions and said: "I shall no longer keep company with animals and insects but advance myself to the Kingdom of man." He built a great system of learning and education, men saw what he did and emulated him; and so by reverse of circumstances which follows men all over the world, this skill was lost to the white man, and until we recover that we cannot get back our position.

U.N.I.A. Has Hopes for
the Black Man

We of the Universal Negro Improvement Association are hoping that the black man will redeem himself to the position of leadership in pursuing human love, pertaining to the divine injunction that we should do unto others as we would that they should do unto us. Meaning that we should bear our brothers' burden. When civilization reaches that point where we become our brothers' keepers, then we shall be perfect as men ready for the companionship of God's angels. I do hope that the black man will reach that position first, so that God from His Judgment Seat will say: "Come unto me thou child of Ethiopia indeed thou has stretched forth thy hands unto Me, and Princes have come out of Egypt." (Applause). I believe that the inspiration of the Psalmist will not fall to the ground, but as a symbolism, it means that the rejected stone will become the head of the corner, the permanent stone to erect a magnificent building that shall last forever. Man is not an independent creature by himself but a child of God; and when God calls him to give an account of Himself, I do hope that among men the black man will reach that unique position befitting a child of God. But on the journey let us not lose the respect of others. Coming in contact with other men, we must never forget our decorum; we must never forget we are soldiers in life's warfare. We must fight our battles with character, and as a soldier will take no affront from any soldier of the other army, so must we not take any from the other people. Be courageous and march towards the goal, towards the destiny of an emancipated race. We must march steadily on, until we reach the front where there shall be a greater victory.

Face Your Difficulties
Like Men

You black men, you Negro men, you coloured men and women whatsoever may be your surrounding difficulties bow not down before them, but face them, because when you summon your soul to duty, you can rise with the sun, and become one of God's elected children. I see no reason why you cannot look forward and become what your fathers were. That is my advice tonight to you, and I do hope that you will get this Creed, and read the words written on it, and so imitate the men who never became discouraged; never gave up, and were able to build up structures that last down the ages. If they could do it, why should you become discouraged. Although you may be going to the grave in age, you may be able to give your children the inspiration to be a Plato, or a Socrates of Africa and another generation will be able to bless your memory; as they bless the memory of the parent of Napoleon; as they bless the memory of the parent of Plato for giving to the world such illustrious characters. I do hope that by another hundred years by the inspiration that we gather from this Creed another generation will be able to bless you mothers and fathers for giving to the world an illustrious son, whom we hope to follow under the colours of the Red, the Black and the Green. May God help you to see the light and to develop so that you may become a greater and grander race marching to destiny. (Applause).

SOURCE NOTES

Printed in the *Blackman* (Kingston), 11, 18, and 25 October and 1 November 1930. Original headlines and editorial prefaces and postscripts omitted. Reports of 11 and 25 October and 1 November 1930 based on stenographic notes.

GOVERNING THE IDEAL STATE

ESSAY

By Marcus Garvey

Our modern systems of Government have partly failed and are wholly failing.

We have tried various forms, but none has measured up to the Ideal State. Communism was the last attempt, and its most ardent advocates have acknowledged its limitations, shortcomings and impossibility.

The reason for all this failure is not far to seek. The sum total of Governmental collapse is traceable to the growing spirit of selfishness, graft and greed within the individual. Naturally, the state cannot govern itself: it finds expression and executes its edicts through individuals, hence the State is human. Its animation is but the reflex of our human characters. As a Nero, Caesar, Alexander, Alfred, William, Louis, Charles, Cromwell, Napoleon, Washington, Lincoln, Roosevelt or Wilson thinks, so expresses the majesty of the State.

If we must correct the maladministration of the State and apply the corporate majesty of the people to their own good, then we must reach the source and there reorganize or reform.

Under the pressure of our civilization, with its manifold demands, the individual is tempted, beyond measure, to do evil or harm to others; and, if responsible, to the entire State and people, and if by thus acting he himself profits and those around him, there arises corruption in Government, as well as in other branches of the secular and civil life.

All other methods of Government having been tried and failed, I suggest a reformation that would place a greater responsibility upon the shoulders of the elect and force them either to be the criminals, that some of us believe they are, or the good and true representatives we desire them to be.

Government should be absolute, and the head should be thoroughly responsible for himself and the acts of his subordinates.

When we elect a President of a nation, he should be endowed with absolute authority to appoint all his lieutenants from cabinet ministers, governors of States and Territories, administrators and judges to minor officers. He should swear his life as a guarantee to the State and people, and he should be made to pay the price of such a life if he deceives, grafts, bows to special privilege or interest, or in any way undermines the sacred honor and trust imposed upon him by acts of favoritism, injustice or friendly or self interests. He should be the soul of honor, and when he is legally or properly found to the contrary, he should be publicly disgraced, and put to death as an outcast and an unworthy representative of the righteous will of the people.

A President should, by proper provisions made by the State, be removed from all pecuniary obligations and desires of a material nature. He should be voted a salary and other accommodations so large and sufficient as to make it reasonably impossible for him, or those dependent upon him, to desire more during his administration. He and his family should be permanently and substantially provided for after the close of his administration, and all this and possibly more should be done for the purpose of removing him from the slightest possible material temptations or want. He, in turn, should devote his entire time to the sovereign needs and desires of the people. He should, for all the period of his administration, remove himself from obligatory, direct and fraternal contact with any and all special friends. His only friends outside of his immediate family should be the State. He should exact by law from all his responsible and administrative appointees a similar obligation, and he should enforce the law by penalty of death.

His administrators and judges should be held to strict accountability, and on the committing of any act of injustice, unfairness, favoritism or malfeasance, should be taken before the public, disgraced and then stoned to death.

This system would tend to attract to the sacred function of Government and judicial administration, only men and women of the highest and best characters, whom the public would learn to honor and respect with such satisfaction as to obliterate and prevent the factional party fights of Socialism, Communism, Anarchism, etc., for the control of Government, because of the belief that Government is controlled in the interest of classes, and not for the good of all the people. It would also discourage the self-seekers, grafters, demagogues and charlatans from seeking public offices, as the penalty of discovery of crime would be public disgrace and death for them and their families.

The State should hold the wife of a President, and the wives of all administrative officials, solely responsible for their domestic households, and they should be required by law to keep a strict and accurate public account of all receipts and disbursements of their husbands during their administrative terms, and if any revenue comes into the household other than provided by law, should be promptly reported to the responsible officer of the State for immediate action, and should the wife conceal or refuse to make such a disclosure, and that it be discovered afterwards, and it was an act of crime against the dignity and high office of the incumbent, she and her husband should be publicly disgraced and put to death, but any child or member of the family who, before discovery, reports the act, should be spared the disgrace and publicly honored by the populace for performing a duty to the State.

The State should require that the husband and his consort under the severest penalty for non-performance, report the full amount of his entire wealth to the State before taking office, and that all incomes and salaries legally authorized be reported promptly to the wife to enable her to keep a proper public account.

Whenever a President or high official during his term has performed solemnly and truly all his duties to the people and State, and he is about to retire, he should be publicly proclaimed and honored by the populace, and all during his life he and his family should occupy a special place of honor and respect among the people. They should be respected by all with whom they come in contact, and at death they should be granted public funerals and their names added to the niche in the Hall of Fame of the Nation. Their names should be placed on the Honor Roll of the Nation, and their deeds of righteousness should be handed down to the succeeding generations of the race, and their memories sung by the poets of the nation.

For those who have abused their trust, images of them should be made and placed in a national hall of criminology and ill fame, and their crimes should be recited and a curse pronounced upon them and their generations.

Government left to the free and wanton will and caprice of the individual in an age so corrupt as this, without any vital reprimand or punishment for malfeasance, other than ordinary imprisonment, will continue to produce dissatisfaction, cause counter agitations of a dangerous nature and upheavals destructive to the good of society and baneful to the·higher hopes and desires of the human race.

This plan I offer to the race as a means to which we may perfect the establishment of a new system of Government, conducive to the best interest of the people and a blessing to our disorganized society of the twentieth century.

SOURCE NOTES

Printed in *Philosophy and Opinions of Marcus Garvey,* edited by Amy Jacques Garvey, vol. 2 (December 1925). Written by Marcus Garvey in Atlanta Federal Penitentiary.

AUTOBIOGRAPHY

Articles from the *Pittsburgh Courier*

ARTICLES

By Marcus Garvey

I was born on the 17th of August, 1887, in the island of Jamaica, British West Indies. My parents were Negroes. My father was a man of brilliant intellect, and in his youth, of dashing courage. Up to his mature years, he was unafraid of consequences. In life he took human chances, as most bold men do, but at the end he failed in his career. He was once independent. He died poor. My mother was a sober and conscientious Christian of the soft and good-natured kind. She was the direct opposite of my father, who was severe. To this strange combination I owe my birth.

I grew up in my home town, St. Ann's Bay, to the age of 14. There I attended grammar, public and high schools. I found myself afterward in the metropolis of the island, where I lived for some time continuing my studies. At the age of 18 I started to take interest in public affairs. The politics of my country so disgusted me that I started to travel, in which course I visited several countries in South and Central America and in Europe. By the age of 21 I had further added to my education. I spent three years in Europe, which broadened my outlook on human affairs, particularly the affairs of the Negro race.

From early youth I discovered that there was prejudice against me because of my color, a prejudice that was extended to other members of my race. This annoyed me and helped to inspire me to create sentiment that would act favorably to the black man. It was with this kind of inspiration that I returned from my trip to Europe to Jamaica in 1914, where I organized the Universal Negro Improvement Association and

African Communities League.

When I organized this movement in Jamaica it was treated with contempt and scorn by a large number of the highly colored and successful black people. In Jamaica the colored and successful black people regard themselves as white. This is also true of the other British West Indian islands. The result is that racial movements tending to the betterment of the Negro have to undergo great difficulties. Such difficulties I encountered with the new organization. I labored in Jamaica with the hope of making the movement successful for two years. Seeing how difficult it was to succeed with only a limited amount of money at my disposal, I communicated with Dr. Booker T. Washington of Tuskegee. He encouraged me to go to the United States on a lecture tour and promised me his help. Unfortunately, he died before I was able to reach America.

However, I arrived in America in the spring of 1916, after which I started to study the sociological, economical and political status of the Negroes of America. This took me through 38 states. It was after my return from these trips to New York that I founded in New York the New York division of the Universal Negro Improvement Association. I had great difficulty in New York in holding the organization, in that as often as I organized it there would come into the movement scheming politicians of the Harlem district, who would attempt to turn the organization into a political club. I can remember well the activities of Mr. Isaac B. Allen, Messrs. Samuel Duncan and L. Lavelle and others who had political designs and who thought that they could work them out through the newly formed organization I had created. To throw off the political influence of these men I was even forced into court, for I had to somewhat beat up Duncan in detaching him from the presidency of the newly formed division of New York. After this happened those who were following me and myself had to make desperate efforts to have the organization incorporated in New York, so as to prevent Samuel Duncan overreaching us and taking away the organization from us. The organization was incorporated by Attorney Conway, who was one of the charter members. The first lady president of the New York organization was Mrs. Irene Morman Blackston [Irena Moorman Blackstone]. For safety I also was elected president of the incorporated organization. In the space of a couple of months the organization grew from a membership of 600 to 12,000.

Just at this time we started to secure our own premises after having rented a portion of the Lafayette lodge rooms for a short while. Immediately after the growth of the New York organization I started the celebrated newspaper, "The Negro World," in which was published my speeches made before the New York organization and in which also was published special feature articles of mine. Through the speeches and articles, circulated over the world, applications were made for the organization of branches of the association. I was therefore in immediate requisition to visit different centers of the country to form branches. In the space of six months I had formed 30 branches in America and had issued charters to several abroad. All this happened in the latter part of 1918 and the early part of 1919. By the middle of 1919 the organization had over 300 branches in America and abroad. It was at this time that we launched the idea of the Black Star Line Steamship Corporation.

The Black Star Line Steamship Corporation that I organized in 1919, under charter from the State of Delaware, was the great attraction that brought to the Universal Negro Improvement Association millions of supporters from Central America, South America, Africa and the West Indies.

The idea became immediately popular—that of having ships. The Negroes of the West Indies, Central America and Africa could better appreciate the scheme of steamships than the Negroes of America. And so at that time with very little persuasion they subscribed the major portion of the money and purchased the first ship of the Black Star Line. Most of this money came from Cuba, Panama, Costa Rica, and from among the British West Indian Negroes laboring in those countries. It was not until after the first ship, the S.S. Yarmouth, afterwards christened "Frederick Douglass," was launched in New York that the American Negroes got to know what it was all about, and subscribed speedily their quota to help to purchase the other ships.

Most of the money subscribed in America came from Negroes who lived in Boston, New York, Philadelphia and New Orleans. The moment the first ship of the Black Star Line was launched the whole movement of the Universal Negro Improvement Association was referred to as The Black Star Line Movement.

The fact that Negroes had launched a ship in New York became a world sensation, and the news was flashed from one centre of our civilization to the next. Thousands of letters of inquiry came from all parts of the world. The result of which tended to create more branches for the Universal Negro Improvement Association.

The state of world enthusiasm having reached to such a height, I thought the best thing to do was to call a world convention of the Negro race. Notice was therefore served throughout the world that on the first of August, 1920, an international convention of the Negro peoples of the world was to be called to assemble at New York, to which each Negro community was to send delegates. Between the launching of the first ship in October, 1919, and the first of August, 1920, several hundred branches of the Universal Negro Improvement Association were organized in the West Indies, Central America, South America, Africa and all over the United States.

The immediate success of the Black Star Line also enhanced the success of the Universal Negro Improvement Association. The world was in a state of excitement to witness the first convention of the Negro peoples of the world. So, realizing the importance of the gathering, I undertook to prepare the meeting place for the convention in New York. It was then that the organization acquired the premises known as "Liberty Hall," 120–140 W. 138th street. In addition to the smaller building that we previously occupied at the spot around June, 1920, a purchase was made of the Baptist Church of adjoining lands, and a contract made to erect a temporary building to house the convention. The contractors worked day and night for two months to erect the building, and on the first of August 1920, it was ready for the great convention that really commenced the world history of the Universal Negro Improvement Association.

August 1st, 1920, was the red letter day for the Negro peoples of the world, in that on that day at 9:30 a.m. there assembled in Liberty Hall, New York, 120–140 W. 138th street, [2]5,000 representatives of the race from every known part of the world. They came in groups of one hundred, in scores, dozens, tens and in units.

We had them from Nigeria, the Gold Coast, Sierra Leone, Liberia, West Africa, from Cape Town and Johannesburg, South Africa, and from East and Central Africa, from every known island in the West Indies, including Cuba, Haiti, Jamaica, Barbados, Trinidad, Grenada and all the groups of the Leeward and Windward islands. They came from South and Central America: from Europe and from Asia. Contingents of thousands [c]ame from Philadelphia, Detroit, Chicago, Cincinnati, in the United States, and from every other nook and corner of the republic.

It was at this hour that the famous Black Star Line band of 25 pieces, under the leadership of Prof. Isles, and the celebrated Liberty Hall choir of 100 voices, under the leadership of Prof. Arnold Ford, struck up and sang the celebrated Negro hymn: "O Africa Awaken."

> O Africa Awaken!!
> The morning is at hand,
> No more art thou forsaken,
> O bounteous motherland.
> For far thy sons and daughters
> Are hastening back to thee,
> Their cry rings o'er the waters
> That Africa shall be free.

After the singing of this celebrated hymn, the mighty procession of the robed officials of the Universal Negro

Improvement Association from all parts of the world started up the aisle in Liberty Hall; the whole congregation singing another celebrated Negro hymn, "Shine On, Eternal Light."

> Shine on Eternal Light.
> To greet our souls this day;
> Dispel the gloominess of night,
> And drive our doubts away.

The singing of the hymn was enough to inspire the most mute soul. It was an occasion that could not fail to stir, and everybody there among the 25,000 was stirred. When the procession reached the celebrated Liberty Hall platform that accommodated 200 persons the picturesqueness of it was marked. It reminded one of the great ceremonials at the courts of Europe, or one of the coronation celebrations at Westminster Abbey, London. The people were greatly impressed—the thousands inside of Liberty Hall, and numerous thousands peeping through the windows on the outside.

The morning service at Liberty Hall on this day opened the day's celebrations at New York. Speeches were made and the official sermon preached by the Rev. J. W. Eason, who was then acting chaplain general of the organization, and who was subsequently at the convention elected leader of the American Negroes.

After the morning display at Liberty Hall there was the parade and review throughout the streets of Harlem, in which 50,000 members of the organization, along with the legionary and uniform ranks, including Black Cross nurse[s,] motor corps, Juvenile [divisions] and African Guards[,] marched. The military spectacle of these auxiliaries was wonderful. Eighteen bands of music were in line and marched.

Fully 30,000 people saw the parade from the streets and homes in Harlem. The demonstration was of such as never seen in Harlem before and probably not to be seen again.

The parade started at 1 o'clock and ended at 4 o'clock. Those who marched in line made a circuit of Harlem from the headquarters, 35 W. 135th street, where the first line marched off from, taking in Lenox avenue up to 125th, to 7th avenue, to 125th street, down Lenox avenue, back to 35 West 135th street. When the first line of the parade returned to 135th street the last line was just leaving the same spot to make their circuit in the parade.

The great excitement of the day was climaxed with the mass opening of the convention, at the old Madison Square Garden at 12th and 14th street at night. At 8 o'clock every available seat in the garden was taken. Fifteen thousand people were seated inside and another 10,000 were found accommodations in other ways. It was at the garden that night that the auxiliaries of the Universal Negro Improvement Association came into full play. The wonderful review took place, in which every unit of the organization was in line. It was wonderful to see the coloring effect of the Legions, Black Cross Nurses, African Guards and other auxiliaries. The New York and Philadelphia contingents of auxiliaries took the first prize; but sections like Boston, Cincinnati, Newark and Cleveland came in for good second places.

It was said in reviewing the history of the old Madison Square Garden, by a writer in the New York Times, that the thirteenth great historical feature in the garden in all its years was the historical opening of the convention of the Universal Negro Improvement Association in 1920.

It was at the Madison Square Garden that I made the famous speech that brought me into the limelight of the political world. At 11 o'clock this night I made the official speech in opening the convention, in which I declared in the height of my enthusiasm that: "Four hundred million Negroes were sharpening their swords for the next world war." Among all the things I said these words were taken out and cabled to every capital in Europe and throughout the world. The next morning every first class newspaper proclaimed me as the new leader of the Negro race and featured the unfortunate words I used. Words which have been making trouble for me ever since 1920. Despite what I said otherwise then and often after as a manifestation of my

good faith, I am still held as a dangerous man. It is because
of this danger why France closed her doors against me in
Africa; and Italy and Portugal also and England became so
scared and America watched me at every move.

Six months prior to the gathering of the first
International Convention of the Negro Peoples of the World
I issued invitations to most of the prominent Negroes of
America and elsewhere to attend in that it was my desire
to bring the most prominent members of the race together
when they themselves would elect the officials of the new
organization we were endeavoring to form, so that the past
dissensions in the ranks of the race would be eliminated and
we would pull together as one big organization under world
recognized leadership.

Invitations were sent to such men as Dr. W. E. DuBois,
Prof. Kelly Miller and others in America; among those who
declined to participate in the convention were the two above
named gentlemen. Prof. Miller wrote to say that he was not
prepared to give up hi[s] position at Howard and Dr. DuBois
in his reply suggested contempt more than anything else.
This, in my mind, eliminated the two gentlemen from serious
race leadership in America.

With Professor Miller one could somewhat sympathize,
because he has always been a professional teacher and has
never seriously projected himself forward as a race leader;
but the hypocrisy of Dr. Dubois was made manifest in that
he no doubt under-rated the success of the Universal Negro
Improvement Association at the time when he answered the
invitation of the First Convention, but after the movement
became established and regarded as more than a serious
competitor of the N.A.A.C.P. he started to oppose the
movement with might and main.

We are able to get on without the aid of Dr. Dubois and
the leaders of his stamp. The first ten days of the convention
were occupied with reports of the delegates from all parts of
the world, each delegate was given from five to ten minutes
to report on the state of affairs in his part of the world.
Horroring [Harrowing?] tales were told from Africa, the

West Indies, and the southern sections of the United States; the outcome of which was the drafting and adopting of a Bill of Rights setting forth the grievances of the race to be remedied. The following constituted the drafted and adopted Bill of Rights:

PREAMBLE

Be it resolved, That the Negro people of the world, through their chosen representatives in convention assembled in Liberty hall, in the city of New York and United States of America, from Aug. 1 to Aug. 31, in the year of our Lord one thousand nine hundred twenty, protest against the wrongs and injustices they are suffering at the hands of their white brethren, and state what they deem their fair and just rights, as well as the treatment they promise to demand of all men in the future.

We complain[:]

I. That nowhere in the world, with few exceptions, are black men accorded equal treatment with white men, although in the same situation and circumstances, but on the contrary, are discriminated against and denied the common rights due to human beings for no other reason than their race and color.

We are not willingly accepted as guests in the public hotels and inns of the world for no other reason than our race and color.

II. In certain parts of the United States of America our race is denied the right of public trial accorded to other races when accused of crime, but are lynched and burned by mobs, and such brutal and inhuman treatment is even practiced upon our women.

III. That European nations have parceled out among themselves and taken possession of nearly all of the continent of Africa, and the natives are compelled to surrender their lands to aliens and are treated in most instances like slaves.

IV. In the southern portion of the United States of

America, although citizens under the federal constitution, and in some states almost equal to the whites in population and are qualified land owners and taxpayers, we are, nevertheless, denied all voice in the making and administration of the laws and are taxed without representation by the state governments, and at the same time compelled to do military service in defense of the country.

V. On the public conveyances and common carriers in the southern portion of the United States we are jim-crowed and compelled to accept separate and inferior accommodations and made to pay the same fare charged for first-class accommodations, and our families are often humiliated and insulted by drunken white men who habitually pass through the jim-crow cars going to the smoking car.

VI. The physicians of our race are denied the right to attend their patients while in the public hospitals of the cities and states where they reside in certain parts of the United States.

Our children are forced to attend inferior separate schools for shorter terms than white children, and the public school funds are unequally divided between the white and colored schools.

VII. We are discriminated against and denied an equal chance to earn wages for the support of our families, and in many instances are refused admission into labor unions, and nearly everywhere are paid smaller wages than white men.

VIII. In the Civil Service and departmental offices we are everywhere discriminated against and made to feel that to be a black man in Europe, America and the West Indies is equivalent to being an outcast and a leper among the races of men, no matter what the character attainments of the black man may be.

IX. In the British and other West Indian islands and colonies, Negroes are secretly and cunningly discriminated against, and denied those fuller rights of government to which white citizens are appointed, nominated and elected.

X. That our people in those parts are forced to work for lower wages than the average standard of white men and are kept in conditions repugnant to good civilized tastes and customs.

XI. That the many acts of injustice against members of our race before the courts of law in the respective islands and colonies are of such nature as to create disgust and disrespect for the white man's sense of justice.

XII. Against all such inhuman, un-Christian and uncivilized treatment we here and now emphatically protest, and invoke the condemnation of all mankind.

In order to encourage our race all over the world and to stimulate it to a higher and grander destiny, we demand and insist on the following declaration of rights:

1. Be it known to all men that whereas all men are created equal and entitled to the rights of life, liberty and the pursuit of happiness, and because of this we, the duly elected representatives of the Negro peoples of the world, invoking the aid of the just and almighty God, do declare all men, women and children of our blood throughout the world free citizens, and do claim them as free citizens of Africa, the motherland of all Negroes.

2. That we believe in the supreme authority of our race in all things racial; that all things are created and given to man as a common possession; that there should be an equitable distribution and apportionment of all such things, and in consideration of the [fact] that as a race we are now deprived of those things that are morally and legally ours, we believe it right that all such things should be acquired and held by whatsoever means possible.

3. That we believe the Negro, like any other race, should be governed by the ethics of civilization, and, therefore, should not be deprived of any of those rights or privileges common to other human beings.

4. We declare that Negroes, wheresoever they found a community among themselves, should be given the right to elect their own representatives to represent them in legislatures, courts of law, or such institutions as may exercise control over that particular community.

5. We assert that the Negro is entitled to even-handed

justice before all courts of law and equity in whatever country he may be found, and when this is denied him on account of his race or color such denial is an insult to the race as a whole and should be resented by the entire body of Negroes.

6. We declare it unfair and prejudicial to the rights of Negroes in communities where they exist in considerable numbers to be tried by a j[u]dge and jury composed entirely of an alien race, but in all such cases members of our race are entitled to representation on the jury.

7. We believe that any law or practice that tends to deprive any African of his land or the privileges of free citizenship within his country, is unjust and immoral, and no native should respect any such law or practice.

8. We declare taxation without representation unjust and tyrannous, and there should be no obligation on the part of the Negro to obey the levy of a tax by any law-making body from which he is excluded and denied representation on account of his race and color.

9. We believe that any law especially directed against the Negro to his detriment and singling him out because of his race or color is unfair and immoral, and should not be respected.

10. We believe all men entitled to common human respect, and, that our race should in no way tolerate any insults that may be interpreted to mean disrespect to our color.

11. We deprecate the use of the term "nigger" as applied to Negroes, and demand that the word "Negro" be written with a capital "N."

12. We believe that the Negro should adopt every means to protect himself against barbarous practices inflicted upon him because of color.

13. We believe in the freedom of Africa for the Negro people of the world, and by the principle of Europe for the Europeans, and Asia for the Asiatics, we also demand Africa for the Africans at home and abroad.

14. We believe in the inherent right of the Negro to possess himself of Africa, and that his possession of same shall

not be regarded as an infringement of any claim or purchase made by any race or nation.

15. We strongly condemn the cupidity of those nations of the world who, by open aggression, or secret schemes, have seized the territories and inexhaustible natural wealth of Africa, and we place on record our most solemn determination to reclaim the treasures and possession of the vast continent of our forefathers.

16. We believe all men should live in peace one with the other, but when races and nations provoke the ire of other races and nations by attempting to infringe upon their rights[,] war becomes inevitable, and the attempt in any way to free one['s] self or protect one's rights or heritage becomes justifiable.

17. Whereas, the lynching, by burning, hanging or any other means, of human beings is a barbarous practice, and a shame and disgrace to civilization, we therefore declare any country guilty of such atrocities outside the pale of civilization.

18. We protest against the atrocious crime of whipping, flogging and overworking of the native tribes of Africa and Negroes everywhere. These are methods that should be abolished, and all means should be taken to prevent a continuance of such brutal practices.

19. We protest against the atrocious practice of shaving the heads of Africans, especially of African women or individuals of Negro blood, when placed in prison as a punishment for crime by an alien race.

20. We protest against segregated districts, separate public conveyances, industrial discrimination, lynchings and limitations of political privileges of any Negro citizen in any part of the world on account of race, color or creed, and will exert our full influence and power against all such.

21. We protest against any punishment inflicted upon a Negro with severity, as against lighter punishment inflicted upon another of an alien race for like offense, as an act of prejudice and injustice, and should be resented by the entire race.

22. We protest against the system of education in any country where Negroes are denied the same privileges and advantages as other races.

23. We declare it inhuman and unfair to boycott Negroes from industries and labor in any part of the world.

24. We believe in the doctrine of the freedom of the press, and we therefore emphatically protest against the suppression of Negro newspapers and periodicals in various parts of the world, and call upon Negroes everywhere to employ all available means to prevent such suppression.

25. We further demand free speech universally for all men.

26. We hereby protest against the publication of scandalous and inflammatory articles by an alien press tending to create racial strife and the exhibition of picture films showing the Negro as a cannibal.

27. We believe in the self-determination of all peoples.

28. We declare for the freedom of religious worship.

29. With the help of almighty God we declare ourselves the sworn protectors of the honor and virtue of our women and children, and pledge our lives for their protection and defense everywhere, and under all circumstances from wrongs and outrages.

30. We demand the right of an unlimited and unprejudiced education for ourselves and our posterity forever.

31. We declare that the teaching in any school by alien teachers to our boys and girls, that the alien race is superior to the Negro race, is an insult to the Negro people of the world.

32. Whereas Negroes form a part of the citizenry of any country, and pass the civil service examination of such country, we declare them entitled to the same consideration as other citizens as to appointments in such civil service.

33. We vigorously protest against the increasingly unfair and unjust treatment accorded Negro travelers on land and sea by the agents and employes of railroad and steamship companies[,] and insist that for equal fare we receive equal privileges with travelers of other races.

34. We declare it unjust for any country, state or nation to enact laws tending to hinder and obstruct the free immigration of Negroes on account of their race and color.

35. That the right of the Negro to travel unmolested throughout the world be not abridged by any person or persons, and all Negroes are called upon to give aid to a fellow Negro when thus molested.

36. We declare that all Negroes are entitled to the same right to travel over the world as other men.

37. We hereby demand that the governments of the world recognize our leader and his representatives chosen by the race to look after the welfare of our people under such governments.

[38. We demand complete control of our social institutions without interference by any alien race or races.]

39. That the colors, red, black and green, be the colors of the Negro race.

40. Resolved, That the anthem, "Ethiopia, Thou Land of Our Fathers," etc., shall be the anthem of the Negro race.

UNIVERSAL ETHIOPIAN ANTHEM
(POEM BY BURRELL AND FORD)

I

Ethiopia, thou land of our fathers,
Thou land where the gods loved to be,
As storm cloud at night suddenly gathers
Our armies come rushing to thee.
We must in the fight be victorious
When swords are thrust outward to glean;
For us will the vict'ry be glorious
When led by the red, black and green.

CHORUS

Advance, advance to victory,
Let Africa be free;
Advance to meet the foe

With the might
Of the red, the black and the green.

II

Ethiopia, the tyrant's falling,
Who smote thee upon thy knees
And thy children are lustily calling
From over the distant seas.
Jehovah, the Great One, has heard us,
Has noted our sighs and our tears,
With his spirit of love he has stirred us
To be one through the coming years.

CHORUS—Advance, advance, etc.

III

O, Jehovah, thou God of the ages
Grant unto our sons that lead
The wisdom Thou gave to Thy sages
When Israel was sore in need.
Thy voice thro' the dim past has spoken,
Ethiopia shall stretch forth her hand,
By Thee shall all fetters be broken,
And Heav'n bless our dear fatherland.

CHORUS—Advance, advance, etc.

41. We believe that any limited liberty which deprives one of the complete rights and prerogatives of full citizenship is but a modified form of slavery.

42. We declare it an injustice to our people and a serious impediment to the health of the race to deny to competent licensed Negro physicians the right to practice in the public hospitals of the communities in which they reside, for no other reason than their race and color.

43. We call upon the various governments of the world to accept and acknowledge Negro representatives who shall be

sent to the said governments to represent the general welfare of the Negro peoples of the world.

44. We deplore and protest against the practice of confining juveniles in prisons with adults[,] and we recommend that such youthful prisoners be taught gainful trades under humane supervision.

45. Be it further resolved, that we as a race of people declare the League of Nations null and void as far as the Negro is concerned, in that it seeks to deprive Negroes of their liberty.

46. We demand of all men to do unto us as we would do unto them, in the name of justice; and we cheerfully accord to all men all the rights we claim herein for ourselves.

47. We declare that no Negro shall engage himself in battle for an alien race without first obtaining the consent of the leader of the Negro people of the world, except in a matter of national self-defense.

48. We protest against the practice of drafting Negroes and sending them to war with alien forces without proper training, and demand in all cases that Negro soldiers be given the same training as the aliens.

49. We demand that instructions given Negro children in schools include the subject of "Negro History" to their benefit.

50. We demand a free and unfettered commercial intercourse with all the Negro people of the world.

51. We declare for the absolute freedom of the seas for all peoples.

52. We demand that our duly accredited representatives be given proper recognition in all leagues, conferences, conventions or courts of international arbitration wherever human rights are discussed.

53. We proclaim the thirty-first day of August of each year to be an international holiday to be observed by all Negroes.

54. We want all men to know that we shall maintain and contend for the freedom and equality of every man, woman and child of our race, with our lives, our fortunes and our sacred honor.

These rights we believe to be justly ours and proper for the protection of the Negro race at large, and because of this belief we, on behalf of the four hundred million Negroes of the world, do pledge herein the sacred blood of the race in defense, and we hereby subscribe our names as a guarantee of the truthfulness and faithfulness hereof, in the presence of almighty God, on the thirteenth day of August, in the year of our Lord, one thousand nine hundred and twenty.

[SIGNATURES:]

Marcus Garvey, Jane [James] D. Brooks, James W. H. Eason, Henrietta Vinton Davis, Lionel Winston Greenidge, Adrion [Adrian] Fitzroy Johnson, Rudolph Ethelbert Brisaac Smith, Charles Augustus Petioni, Thomas H. N. Simon, Richard Hilton Tobitt, George Alexander McGuire, Peter Edward Batson, Reynold R. Felix, Harry Walters Kirby, Sarah Branch, Marie Barrier Houston, George [Georgiana] L. O'Brien, F. O. Ogilvie, Arden A. Bryan, Benjamin Dyett, Marie Duchaterlier, John Phillip Hodge, Theophilus H. Saunders, Wilford H. Smith, Gabriel E. Stewart, Arnold Josiah Ford, Lee Crawford, William McCartney, Adina Clem. James, William Musgrave LaMotte, John Sydney de Bourg, Arnold S. Cunning, Vernal J. Williams, Francis Wilcome [Wilcem] Ellegor, J. Frederick Selkridge, Innis Abel Horsford, Cyril A. Crichlow, Samuel McIntyre, John Thomas Wilkins, Mary Thurston, John G. Befue, William Ware, J. A. Lewis, O. C. Kelly, Venture R. Hamilton, R. H. Hodge, Edward Alfred Taylor, Ellen Wilson, G. W. Wilson, Richard Edward Riley, Nellie Grant Whiting, G. W. Washington, Maldena Miller, Gertrude Davis, James D. Williams, Emily Christmas Kinch, D. D. Lewis, Nettie Clayton, Partheria Hills, Janie Jenkins, John C. Simons, Alphonso A. Jones, Allen Hobbs, Reynold Fitzgerald Austin, James Benjamin Yearwood, Frank O. Raines, Shedrick Williams, John Edward Ivey, Frederick Augustus Toote, Philip Hemmings, F. F. Smith, E. J. Jones, Joseph Josiah Cranston, Frederick Samuel

Ricketts, Dugald Augustus Wade, E. E. Nelom, Florida Jenkins, Napoleon J. Francis, Joseph D. Gibson, J. P. Jasper, J. W. Montgomery, David Benjamin, J. Gordon, Harry E. Ford, Carrie M. Ashford, Andrew N. Willis, Lucy Sands, Louise Woodson, George D. Creese, W. A. Wallace, Thomas E. Bagley, James Young, Prince Alfred McConney, John E. Hudson, William Ines, Harry R. Watkins, C. L. Halton, J. T. Bailey, Ira Joseph Touissant [Toussaint] Wright, T. H. Golden, Abraham Benjamin Thomas, Richard C. Noble, Walter Green, C. S. Bourne, G. F. Bennett, B. D. Levy, Mary E. Johnson, Lionel Antonio Francis, Carl Roper, E. R. Donawa, Philip Van Putten, I. Brathwaite, Jesse W. Luck, Oliver Kaye, J. W. Hudspeth, C. B. Lovell, William C. Matthews, A. Williams, Ratford E. M. Jack, H. Vinton Plummer, Randolph Phillips, A. I. Bailey, duly elected representatives of the Negro people of the world. Sworn before me this fifteenth day of August, 1920. (legal seal) JOHN G. BAYNE New York County Clerk's No. 37[8?,] New York County Register's No. 12102. Commission expires March 30, 1922.

Among the many things discussed at the first International Convention of the Negro Peoples of the World, held under the auspices of the Universal Negro Improvement Association, was the great need for steamship communication among the different branches of the Negro race scattered in Africa, the Americas and the West Indies. It was in keeping with this need that I founded the Black Star Line in 1919.

Having traveled extensively throughout the world and seriously studying the economical, commercial and industrial needs of our people, I found out that the quickest and easiest way to reach them was by steamship communication. So immediately after I succeeded in forming the Universal Negro Improvement Association in America, I launched the idea of floating ships under the direction of Negroes. Growing up as I did in my own island, and traveling out to the outside world with open eyes, I saw that the merchant marines of all countries were in the hands of white men. Captains and officers of ships were all of the white race, and their very presence in ports, dressed up in the uniforms of their respective company or nation tended to lend a prestige to the white race and compelled an impression upon the black race that aimed to lift the respect for the white race to a higher state of appreciation among the blacks. I thought if we could launch ships and have our own black captain and officers of our race, too, [we] would be respected in the mercantile and commercial world, thereby adding appreciative dignity to our down-trodden people.

With this aim in view I circularized the whole world for support of the Black Star Line. My appeal was heard and responded to immediately in such places like Cuba, Panama and Costa Rica and other Central American republics. Most of the people who responded were West Indians who could appreciate the value of steamship communication. The call to distant Africa was answered also. In the space of two or three months the corporation of the Black Star Line was able to purchase its first ship, the "S.S. Yarmouth," which was rechristened the "S.S. Frederick Douglass."

To do this, however, entailed a great deal of trouble and difficulties. First, my enemies in New York, namely, Samuel Duncan, Richard Warner, Edgar Grey and one Adolphus Domingo, did everything to influence the district attorney's office in New York to prevent me carrying out the idea of launching ships for the Negro race. Mr. Edwin P. Kilroe was then assistant district attorney. He on several occasions threatened me with imprisonment if I continued in the idea. He demanded from the organization our books, had them examined and when he found that he could not do anything legally he somewhat left us alone. Yet by his influence I was arrested two or three times; once for criminally libeling him, but I had the good fortune of escaping from any serious consequences.

As a retort to Kilroe and all those who were endeavoring to intimidate me, I stated that "we would launch our ships even if we had to do so in an ocean of blood." This statement somewhat scared those who were trying to intimidate us, the result of which was on a day in October, 1919, we launched in the New York harbor the first boat of the line. That was a day never to be forgotten. It was on a Sunday. Hundreds of thousands of people gathered at the foot of 135th street pier at the North River to see the boat sail under the black captain. People also gathered in thousands on the Riverside drive to witness the wonderful spectacle.

The first captain was a man by the name of Josiah [Joshua] Cockburn. This man had in his hands the destiny of the Negro race on the high seas. If he had proved true and sincere the Negro race today would be regarded as a serious competitor in maritime affairs; but Cockburn deceived and sold me. He deliberately, by his conduct, ruined the success of the Black Star Line and piled up for me along with others troubles that ultimately landed me in the Atlanta Federal Penitentiary.

I never knew that individuals of the Negro race were so evil and wicked at heart until I was able to gather, from different sections of the world, reports bearing on the conduct of certain people. As my readers still remember, when the organization of the Universal Negro Improvement Association was started in New York I had altercations with Samuel Duncan, whom I had to depose from the position of president of the first New York organization. This man's revenge ran so far that he wrote confidential letters to all the British colonial governments, as well as the imperial government, and the French colonial and imperial governments, warning them that one "Marcus Garvey, a dangerous Negro agitator, who desired to stir up hatred between the colored and white people, had now made a serious attempt to get in touch with the colored people of the world through the launching of steamships, and that it would be wise for all good governments to undertake to prevent the entry of the ships of the Black Star Line into the ports of their countries." Letters to this effect, as stated, were dispatched to different governments of the world, which worked incalculable harm to the early maritime enterprise of our race.

Associated with Duncan in this was Adolphus Domingo, already referred to. Domingo was first associated with me as editor of the "Negro World." We were friends from boyhood, but because of my success he became jealous of me and, being a Communist, while editing my paper he attempted to impress his Communistic views upon the readers and myself, even though he knew we had no inclinations toward Communism; we disagreed on policy and he left the paper. To show me that I was wrong and that he was right, with his Communistic ideas, he did everything to destroy me by denouncing me as capitalistic in my ideas. He linked up with other Communists like Cyril Briggs, who was running a magazine called "The Crusader," and Chandler Owen, another red Socialist. They kept up a continuous tirade against me; in fact, Domingo and others did everything to sabotage the Black Star Line. They were never satisfied until the venture went under.

My great difficulties in leading the Universal Negro Improvement Association and directing the affairs of the Black Star Line came really through the invisible influences that were operating against me all over the world, caused through the secret propaganda of other Negroes against me in impressing prominent members of the white race and their governments that I was a bad man. It is not possible for me to publish all the letters that have come into my hands that have been written to these governments and prominent persons by Negroes, with the object of their using their powerful influences against me; but a reproduction of the following letter, written by well-known persons in America, may supply to the public a faint idea of the tremendous oppositions I had to face to carry on the work of the Universal Negro Improvement Association and the enterprises allied thereto.

I have long forgiven these persons for writing this letter; nevertheless it may help those desiring to do as much as I attempted to realize the difficulties ahead.

The Letter:

2305 Seventh Ave.
New York City
Jan. 15, 192[3]

Hon. Harry M. Daugherty,
United State[s] Attorney General,
Department of Justice,
Washington, D.C.

Dear Sir:

(1) As the chief law enforcement officer of the nation, we wish to call your attention to a heretofore unconsidered menace to harmonious race relationships. There are in our midst certain Negro criminals and potential murderers, both foreign and American born, who are moved and actuated by intense hatred against the white race. These undesirables continually proclaim that all white people are enemies to the Negro. They have become so fanatical that they have threatened and attempted the death of their opponents, actually assassinating in one instance.

(2) The movement known as the Universal Negro Improvement Association has done much to stimulate the violent temper of this dangerous element. Its president and moving spirit is one Marcus Garvey, an unscrupulous demagogue, who has ceaselessly and assiduously sought to spread among Negroes distrust and hatred of all white people.

(3) The official organ of the U.N.I.A., The Negro World, of which Marcus Garvey is managing editor, sedulously and continually seeks to arouse ill-feeling between the races. Evidence also has been presented of an apparent alliance of Garvey with the Ku Klux Klan.

(4) An erroneous conception held by many is that Negroes try to cloak and hide criminals. The truth is that the great majority of Negroes are bitterly opposed to all criminals, and especially to those of their own race, because they know that such criminals will cause increased discrimi-

nation against themselves.

(5) The U.N.I.A. is composed chiefly of the most primitive and ignorant element of West Indian and American Negroes. The so-called respectable element of the movement are largely ministers without churches, physicians without patients, lawyers without clients and publishers without readers, who are usually in search of "easy money." In short, this organization is composed in the main of Negro sharks and ignorant Negro fanatics.

(6) This organization and its fundamental laws encourage violence. In its constitution there is an article prohibiting office-holding by a convicted criminal[,] EXCEPT SUCH CRIME IS COMMITTED IN THE INTEREST OF THE U.N.I.A. Marcus Garvey is intolerant of free speech when it is exercised in criticism of him and his movement, his followers seeking to prevent such by threats and violence. Striking proof of the truth of this assertion is found in the following cases:

(7) In 1920 Garvey's supporters rushed into a tent where a religious meeting was being conducted by Rev. A. Clayton Powell in New York City and sought to do bodily violence to Dr. Charles S. Morris, the speaker of the evening—who they had heard was to make an address against Garveyism—and were prevented only by the action of the police. Shortly afterward members of the Baltimore branch of the U.N.I.A. attempted bodily injury to W. Ashbie Hawkins, one of the most distinguished colored attorneys in America, when he criticized Garvey in a speech. During the same period an anti-Garvey meeting held by Cyril Briggs, then editor of a monthly magazine—The Crusader—in Rush Memorial Church, New York City, on a Sunday evening, was broken up by Garveyites turning out the lights.

(8) Several weeks ago the Garvey division in Philadelphia caused such a disturbance in the Salem Baptist Church, where Attorney J. Austin Norris, a graduate of Yale University, and the Rev. J. W. Eason were speaking against Garvey that the police disbanded the meeting to prevent a riot of bloodshed. Reports state the street in front of the church was blocked by Garveyites, who insulted and knocked down pedestrians who

were on their way to the meeting.

(9) In Los Angeles, Cal., Mr. Noah D. Thompson, a distinguished colored citizen of that city, employed in the editorial department of the Los Angeles Daily Express, reporting adversely on the Garvey movement as a result of his visit to the annual convention, was attacked by members of Garvey's Los Angeles division, who, it is alleged, had been incited to violence by Garvey himself, and only through the help of a large number of police officers was Thompson saved from bodily harm.

(10) A few months ago, when some persons in the Cleveland (O.) division of the U.N.I.A. asked Dr. LeRoy Bundy, Garvey's chief assistant, for an accounting of funds, a veritable riot took place, led, according to the Pittsburgh American, by Bundy himself.

(11) In Pittsburgh, Pa., on Oct. 23 last, after seeking to disturb a meeting conducted by Chandler Owen, editor of the Messenger magazine, Garveyites who had lurked around the corner in a body rushed on the street car after the meeting, seeking to assault him, but were prevented by the intervention of the police.

(12) When William Pickens, who had co-operated in the exposé of the Garvey frauds, was to deliver an address in Toronto, Canada, Garveyites met him on the steps of the church, with hands threateningly in their hip-pockets, trying to intimidate him, lest he should further expose the movement.

(13) In Chicago, after seeking to break up an anti-Garvey meeting, a Garvey supporter shot a policeman who sought to prevent him from attacking the speaker as he left the building.

(14) In New York last August during a series of meetings conducted by the Friends of Negro Freedom to expose Garvey's schemes and methods, the speakers were threatened with death. Scores of Garveyites came into the meetings with the avowed intention of breaking them up. This they were prevented from doing by the stern determination on the part of the leaders, the activities of the New York police and the great mass of West Indians and Americans, who clearly

showed that they would not permit any cowardly ruffians to break up their meetings.

(15) In fact, Marcus Garvey has created an organization which in its fundamental law condemns [condones?] and invites to crime. This is evidenced by section 3 of article V of the constitution of the U.N.I.A., under the caption, "Court Reception At Home." It reads, "No one shall be received by the potentate and his consort who has been convicted of felony, EXCEPT SUCH CRIME OR FELONY WAS COMMITTED IN THE INTEREST OF THE UNIVERSAL NEGRO IMPROVEMENT ASSOCIATION AND THE AFRICAN COMMUNITIES LEAGUE."

(16) Further proof of this is found in the public utterances of William Sherrill, one of the chief officials in the organization and Garvey's envoy to the League of Nations assembly at Geneva. Speaking at the Goldfield Theater in Baltimore, Md., on Aug. 18, 1922, he is quoted as saying: "BLACK FOLK AS WELL AS WHITE WHO TAMPER WITH THE U.N.I.A. ARE GOING TO DIE."

(17) What appears to be an attempt to carry out this threat is seen in the assault and slashing with a razor of one S.T. Saxon by Garveyites in Cincinnati, O., when he spoke against the movement there last October.

(18) On Jan. 1, this year, just after having made an address in New Orleans, the Rev. J.W. Eason, former "American leader" of the Garvey movement, who had fallen out with Garvey and was to be the chief witness against him in the federal government's case, was waylaid and assassinated, it is reported in the press, by the Garveyites. Rev. Eason identified two of the men as Frederick Dyer, 42, a longshoreman, and William Shakespeare, 29, a painter. Both of them are prominent members of the U.N.I.A. in New Orleans, one wearing a badge as chief of police and the other as chief of the fire department of the "African Republic." Dr. Eason's dying words, identifying the men whom he kn[e]w from long acquaintance in the movement, were:

(19) "I had been speaking at Bethany and was on my way home when three men rushed out at me from an alley. I saw their faces and (pointing at Dyer and Shakespeare) I am

positive that these two men here are two of the three."

(20) The vicious inclination of these Garvey members is seen in their comments in an interview:

(2[1]) (The N.Y. Amsterdam News reports:) "Both Dyer and Shakespeare have denied the attack, but declared they were glad of it, as they said Eason richly deserved what he got. 'Eason,' said one of them, 'was a sorehead. The association made him what he was. When he was expelled because of misconduct he went up and down the country preaching against Marcus Garvey, who is doing great good for our race. Someone who evidently thought it was time to stop his lies took a crack at him. I don't blame the one that did it. Eason richly deserved what he got.' "

(22) Eason says he knew the men who shot him were directed to do so. Insomuch, however, as the assassination of Mr. Eason removes a federal witness, we suggest that the federal government probe into the facts and ascertain whether Eason was assassinated, as the result of an interstate conspiracy emanating from New York. It is significant that the U.N.I.A. has advertised in its organ, The Negro World, the raising of a defense fund for those indicted for the murder, seemingly in accordance with its constitution.

(23) Not only has this movement created friction between Negroes and whites, but it also has increased the hostility between American and West Indian Negroes.

(24) Further, Garvey has built up an organization which has victimized hordes of ignorant and unsuspecting Negroes, the nature of which is clearly stated by Judge Jacob Panken of the New York Municipal Court, before whom Garvey's civil suit for fraud was tried; Judge Panken says: "It seems to me that you have been preying upon the gullibility of your own people, having kept no proper accounts of the money received for investments, being an organization of high finance in which the officers received outrageously high salaries and were permitted to have exorbitant expense accounts for pleasure jaunts throughout the country. I advise those dupes who have contributed to these organizations to go into court and ask for the appointment of a receiver."

(25) For the above reasons we advocate that the attorney general use his full influence completely to disband and extirpate this vicious movement, and that he vigorously and speedily push the government's case against Marcus Garvey for using the mails to defraud. This should be done in the interest of justice; even as a matter of practical expediency.

(26) The government should note that the Garvey followers are for the most part voteless, being either largely unnaturalized or refraining from voting because Garvey teaches that they are citizens of an African republic. He has greatly exaggerated the actual membership of his organization, which is conservatively estimated to be much less than 20,000 in all countries, including the United States and Africa, the West Indies, Central and South America. (The analysis of Garvey's membership has been made by W.A. Domingo, a highly intelligent West Indian from Jamaica, Garvey's home, in "The Crusader" magazine, New York City; also by Dr. W. E. DuBois, a well known social statistician, in "The Century Magazine," February, 192[3], New York City.) On the other hand, hosts of citizen voters, native born and naturalized, both white and colored, earnestly desire the vigorous prosecution of this case.

(27) Again[,] the notorious Ku Klux Klan, an organization of white racial and religious bigots, has aroused much adverse sentiment—many people demanding its dissolution as the reconstruction Klan was dissolved. The Garvey organization, known as the U.N.I.A., is just as objectionable and even more dangerous, inasmuch as it naturally attracts an even lower type of cranks, crooks and racial bigots, among whom suggestibility to violent crime is much greater.

(28) Moreover, since in its basic law—the very constitution of the U.N.I.A.—the organization condones and encourages crime, its future meetings should be carefully watched by officers of the law and infractions promptly and severely punished.

(29) We desire the Department of Justice to understand that those who draft this document, as well as the tens of thousands who will indorse it in all parts of the country, are

by no means impressed by the widely circulated reports which allege certain colored politicians have been trying to use their influence to get the indictment against Garvey quashed. The signers of this appeal represent no particular political, religious or nationalistic faction. They have no personal ends or partisan interests to serve. Nor are they moved by any personal bias against Marcus Garvey. They sound this tocsin only because they foresee the gathering storm of race prejudice and sense the imminent menace of this insidious movement, which cancer-like, is gnawing at the very vitals of peace and safety—of civic harmony and inter-racial concord.

The signers of this letter are:
Harry H. Pace, 2289 Seventh avenue, New York City.
Robert S. Abbott, 3435 Indiana avenue, Chicago, Ill.
John E. Nail, 145 West 135th st., New York City.
Dr. Julia P. Coleman, 118 West 130th street, New York.
William Pickens, 70 Fifth avenue, New York City.
Chandler Owen, 2305 Seventh avenue, New York City.
Robert W. Bagnall, 70 Fifth avenue, New York City.
George W. Harris, 135 West 135th street, New York City.

There is no doubt that the Negro is his own greatest enemy. He is jealous of himself, envious and covetous. This accounts for most of our failures in business and in other things. This I know was responsible for the collapse of the Black Star Line, in addition to the dishonesty of the race to itself.

In calling our people dishonest to ourselves I do not mean to infer that the white or other races are not dishonest; but they are dishonest with a method or a system. The Negro has no method or system in his dishonesty. Environed as the Negro is in our civilization, handicapped, abused, limited in opportunities and prejudiced against, he cannot well afford to be as lax in his racial dishonesty as other people who have reached a higher state of civilization or progress without any surrounding handicaps or barriers. The Negro should, like the Jew, adopt a method of dealing with himself. If he is to steal, he should, like the Jew, steal from others but not from himself.

Unfortunately the Negro is growing up with the disposition of playing dishonest with himself, hence, the great difficulty to promote successful Negro enterprises on a large scale.

When I started the Black Star Line I had the greatest confidence in every Negro—first, I believed every Negro felt like I did—a great enthusiast to see the race go forward to success. Speaking to large groups under the auspices of the Universal Negro Improvement Association, I felt their enthusiasm, their earnestness, and, therefore, I concluded, that as much as I felt to be racially true and patriotic they also felt like myself. Therefore, in selecting directors and officers of the Black Star Line, I did so with an open mind to everybody. I had Americans on the directorate, I had West Indians, I had South Americans, I gave everybody a chance, and the sad story is that very nearly every one that I placed in a responsible position fleeced the Black Star Line.

The fellow that I made secretary for the first few months [E.D. Smith-Green] (a clever, well-trained accountant from British Guiana, who could not be eclipse[d] for competency anywhere), after three months when we called our first quarterly meeting was unable to account for 50,000 shares of the stock of the Black Star Line. I will give you the history of this man. He was one of the original members of the New York division of the Universal Negro Improvement Association. I discovered his ability and made him secretary of the New York division. It was during the war period, and he could earn much more money at Trenton, N.J., working in ammunition factories than he could in New York. He left New York and went to Trenton. When the Black Star Line was formed and I was looking for men of ability, it was then I thought of him. I offered him a position. There was no raised capital to the Black Star Line, except my personality and the confidence the people had in me. He knew that I was not offering him a job in a corporation that was already established, but to something to be made on the confidence of the public in us. He accepted the offer, but stated to me that he had not enough money to pay the railroad fare to New York. I sent him the money. The fellow, through his poor financial condition, could be rated just an ordinary working man with about three or four suits of clothes. He came to New York, I coun[s]elled him; I took him into my confidence and told him what could be accomplished in the interest of the people in starting this steamship line. He was inducted into office as secretary of the corporation.

We started to sell stock and the people bought it with a tremendous go. Thus this man, earning $50 a week, started to handle thousands of dollars daily. He was the man who received all cash. Sometimes $15,000 would pass through the mails—as fast as I could gath[er—]and sometimes he would take over the counters at the office in New York and at Liberty Hall—$10,000 a day. I myself saw the people who were buying stock although I never sold a single share. I believed in this man, and I trusted his honesty. About one month after he was with us, I noticed a great change in his personality; he had become a fashionable sport, he used to change his suits almost twice a day. At the end of the second month he came to me and said: "Mr. Garvey, what are you doing; aren't you going to buy an automobile?" I replied: "Buy an automobile? For what, and with what?" I was then getting $50 a week also. I said: "I can't afford to buy an automobile." He said: "Chief, I would like to buy a 'knock-about,' but I was watching you." I became suspicious of the man, and after three months when an inventory was made, we found that 50,000 shares could not be accounted for. The usual excuse: "There must be a mistake somewhere." Just as the Negro always says when he is asked to explain himself. The blame is always on somebody else, or else on circumstances that cannot be explained, or understood.

The assistant secretary [Richard Warner?], who was a native of North Carolina, who knew more about what the secretary was doing than I, was jostling the secretary to get for himself equal authority to handle the money of the corporation. I couldn't understand what the reason was, I never did, until the tria[l] of my case for "Using the mails to defraud," when this assistant secretary was one of the principal witnesses against me, in that in spite he never pardoned me for not originally giving him equal authority with the secretary so that he could manipulate things as the secretary did. His latitude was not as great, under the rules and he wanted a big latitude to do what the other man did. The thing that startled me in his evidence was when he tol[d] the court that: "I placed the cold hand on him." Meaning that I restrained him from being able to make away with as much as the other secretary did. This statement I believe won for me sympathy from the jury.

For one year I unreservedly gave over my entire self to talking for the Black Star Line, so as to influence the people in buying stock—a penny's worth of which I never sold myself, and a dollar of which money I never handled. My position can be properly understood when I state that all the money for the Black Star Line went through the New York office, from which office I was generally absent nine months out of the year. The hand[l]ing of the money took place generally when I was 2,000 or 3,000 miles away. I had, therefore, to rely on the honesty of the other officers, such as the secretary, the treasurer [George Tobias], and the vice president [Jeremiah Certain]. They betrayed me and destroyed the [hop]es I had in view, as made manifest by the fact that with such a splendid start, with the accumulation of nearly $750,000 in ten months, [t]he Black Star Line is nowhere today.

The treasurer of the Black Star Line was a man I had also great confidence [in]. This man has remained to me a mystery up to now. I really cannot say that this man has been a dishonest man, a knave, a fool, or an honest man. He has played such a game that with as much as I understand human nature, I don't know how to place him. He has been one of those characters who never knew anything, from whom you could never get any positive information, therefore, one has to do nothing else but assume [h]is responsibility if he was wrong or curse him as a d... fool, which [h]e wasn't. He had such a disposition you couldn't believe he would do a wrong.

He was never vexed. But between this man, the secretary and other prominent persons in the corporation I found myself as one who rested "between the devil and the deep blue sea."

The Black Star Line, as everybody knew, was the first really big business venture in America. In one way it has fai[l]ed, but in another way it has not, in that its very organization has been an inspiration to thousands of N[e]groes in America to l[a]unch out in business on a bigger scale. If in no other direction, this has been a good, and I am sati[s]fied even to have suffered a penitentiary sentence for this.

The vice president of the Black Star Line was an American; a very fine type of man; but one who probably like myself allowed an organized group of sharpers to take him in. These sharpers were West Indians and Americans of the same type of the Secretary, fellows who wanted to get rich over night. Well-trained fellows, but discovered rascals.

There is another fellow whom I may bring out pointedly, whom I gave the position of passage and traffic superintendent. This man, although possessing very fine qualifications like the secretary couldn't do better than work in a factory. It was out of a factory I took him. He was in ordinary circumstances when he came to us, his clothes were not of the best, but after two months this Negro was the best d[r]essed man in Harlem, a fashion plate. He had all the women around and [to] my surprise after a while, he also had under his influence my first wife [Amy Ashwood Garvey].

Unfortunately, this type of Negro is too much at large. With their very intelligence, which is wrongly directed, they are able to do a great deal of harm to our business institutions, and so not only the Black Star Line suffers, but other institutions, like our banks, our insurance companies, have suffered and are suffering. It is a pity bec[a]use when fellows like these destroy these [o]rganizations the confidence of our people is weakened, and so it becomes more difficult for the honest Negro business man to succeed in helping his race.

It must be understood that [t]hose Negroes who robbed the Black Star Line did so, not only by themselves but by the inspiration and protectio[n] they got from those white men in authority who could punish them when brought to justice, but who would not punish them, because they had carried out just what the white men wanted them to do—destroy an institution like the Black Star Line, that sought to give the Negro business people self-reliance and demonstrate Negro initiative.

Among those who robbed the Black Star Line was a stock salesman, who defrauded the corporation of $300. I caught him red-handed. I took him before the magistrate— it was Magistrate Simpson—he was good enough, seeing the evidence was so clear, to hold him for the grand jury. When the case was sent down to the district attorney's office, M[r.] Edwin P. Kilroe, who had great influence as assistant district attorney, used that influence against an indictment. The man was not indicted. He was advised by my enemies to bring a suit against me for false imprisonment in that he was arrested; when the case was tried, the white jury's passion was played upon and immediately through prejudice they returned a verdict against me for damages of $2,000 and against the Black Star Line for $500. Yet, in a Federal Court, two years after, I was indicted and convicted for using the mails to defraud, because the Black Star Line had failed, through the acts of such men, whom I could not succeed in punishing even though I caught them with the goods. Since my deportation to Jamaica efforts have been made to collect the $2,000 judgment from me here.

The interested or inquiring person may ask: "How is it your secretary was able not to account for 50,000 shares and your treasurer and other officials were able to do so many things to [contribute to] the failure of [*words repeated*] the Black Star Line; did you not keep [p]roper books?" The answer is: "Yes." In the history of [t]he Black Star Line I had two of the best firms of chartered accountants in New York to open and start the sets of books to be used by the corporation and to audit them. The books were laid out. I had competent men to keep the books in keeping with the instructions and advice of the accountants. But this is what happened, as generally happens among our people when they are disposed to do wrong. They would not make the regular and proper entries in the books. They made an entry on Monday and on Tuesday part of the day they have forgotten three times; by others, and by the end of the week they had forgotten th[re]e times; by the end of the month they had forgotten a dozen times. Now, how am I to know that the books are not kept, that the records are not kept in the proper way, when I happen to be away six months from my office depending upon other men to see that the work is properly done. Whenever I call in an outside party to give me expert information the rest of the fellows in the inside would organize themselves against the person getting the right kind of information. Even the accountants couldn't get the proper books from them to audit. It was always a case of Mr. So and So has been using it and it can't be found, or some such excuse. Whenever anyone suspects that an investigation is going to be made by me that person would find an excuse to leave the position, another one takes charge and then whatever the wrong it is shifted to some other person or persons not to be identified. For me to find out meant I had to do the work myself.

If Jesus was the accountant or president of the Black Star Line He could not have done better than I or the accountant did, because the men had the disposition to steal and hide. They did everything to embarrass an honest investigation, and because I was president of such a corporation[,] I had to bear the b[r]unt.

I am giving this rehearsal of what ha[s] happened to the Black Star Line with the hope of helping other business men. Many another Negro will go to the State or Federal penitentiary in trying to do good, if he places too much confidence in the loyalty of other men, because we are all of the same race; it is difficult even to sort men. This must not be regarded as a discouragement, it is only a suggestion to be careful; but when it is considered that the environment in which our people live and the kind of teachings they are getting are destroying them, we have to be careful how we place confidence in those who help us to carry out our proposition of usefulness to the race.

Some Negroes have the idea that they must become rich over night, and at somebody else's expense. They will take no chances with the white man, but they are most desperate with their own. It would be a good thing if our colleges started to train our students to the disposition of becoming rich only when they have honestly worked for its accumulation.

The Black Star Line was such an important business venture for the Negro that I feel it my duty to continue explaining why it was a financial failure.

As stated before, the directorate was made up of all nationalities of Negroes. Among the officers, we had the president, who was myself, a Jamaican; the first and second vice presidents, American; the secretary, a British Guianese; the assistant secretary, an American; [the] treasurer, an Antiguian; others of the directorate were from the Americas and the West Indies. It cannot be said, therefore, that the blame is more for the Americans, the West Indians or the South and Central Americans. The blame of the failure is traceable to everybody, which proves that the Negro is characteristically the same everywhere in our present civilization. He has the wrong outlook; his education is bad, hence the greater need for universal re-education. As time went on the personnel of the directorate changed as also the officers.

Nineteen hundred and twenty was a banner year for the Black Star Line. We had ships on the seas and were engaged in active business. But this is the result of it: In the early part of January, I was in Canada on my honeymoon, having been married [to Amy Ashwood Garvey] on the 25th of December, 1919. Whilst in Canada several scheming white business sharpers from Wall Street, who had, during my presence in New York, tried to involve me and the Black Star Line in shady transactions that would have led to the embarrassment of the company, took advantage of my absence in striking up some arrangements with the secretary and treasurer o[f] the company—who, like most Negroes, working with other Negroes—felt that they had as much right as their superior officers to negotiate and handle vital business matters without any advice or guidance.

My methods of doing business have always been to investigate and scrutinize well the parties to be dealt with, and all their agreements and arrangements before committing myself. This kind of a caution enabled me, up to the present, to survive in my independent business transactions; but my associates who adopted no method or system of care, probably because they were not as deeply interested in the results as myself, regarded men more from their s[ua]vity and bluff, than from the truth and facts behind them. While I refused to do any business with the men who wanted to involve me before I left New York, my associates in my immediate absence started negotiations with them. The result was that our first ship, the "S.S. Frederick Douglass," [*also known as the S.S. Yarmouth*] was chartered to a company of irresponsible brokers for the removal of general cargo from New York, to Havana within certain specified dates.

When the question of removing the cargo really came up, it was found to be a cargo of whiskey and other spirituous liquors, under prohibition by the 17th of the month. The S.S. [*line missing*] [ac]cording to the new prohibition law, that was to come into effect. Everyone in America knows what the new prohibition law was. All spirituous liquor had to be disposed of in a limited time in the United States or be confiscated.

The secretary and treasurer of the Black Star Line actually involved the company in a removal of a cargo of $5,000,000 worth of Green River whiskey from the port of New York, by the 11th of the month. The S.S. Frederick Douglass had not returned to New York, but was in the West Indies completing its second voyage. When the ship returned a few days before the agreed time for removal of the whiskey, I was notified in Canada of the complications. It must be remembered I knew nothing about the contract when it was negotiated, no one mentioned anything to me about it, not until it was discovered that the company was to receive $7,000 for removing the cargo that was valued at $5,000,000, at the tremendous risk of being responsible for the cargo to its full value and with the possibility of losing our ship if the ship did not sail an hour before the prohibition law went into effect. It was only when the secretary and treasurer got themselves into this trouble that I was notified, and had to cut short my honeymoon in Canada and return to New York to see what could be done to extricate the company from the great trouble these two men had created around it.

When the captain of our ship returned to port, just a few days before the day that the ship was to sail with the cargo of whisky, he found that it was a chance for him to make his fortun[e]. He found out that the secretary and treasurer had agreed to collect $7,0[00] on the freight, that the freight was worth $5,000,000, and so without any regard for the interest of the company, he said that the ship could not sail for three weeks, because there were repairs to be done. This was served as a kind of ultimatum to the secretary and treasurer. The captain also found out who the shippers of the cargo were and got them worked up to a state of excitement, the result of that was that they themselves offered the captain and secretary of the company a side cheque to remove the cargo within the prescribed period; in that it was worth that much to them to have the $5,000,000 worth of cargo removed for $7,000 to the owners of the ship and pay a few thousand dollars more on the side for the accommodation.

On my arrival in New York I found the Black Star Line was tied up owing to the grave blunder of the secretary and treasurer. There was only one thing for me to do, that was to see that the contract was immediately executed so as to avoid other liabilities. I called upon the captain, therefore, to make preparations for the ship to sail with the cargo. After he had entered into the agreement with the shippers to get his side cheque, the limit set for repairs was cancelled, and I was told that the repairs could be done in a couple of days. It turned out that under the direction of the captain, $11,000 had to be spent for repairs. I was, therefore, called upon to spend $11,000 for repairs in order to have the ship sail with the cargo valued at $5,000,000, on which the company was [o]nly collecting $7,000 as freight, all because of the disobedience of two officers of the company, who took advantage of my absence in dealing with men whom I had already turned down.

After this my suspicion in all things was aroused and I made certain investigations, and found out that the Black Star Line and I as its president, have often been called upon to pay repair bills for the ships running into the thousands, on which certain officers of the ships collected percentages of from 20 to 30 per cent, from the engineers, on repairs that were called upon to be done that were not necessary, unless to supply the officers with their percentages. This kind of a fraud was also practiced in buying supplies for the ships, when ship-c[h]andlers were given orders running into thousands of dollars, out of which they had to pay officers of the company on the ships responsible between 15 and 35 per cent commission. These were the things I never knew of and which I found out too late.

After the captain of the Frederick Douglass sailed with the cargo of whiskey and returned to New York there was a loss of $70,000 [on] the one trip. The ship was tied up to Havana and could not unload for over three weeks. The secretary was dispatched simultaneously with the boat to see to the unloading of the ship, in that he entered into the contract with the shippers. But the contract was so loose that there was no protection for the owners to collect demurrage at Havana if it was not possible to unload immediately on the arrival the boat.

I was so completely disgusted that I was determined to bring the employment of the captain and the secretary to an end. The secretary was bonded. When I presented his defalcations and tried to collect, the bonding company refused to pay. The captain had already made his fortune and, therefore, w[as] as ready to leave the company as I was to get rid of him. But in the separation [of] the captain and secretary from the Black Star Line a loss [wa]s left behind of hundreds of thousands of dollars which, as president, fell on my head, and which contributed to the ultimate collapse of the company, on which I was indicted and sent to prison.

After we succeeded in getting rid of the first secretary, the next was a Haitian Negro of high attainments in accountancy [Elie Garcia]. I learned afterwards that this man once held a high position in the Haitian government; the vice president also changed to a Barbadian [Orlando M. Thompson], a man also of high attainments in accountancy, having had special training [f]or over twenty years as a practical business man. It was with this latter [outing] that the Black Star Line foundered.

After having gotten rid of one group, I thought I would have been safe in the hands of another. This Barbardian whom I made first vice president and general manager of the Black Star Line, came to me with first a sad story, that through certain misfortunes, he was in such a position that he could not find even shoes for his children, and that he wanted me to give him a chance, which I was glad to do.

There was no doubt that this man had the qualifications; if he were a white man and honest, he could have made his fortune for his company and himself in Wall Street. I felt that because this man was colored, he was handicapped and, therefore, I thought I would give him a chance. He was inducted into office as vice president and general manager.

After the management was passed over to this man, who had so much business experience, I had to take my circuit on the road in helping to improve my organization as usual. This man in whom the entire board of directors had confidence, went about and made connections in the shipping and commercial areas which turned out to be connections with the very white men who were desirous of destroying the Black Star Line. This was not known to me until some time after.

We had now reached 1921, just about the time when we were to float our African Trans-Atlantic Liner. This new manager and vice president presented to us the possibility of securing a ship from the Holt Line. I believe it was the S.S. Byron. I believe it could be purchased for $100,000 or more. I can't remember; but of this amount $30,000 should be paid on a certain date. So as to be able to raise this amount of money, we decided on a campaign to be started, which in America would be carried on by certain individuals on the American field, and I would go to South and Central America and the West Indies. We felt sure that the money would be accumulated on the particular day.

At this time we had under repairs at the Morse dock in Brooklyn the S.S. Antoni[o] Mace[o], a yacht that we had bought from the interests of H. H. Rogers, which we were reconditioning for passenger service between Central America and the West Indies. I was to have sailed on this boat on the trip contemplated to Central America and the West Indies. It happened, however, that whilst I made an arrangement with Morse to repair the boat for $15,000 and left for a trip to California and the West, Morse found out that his profit would not have been enough at $15,000, so during my absence he entered into an agreement with the vice president of a loose nature which he never brought to my notice, and which I never knew about until months after. This new agreement gave Morse the option to violate the first agreement I made, not only concerning the boat, but the specified time and for $15,000, which he changed to an indefinite time and an unlimited amount for the repairs.

The result was that when I returned from the West to New York, ready to sail to the West Indies, and asked the vice president to have the boat ready, he said that Morse had not completed the work. I was surprised; but he argued me out of realizing that he had changed the agreement, but promised that the boat would be ready in a couple days. He knew I had already made dates for appearing in the West Indies and Central America, and could not remain. I, therefore, had to leave for Cuba via Key West with the hope of having the boat pick me up at Santiago.

This was the unfortunate trip that really gave the vice president, whom I found out to have been my enemy, other officers of the B[l]ack Star Line, executives of the Universal Negro Improvement Association, and my enemies on the outside the chance to influence the Secretary of State's department [Sec. Charles Evans Hughes] and the Department of Labor [Sec. James J. Davis] not to have me return to the United States. My trip was to have been one of 30 days, I was kept out by machinations of these men for over four and one-half months. Nowhere in the West Indies nor in Central America would any of the American consuls vise my passport. They had all had definite instructions not to do so.

The part many of my co-officers played in this matter will be related later.

I had hardly sailed away from the United States, in March, 1921, via Key West, Florida, before the other men who were associated with me in promoting the Black Star Line and the Universal Negro Improvement Association conspired to permanently eliminate me from being head of the organizations, by having me exiled from the United States. This I believed was contemplated, not because I was personally objectionable to the men, but because they wanted my position; they desired to share among themselves the honor that had been conferred upon me. This I take to be a common disposition among human beings; there are some people even closely related to one by blood, as well as others, not so closely related, who would have no objection to even seeing an associate or friend in business die[,] if by the death of the individual it meant promotion for them. Those of us who understand human nature know that this happens among people generally, and without regard to race.

I am only reciting the incident here to prove to you how human beings treat each other. The men who are identified with me in the Black Star Line and the Universal Negro Improvement Association owed their positions to me. Some I elevated to positions of responsibility and honor, such as no other person in the world would have done for them; others were professional men whom I introduced into the organization and offered them better opportunities than they had before. These persons should regard me more as a friend than as an enemy, in fact, they did not regard me as an enemy, only that they were jealous of my position, and with an evil genius, such as the vice president of the Black Star Line, who was scheming to get control, to inspire them, one can readily understand how easy it was for them to lend themselves to the scheme in exiling me from the United States after I had sailed away in the interest of the organization for only a period of 30 days.

To explain some of the methods used to get me out of the United States, and to keep me uninformed, I will state the following: The vice president of the Black Star Line had associated himself with some of the enemies of the corporation in Wall Street who used their influence to get the order issued against me for my non-return to the United States; other agencies such as the National Association for the Advancement of Colored People also made reports to the secretary of state and the Labor Department; but I believe the greatest harm was done by the people who were closely associated with me and who wanted my position.

For several years before the Black Star Line reached its zenith of prosperity I had a private secretary [Gwendolyn Campbell] who was a Jamaican like myself. She was the first female secretary of the Universal Negro Improvement Association. I had great respect for this young lady, because she was the fiancee of a friend of mine who also was the first male secretary of the organization. I always treated her with respect and consideration. When the organization and the Black Star Line became so successful she had under her control all of my confidential business, she was permitted to sign my name for me in issuing orders and she was authorized not to allow any transaction where my name was necessary, to be consummated without her being satisfied that it was correct or by notifying me personally.

When the vice president and the Haitian who succeeded the secretary of the Black Star Line as secretary found out that this young lady had such an important position, they started to make love to her and succeeded in their designs, even though they were two married men. All this was not known to me for a long while. After they had succeeded in getting the love of this young lady they had access to all my confidential reports. Whatsoever information I had gathered about the activities of these two men was related to them by my private secretary, so that they were always in a position to dismiss my informants who were other employes, or head of[f] the reports, in that most of them never reached my hands.

On leaving the United States for the trip to South and Central America and the West Indies, this young lady had complete charge of my private office. She was instructed by me to give me detailed reports of what was transpiring in my absence. This she withheld from me during the time I remained out of the United States. The secretary and vice president were able to influence her to sign my name to any document they wanted. It was on her order that the fatal $25,000 was taken from the Black Star Line and handed to a Jew named Silvertone [Silverston], who, along with the vice president, kept the money in their possession, which money was intended to go toward the amount I was collecting in South and Central America and the West Indies for the purchase of the African ship, but which amount was dissipated either by a split among the men or interested parties or otherwise so that when I secured a re-entry to the United States in July I found out that up to then only $2,500 of the money had been lodged with the United States Shipping Board, under the guise of securing a ship in lieu of the one that was to be purchased from the Holt Steamship Corporation, and for which I went to the West Indies.

I must state that among those who did not take part in the conspiracy to keep me out of the United States were Mr. Wilford Smith, consul general, and Mr. William Matthews, the assistant consul general, of the U.N.I.A. It was really due to their influence and to the efforts I made that I re-entered the United States, much to the surprise of the other executive officers of the organization and the Black Star Line. When it was reported that I had arrived in the United States in the last week of July, it was like a bombshell to these officers, because they had made sure that the secretary of state would not vise my passport either in the West Indies or for South or Central America. In fact, when the ship on which I was returning entered the port of New Orleans and the immigration officers boarded her, they were surprised to see me with a vised passport, and so as to make sure I had not got it by fraud I was detained at the immigration office for four hours. I had to telegraph President Harding, and the secretary of state, Mr. Charles Evans Hughes, before I was permitted to leave the immigration station.

During the time spent in the West Indies and South and Central America, the vice president of the Black Star Line mortgaged and complicat[ed] everything we had by way of assets. He had tied up the corporation so with the sharks of Wall street that it would have taken Jesus himself to extricate the company.

After I got information about the handing over of the check of $25,000 to the man Silvertone—whom I previously had refused to do business with before I left—I started to investigate the whole matter of the ship that was to have been bought for the African trade. As stated before, it was revealed that $25,000 which was to the credit of the Black Star Line was taken away. I therefore called a meeting of the directors and presented to them the information I had received from the United States Shipping Board. The vice president stated that the rest of the money not deposited with the United States Shipping Board was in escrow and could be obtained at any moment, but if I personally interfered with the matter the parties who were getting the boat for him would not continue to do so. This boat should have been purchased from April, of the same year; the money was taken from the Black Star Line in March; we were then in August and up to then when I inquired of the money in escrow, it was found that no money was there. I gave the vice president two weeks to produce the boat or the $25,000. The result was that after continuous correspondence with the shipping board and addressing letters to certain individuals, $22,500 was subsequently deposited with the shipping board.

I found out afterward that the vice president, at the convention of the Universal Negro Improvement Association, held in August of that year, got me to sign a document, which he told me was to be used in securing a bond for the balance of the money to be paid on the ship, which was to be allotted by the shipping board, the name of which was the steamship Orion. I interrogated him on the matter and he told me all that was necessary was for the treasurer and myself to sign the document and the ship would be awarded. But the document was used by the vice president and his confederates to borrow $10,000 on the steamship Antonio Maceo of the Black Star Line, which money was secured from the Massachusetts Bonding Co. and used to make up the amount of $22,500 that they subsequently lodged with the shipping board to deceive me. It was when I got the information that I took definite steps in November to prosecute the vice president. The information got out and I was circumvented by the influences that surrounded him.

One Sunday morning in December I went out to the Tombs Court to secure a warrant, which I was denied. The information went out that I made the attempt, and the result was that in January of 1922 I was indicted for using the United States mails to defraud.

It was this combination I had to fight when I appeared before the Federal Court and tried [my] own case before Judge Julian Mack. In my next article I will relate some of the incidents of the trial.

My indictment for using the United States mails to defraud occurred as follows:

First, I was the only person indicted, in that I was the only person wanted; on my first indictment, as explained before, the secretary of the Black Star Line handed over all the books and documents of the corporation to the district attorney's office.

I was arrested around 4 o'clock in the afternoon, and between my being taken from my home to the U.S. Commissioner's office for bail, the secretary handed over these books. When I returned to the office I found out that he had done so without my instructions or any information to me. This made me feel that there was a conspiracy somewhere, while it was apparently the desire to "get me alone." When the matter was thoroughly gone into, it probably was discovered that the attempt to "get me alone" was too glaring, in that I was only president of the corporation and there were other officers who took as prominent part, if no more than myself, in the daily routine of the corporation's business, so several months after there was another indictment which included the vice president [O.M. Thompson], the secretary [Elie Garcia], the treasurer [George Tobias], with myself. Through private information I knew, however, that the other men were only brought in to take off the suspicion of wanting to "get me singly."

It was rumored that during the time of my indictment and the preparation for the trial, Dr. W.E. DuBois was often seen in consultation with the prosecuting district attorney. It was stated that he was supplying him with information how to go about the prosecution. Prof. William Pickens was alleged to have been in consultation with the district attorney [Maxwell Mattuck]. To explain the attitude of Prof. William Pickens is somewhat surprising. At one time when Prof. Pickens was not on such good terms with the National Association for the Advancement of Colored People, he sought my presence and discussed with me the possibility of his being employed by the Universal Negro Improvement Association. I readily sympathized with him and offered him a position. At this time he visited my home as well as my office. When we expected him to report for work we found out that he had used the offer made him to induce the National Association for the Advancement of Colored People to increase his salary under more secured arrangements. It was after all this was done that Prof. Pickens got in co-operation with the district attorney against me.

During the time of the indictment, I had occasion also to have the secretary of the Black Star Line arrested for forgery and embezzlement as auditor-general of the Universal Negro Improvement Association. The incident that caused the arrest is explained as follows: The chancellor [G.E. Stewart] of the Universal Negro Improvement Association one day made up his lodgment of the Association's funds for the bank. He had the money resting on the sideboard of his desk made up of cheques, and American green-backs. The auditor-general who is the Haitian I explained about in a previous article, came down from his office to the chancellor's office and engaged him in a conversation, sitting near the sideboard where the money was. Whilst the chancellor was not looking the auditor-general slipped in among the lodgment money a forged cheque for fifty dollars, made out in the name of a man whose name I cannot very well remember, but who resided in Kansas and was formerly an official of the Kansas division of the Universal Negro Improvement Association, and a barber well known to me. The auditor-general took out fifty dollars of American green-backs and slipped in the cheque for fifty dollars.

Immediately after this was done it happened that I entered the chancellor's office[, j]ust by curiosity to find out what the amount of lodgment for that day was, as I had before me in my office several bills to be paid for the corporation on the same day. The chancellor immediately turned to the amount of money he had for lodgment and started to check over. I watched carefully and I saw a peculiar looking check. I asked him where he got it from. He could not ex[pla]in. He said he could not remember seeing it before. I looked at the check (and by the way I just remember) the signature on the check was that of James Moore, but the writing I discovered immediately was that of the secretary of the Black Star Line, who also was the auditor-general of the Universal Negro Improvement Association. I had suspicions of the man that he was doing wrong things before. I took the check from the chancellor and a half-hour after I called down the stenographer from the secretary's office to inquire where the secretary was. The young lady said he was out for about a half-hour. I immediately ordered his office closed. The two young women working in his department were advised to shift themselves to other departments, whilst I nailed up the door.

It was evident that the news of my discovery got to

him, because he kept away all the day. I remained in my office up to 6 o'clock that afternoon. The ordinary staff left at 5. As I was about to leave, he came into the building in a crestfallen and crying attitude. I stared at him and he voluntarily confessed in the following words:

"Mr. Garvey, I did it; I cannot say why I did it, but I did it."

I replied and said: "I am surprised that a man of your responsibility should do a thing like this. I have investigated and found out that this is only one of several checks you have so cashed on the bank, which have been returned by them, but which came into your hands as auditor-general, which you have not brought to my attention. I cannot pardon you for this and I cannot promise you I will not take immediate action."

He beseeched me to give him another hearing before I took steps to prosecute. I promised him I would give him an interview at 9 o'clock the next morning at my home. The next morning he brought with him three other men, officers of the corporation, all with the attitude of influencing me not to prosecute. He offered to give up the securities he had in the organization and immediately vacate his position. I told him I could not accept that because it was a bad example. I therefore summoned him before the magistrate at the Highgate court, where he was examined and held for the grand jury. He was indicted and tried in the Petty Sessions Court and found guilty and was to be sentenced at a later hearing. During his conviction, at a later hearing, the combination of my enemies and those working against me became his protectors, the result was at the second hearing he was acquitted.

It is to be explained that this man as auditor-general and secretary of the Black Star Line had under his control all the books of the corporation for two years. He had been carrying on that kind of practice as explained above with no one to check him, so it was only by accident that I discovered the one incident; and it was because I know who James Moore was and that he had no checking account why I regarded the check as a forgery, and knowing that the secretary was capable of writing several different hands, I was able to detect the signature on the check.

What the secretary did in his way is an indication of what the vice president did in his other way. So when I stood indicted along with these men I found myself in the company of enemies who were working with my outside enemies to defeat me and to send me to prison, because I stood in their way of making easy fortunes.

At the trial I was represented by an array of counsel, but after the first day's hearing I discovered that there was an arrangement whereby I was to be found guilty and disposed of as the court felt, after my attorney made the plea for mercy to further humiliate me. I detected that I would have been sent to prison on the 26 counts on which I was to be tried, each of which carried five years' imprisonment and a fine of $1,000. I suggested to my counsel on the first day to adopt a certain course in questioning the witnesses of the government.

Richard Warner and Edgar Gray [Grey] testified the first day and counsel made me to understand that it was not necessary to keep the witnesses on the stand all day and over for the second day, but that I could recall them the next day. When the next day came he told me I could only recall them as my witnesses and not under cross-examination as crown witnesses. I immediately lost faith in my counsel and urged him to retire from the case, which I tried myself. I found out that the counsel had arranged with the district attorney to give him two weeks for the prosecution and to take one week for me in my defense, so as to allow the judges and others to go on their vacations. When this was revealed to me through the exhaustive and careful conduct of my case by myself, which suggested to the court that it would take longer than three weeks, I felt indignant that my liberty was to be so jeopardized without consulting me on the matter.

The trial took five and one-half weeks, and every day of it was a terrible fight between myself and the district attorney, one Mr. Maxwell Mattock [Mattuck]. As I went through the trial I saw where it was almost an impossibility for me to escape the traps that were laid for me, in which the press, rival organizations, personal enemies, big businesses, foreign and other governments were interested to the point of seeing me convicted, so that my career as leader of the Negro peoples of the world would be doomed. It was really a question of international, national, state, municipal and ward politics. There were governments watching this conviction so as to be able to close their doors against me as being a convicted person. Cuba was watching for the opportunity, Guatemala was watching for the opportunity, Panama was watching for the opportunity, all the Central American republics were watching for the opportunity, because that was the only way they could keep me out of those countries. The United Fruit Co. was instrumental in seeing me placed in such a position because my freedom to visit the Central American countries might influence the hundreds of thousands of Negro laborers that they had under their control who were members and sympathizers of my movement.

The real importance of this trial may never be appreciated by the people of our race in America because the plot was so deeply laid and the forces aligned against me were so influential. It was with the fullest realization of this in my mind which made me fight as I did for the five and one-half weeks.

No one, not even the ablest attorney, could have fought for me as I fought for myself, unless I was in a position to pay him millions of dollars to make him comfortable for the rest of his life, because he would be risking the friendship and good will of the powerful influences that were aligned against me. During the trial I had to practically separate myself from my co-defendants because I could only properly plead my case by showing that whatsoever happened was the result of the complicity of others and not by any fault of my own. This my counsel did not want me to do, because my counsel was in sympathy with the others who were defending my co-defendants in the case. There was an arrangement that I was to be sacrificed and this would only be done by keeping the proper information from the jury. I therefore took the only course which was left for me, and that was to honestly defend myself. The result was that instead of having me convicted before the white jury on 26 counts, as I was indicted for, I was only convicted on one, and everybody knew that it was a verdict arrived at in satisfying the atmosphere of the court and not because I was really guilty. In support of this, after I was in prison for two years, all the jurymen signed a petition for my release, except one, who said that he could not do so unless advised to do so by his friend, the district attorney who tried the case against me, and this he refused to do. The trial was really a fight between the high ideals of justice and the desire to destroy a man who was not in favor among his enemies.

As a foreigner, I had the extreme prejudice of being an alien against me; this was worked upon by the district attorney. The evidence on which I was convicted is told as follows: A man by the name of Benny Dancy, working at the Pennsylvania Railroad in the postal department, testified that he received a letter from the Black Star Line. He could not tell what was contained in the letter nor could he identify the letter, but he could identify an empty envelope with his name typed on it and which bore in the corner the rubber stamp of the Black Star Line. He testified having received the envelope through the mail. It was on this evidence only that I was convicted of using the mails to defraud. It isn't necessary to go into the merits of the evidence here, but when it is considered that there was no testimony to identify the rubber stamp of the Black Star Line, and when it can be assumed that even in the office I had enemies, it could have been easy for my enemies to have made the rubber stamp of the Black Star Line, had it affixed to the envelope and posted it to the man. The evidence in the case is tantamount to that.

In the trial the principal witness to state the fact that letters were mailed from the office of the Black Star Line to different places and parties was a boy [Schuyler Cargill], who I never saw, never knew in my life and who could not even remember the persons employed to the Black Star Line during the time he was supposed to be employed there. When I tried to bring out the fact that he was only brought in to testify without knowing the facts, because on cross-examination he was unable to tell where the general post office of Harlem was, I was prevented from cross-examining him. So, up to the present, no one knows whether the boy was employed to the Black Star Line or not. He could not even tell who used to pay him during the time he was supposed to be working with the Black Star Line. Nevertheless, with all that was said and done, I was convicted on one count—the penalty, a sentence of five years or a fine of $1,000 or both, the passing of sentence resting with the discretion of the judge. I could have been given a day, a month or a year or could have been fined alone. The judge, however, sentenced me for five years, with a fine of $1,000 and cost of the trial. He also denied me the right of bail, pending appeal to the District Court of Appeals. I was therefore confined in the Tombs Prison for several months, awaiting the decision of the Appellate Court. It was only through the good offices of President Harding that I was allowed out on bail, and when the question of bail came up[,] the trial judge, who was then in Palestine, insisted on a bond of $50,000, but the wishes of President Harding prevailed with the district attorney, who was then Colonel Haywood [William Hayward], and I was released on a bond of $1,500.

I shall continue in my next article further explanations of my trial and imprisonment.

It was rumored during my conviction and pending appeal before the District Court of Appeal that if I would keep quiet the appeal would not be heard, or would be decided in my favor. The idea was no doubt to scare me from continuing my propaganda among the Negro peoples of the world—a propaganda that was working havoc among the enemies of the Negroes in Africa principally, and in the United States of America, and other parts of North and South America and the West Indies. There was no doubt that several of the governments of Europe were feeling the effects of the new spirit of racial consciousness that had come over the Negro peoples of the world. Big commercial houses in America were also afraid of the result of my encouraging Negroes to develop their own business enterprises and trading among themselves.

It was felt that I was a danger and would continue to be a greater one if allowed to continue my propaganda unmolested. The big companies that were engaged in the shipping business were also determined to keep the Negro off the high seas. When I was told of what would happen if I kept quiet, I became more determined to prosecute the idea that was uppermost in my mind, so I launched out immediately to organize a new line of steamships—the Black Cross Navigation and Trading Company.

When the forces fighting me heard about it they became irate and they launched another propaganda against me. But not two months after my release from the Tombs, the people rallied around me and we purchased our then biggest ship the S.S. General Goethals, afterwards re-christened the S.S. Booker T. Washington. This splendid boat was bought from the Panama Railroad Company, in A1 condition. When the boat was acquired the sentiment of my enemies was stirred to force the decision of the District court of Appeal, and so the decision was timed and given. The very day that the S.S. General Goethals was to sail from Norfolk, Va., on a trip to the West Indies to engage in the Panama business and the conveyance of general freight, the decision was given against me in the appeal. Two days after I had to surrender for imprisonment.

The enemies knew well that if I was confined to prison whilst the ship was at sea, it would be only a matter of time when they would be able to influence those representing me to the extent of destroying the new venture. They were not wrong in this. Two months after I was confined at Atlanta, they succeeded in taking away the ship from the unfaithful man who represented me, for $25,000. It came about in this way: The same group of men in Wall Street who had their eyes on the Black Star Line and who used the old officers to destroy the corporation maneuvered to get the officers of the Black Cross Navigation and Trading Company to sign up with them to accept a cargo to Miami, Fla., through a Negro broker [Anthony Crawford]. This Negro broker influenced the men to allow him to accept the freight and this was done without saying a word to me in Atlanta. The result was, in the working out of the scheme to get the ship, they got one or two shippers to place aboard the boat a small tonnage of cargo and then they went around to prospective shippers and influenced them not to ship any freight on the boat to Miami. That meant that the ship could not sail with the small amount of cargo, they in turn libelled the boat for non-performance of contract with a demand to the extent of $25,000. They maneuvered for time against the absolutely incompetent men who were representing me, the result being that I was notified that the boat was sold in New York at an auction sale for $25,000 to cover damages for nonperformance of contract by the ship. So the boat that was purchased and equipped for $260,000 was taken away while I was in prison for $25,000. I may mention here, that the trick was played during the time I was in prison to take away the building of the Black Star Line, 52–54–56 W. 135th street, and Liberty Hall, 120–140 W. 138th street, New York. Efforts were also made to get the $22,250 lodged with the Shipping Board for the Black Star Line.

When I was sent to Atlanta my enemies made sure that that would have been the last of me. From what I could gather it seemed that they had reached even the Deputy Warden [Julian A. Schoen] of the Federal Prison with their influence, with the suggestions of making it hard for me whilst there. The Deputy Warden of the institution made every effort to carry out the wishes of my enemies. When I was drafted for work he gave me the hardest and dirtiest task in the prison, thinking that that would have ruffled my spirits to cause further punishment. But I philosophically accepted the duties and executed them to the best of my ability. After being so engaged for a short while, the Warden (a high-typed man of character and consideration), Mr. J. W. Snooks [Snook], called me into his office and had me transferred to the best position that a colored man could have in the prison; this I also executed to the best of my ability during the entire time that I remained there. The Warden of the prison made everything comfortable for me. I have absolutely no complaint to make during the time I spent at Atlanta under Warden Snooks.

Whilst I was confined efforts were made to secure for me a pardon or commutation. I was informed that President Coolidge would have acted immediately upon the application for pardon a few months after I was in Atlanta but for the pressure brought to bear upon him by my enemies. Instead of signing the papers for my release he returned them with a statement of "Premature." It was not until two years after, he finally granted me commutation.

I had hoped that on my release from Atlanta I would have had the opportunity of returning to New York to straighten out the affairs of the Universal Negro Improvement Association, the Black Star Line and the Black Cross Navigation and Trading Company, but my enemies made sure of their game in not allowing me to return to New York. They had already swallowed up all the assets of the companies, which could be recovered only by my presence in New York. So they skillfully influenced the Department of Labor and the Department of State to deport me to Jamaica. On the order of President Coolidge I was shunted to New Orleans, and from there to my homeland—Jamaica.

The plotters and robbers have had things their own way, because I have been unable to defend myself from this far distance. I was able, however, to hold up the distribution among them of the $22,250 lodged with the Shipping Board, although several motions have been made before the Senate to distribute it. Up to the present I do not know what has happened; but the public can gain an idea of the state of affairs when it was published broadly at the trial that the Black Star Line had not a penny to its credit, when, in fact, up to the present (except something has happened), there is a large amount on deposit to the corporation's credit of a ship with the U.S. Shipping Board.

The Black Star Line and the Black Cross Navigation and

Trading Company were the two big ventures that could have succeeded but for the disloyalty of members of our own race to themselves. In competition we must expect anything from others but we ourselves should close ranks in the promotion and conduct of enterprises of the kind, the success of which would mean so much to the race.

If the people I have mentioned and others not mentioned of our race did not constitute themselves stumbling blocks in the way of our enterprises, today the Negro would occupy a high rating in the marine and mercantile world. The enthusiasm that the people started with to support the Black Star Line, if they who had the management had proved loyal, sincere and honest, today our race would have on the ocean, on the high seas no fewer than 50 first-class ships; our trade relationship would have been established between our races in Africa, in the United States, in South and Central America and the West Indies; we would have been removing raw materials from plantations of far-off Africa, from South and Central America, and the West Indies, to our factories in the United States, thus giving employment to millions of Negroes in America in the factories and clearing houses and giving employment to millions more in tropical Africa and South and Central America, and the West Indies. Today the Negro would not be still dependent upon the white man for a pittance of existence but would be his own employer. The Negro today, like the Jew, would be holding his head high in the commercial world and men would be respecting him everywhere. That was my hope! That was my dream when I started the Black Star Line and the Black Cross Navigation and Trading Company, but the men of little vision in the race who were small and petty, malicious and envious did everything to destroy such a possibility.

I can never pardon Dr. DuBois, Prof. Pickins [Pickens], Cyril Briggs, Chandler Owen, Samuel Duncan and Adolphus Domingo for the treacherous part they played in preventing the success of the Black Star Line, thereby making it impossible for the Negro to find a prominent and settled place in our industrial world at the present time. These men, because of their limited intelligence, might not have known what they were doing then, but surely if they could do no good they should have done no harm to their own race for they had intelligence enough to know that they were doing harm to their own race when they made such strenuous efforts to defeat the Black Star Line. And these men, everyone of them, had the opportunity (because they were invited into the organization), to do good if they were sincere. But you will remember that Dr. DuBois declined the invitation he received; all the other men were identified with the movement in some way or the other, and yet they fought it with the idea of destroying it, prompted by malicious motive. They thought they were destroying me, but they ought to have realized they were destroying themselves and their race.

In my next article I shall give you an idea of the trials and troubles I had in promoting and conducting the affairs of the Negro Factories Corporation and the African Communities' League.

The Negro Factories Corporation and the African Communities League we[re] two auxiliary corporations, offshoots, of the Universal Negro Improvement Association, like the Black Star Line, and the Black Cross Navigation and Trading Company. The purpose of the Negro Factories Corporation was to establish factories all over the United States of America for the manufacture of such articles and commodities that were needed for the consumption of the Negro peoples of the world.

I have calculated that the American Negro could be put to work in the factories to manufacture clothing, toilet, mechanical and other articles necessary for distribution among Negroes, as well as canning the different foodstuffs that they do consume, and that these factories would supply the hundreds [of] millions of our people in the West Indies, South and Central America and Africa with things thus manufactured. In turn, the steamships of the Black Star Line would have conveyed these articles to these foreign places and in returning take from Africa, the West Indies and South and Central America the raw materials produced by Negroes in those parts on their plantations and farms. In this way we would be feeding the mills of industry in America and finding employment in the agricultural regions for millions of our people all over the world.

The African Communities League was organized for the purpose of trading. We were to have commercial houses, distributing houses and also to engage in business of all kinds, wholesale and retail. The start was made in this direction in Harlem, where the Negro Factories Corporation acquired a large steam laundry in 142d street, wherefrom we were to spread out in our larger enterprises. We had about 50 people employed at the laundry, but the result was that after a few months they created such a confusion among themselves, entailing great financial loss, that we had to close down the outfit. The laundry men who collected the laundry abused the people whom they collected from; the workers on the inside tore up the people's garments, they misplaced them, and when we came to collect for the work done we found that the company was robbed of half of what it was entitled to. It was impossible to continue, therefore we closed down the laundry.

The African Communities League purchased a large printing outfit, the object of which was to publish our first daily newspaper, the Negro Times. Over $35,000 was spent in equipping the printing plant. We had linked up to it the United Press service and the latest and best in the publishing art. There again we suffered through bad management. The men who would work honestly and uprightly with white men started to work as they felt like when they came into our plant. They worked on our linotype machines (six of them) with such indifference that they were out of order nearly all the time, although they were new machines. Although we paid good proofreaders, the paper published each morning was a disgrace. The men would not obey each other, they would not report on the proper time and the result was that the Daily Negro Times had to go out of business.

At the same time the African Communities League started a chain of groceries and restaurants in Harlem, and here we had a greater amount of trouble than ordinary. The men in the groceries and restaurants would rob the sales between them and the collectors, who were supposed to check them up each morning, would connive with each other to give in wrong returns of the sales or takings for the day, and then split between themselves. We simply could not get the men of our race to realize that they were doing themselves a great injury in not working for Negro corporations as honestly as they worked for white ones. The idea behind each Negro's mind was that he had to get rich overnight. So they had no scruples to rob as much as they could get, hence in the space of three or four months, we found that the company had lost so much between the groceries and the restaurants that they could not be kept up, and we had to close them. But behind all this was the organized campaign of those who did not want to see the Negro in business and who were determined to destroy us so that we could still remain a dependent people. The people employed by us seemed to have been under the influence of such people who promised them protection, and so they did these things with impunity, knowing that they would not be prosecuted.

This is where the American Negro must be careful; he is environed by a hostile population, a population not of his own race, a population of people who have long regarded the Negro only as a slave, as a menial servant. This population is not disposed to see the Negro develop in its midst—is not disposed to see the Negro become economically independent. Like everywhere else, wherever the Negro had been a slave, his old slave master feels that if there is to be any relationship between them it must continue to be that of master and servant; and unless the Negro is in a position from a numerical point of view, he is almost certain to fall under the influence and environments set for him.

From my study in America I have learned that it is the part of the American white man to encourage the Negro in non-essentials. He will give him money to build up churches, to equip his Y.M.C.A.'s, or give him protection in minor things where great issues are not involved, but he is not interested in seeing the Negro go ahead in industrial enterprises. He would not allow him to become independent. There is always a check on the Negro when he attempts to launch out on anything independent. So movements like mine will always suffer the disadvantage of being objectionable to the white man and become targets for their destruction, whether directly or indirectly.

My movement seeks to make the Negro independent from an economic point of view and later from a political point of view. That is the only way I see for the salvation of the Negro. This means that greater efforts must be made to make movements of the kind successful. This is not going to be tolerated by the enemies and therefore there must be a fight for the survival of the idea.

Simple enterprises that the white man controls, whether directly or indirectly, in which the Negro is engaged, may continue, because he realizes that such enterprises cannot succeed without him and ultimately he will get the major portion of what is produced. Negroes who are engaged in such enterprises will succeed, but success in that direction will not take the race very far, but will still make it a dependent race. That is my fear! That is why I appear different to many of the leaders. Whether I succeed or not, I believe firmly and sincerely that the Negro will only amount to something in the world when he is able to do things independently, as the white men and as the yellow men have done. It is by virtue of their independence that they are so progressive. If any branch of the white people were dependent on the other peoples, they would not be as successful as they are today. If Japan were dependent on the other countries she would not be as successful as she is today; and so long as the Negro is dependent on other groups, he will remain lowest down.

My program seeks to make the Negro an independent person in every walk of life, and that is where the conflict comes in. It is left to the Negro to see that he succeeds in his own enterprises, man them honestly so that they may succeed, so that he may climb the heights as other men. This program also seeks to impress the Negro that he also has his part to play and must play it well. He has been too easily influenced by the white man, who seeks to destroy him, and so, as a people, we have been battered from pillar to post, hence we have not reached the objective that we should set before us. But the Black Star Line, the Black Cross Navigation and Trading Company, the Negro Factories Corporation, [and] the African Communities League have in a way played their part in preparing the Negro for bigger things.

When it is considered that the failure of these enterprises did not amount to more than a million dollars and that we got almost fifty millions worth of lessons and experience out of them, we cannot say that they have failed completely, because the lessons will go to set others right in conducting bigger affairs for the good of the race. At the present time, with the experiences we have had, we will be able to launch out on a bigger scale, and the mistakes we made previously will not be made in the future. Thus these corporations have done good for the race; and it is hoped that other race leaders will profit by the story I am relating about them.

What is true of these organizations also is true of others that are not so prominently brought before the public in America; hundreds of other enterprises have gone under in similiar ways, but the only difference is that I am more courageous than many to relate the real cause. I do so with pride, because I want to see my race well informed; and so I gladly give the information.

As stated before, all these organizations I have mentioned were offshoots of the parent organization, The Universal Negro Improvement Association, which was founded in America in 1918.

In my next article, I will continue my explanation of the activities of this greater organization for the benefit of the American people.

After the holding of the First International Convention of the Negro Peoples of the world, at New York in 1920, the Universal Negro Improvement Association became a world factor as a Negro movement.

The convention elected a responsible group of officials to

lead, including the following: The Potentate, the Provisional President of Africa, the President General, the Leader of the American Negroes, the Supreme Deputy Potentate, an Assistant President General, a Secretary General, a High Chancellor, an International Organizer, a Surgeon General, the Leader of the Western Province of the West Indies, South and Central America, the Leader of the Eastern Province of the West Indies, a Chaplain General, an Auditor General, a Counsel General, an Assistant Counsel-General, an Assistant Secretary-General, a High Commissioner-General, a Minister of Legions, a Minister of Labor and Industry and a Speaker in Convention. All these officials formed the Executive Council of the new organization. All of them were educated persons. The Potentate [Gabriel M. Johnson] came from Liberia: he was a Mayor of Monrovia. The Deputy Potentate [G.O. Marke], an highly educated man, who was a Town Clerk at Sierr[a] Leone, also came from Africa. The rest of the officials were from the Americas, and the West Indies; nearly every section of the Negro world had a representative on the executive body, so that the organization was truly universal in its scope, from an executive point of view.

This was the first big attempt at world organization among Negroes. There was a hope that every unit of the Negro race throughout the world would be brought under the influence of this organization to work out the plan of true race emancipation and national redemption.

The start in this direction was wonderful because in the space of two years the organization had covered the entire world and had become a power to be reckoned with by national and imperial forces. But the great difficulty was the inability of most of the leaders of the movement and the other Negro leaders on the outside to grasp fully the significance of the organization. Those who were in, apparently were more concerned with the opportunity of having big positions to which large salaries were attached than to do their little to justify and maintain them; while those on the outside being envious, and jealous, sought to destroy without consideration the good or ill effects thereof. Those of us on the inside who were sincere had a tremendous responsibility upon our shoulders, that of disciplining and restraining the leaders from within and defending ourselves against enemies from without. It has been a kind of tug-of-war and in the end, but few of us have survived.

From within a large number of those who started with [us] have been eliminated; from without the other leaders harrassed us to the point where they have not only weakened us, but have weakened the whole race. Some of those who tried to damage the Universal Negro Improvement Association from the outside must be regarded not as race leaders but more as iconoclasts than anything else.

We cannot ignore the evil influences of leaders like Dr. DuBois, [*words missing?*] Owen, but their opposition to us may be regarded as the opposition of leaders of one group to leaders of another; but fellows like Adolphus Domingo and Cyril Briggs, who had no policy, but whose purpose was to criticise and condemn leaders whether they be Dr. DuBois, Moton or Garvey may be regarded as iconoclasts.

Out of the great confusion of ideas among leaders and the destructive criticisms of the iconoclasts the race stands today weeping and sorrowing. We must admit that conditions are worse today in America than they ever were within the last 20 years. This is evidence positive that the iconoclasts and the jealous and malicious leaders have hurt none other than the people. In destroying movements like the Universal Negro Improvement Association they do not only destroy the individual that may be hateful to them, but they destroy ideals upon which are founded the hopes of the people. And what are the ideals of the Universal Negro Improvement Association[?] These are they:

To establish a Universal Confraternity among the race;

To promote the spirit of pride and love; To reclaim the fallen; to administer and assist the needy;

To assist in civilizing the backward tribes of Africa;

To assist in the development of independent Negro nations and communities; To establish commissionaries or agencies in the principal countries and cities of the world for the representation and protection of all Negroes, irrespective of nationality;

To promote a conscientious spiritual worship among the native tribes of Africa;

To establish universities, colleges, academies and schools for the racial education and culture of the people;

To conduct a world-wide commercial and industrial intercourse for the good of the people;

To work for better conditions in all Negro communities.

When the other leaders fought us and the iconoclasts sought to destroy us, these were the things that they were fighting and working to destroy. What satisfaction they got out of it one doesn't know. Yet those who have followed my career in the United States must recall the tremendous amount of opposition that was organized against me to make these objects a reality.

Now when it is considered that the Universal Negro Improvement Association is a membership organization and that anyone could join so long as he was of Negro blood and that an invitation was given to those recognized leaders of the race to become members, it seems almost hard to understand how anyone could justify his opposition to me, because I was only a unit in the organization under its constitution. Therefore, if the opponents were really interested in the race they would not have opposed me from the outside[,] but they would have become members of the Universal Negro Improvement Association to co-operate and bring about a realization of the objects. In not doing this there is but one logical conclusion to be arrived at, and that is, that they intended to destroy not only me, not only the Universal Negro Improvement Association, but anything, caring not how idealistic it may be, and promising in behalf of the race so long as they were not the chief beneficiaries or creators of its existence.

Since writing this series of articles, I have seen one or two press releases by Prof. Pickens in which he continues to lambast me and to hold me up to ridicule. I have also seen a letter written by Mr. Adolphus Domingo stating that the references I made to him in previous articles were not true. Prof. Pickens is well known for his "mouth usefulness." I[f] we were [to] analyze the work of the professor we would find that he has done more harm to the American Negro than half of the white population put together because his criticisms have always been destructive. If we were [to] analyze the work of Prof. Pickens with that of Madam C. J. Walker or Mrs. Malone of the Poro College, it would be like weighing a mouse in a scale against an elephant. These two women have employed thousands of Negroes and found bread for them, thereby helping to lif[t] the economic standard of the race. Prof. Pickens with all his "froth and noise" has not helped three people of his race to earn a livelihood; so much for his race leadership, but he has caused many a Negro to be lynched and to lose his job by following his "fool talk" that only tends to create dissatisfaction, when there is no balancing effort to help the dissatisfied person.

Let me explain myself clearly here: We must agitate, we must protest since we are living in the midst of a hostile environment; but when we stir the people to dissatisfaction through protest, it is good common sense to suggest a way out of all this dissatisfaction. If a man is dissatisfied with his employment, you must find one for him; if he is dissatisfied with his political condition, you must create a new condition for him. In agitating that was what the Universal Negro Improvement Association sought to do, hence our program as above. We did not only talk but we were trying to lay a foundation for the [e]conomic existence which would save the race from all their trials, troubles and tribulations.

Mr. Pickens has denounced all these efforts in denouncing me and so, after he has eliminated me, as he says, and has the field for himself, we find him still talking, still protesting, still encouraging the Negro people to be dissatisfied over their condition, and the people are becoming poorer and poorer by not being able to find employment. This is the kind of harm that men like Prof. Pickens do to the race.

I may bring out the following pointedly, not because I want to injure him but because I want to bring home to him the evil of his ways. He hates me because I am a West Indian. What this is to do with my being a race leader I do not know. Alexander Hamilton was a West Indian, but one of the saviours of the American nation. The Negro, as I have always pointed out, owes his nationality in the Western world to accident, so whether he be an American or West Indian should not count when we have before us the big idea of rescuing ourselves from the common enemy.

The Universal Negro Improvement Association seeks to break down the prejudice that exists between the different groups within our race; we seek to link South Carolina with North Carolina, the Carolinas with the Virginias; the entire South with the entire North, and all America with the West Indies and Africa in one great racial movement tending towards our complete emancipation. This is what the enemies, the foolish and the sinister have raced [raged?] against.

As far as Mr. Adolphus Domingo is concerned, I have but to draw the attention of the public to the following to prove the insincerity of the man in his reference and his attack upon me: Mr. Domingo is well known to me, we grew up as young men together. I am glad to know that he has now found a useful occupation in being an importer; but I can just imagine what that importation is; I hope no one will believe that he is the big business man, as would be suggested by the statement that he is an importer. My knowledge of Mr. Domingo is complete in knowing that he has always been a mischief maker and a barber shop and tailor shop philosopher who recently drifted into Communism. Whatever he wants to make himself out to be otherwise, is left to the public's benefit; but in criticising me and in stating that I lied against him I will go to no other authority to prove my case that he is an iconoclast, but his own letter to "The Pittsburgh Courier," which was published on the 12th of April [see following appendix], in which, among other things, he stated: "When I was actively opposing Mr. Garvey I did so openly and publicly." He, therefore, admits his opposition to me. He again states in another paragraph the following: "It is not my practice to take notice of statements emanating from people whose reputation for truth telling and honesty is 'zero.'" Mr. Domingo evidently means to suggest that my reputation for truth telling and honesty is "zero," yet, in the world, I occupy a higher social and commercial standing than Mr. Domingo, and in addition to this, by election, I am head of a world organization recognized by all the governments of the world, while Mr. Domingo is only known by the mischief he can make around people of repute and by telling how honest and reputable he is himself. The people who know Mr. Domingo in New York could tell you if they care to whether Mr. Domingo opposed me always openly and publicly; but Mr. Domingo is very artful, and so he suggested that you should not publish the series of articles I am writing. The purpose is evident, for the truth would never be known from my side and this very suggestion of Mr. Domingo's reveals the character of the man. If he would suggest that to you logically, what would he not be capable of doing otherwise undercover[?]

I desire it to be emphatically understood that I have no other purpose in writing these articles than to give honest information to the public, so that any other Negro coming after me, would, by the information be better able to deal with the opposition that will be found among certain Negroes to anything started on behalf of the race.

As far as I am personally concerned those who have opposed me and who are still doing so could have n[o] better opportunity in the world than I personally have. I could have selected to be a "frothy lecturer" like Prof. Pickens, without assuming any responsibility to anybody. I could assume to be an iconoclast without any responsibility to anybody; but I felt when I started my career that one should not live entirely to himself, hence, I attempted like other far-seeing members of the race to assume my responsibility. If in doing so I am to be called a liar, I am to be charged, as Prof. Pickens and Mr. Domingo charge me, with going to jail, what must I do but be satisfied. The only difference is that I had the courage to go to jail in rightly or wrongly fighting for a cause that I believe dear to my heart; whilst Mr. Pickens is too cowardly to place himself in that position. It seems almost surprising that a man like Mr. Pickens should refer to my being in jail several times when he ought to know that a cause like the Negro's can't be won unless not one, but hundreds go to jail on principle. He has forgotten that Gandhi has gone to jail, and De Valera has gone to jail; but I suppose he will say that they did not go to jail for using the U.S. mails to defraud; but if De Valera had Irish men to deal with in Ireland, as I had Negroes to deal with in America he would not have gone for five years but 10 over the Republican Irish bond issues. The Negro will never amount to anything so long as he has leaders like Pickens who play safe by not assuming the kind of responsibility that would really allow them to amount to anything. Anybody can talk or write, but writing and talking are not going to save the Negro. The men who are really going to make the race are the big business men, who take chances; men like Jesse Binga, R.R. Wright, Watt Terry, the heads of our insurance companies and our banks and corporations; women like Mrs. Maggie Walker, Madam C. J. Walker, Mrs. [Annie] Malone; these are the people who are constructively building to help the race because out of their efforts (which is a great risk) employment is being found for the people and opportunity is being given for them to exist. Many another such daring, but useful person, has failed; many have been sent to prison, probably, as I was, for innocently trying to do more concrete and substantial good for the race. If they had elected like Prof. Pickens to only [talk?] and write[,] they would not have probably failed or suffered; but when we consider that our civilization is built up of men who are willing not only to go to prison but to die in doing good for the race we can well look down on Prof. Pickens as an idiot for his suggestion that I have been recently out of jail in Jamaica. I went to jail in Jamaica for supposedly contempt of court—standing upon a principle. Probably Prof. Pickens would have been too cowardly to stand up in a similar court, even though a principle was involved, and commit contempt.

I do not want to enter into any controversy with anybody, but I won't allow anybody to hide the truth at my expense. With all that the enemies have done the Universal Negro Improvement Association is still alive, and its membership is still open to enemies and friends alike. My position is also open to anyone who thinks he would better fill it than myself. I have never, to the exclusion of any other, sought the position. Mr. Pickins or any other can have it any time that they feel that they can honestly and sincerely do what is right by the people. I hold my position not by myself but by election, which shows that the people still have confidence in me. Any time they feel to transfer that confidence to Prof. Pickens or Mr. Domingo they are welcome to do so, and until then I think it unfair for Prof. Pickens to condemn me. I would suggest to Brother Pickens that he think of himself in the manner how he would like to be treated, and thus try to treat others in the same way. That is: Practice the Golden Rule.

At the outset, I had hoped to write more extensively about the operations of the Universal Negro Improvement Association, but unfortunately, I have been so inundated with new matters and pressed for time in keeping up with my regular organization's work and business that I have to conclude my series of articles with this one, in which I will, incidentally, touch upon the organization's work—past and present—as well as give a few suggestions as to what we hope to do in the future.

The Universal Negro Improvement Association was actively brought into existence in the year 1914 in Kingston, Jamaica, B.W.I. From Jamaica, as stated before, I journeyed to the United States and founded there our American unit of the organization in 1918.

The American organization became after one year the dominant force in the organization's life. All the branches and divisions that were organized all over the world—in Africa, South and Central America and the West Indies [—]looked to New York as the parent of the organization. And so, our international headquarters was established there until it was transferred, after my deportation, to Jamaica. The headquarters of the organization is now at Edelweis[s] Park, 67 Slip[e] Road, Cross Roads P.O., St. Andrew, Jamaica, B.W.I.

My activities in America are well known to a large number of the people, but there are certain things that no one can know, except I, as the head of the movement[,] reveal them. For the good of the organization in America and elsewhere, I must state that our greatest difficulty has been that of finding honest and upright leaders within the movement.

In my previous articles I referred to the harm done by my enemies from without. Among the methods used by these enemies is that of approaching every new convert of the Universal Negro Improvement Association and possible leader of the movement, in showing him, either he, by himself, can better lead the movement than Garvey, or that he would do much better if he double-crossed the organization to secure a better position in some outside movement backed by white patronage, or to secure the patronage of some wealthy white person. This propaganda has worked havoc in some of our big enterprises; and it is in this consideration that I cannot pardon Mr. Domingo, who in New York was one of the chief propagandists in turning the leaders of the movement against the movement and me. Up to the present we have not entirely succeeded in getting upright and honest men. The few leaders we have had recently, came in quite all right but after a while they started to do and play the same tricks as others did before them. Among those whom I can recommend as being most honorable and consistent leaders of the movement are two women who have done exceedingly well, when nearly all the men have failed, and they are still in active s[e]rvice—Madame M.L.T. DeMena, who is our present international organ[iz]er, and Lady Henrietta Vinton Davis, who is our present secretary general. We have had very little trouble with the women in the movement; with the exception of one or two, we have never had a dishonest woman in the leadership of the organization. Every wom[a]n has played fair and true. But it is sad to say, that nearly every man we placed in [a] position of trust ha[s] abused that confidence and proven a scamp. They always see the selfish "I," the desire to exploit the people willing to support the cause, for their own purpose. That is the great difficulty with Negro organizations and the great difficulty that the Universal Negro Improvement Association has not been able to overcome entirely.

I make bold to make these statements of truth because I want to guide my people right. Everybody who has watched Negro movements knows that sooner or later most of them get foundered on the same rock—inconsistency, dishonesty, swell-headedness, and the desire to usurp authority—everybody wanting to be boss, wanting to be head.

At the present time I am having difficu[l]ty in the organization, caused from the same evil disposition. Whilst I am president general of the organization and whilst we have our headquarters here from which all instructions must go, we have a vice president general, without any authority[,] calling a conference of all the presidents of the movement and without any information or instruction from the president general. These are the things that ruin Negro movements, but still, because of the deep-seated principles of the Universal Negro Improvement Association and its glorious ideals, the movement moves on, overcoming all difficulties, destroying all handicaps. And so today the movement is entrenched in the hearts of hundreds of millions of Negroes throughout the world. We have done wonderful work in Africa. And if our work in the 15 years was to be measured by profits and dividends, we could fairly say that the Universal Improvement Association has been the most successful movement not only among Negroes but among all races during that period of time. The dividends we have paid are that we have stirred Africa from center to circumference. In every section of the homeland, the Negro is now awakened through our propaganda of "Africa for the Africans, at home and abroad."

Despite what the world may say in criticism of me,

we have rendered more service as an organization than all the Negro organizations put together have done in the last 100 years. We have given a national consciousness to the Negro; we have emblazoned his name on the banner of liberty and today he is carrying that banner throughout the world fearlessly. He is stirred in Africa and in the West Indies; he is alive in South and Central America; and all that is needed today is the unifying of our forces so that the great objective that we aim at may become a reality. By our propaganda Negroes have been granted positions in Africa they never would have received from the French, the Spanish and the English. In America compromises have been struck that never would have been arrived at, but for my presence in America and that of the Universal Negro Improvement Association. Even the National Association for the Advancement of Colored People has had a better time, because of my presence in America, because they were able to use my name and the organization[']s in approaching white men for their patronage—because if they did not support the middle mean—that is the National Association for the Advancement of Colored People—they would have to grapple with the extreme movement of the Universal Negro Improvement Association and the uncompromising radicalism of Marcus Garvey. This scare brought more money into the coffers of the N.A.A.C.P. than they would have gotten otherwise. Many men opposed me because it was profitable to them. Large amounts by way of philanthropy, charity and gifts were given by white men to double-crossing Negroes under such consideration. That is why certain white people looked upon me as a dangerous man because they were prompted to that belief by my enemies to take money out of them.

What is true of America is also true of the West Indies. My name has been used as a kind of cashier's cheque for certain people. But with all that has happened, I can honestly say I have done my best for my race; and God has so blessed us that the Universal Negro Improvement Association has survived. We have not only made our impress on the nations, but have attracted the attention of the League of Nations, and today many things that are working for the good of the Negro in Africa are because of our determination to press our cause before the League. There is nothing like proper education. It will fit the man for his future. And so the education in the Universal Negro Improvement Association's propaganda has done such great work that today many a Negro owes his position to this source.

We are now launching out in America, in keeping with our original objects, on the proposition of building factories in the United States and developing plantation[s] in the West Indies and in Africa. This is going to take a tremendous outlay of money and co-operation, but we are laying a proper foundation. With the plan we have in view, we hope that in 10 years the Negro will be on the right road to the solution of his problems. We are anticipating opposition from the same group of men, who do nothing but oppose. They have not up to now brought out any economic solution of our race problem. Yet, they agitate to oppose anything undertaken by others for the good of the race.

We must realize that our greatest enemi[es] are not those on the outside, but those in our midst, because when we can readily recognize the enemies on the outside and do not allow them to pass, we have those on the inside working with us to destroy us without our knowing.

In concluding these series of articles, I am appealing to Prof. Pickens and those of his kind to stop and consider the g[re]at injury they do to the race by opposing everything, because they are not in it, or personally profiting by it. If these men are to continue their iconoclastic criticisms of Negro movements, ultimately when the race becomes more independent and intelligent their names will be blasted in derision, because they had been traitors. I have no other feeling than that of brotherhood for Prof. Pickens, for I feel that we are all Negroes and as such we should work hand in hand to foster our cause. In considering that there is a terrible opposition against us, we should forget self and see the one big, glorious cause to which all of us should be attracted. Let everybody understand that the Universal Negro Improvement Association is very much alive. We have gained and covered much ground, linked up many continents; and we are now on the march toward executing the great ideals that brought us into existence.

I cannot close these series without returning my personal thanks to the millions of American friends who have rallied around the Universal Negro Improvement Association. But for the splendid loyalty of the American Negroes the Universal Negro Improvement Association would be still in its swaddling clothes. If the movement comes to anything it is due to the stalwart, loyal and race-loving American Negro who allows nothing to divide him from the truth. It is such a Negro that has helped me to make the Universal Negro Improvement Association and if I live and my name lives in history, this will be due to the help of my American brothers. They must share the credit, the glory, [as] well as I. No one can take it away from them. I do hope the time is not far distant when I will be able to meet the millions of my friends again in America. I hope to visit the country from time to time in promulgation of the cause and in representing the interest of the organization. Probably between now and next year I shall visit not only America but Africa and other sections of the world, such as I used to do before. And at that time, I do hope to renew my friendship and acquaintanceship with the many who have supported me in America.

I have to thank you, Mr. Editor, for the opportunity you presented to me to somewhat explain the activities of the Universal Negro Improvement Association and its auxiliary corporations—an opportunity that heretofore was closed to me, because of prejudice. Whilst my enemies have had the right of way to abuse me, I never had the opportunity to reply. Even now, I understand that my enemies are trying to destroy me; but as you know truth cannot die, it shall never perish from the earth; and as you have given me the opportunity to explain the truth, I must thank you, believing with that great American, Theodore Roosevelt: "No man is worth his salt who is not ready at all

times to risk his body, to risk his well-being, to risk his life
in a great cause."

SOURCE NOTES

Printed in the *Pittsburgh Courier*, 22 February, 1 March, 15 March, 22 March,
29 March, 5 April, 12 April, 19 April, 26 April, 3 May, 10 May, 17 May, and
31 May 1930. Original headlines omitted.

APPENDIX

W.A. Domingo to the Editor
of the *Pittsburgh Courier*

W.A. Domingo, importer and exporter, of 110 West 143d Street, New York City, takes exception to certain statements of Marcus Garvey in his series of "My Experiences in America," running exclusively in the Pittsburgh Courier. Mr. Domingo's letter follows:

[Robert L. Vann]
Editor of The Pittsburgh Courier,
428 Center Avenue
Pittsburgh, Pa.

Dear Sir:

My attention has been drawn to the installment of the alleged autobiography of Mr. Marcus Garvey which appeared in your issue of March 29th. In this article the author makes certain grave and unsupported charges against several persons who at various times have had occasion to disagree with him, and in keeping with his usual customs these men, including myself, are described as being wicked enemies of our race.

It is not my practice to take notice of statements emanating from people whose rep[ut]ation for truth-telling and honesty is zero, nor would I under ordinary circumstances pay any attention to the poisonous outpourings [of] Mr. Garvey's romantic imagination, but in this instance he has overstepped the bounds of unadulterated fiction and indulged in the most vicious kind of libel thinkable.

At the outset, may I not point out that Mr. Garvey's [re]putation for veracity is best g[au]ged by the fact that in his spectacular c[are]er as race leader, business genius, genius, orator, would-be Napoleon and other mirth-provoking and race-impoverishing poses, he has been compelled to make abject apologies and crawling retractions of libelous statements not less than six times. I mention that he had to apologize to Kilroe, Grey, Warner, B[r]iggs, and since his deportation to Jamaica he had to apologize cravenly to the Chief Justice in open court. Later he had to admit being a liar in statements he published a[b]out the magistracy of the island. These are absolutely indisputable facts and give a "close-up" on Mr. Garvey's character.

In his article, he insinuates that I, along with the late S. A. Duncan, wrote to various governments warning them against him. It is this particular charge that I am writing you about.

I take it that your newspaper is not alone concerned with building up its circulation. You, I presume, realize that you owe a duty to your readers. In view of the fact that I desire no kind of legal dispute with you, and since I credit you with a lofty sense of public responsibility, I am asking you to publish all if any evidence submitted to you in substantiation of the charges made against me by Mr. Garvey. You owe this to me and to your readers.

If your readers will only take the trouble to make comparisons they will notice that in the installment of the autobiography in the April 5 issue the author gives another reason for the failure of his mental abortion, the Black Star Line, namely, the dishonesty of the men he selected as his assistants. At one time it was due to propaganda, now to dishonesty. I submit that the court records of his famous trial for defrauding his trusting followers (a record that was adequately covered daily by a reporter of The Courier) shows that the real cause of the early debacle of the steamship company was the gross incompetency of Mr. Garvey, his ignorance, his gullibility, the fact that he gave two Black Star Line checks each for $500 to his fiancee, his paying a fabulous price for old tubs that were unseaworthy and only fit for the junk heap, and wholesale mismanagement of a project that had as much chance of success as Mr. Garvey has of being manly enough to accept responsibility for his myriad failures or of him overcoming his constitutional limitations and surprising himself by telling the truth even once.

I submit that for intelligent and impartial people, those not blinded by fanaticism, there exists ample evidence to disprove most of the statements made by Mr. Garvey.

You, I am sure, will note that Mr. Garvey has departed from the legitimate purpose of an autobiography and has used the circulation of your journal as a means to defame, attack, libel and denounce those whom he dubs his "enemies." His asseverations lack authentication and that very fact impels me to request that in my case you be fair enough to advise the public whether or not Mr. Garvey, who has six times been compelled to retract libellous statements, has furnished you with a single bit of proof in substantiation of his charges made against me with reference to my alleged acts dealing with the defunct Black Star Line.

When I was actively opposing Mr. Garvey I did so openly and publicly, both on the platform and through the press. I never concealed my views for I was not afraid to speak my mind.

That being so, I resent the fact that a paper of your influence, which I have never at any time injured in any way, should depart from the high standards I credited it with possessing and throw open its columns to a confessed libeller to be used for his malign purpose of defaming persons with reputations to protect.

Believing that your newspaper is more than a mere medium for calumny and that your instincts of fair play are antipodal to those of Mr. Garvey, and not desiring to have any avoidable dispute with you, I am asking you to give this letter as favorable publicity as that given the articles written by Mr. Garvey. Yours for clean controversy,

W. A. DOMINGO

SOURCE NOTES

Printed in the *Pittsburgh Courier*, 12 April 1930. Original headlines omitted.

THE
WHITE MAN'S GAME

His Vanity Fair;

or,

The Tragedy of White Injustice

FOREWORD

By Marcus Garvey

Because of the circumstances of time, it is thought that the representation of this little pamphlet would not be amiss in somewhat achieving the original object that it was designed to accomplish—that of giving the Negro a thought, with the hope of inspiring him toward the freeing of himself from the ugly octopus of race prejudice and exploitation, which has been devouring him in his universal association with certain members of the white race.

All good psychologists realize that if you can set a man thinking you are likely to produce, through him, results that never would have been possible otherwise. The object I have in view is to get the Negro to accomplish much for himself out of his own thoughtfulness. To arouse that thoughtfulness, he must be shocked or otherwise he must be driven to see the unusual that is operating against him, and so this little pamphlet was written during a time of leisure in jail in 1927, in the peculiar form in which it appears. It is not verse, neither is it orthodox prose, but it is a kind of mean adopted for the purpose of conveying the desired thought.

The first and second editions of this pamphlet were published in the United States by Mrs. Amy Jacques Garvey, whilst I was doing a five-year sentence at Atlanta, Ga., as the result of the white man's prejudice in America, and thousands of copies have been circulated all over the world. There has been constant demand for more copies, but it has just been found convenient to publish the third edition. This was chiefly inspired by the present war conditions, where another section of the white race—the

Italians, under their mad leader, Mussolini—has seen it customarily proper, to again invade free African territory. Following the course of the old land thieves, Mussolini has organized an unusual savagelike military outfit to conquer Abyssinia, the avowed purpose being to afford Italy economic and political expansion, disregarding all the rights of the Abyssinians to the peaceful possession of their native land. It is evident, therefore, that some of the white race have not changed much during the centuries. They are still barbarous, savage, and in every way inhuman and unjust. The war in Abyssinia proves their modern barbarism and savagery, hence, no one may say that what is contained in this little pamphlet is not really true of the character and disposition of the white man in his association with the weaker, and particularly the darker peoples of the world. Probably, if he reads this he himself may get a conscious thought in realizing how unworthy is his character as is shown by his conduct among other people. If it could achieve no other good than that of making him realize how unworthy he is of being a real human being, and more so a Christian, the publication would not have been in vain. It must be remembered that this is not an attempt at poetry: it is just a peculiar style of using facts as they impress me as I go through the pages of history and as I look at and note the conduct of the white race.

MARCUS GARVEY

2 Beaumont Crescent,
West Kensington, London, W.14
England
November, 1935

THE TRAGEDY
OF WHITE INJUSTICE

By Marcus Garvey

(1)

Lying and stealing is the whiteman's game;
For rights of God nor man he has no shame
(A practice of his throughout the whole world)
At all, great thunderbolts he has hurled;
He has stolen everywhere—land and sea;
A buccaneer and pirate he must be,
Killing all, as he roams from place to place,
Leaving disease, mongrels—moral disgrace.

(2)

The world's history of him is replete,
From his javelin-bolt to new-built fleet:
Hosts he has robbed and crushed below;
Of friend and neighbour he has made a foe.
From our men and women he made the slave,
Then boastingly he calls himself a brave;
Cowardly, he steals on his trusting prey,
Killing in the dark, then shouts he hoo ray!

(3)

Not to go back to time pre-historic,
Only when men in Nature used to frolic,
And you will find his big, long murder-list,

Showing the plunderings of his mailed fist;
Africa, Asia and America
Tell the tale in a mournful replica
How tribesmen, Indians and Zulus fell
Fleeing the murdering bandit pell mell.

(4)

American Indian tribes were free,
Sporting, dancing, and happy as could be;
Asia's hordes lived then a life their own,
To civilization they would have grown;
Africa's millions laughed with the sun,
In the cycle of man a course to run;
In stepped the white man, bloody and grim,
The light of these people's freedom to dim.

(5)

Coolies of Asiatics they quickly made,
In Africa's blacks they built a world trade,
The Red Indians they killed with the gun,
All else of men and beasts they put to run;
Blood of murderer Cain is on their head,
Of man and beast they mean to kill,—dead;
A world of their own is their greatest aim,
For which Yellow and Black are well to blame.

(6)

Out of cold old Europe these white men came,
From caves, dens and holes, without any fame,
Eating their dead's flesh and sucking their blood,
Relics of the Mediterranean flood;
Literature, science and art they stole,
After Africa had measured each pole,
Asia taught them what great learning was,
Now they frown upon what the Coolie does.

(7)

They have stolen, murdered, on their way here,
Leaving desolation and waste everywhere;
Now they boastingly tell what they have done,
Seeing not the bloody crown they have won;
Millions of Blacks died in America,
Coolies, peons, serfs, too, in Asia;
Upon these dead bones Empires they builded,
Parceling out crowns and coronets gilded.

(8)

Trifling with God's Holy Names and Law,
Mixing Christ's religion that had no flaw,
They have dared to tell us what is right,
In language of death-bullets, gas and might.
Only with their brute force they hold us down,
Men of colour, Yellow, Red, Black and Brown:
Not a fair chance give they our men to rise.
Christian liars we see in their eyes.

(9)

With the Bible they go to foreign lands,
Taking Christ and stealth in different hands;
Making of God a mockery on earth,
When of the Holy One there is no dearth:
They say to us: "You, sirs, are the heathen,
"We your brethren—Christian fellowmen,
"We come to tell the story of our God";
When we believe, they give to us the rod.

(10)

After our confidence they have thus won,
From our dear land and treasures we must run;
Story of the Bible no more they tell,

For our souls redeemed we could go to hell.
Oil, coal and rubber, silver and gold,
They have found in wealth of our lands untold;
Thus, they claim the name of our country—all:
Of us they make then their real foot-ball.

(11)

If in the land we happen to tarry,
Most of us then become sad and sorry,
For a white man's country they say it is,
And with shot, gas and shell, they prove it his:
What can we do who love the Gracious Lord,
But fight, pray, watch and wait His Holy word:
His second coming we know to be true,
Then, He will greet the white man with his due.

(12)

This Christ they killed on Calvary's Cross,
After His Person around they did toss:
White men the Saviour did crucify,
For eyes not blue, but blood of Negro tie;
Now they worship Him in their churches great,
And of the Holy Ghost they daily prate;
"One God" they say, enough for all mankind,
When in slavery the Blacks they entwined.

(13)

Their churches lines of demarcation draw;
In the name of Christ there is no such law,
Yet Black and White they have separated,
A Jim Crow God the preachers operated,
Then to Heaven they think they will all go,
When their consciences ought to tell them NO.
God is no respecter of persons great,
So each man must abide his final fate.

(14)

We'd like to see the white man converted,
And to right and justice be devoted;
Continuing in land-values to lie and steal,
Will bring destruction down upon his heel.
All that the other races want, I see,
Is the right to liberty and be free;
This the selfish white man doesn't want to give;
He alone, he thinks, has the right to live.

(15)

There shall be a bloody mix-up everywhere;
Of the white man's plunder we are aware:
Men of colour the great cause understand,
Unite they must, to protect their own land.
No fool's stand on argument must we make;
Between Heaven and earth an oath we take:
"Our lands to deliver from foreign foes,
Caring not of trials and maudlin woes."

(16)

The privilege of men to protect home
Was established before the days of Rome.
Many gallant races fought and died,
Alien hordes in triumph thus defied.
Carthage did not crush Ancient Greece
For their believing in the Golden Fleece.
No other race shall kill the sturdy Blacks
If on their tribal gods we turn our backs.

(17)

From Marathon, Tours, Blenheim and the Marne
A braver courage in man has been born
Africans died at Thermopylae's Pass,

Standing firm for Persia—men of Brass.
The Black Archers of Ethiopia stood
At Marathon, proving their stern manhood;
Senegalese held their own at Verdun,
Even though their praises are not now sung.

(18)

In the Americas' modern warfare
The Blacks have ever borne their share;
With Cortez, Washington, too, and the rest,
We did for the others our truthful best;
At St. Domingo we struck a clear blow
To show which way the wind may one day go.
Toussaint L'Ouverture was our leader then,
At the time when we were only half-men.

(19)

Italians, Menelik put to chase,
Beating a retreat in uneven haste;
So down the line of history we come,
Black, courtly, courageous and handsome.
No fear have we to-day of any great man
From Napoleon back to Genghis Khan;
All we ask of men is "Give a square deal,"
Returning to others same right we feel.

(20)

With a past brilliant, noble and grand,
Black men march to the future hand in hand;
We have suffered long from the white man's greed,
Perforce he must change his unholy creed.
Stealing, bullying and lying to all
Will drag him to ignominious fall;
For men are wise—yes, no longer are fools,
To have grafters make of them still cheap tools.

(21)

Each race should be proud and stick to its own,
And the best of what they are should be shown;
This is no shallow song of hate to sing,
But over Blacks there should be no white king.
Every man on his own foothold should stand,
Claiming a nation and a Fatherland.
White, Yellow and Black should make their own laws,
And force no one-sided justice with flaws.

(22)

Man will bear so much of imposition,
Till he starts a righteous inquisition.
History teaches this as a true fact,
Upon this premise all men do act.
Sooner or later each people take their stand
To fight against the strong, oppressive hand;
This is God's plan, raising man to power,
As over sin and greed He makes him tower.

(23)

This trite lesson the white man has not learnt,
Waiting until he gets his fingers burnt.
Millen[n]iums ago, when white men slept,
The great torch of light Asia kept.
Africa at various periods shone
Above them all as the bright noonday sun;
Coming from the darkened cave and hut,
The white man opened the gate that was shut.

(24)

Gradually light bore down upon him,
This ancient savage who was once dim;
When he commenced to see and move around,

He found the book of knowledge on the ground;
Centuries of wonder and achievements
Were cast before him in God's compliments;
But, like the rest, he has now fallen flat,
And must in Lord's cycle yield for that.

(25)

We shall always be our brother's keeper,
Is the injunction of the Redeemer;
Love and tolerance we must ever show,
If in Grace Divine we would truly grow:
This is the way clear to God's great kingdom—
Not by the death-traps of Argonne or Somme,
When the terrible white man learns this much,
He will save even the African Dutch.

(26)

South Africa has a grave problem now
In reducing the Negro to the plow;
White men are to live in their lazy ease,
While the patience of the goodly natives tease;
They make new laws to have Africa white
Precipitating righteous and ready fight:
Around the world they speak of being so just,
Yet, in fact, no lone white man can you trust.

(27)

In Australia the same they have done,
And so, wherever man's confidence won:
This they call the religion of the Christ,
And upon their willing slave try to foist.
Only a part of the world may you fool,
And easily reduce to your foot-stool;
The other one-half is always awake,
And from it you cannot liberty take.

(28)

"And now valiant Black men of the west
Must ably rise to lead and save the rest":
This is the ringing call Africa sounds,
As throughout the Godly world it resounds;
Clansmen! black, educated, virile and true!
Let us prove too that we are loyal blue.
We must win in the blessed fight of love,
Trusting on the Maker of men above.

(29)

The Christian world is yet to be saved!
Man, since the risen Christ has not behaved!
Wanton, reckless, wicked, he still remains,
Causing grief, sorrow, tears and human pains!
Can we show the Godly light to anyone
Seeking for earnest truth while marching on?
If so, friend, let us tell you now and here,
For love, freedom, justice, let's all prepare!

(30)

God in His Glorious Might is coming,
Wonderful signs He is ever showing,
Unrest, earthquakes, hurricanes, floods and storms
Are but revelations of Heavenly Forms:
The proud white scientist thinks he is wise
But the Black man's God comes in true disguise,
God is sure in the rumbling earthquake,
When He is ready, the whole world will shake.

(31)

The Armageddon is gathering now;
The sign is on every oppressed man's brow:
The whites who think they are ever so smart

Do not know other men can play their part:
When the opportune time is almost here
Black, Yellow and Brown will be ev'rywhere,
In union of cause they'll stand together,
And storms of the bully boldly weather.

(32)

Their gases and shots, and their rays of death,
Shall only be child's play—a dream of Seth,
For out of the clear, sleeping minds of ages,
Wonders shall be written on history's pages:
Our buried arts and sciences then shall rise,
To show how for centuries we were wise:
Silent tongues we kept, by God's true command,
Until of us, action, He did demand.

(33)

Under the canopy of Nature's law
We shall unitedly and bravely draw,
On the plains of God's green Amphitheatre,
Swords, in rhythm with Divine Meter:
Jehovah's Day will have surely come,
With Angelic strains and Seraphic hum:
The Guide's of Heaven will direct the way,
Keeping us from wandering far astray.

(34)

Like around the high walls of Jericho,
March we, as Rio speeds through Mexico:
Trumpets loud will the Guiding Angels blow,
As scatter the enemy to-and-fro:
Heaven will have given us a battle cry:
"Oh Brave Soldiers you shall never die":
Rally to the command of Heaven's King,
As Cherubim to Him your tidings bring.

(35)

See the deadly clash of arms! Watch! They fall!
There is stillness!—It is the funeral pall!
A sad requiem now is to be sung,—
Not by Angels, but in their human tongue!
The cruel masters of yest'rday are done!
From the fields of battle they have run!
A brand new world of justice is to be,—
"You shall be a true brother unto me!"

(36)

This is a forecast of God's wrath:
White man, will you turn from the evil path?
There is still hope for you, among the good.
If you will seek the bigger-brotherhood:
Stop your tricks, frauds, lying and stealing,
And settle down to fair and square dealing;
If not, prepare yourself for gloomy hell,
As God announces the sorrowing knell.

(37)

Your lies, to us called diplomacy,
Are known by us, a brazen phantasy;
You imprison men for crimes not so great,
While on your silly wisdom you do prate.
The masses are soberly watching you;
They know that you are false and so untrue.
The labourers of your race you oppress,
As well as black and other men you distress.

(38)

If you were wise you'd read between the lines
Of feudal "isms" and others of old times.
Men have fought against ugly royal gods,

Burying them 'neath European sods.
Such to heartless masters the people do,
From Syracuse to bloody Waterloo;
Wonderful lessons for any sober man,
Who worships not idols or the god of Pan.

(39)

In the vicious order of things to-day,
The poor, suffering black man has no say:
The plot is set for one 'gainst the other,
With organization they mustn't bother.
"If one should show his head as a leader,
Whom we cannot use, the rest to pilfer,
We shall discredit him before his own,
And make of him a notorious clown."

(40)

"In Africa we have plans to watch him,
While the native Chiefs of their lands we trim;
The Blacks schooled in England are too smart,
On the I BETTER THAN YOU scheme we'll start,
And have them thinking away from the rest;
This philosophy for them is best—
Easier then we can rob the good lands
And make ourselves rich without soiled hands."

(41)

"We will so keep from them the 'NEGRO WORLD'
That no news they'll have of a flag unfurled;
Should they smuggle copies in, and we fail,
We will send the sly agents all to jail."
This is the white man's plan across the sea.
Isn't this wily and vicious as can be?
In other lands they have things arranged
Differently, yet they have never changed.

(42)

In America they have Coloured to tell
What they know of the rest, whose rights they sell;
The Blacks they do try to keep always down,
But in time they will reap what they have sown.
No Negro's good life is safe in the STATES
If he tries to be honest with his mates;
In politics he must sell at the polls,
To suit the white man in his many roles.

(43)

The West Indian whites are tricky, too;
They have schemes curved like the horse's shoe:
There is only one opening for the black—
Three other sides are close up to his back;
Hence he never gets a chance to look in
Whilst staring at the world of mortal sin.
Yes, this is the game they play everywhere,
Leaving the Negro to gloom and despair.

(44)

And now, white man, can we reason with you,
For each race in the world to give its due?
Africa for Africans is most right;
Asia for Asiatics is light;
To Europe for the Europeans,
America for the Americans:
This is the doctrine of the goodly Klan.
Now fighting for the alien ban.

(45)

Blacks do not hate you because you are white;
We believe in giving to all men right;
Some we do keep for ourselves to protect,

Knowing it as a virtue to select.
We are willing to be friends of mankind,
Pulling all together with none behind,
Growing in sane goodness and fellowship,
Choosing but the Almighty to worship.

(46)

Let justice prevail, at home and abroad;
Cease over the weak your burdens to lord;
You're but mortal man, like the rest of us—
Of this happy truth we need make no fuss.
All Nature's kindly gifts are justly ours—
Suns, oceans, trees, to pretty flowers—
So we need not doubt the marvellous fact
That God has given to each man his tract.

(47)

The common thief now steals a crust of bread,
The law comes down upon his hungry head;
The haughty land robber steals continents,
With men, oil, gold, rubber and all contents.
The first you say is a hopeless convic',
While the latter escapes the law by trick;
That grave, one-sided justice will not do—
The poor call for consideration, too.

(48)

The rich white man starts the unholy war,
Then from the line of action he keeps far;
He pushes to the front sons of the poor,
There to do battle, die, suffer galore.
As the guns rage, liberty loans they raise,
And in glorious tones sing freedom's praise.
This is the method to gain them more wealth,
Then, after vict'ry they practice great stealth.

(49)

Those who make wars should first go to the front,
And of gas, shot and shell bear there the brunt;
In first lines of action they are all due,
If to their country and people they are true:
When this is demanded in right of all,
There will be no more deadly cannon ball:
The downtrodden poor whites and blacks should join
And prevent rich whites our rights to purloin.

(50)

Weeping mothers, tricked in patriotism,
Send their sons to fight for liberalism:
Into most far off lands they go with pride,
Thinking right and God be on their side:
When they get into the bloody trenches,
They find of lies they had awful drenches:
The people they were all supposed to kill,
Like themselves, had gotten of lies their fill.

(51)

In the private club and drawing room,
White schemes are hatched for the nation's doom:
Speculators, grafters, bankers—all,
With politicians join to hasten the fall,
By stealing rights from other citizens,
As if they weren't fit or true denizens:
How awful is this daring story
That we tell to men young and hoary.

(52)

Crooked lawyers, friends and politicians,
Corrupt the morals of the good nations:
Between them and others, fly plots they make,

Innocent citizens' money to take:
From banks they find out your real account,
Then have you indicted on legal count:
Large fees they charge, to have you surely broke,
Then, to prison you go—what a sad joke!

(53)

The white man controls cable and wireless,
Connections by ships with force and duress:
He keeps black races of the world apart,
So to his schemes they may not be smart:
"There shall be no Black Star Line Ships," he says,
"For that will interfere with our crooked ways:
"T'll disrupt their business and all their plans,
"So they might not connect with foreign lands."

(54)

Black women are raped by the lordly white,
In colonies, the shame ne'er reaching light:
In other countries abuses are given,
Shocking to morality and God's Heaven.
Hybrids and mongrels are the open result,
Which the whites give us as shameful insult:
How can they justify this? None can tell;
Yet, crimes of the blacks are rung with a bell.

(55)

White men newspapers subsidize and own,
For to keep them on their racial throne:
Editors are slaves to fool the public,
Reporters tell the lie and pull the trick;
The papers support only what they want,
Yet truth, fair play, and justice, daily flaunt:
They make criminals out of honest men,
And force judges to send them to the Pen.

(56)

Capitalists buy up all bank space
To advertise and hold the leading place
For to influence public opinion
And o'er Chief-editors show dominion.
The average man is not wise to the scheme,
He, the reformer, must now redeem;
This isn't a smooth or very easy job,
For, you, of your honour and name, they'll rob.

(57)

The bankers employ men to shoot and kill,
When we interfere with their august will;
They take the savings of deaf, dumb and poor,
Gamble with it here and on foreign shore:
In oil, gold, rum, rubber they speculate,
Then bring their foreign troubles upon the State:
Friends in Government they control at will;
War they make, for others, our sons to kill.

(58)

The many foundations of researches,
And the foreign missions and their churches,
Are organized to catch the mild converts
Who don't understand the way of perverts.
Our wealth when discovered by researchers,
In lands of Native occupiers
Is surveyed and marked to the river's rim
Till they dislodge a Premprey or Abd-El-Krim.

(59)

It is not freedom from prison we seek;
It is freedom from the big Christian freak:
All life is now a soulless prison cell,

A wild suspense between heaven and hell:
Selfish, wicked whites have made it so;
To the Author and Finisher we'll go,
Carrying our sad cares and many wrongs
To Him in prayers and holy songs.

(60)

This is the game that is played all around,
Which is, sure, one day, to each race rebound:
The world is gone mad with the money craze,
Leaving the poor man in a gloomy haze:
There must be world reorganization,
To save the masses from exploitation:
The cry is for greater democracy,
A salvation from man's hypocrisy.

(61)

Out in this heartless, bitter oasis,
There's now very little of human bliss;
The cold capitalists and money sharks
Have made life unsafe, like ocean barks
The once dear, lovely Garden of Eden
Has become the sphere of men uneven;
The good God created but an equal pair,
Now man has robbed others of their share.

(62)

Shall there be freedom of liberal thought?
No; the white man has all agencies bought—
Press, pulpit, law and every other thing—
Hence o'er public opinion he reigns king.
This is indisputable, glaring fact;
You may find it out with a little tact.
College tutors and presidents are paid,
So that in universities schemes are laid.

(63)

Cleopatra, Empress Josephine,
Were black mongrels like of the Philippine:—
Mixtures from black and other races they,—
Yet, "true," the white man's history will not say
To those who seek the light of pure knowledge
In the inquiring world, school or college.
Napoleon fell for a Negro woman;
So did the Caesars, and the Great Roman.

(64)

Anthony lost his imperial crown
To escape Cleo's fascinating frown.
This truth the New Negro knows very well,
And to his brothers in darkness he'll tell.
No one can imprison the brain of man—
That was never intended in God's plan;
You may persecute, starve, even debase—
That will not kill truth nor virtue efface.

(65)

The white man now enjoys his "Vanity Fair";
He thinks of self and not of others care—
Fratricidal course, that to hell doth lead—
This is poison upon which the gentry feed.
Blacks should study physics, chemistry, more,
While the "gold god" all such sinners adore;
This is no idle prattle talk to you;
It has made the banners red, white and blue.

(66)

Out of the clear of God's Eternity
Shall rise a kingdom of Black Fraternity;
There shall be conquests o'er militant forces;

For as man proposes, God disposes.
Signs of retribution are on every hand:
Be ready, black men, like Gideon's band.
They may scoff and mock at you to-day,
But get you ready for the awful fray.

(67)

In the fair movement of God's Abounding Grace
There is a promised hope for the Negro race;
In the sublimest truth of prophecy,
God is to raise them to earthly majesty.
Princes shall come out of Egypt so grand,
The noble black man's home and Motherland,
The Psalmist spoke in holy language clear,
As Almighty God's Triune will declare.

(68)

In their conceit they see not their ruin;
You soldiers of trust, be up and doing!
Remember Belshazzar's last joyous feast,
And Daniel's vision of the Great Beast!
"Weighed in the balances and found wanting"
Is the Tekel to which they are pointing.
This interpretation of the Prophet
Black men shall never in their dreams forget.

(69)

The resplendent rays of the morning sun
Shall kiss the Negro's life again begun;
The music of God's rhythmic natural law
Shall stir Afric's soul without Divine flaw.
The perfume from Nature's rosy hilltops
Shall fall on us, spiritual dewdrops.
Celestial beings shall know us well,
For, by goodness, in death, with them we'll dwell.

(70)

AND HOW SAD A FINIS!

With battleship, artillery and gun
White men have put all God's creatures to run;
Heaven and earth they have often defied,
Taking no heed of the rebels that died.
God can't be mocked in this daring way,
So the evil ones shall sure have their day.
"You may rob, you may kill, for great fame,"
So says the white man, FOR THIS IS HIS GAME.

SOURCE NOTES

First printed in the *Negro World* under the title "The White Man's Game: His Vanity Fair (With Apology to All Honest Friends)," 11 June and 18 June 1927. Reprinted as a UNIA pamphlet, first edition copyrighted by Amy Jacques Garvey, 1927. Transcription is of the third, revised, edition of the UNIA pamphlet, with foreword by Marcus Garvey, published by the Black Man Publishing Co., London, 1935. Minor variations from the original 1927 text occur in the 1935 edition. "Hail! United States of Africa!" and "Africa for the Africans," included in the 1935 pamphlet, have been omitted.

DIALOGUES

From the *Black Man*

A DIALOGUE:
WHAT'S THE DIFFERENCE?

By Marcus Garvey

CHAPTER I

SON: Say, father, why is it I am born black and placed at such a disadvantage among other boys in the world?

FATHER: My son, to be born black is no disgrace nor misfortune. It is an honour. Nature never intended humanity to be of one colour or complexion, and so there are different races or types of people in the world. There are standard types and the Negro is one of them. In the history of the world the Negro has had a glorious career. In the centuries past he was greater than any other race, but, unfortunately, to-day he occupies a position not as favourable as that of his fathers.

SON: But father, everywhere I go I hear and see people speaking and acting disrespectfully toward the Negro.

FATHER: That is true, my son, but that doesn't mean that to be black is to be really inferior. It is only because the economic condition of the blackman is so low to-day why other peoples do not entirely respect him. It is, therefore, due to his own neglect, and not to any cause of natural inferiority.

SON: Does that mean, father, that if the Negro wants he can be as honourable, progressive and dignified as any other race?

FATHER: Yes, my son, that's it. In this world we are what we make ourselves. The Negro is just an individual like anyone else, and, individually, he can make himself what he wants to be. In the same respect the individuals of a race becoming a congregation of a whole can make themselves what they want to be.

SON: Do you mean by that, father, that if I want to be a great man I can be?

FATHER: That's just it, my son. If in your mind you develop the thought and the ambition to be a useful and great man rather than a pervert, imbecile or hopeless dependent, you can be so, and in the same way you can do that as an individual; if the race becomes inspired it can climb to heights of greatness and nobility.

SON: So, father, the only difference between me and the white boy is mind and ambition.

FATHER: That is right, my son. The white boy who has the ambition through dint of perseverence, energy and labour may climb from his lowly surroundings to become President of the United States or a Prime Minister in England. The biographies and auto-biographies of individuals have shown that some of the humblest boys in the world became the world's greatest men.

SON: I am glad of this explanation, father, because at school and wherever I went I was made to feel that the Negro was never anybody and could never be anybody.

FATHER: I can well understand that, my boy. That is the kind of wicked influence that has been used against the race to deny it of its character for higher development. But we must never fall entirely to our environment. We must create the environments we want, and I do hope you will endeavour all during your lifetime to create the environments you would like to live in.

SON: But what about the millions of other Negroes, father, who do not know this?

FATHER: The lack of this knowledge, my boy, is the great disadvantage of the race as a whole. Most of our people born to modern environments in our civilization seem to think that they were destined to be an inferior people. Their school and education was based upon this assumption.

SON: But why so, father?

FATHER: Because under our present civilization the Negro was forced to accept his educational code from other peoples who were not disposed to give him credit for anything. They wrote books quite disparaging to the Negro. Their literature was intended to bolster up their particular race and civilization and down that of the blackman. Historians who have written have all twisted the history of the world so as to show the inferiority of the blacks. The blackman has not written recently his own history, neither has he yet engaged himself in writing his own literature; and so, for the last hundred years, he has been learning out of the white man's book, thereby developing the white man's psychology.

SON: I can see, father, that is why at school I wanted to be a white man, because the books I read all told me about the great deeds of white men. I wanted to be like Abraham Lincoln and George Washington and Napoleon, but I thought I could only be that by being white.

FATHER: That is a mistake, my boy. Greatness has no colour. You must never want to be a white man. You must be satisfied to be what nature made you and to excel in that respect, so that the credit for your achievements will go to your race.

SON: What a wonderful thing it would be, father, if all the Negroes thought this way.

FATHER: That is it, my boy. There is a new effort to inspire all the blacks to think this way, so that in another hundred years our children will not want to be white but will be proud to be black. Instead of wanting to be George Washington and Abraham Lincoln or a Disraeli or Lord Chatham you should try to be a Toussant L'Overture [Toussaint L'Ouverture], a Hannibal, a Booker T. Washington.

SON: These were all black men father?

FATHER: Yes, my son. Hannibal, the Carthagenian, was a blackman, but the white history will tell you he was white.   Toussant L'Overture, the slave of Santa Domingo, was also a blackman, and if it were not for men like Rendell [Wendell] Phillips probably the records would show in another hundred years that he was white. Even up to now some people are trying to make out that Booker T. Washington was more white than he was Negro.   That shows how certain white historians and others are disposed to rob the Negro of any glory that he may have.

SON: So all the books we read, father, are not true?

FATHER: That's right, my boy.   Most of the books that are written are for propaganda purposes.   Each nation has its own propaganda method.   The Anglo-Saxon race will boost the Anglo-Saxon, the Teutonic race will boost the Teutons, the Latin races will boost the Latins.   None is impartial enough to give real credit to other peoples for what they have done and are accomplishing, so that the books that the Negro has been reading written by the Anglo-Saxon, Teutonic and Latin races were not intended for him at all, except to give him the idea that in the history of the world he was never anybody.   The time will come when our historians and writers will reveal the truths of history.   At that time we will learn that our race was once the greatest race in the world.   That, when we had a glorious civilization on the banks of the Nile in Africa the white races were living in caves and among the trees and bushes of Europe.   They were savages and barbarians when our fathers held up the torch of civilization in Africa.

SON: So there is no need, father, for me to hold down my head any longer?

FATHER: No, my son, you should hold up your head and be as proud as any other boy in the world.   The English boy wants to be Prime Minister of England, the French boy wants to be President of France, the American white boy wants to be President of the United States.   You, my boy, and all other black boys should have a similar ambition for a country of your own.

SON: Is that the reason why, father, the Japanese refuse to accept the leadership of Western civilization?

FATHER: That is so. The Japanese are a proud people. They are of the yellow race and they feel that they should develop a civilization of their own, and so they have their own Empire, their own Prime Minister, their own Ambassadors, their own Army and Navy. They have a Japanese Empire.

SON: But can the Negro have an Empire, father?

FATHER: Yes, my son. It is difficult, to-day, for him to have a political Empire, because the world is almost taken up by the white and yellow races. In fact, the white races have robbed the homelands of the blacks, particularly in Africa. The English, the French, the Italians, the Spaniards, the Belgians, and the Portuguese have, within one hundred years, gone from Europe into Africa, and have robbed every square inch of land from our fathers; so it is very difficult under existing conditions, where these countries use brute force to conduct their Government, for the Negro to politically become an imperial force. But, culturally, the Negro can become imperial. That is to say he can have an imperial ideal and culture and fellowship of love, which may ultimately end in political imperialism.

SON: But how can this be possible, father?

FATHER: You see, my boy, the world undergoes changes time over and again. Just as the Negro ruled once and lost his power, so some of the races that are ruling now will in the cycle of things lose their power. Nature intended this. When this happens unfortunate and oppressed peoples rise into power, so that there is great hope for the Negro to be restored to his true political position, because sooner or later some of these dominant nations and races will fall.

SON: So there is great hope for us politically, father?

FATHER: Sure, my son. But whatever hope we may have must be backed up by our own effort and energy. We must never go to sleep. We must always keep before us steadfastly the object we desire. Like the Jews, we should never lose our purpose. The Jews have been very much outraged by other nations and races of the world, but they ever clung to their religious ideals. The Negro must have a religion that is binding. He must have some ideal that is unchangeable and outstanding and when this ideal is universalized, being meritorious and worthy, he will in time accomplish the end.

SON: I am glad father that there is a real hope. I shall tell all the other boys about this and shall make myself a missionary to preach the eternal hope of racial salvation.

FATHER: That's right, my boy, be ever vigilant in the maintenance of the honour, dignity and integrity of your race.

CHAPTER II

SON: I intend to ask your advice, father, on many things affecting my life, for I have come to realize that one profits very much by experience. You have had more experience than I, therefore I ought to profit by what you honestly tell and teach me.

FATHER: I see you are becoming very philosophic, my boy.

SON: Yes, father, I also think that it is a good thing to start life with the right philosophy, and if I can get an honest introduction into the right philosophy my life will not be lived in vain.

FATHER: I am indeed glad to hear of your decision. I shall do everything to properly advise you, so that your mistakes in life, if any, may be reduced to a minimum, for it is the things we know not of that hurt us most; for the things we know can be properly measured, negotiated or handled from our best judgment, but when we are entirely ignorant we are at the mercy of that which is.

SON: I quite appreciate that, and that is why I am so anxious to gather information from you to help me in my journey through life. I am really desirous of knowing more about the contact between black and white; I want to find out if there is any positive and irremovable handicap that would prevent the blackman rising to the same eminence as the white man.

FATHER: In my first conversation with you I hinted that there was absolutely no difference but that which is mental. Mind is the thing that rules and the black man to-day falls below the level of a white man only because of the poverty of his mind. He has somewhat subjugated his mind. He has surrendered it to his environments—environments that have been created for him through an exterior civilization. The white man's civilization is an improvement upon other civilizations, and the Negro has been brought within its pale or under its influence and it has succeeded in humiliating and denying him all initiative, but when the Negro recovers himself and starts to think independently and particularly in the direction of building for himself, even to the extent of creating his own improved civilization, he will find that there is absolutely no difference between him and the white man.

SON: Must I take it that the Negro will ultimately emancipate himself through the development of his own mind?

FATHER: Yes, all emancipation is from within. That is to say, real emancipation. As a man thinketh so is he. That means that the man must think for himself and make himself. A race is only a congregation of individual men, so as a race thinketh so will it be.

SON: You mean, therefore, that when the Negro race as a whole starts to think in the higher terms of life there will be a real racial emancipation?

FATHER: That is so. Unfortunately at the present time the Negro's mind is confused. In America, for instance, the American Negro wants one thing, in the West Indies the Negroes there want another thing, and in Africa the natives are quite different even in their separate and distinct tribal outlooks. There is no unity of purpose, there is no common objective with Negroes as with the white man. As for instance, the white man has a dominant idea of control. He feels he must govern, that no one must be above him. Such a feeling inspires him to its accomplishment and so he is a ruler everywhere you find him. The Negro is not yet as bold as that to desire absolute control, he is satisfied to be subservient and so it becomes very easy to reduce him to the various conditions in which he finds himself to-day in America, the West Indies and Africa. The white man is not afraid of responsibility, he is not afraid of any risk, he is adventurous, he is bold, he has daring in his blood. It is this kind of character that gave us discoverers like Columbus, Raleigh, Drake and great conquerors like Napoleon, Nelson, Wolfe, and warriors like Charlemagne, Attila and the Green [Greek] and Roman heroes.

SON: You believe then, father, that the Negro has been too self-satisfied.

FATHER: It is more than that, my son. He has been too lazy and careless with his own life. It is the duty of man not only to protect his own life but to protect the existence of his tribe, his clan or his race, and when it is considered that mankind has always been in universal warfare against each other, leading to tribe against tribe, clan against clan, race against race, nation against nation, it seems suicidal that any tribe, clan, race or nation should become indifferent to the activities of others to the extent of not preparing itself against invasion, attack or subjugation. To do this you must know, you must understand, you must have good information of what others are doing, therefore you must be adventurous, you must go out to seek your information, you must take chances. The Negro has not been doing this and so those who have indulged in this kind of adventure have surpassed him and have ultimately enslaved him.

SON: So there is a great deal of work to be done in recovering ourselves.

FATHER: My boy, we have not even started yet. To-day we are hearing much of unemployment among the white races, of the lack of opportunities in industry and so forth. That is true and that can be explained through the fact that the white man has been a builder for the last one thousand years at least; he has been building his kingdoms, his nations and his empires; he has been building his towns and his municipalities, he has been building his institutions and adding to the growth of his civilization. He has almost reached the apex. There is hardly much more for him to do in the realm of industry. He is now occupied chiefly in the discovery of new things, elemental and scientific. You can very well understand, therefore, that there isn't very much for him to do, but the Negro who hasn't built any nation, kingdom or empire, nor laid the foundation of his industrial and commercial marts is in a different position. He has still to start where the white man started hundreds of years ago, so that if the Negro were conscious of himself he would not accept the conditions imposed upon him of being unemployed. He would find much to do building for himself.

SON: But where could he build, father?

FATHER: He could build just where he is. There are more than two hundred million Negroes in Africa with a continent that is large and resourceful. Let him build there, let him build his own nations, let him build his own civilization, let him show the world a duplicate in Africa of what exist[s] in Europe. The Negro in America has the opportunity of even building where he is if he will think seriously and lay down a proper programme. He forms a part of the American nation. He is fifteen million strong, yet he has a very limited political voice. He is lynched and burnt in that country. He is socially ostracized. Of the 48 States of the American Union he doesn't boss or control one. If the American people refuse to absorb the Negro on equal terms the Negroes could colonize themselves in America and particularly in certain sections of the South, and build themselves such a political, industrial and general economic power that they would be considered a real factor in American national life. Fifteen million Negroes in a population of one hundred and twenty million people in the United States ought to be able to exercise a great influence upon American public opinion. In the West Indies the Negroes form the majority population in each of the islands, yet these Negroes have very little influence and power. If they were thinking right they could build up where they are a powerful political influence that would probably see them one day a free and independent people.

SON: But would the white man tolerate such ideas and progress among Negroes, father?

FATHER: My son, you must understand this. It is not what the other fellow will give you—you must take; it is what you want that you must have. The white man has no more right of interfering with the black man's progress than the black man has to interfere with the white man. Nature or God made black and white free human agents and as such they have a right to the possession of all that nature gives, and when one man interferes with the rights of another and that other submits, he is a coward, he is a fool, and God, Nature and all men must be against him.

SON: The theory then, father, is that the Negro should be self-reliant, self-expressive and self-willed.

FATHER: Yes, this is not only a theory but it must be a practical fact. The man who is dependent upon someone else to do something for him never gets anything done, and any black man who is foolish enough to think that somebody else is going to do something for him, thorough and complete, to his benefit, is but a fool.

SON: How wonderful it must be, father, to have the ambition you have suggested.

FATHER: Ambition, reasonable ambition, is the making of the man and the making of the race. The individual or the nation that has no ambition has no true destiny. It is a positive fact that the majority of Negroes to-day lack ambition.

SON: But it must be aroused in them, father.

FATHER: Yes, but it is a difficult task. The average Negro has submitted for so long in slavery and in general serfdom to the dictates of the white man that he has almost lost hope and confidence in himself. That is why in America it is hard to organize the Negro and still more so in the West Indies where they have no racial consciousness at all. The American and West Indian Negroes were slaves for hundreds of years, and the subjugation of that period seems to have taken out of them all the old African courage and nobility; but scattered here and there among them you will find a few noble and courageous men and women who are doing everything possible to arouse these lethargic and almost unconscious people to a full realization of themselves.

SON: Then there is great hope in that respect, father?

FATHER: Yes, my son. Nature has peculiar ways of speaking to her children in periods. The cycle of things has brought about certain changes, and these changes must affect the Negro as everybody else; probably the white man more than anybody else is doing his best to organize the Negro to a consciousness of himself. The burnings and lynchings in the Southern sections of the United States, the economic oppression in the West Indies, and the inhuman and brutal treatment of the natives of South Africa and in other parts of the continent, and their general exploitation tend to bring out among them a consciousness that probably would not have been evident under any other circumstance. This may be God's way of bringing the Negro out of his bondage.

CHAPTER III

SON: I have been having a serious talk with myself, father, concerning the things we have been discussing, the object being to consciously bring out of myself that which I imagine to be resident in me.

FATHER: That's wonderful. So I see that you have been

developing the personal psychology which enables a man to analyse himself. That is the first duty of every creature to consciously submit himself to a sever[e] test, the object being to find out of what stuff he is made.

SON: That's just it, father. I have been trying to find out if my human mettle is of any worth, and I think I have come to the conclusion that I am possessed with all the powers which will enable me when properly directed to be one of the world's most successful men.

FATHER: Now that is the way to talk. You must fully realize that man on earth is the only absolute power. By the combination of his mind, soul and body he ranks higher than any other animal or creature. The world was given to him as his province of control, and when he becomes conscious of his sovereignty everything material in life is supposed to bend to his will. This power and authority on earth is not confined to any particular man or race of men. Whether a man be white, black or yellow, nature gives him the absolute right of material sovereignty; but, unfortunately, some become conscious of the sovereignty and others fail to recognize or appreciate it, hence they become the subjects of the sovereigns.

SON: Well, I shall surely be a sovereign, father, because I have found out in the questioning of myself that I have the soul, the desire, the ambition to be as good and as able as any man who ever lived. That means that I shall not submit tamely to any conquest over me by another man. If he possesses advantages that I do not have, any attainments, I shall surely make it my duty to add those to my accomplishments so that he may not long have the advantage over me in any particular.

FATHER: That's wonderful. Never allow anyone to get far ahead of you on any natural or human subject of which man should possess a knowledge, because the very fact that he knows more than you in that particular, gives him the opportunity and possibility of reducing you to his will. All knowledge is free to the investigating, probing and analytic mind. As other men have sought knowledge for the value and use of it, seek yours from every avenue of life. When you possess the universal knowledge that is possible to man in the gift of nature, then you will be one of nature's masters. You will, indeed, be a sovereign of your will.

SON: This is hope most cherishing. It makes me feel buoyant and happy because I fully realize there is a world before me to conquer. I only hope there are millions of other Negro boys who will think like me and act like me in the determination to reach the end.

FATHER: That should be our hope, my boy. It is only when the youth of our race is properly trained and inspired that they will realize their true purpose in life. Unfortunately, the home-training of the Negro is as bad as his public training. In fact, he has very little of home-training. Unlike the Jew, there is no family Creed into which the Negro youth is inducted. There is no guiding policy or principle in which he is trained; if nowhere else, even in the home, hence the youth goes out into manhood without an objective or a set purpose. That is why nearly every Negro thinks differently on racial matters. The Jew, as you will observe, thinks collectively on racial matters. He is held together by the philosophy of his religion. The Negro has no such philosophy.

SON: I hope the time is not far distant, father, when there will be such a domestic philosophy, so that every Negro throughout the world will be thinking of the same thing, and doing the same thing, these things being considered by experience as an adopted philosophy, the best in his career toward racial destiny.

FATHER: Some of us who are conscious of our responsibility are endeavouring to create such a philosophy, but it is very difficult to have it universally adopted. I suppose it will take time. Just as you are becoming conscious of your responsibility and duty so other boys are also doing. Sooner or later young men and women of your thought will find something in common. You may, therefore, become either an association or a college of the new thought. The very fact of your coming together may help you to spread the idea until it reaches beyond your immediate circle. That is the way philosophy and new thoughts grow.

SON: As far as I am concerned, I shall always make it my duty in contact with others of my race to inspire them towards racial hopefulness.

FATHER: Yes, that's the proper thing to do. You have missionary work to do, and every Negro who is conscious of himself must do similarly. There is need for this missionary work all through the United States, all through the West Indies and certain parts of South and Central America and particularly the Continent of Africa. Just as the Christians and the Mohammedans are proselyting and spreading the faith here, there and everywhere, so the conscious Negro patriot must scatter his missionary work to the widest fields. He must be willing to make sacrifices, even as the Fathers of the Church have done. The Church has had its Martyrs, its Saints and its good men. Our race must expect to undergo the same experience, because it is a work to save not only the human body, but the soul as well.

SON: Among the Negroes of the world, which section of them do you think is more conscious of the responsibility and duty to be assumed?

FATHER: The American Negroes are the best organized and the most conscious of all the Negroes in the world. They have become so because of their peculiar position. They live in very close contact with organized racial prejudice, and this very prejudice forces them to a rare [race?] consciousness that they would not have had otherwise. Through this consciousness they have been organizing, founding and building and running Institutions of their own, so much so that they stand out to-day, the American Negroes, as the most enlightened of all Negroes. They have attained much in scholarship and general education. In commerce and industry they are better informed. The West Indian Negroes are very much enlightened, not in the majority but among the few. But, unfortunately, the West Indian Negroes of enlightenment do not call themselves Negroes, they call themselves "coloured people," as to suggest that to be coloured—the result of the mixing of black and white blood—constitutes a superiority above black, and so there is absolutely no cohesion racially between the black and coloured people of the West Indies. This tends to weaken them in that in the Islands there is much more prejudice between the black and the coloured people than between the white and the Negro people. All this is due to ignorance, so that great work has to be done among the West Indian Negroes before they will have a proper outlook from the racial point of view. In Africa, tribal differences have somewhat interfered with racial solidarity. The relationship between white and black in Africa with the exception of South Africa, is quite different to that which exists between black and white in the United States and black and coloured in the West Indies. There are not enough white people in the real native settlements to as urgently influence native civilization, as is the case in the Western World, so that the growth in this civilization among Africans is slow, hence their progress cannot be as pronounced as that of the American Negroes, but there has been a gradual increase among the different sections and tribes in the search after the higher education and culture that would place the African in a higher plane of civilization. The universities of England, Germany, France and America have been receiving students from Africa. Young men and women have been studying the professions and have taken academic degrees with the object of going back to their country to lead and inspire others. This will ultimately lead to a greater spread of civilization all over the Continent, so that in time the African Negro because of his wonderful opportunities in his own country will become the natural leader of the race.

SON: Do you mean to say, father, that ultimately the

race problem will be solved in Africa and not in the Western World?

FATHER: That's so, my son. Africa is the hope of the black man. It is there and there only that his mark will be finally made. You see, in Africa he is on his own ground. In the Western world he is only a stranger. He can only fight to a certain point because legally and morally it is suggested that he is without rights or proper claim. In Africa that is just the reverse. He has legal and moral claim, so that when be becomes fully conscious of his rights and his responsibilities, he will stand on those rights or claims and establish himself as a man. It is advisable therefore that the Negroes of the West should link their future or destiny with the Negroes of Africa, because it is only by the strengthening of the racial tie that the work of redemption and accomplishments will be made easy.

SON: But are the Western Negroes conscious of this fraternal responsibility?

FATHER: Not completely, my boy. Much has to be done to destroy a prejudice that has long existed in the Western World, even among Negroes—that of despising the African and looking upon him as somebody different. This was made possible by the introduction of viscious and wicked literature—a literature that has always held up the African as a cannibal and a savage. Contact with the African has proved this to be a lie, but the enlightenment is of slow growth. The Organization known as the Universal Negro Improvement Association has done much to destroy this lie, so that the Negroes of the Western World are much more disposed toward fellowship with the Africans to-day than they were 20 or 15 years ago.

CHAPTER IV

SON: I have been very much worried, father, over Africa's past and present, in that I know so very little of it; yet I am considered by blood an African.

FATHER: Africa's history, my boy, is really not written, and so you may know very little of the past by the reading of present-day books.

SON: I have seen some books, father, about Africa, but they really do not contain anything much complimentary as far as our race is concerned.

FATHER: That is true, my son, and that is why I said that you can gather very little about the truths of Africa from present-day books, because the majority of these books are written by white authors who write with the colouring of prejudice so as to hide the truth about Africa and advance the superiority of European civilization. You cannot, therefore, get the true facts of Africa from the white man's point of view. Historically he is prejudiced and dishonest. He generally glorifies himself at the expense of other peoples. As a fact, the white man is the last to inherit a civilization, and the civilization that he boasts of to-day is really a heritage from Africa, where the first civilization was projected by man. It is this civilization that they desire to hide and for which you and other Negroes must search if you are to know much about your country. Scattered here and there among the pages of white history and literature you may find an accidental admission of Africa's past greatness, but not sufficient to be completely convincing. If you were to go to Homer's "Iliad" you will find that [t]he Greek Poet suggested that at one time in the history of the Greeks their only superiors were to be found among the gods of Ethiopia, the land of the blacks. At that time the superior gods were supposed to have resided in Africa. More recent philosophers, poets and historians have kept shy of anything showing meritorious African origin. In fact they have tried to brutalise Africa. This was purposely done so as to encourage the idea of the inferiority of the black race and the superiority of the white.

SON: Is this what is called propaganda, father?

FATHER: Yes, my son, this is propaganda, and our present

civilization is flooded with it. Every book, magazine or newspaper you take up has propaganda in it, aiming at the glorification of one set of people, and the enthronement of all their ideas. It is this propaganda that has gotten into the system of the Negro that has made him disown his own country—Africa, but even though Negroes may disown Africa that doesn't interfere with the fact that Africa was once the greatest country in the world. It housed the first great civilization. It gave to the world the first thinkers, scholars, statesmen, soldiers and teachers. There is satisfaction to those of us who know, that whilst Europe was inhabited by barbarism and savages, Africa stood out as the cultural light of the world.

SON: Were there centres in Africa, father, where this civilization was evident?

FATHER: Yes, my son, Timbuctu, Benin, Alexandria and several other ancient cities were to be found on the fertile banks of the Nile and other great rivers of Africa. In Egypt our civilization reached a high level, and from that civilization Asia borrowed much that it ultimately bequeathed along with us to Europe. Greece was the first European borrower, and it is through Greece that Europe got its civilization which has marched on to the 20th century. White historians will tell you that Egypt was not a black kingdom. That is as true as if 200 years hence someone were to tell your Great-Great-Great-Grandchildren that I was not a Negro. The Egyptians were Negroes. They afterwards became a mixed population, just as how America to-day is a mixed population, but originally white from the history of settlement. Coloured Egyptians were only the offsprings of miscegenation. The white historians tried to identify these people as the original Egyptians, which is not true. The original Egyptians and the leading peoples of Africa were all black, and it is they who impressed their civilization upon Asia, carrying it into India and China, which civilization subsequently took its course through

Asia Minor into Greece and then into Continental Europe. These are the facts, with the white man's colouring to the contrary. We do not expect the white man to write a true history of the Negro, and so we need not worry about what he says. If we read them we must do so with the opposite prejudice with which he writes them, so that we will not be influenced at all by his opinion.

SON: It means, then, father, that we will have to do a lot of research work to uncover for ourselves the true history of the past.

FATHER: That is so, my son. Never trust to others for the facts that are to guide you. Never let them write your history.

SON: It is a pity, father, that we haven't institutions such as the white people have to finance our research work.

FATHER: That is true, my boy. We have not yet reached that consciousness or sense of responsibility as to cause us to feel that it is our duty to do such things.

SON: But we must hasten that time, father, because much is to be done. We have to do our own research work or investigations. We have to go through the same difficulties as others.

FATHER: Yes, my boy. Not many years ago the white people of England financed Lord Carnarvon to go to Luxor, in Egypt, to do research and archaeological work in discovering the ancient tombs of the Pharoahs. Hundreds of thousands of pounds were spent and he ultimately dug up the body of Tutankumen. That is only one of a series of research and archaeological expeditions running into millions of pounds. A great noise was made over the discovery of the tomb of Tutankumen. The evidence showed that he was a black man, but the white scientists, to suit their own purposes, claimed to the contrary. Tutankumen was only one of the Pharoahs of the Negro race who ruled over Egypt.

SON: Do you think, father, that the Negro will ever realise the seriousness of his position?

FATHER: I think so, but much work has to be done to educate him. You see, he has already been badly educated. His ideas are all foreign to him. His heroes are not his own. He sees life through the eyes of others. To have him change you have to do some hard scolding and then re-cast his mentality. To some it will be difficult, because they are so steeped in the old order of things that nothing can move them, but the younger generation can be saved, so there is hope.

SON: I am glad there is hope, father, because it would seem suicidal that a people as physically strong as the Negro should continue living without a real purpose or object and having themselves thwarted at every turn by those who are calculating in their desire to down them.

FATHER: I cannot promise you that anything immediate will result from the desire to educate the race. It is going to be a long-drawn-out affair, because stumbling blocks will be placed in the way, not only by the Negro himself, but by those who would like to control the Negro's mind. They have many suppressive ways of preventing the new education of the Negro. You see the old school books that made the Negro hideous as an African, that revealed him as a cannibal, and the old literature that has scattered and propagated the suggestion of his inferiority cannot be easily destroyed. Those books, magazines and journals are still in the hands of the people, therefore it takes a long time and excessive counter-propaganda to undo all this evil work. Some have even been vicious enough to use the Bible as a means of discouraging the Negro in his belief of human equality. He has been referred to as a hewer of wood and drawer of water, and Bishops have sanctified this in the Name of the Lord, so you may realise how entrenched is the prejudice towards the Negro and how difficult it must be, therefore, to extricate him.

CHAPTER V

SON: Indeed a calamity has come upon the race, but our

character must show itself and I am one of the youth who will pledge to do everything and anything to retrieve the lost position of our African forebears.

FATHER: I am glad to hear you talk like that, my boy, about Africa. Again I repeat, it is the hope of the race. It is only the foolish Negro who doesn't think highly of the Motherland. Those Negroes who think that they are going to be absorbed in the white or any other race and find a place of equality, will sooner or later find out their tremendous mistake. All honest and honourable races are proud of themselves, and whenever you find any member of a race anxious to transfer himself or herself to another race, that individual represents the lowest in his or her own race, and you may bet that no good will come of him, or her, sooner or later. All animals should love their own kind, and so all peoples of a race should stick together. In fact, the Negro is the only one who has been so divided as not to represent a racial whole, but gradually we will get there, and when that time comes Africa will be indeed united.

SON: Father, can you give any reason why the Negro is so disunited?

FATHER: Yes, my son, and it is a long and complicated story. I do not think at the present time I can [give] you a complete explanation, but I will say enough for you to have at least a fair idea of the reason why there is so little unity among us. First, the Negro race is a scattered one. The Negro is to be found as a subject everywhere. Being such, he falls under the influence of all those who have to deal with him. Naturally, he is used only as a convenience, so that in each community a policy is pursued consistent with the desires of the particular group whose interest must be served. The British Negro, in the different British localities, suffers from the local view point. In some places he is more numerous than the other races. In such a case he must not be taught the consciousness of his own strength, because if he were to realize it he would become the master of such a community. A special programme is therefore mapped out for him. It is generally based upon deception, and in every case he falls into it. So much so that in such a community you will find the Negro doing everything against his own interest. He is generally taught not to think himself a Negro, but only one of the community. He is influenced to think that his opportunities are equal to those of every other race in the community, yet his economic condition is made so low as to prevent him from ever rising ordinarily to the enjoyment of the opportunities that are supposed to be common, and to any kind of true social and other equality with the other races. Wherever he is a minority the treatment is different. He is forced then to realize his inferiority. There is no deception. He must struggle to exist with great difficulty. Everywhere he takes the individualistic point of view, and so he never rises beyond his own selfish view-point in matters of race. Even in this outlook the attitude has been forced upon him. In the United States where he is a minority the attitude is that of general hostility. But even though a minority he is sometimes regarded as a dangerous minority, and so he is educated in his environments to pull against himself and to destroy himself so that in his weakness of division he would not constitute the danger he could be as a solid minority. The education, religious and secular, that the Negro has received was all arranged to destroy his racial consciousness and oneness. What has been done to divide him and almost make him hate himself in the Western world, where he was taken as a slave, is now being done similarly and perfectly in Africa. It is because of this pernicious and wicked kind of teaching that he has not developed the sense of unity. It is by this disunity that he is made an easy prey to those who disrupt him and ultimately destroy him.

SON: In what way then can he throw off this wicked influence that tends to keep him disunited and racially weak[?]

FATHER: By a systematic and steady process of racial education. His education in whatever sphere he finds him-self must be fundamentally racial. Like the Jew, his education should be a religion. It should be taught in the home, if not in the school. It is difficult to teach it in the school because the Negro schools are generally established for him by other people and the curriculum is generally prepared to suit the purpose I have explained before. By his inability to control the policy of Governments he naturally cannot control his own educational system in the public schools; but surely there can be a universal system of education in the home, where each child should be taught the rigid principles of racial love, fraternity, loyalty, devotion. The Jews teach this, and so wheresoever you find them, irrespective of exterior influence, they remain one people even in the midst of persecution.

SON: But how are we to have such an education imparted in the homes[?]

FATHER: Well, that is a problem, my son. It is left to the thoughtful leaders of the race to work out a proper programme. That is what the Organization known as the Universal Negro Improvement Association is trying to do, but it has a difficult task before it.

SON: Why difficult, father?

FATHER: Difficult because they will have to break through the old order of things. The ramifications of the old order are so great that any attempt at reform means desperate opposition. The white Churches will oppose, the white leaders of the white system of education will oppose, and so the Organization will be interfered with in its purpose, and probably even outlawed, because for it to succeed in countries like America, this system of education would mean the emancipation of the people from an old system that has been considered profitable to the creators for centuries.

SON: But father, with all the difficulties something must be done. Difficulties were only made for those who could not move them.

FATHER: What do you mean by that?

SON: I mean this, father, that things only remain difficult when you fail to show initiative and character to make them otherwise.

FATHER: That is wonderful. You could have given no better answer. If all the young men of the race will think like you and then act on the thought the next generation would not have the encumbrances we have to-day.

SON: That is how I feel. I am determined, as I have said before, to play my part and play it well in the redemption and emancipation of the race, and if a proper system of education is to be the first step toward this emancipation, then the rest of my people can count on me.

FATHER: Education, boy, is a mighty force. It is the weapon of human control. If you can educate a people in the idea that you have, they will re-act to your satisfaction whether the education, as a propaganda, is right or wrong. If it is accepted by the masses you have established a control that is difficult to break. That is why all Governments and organized groups have an educational system. It is the vehicle through which they are to put over their special human programme. Religious education is for the purpose of leading man morally and spiritually to his God. It influences him to a sense of goodness and makes him amenable to a broader sense of humanity. This is right. But some of the creators of religion indulged in this kind of education, not for its real good effect upon the human being and for his ultimate salvation in relationship with his God, but to make it easier to exploit that Christian being whose heart is touched with fellowship and sympathy. For such a purpose religion is evil and that is why certain people are rebelling against it. But as far as the individual and his soul's salvation is concerned, religion is the best thing for man, because he ought to know and should know of his God. Some men and some women use secular education to build up a kind of class monopoly that makes them rich at the expense of the ignorant masses whom they have trained to see things in a certain direction. All this, my son, is propaganda, and if the Negro is to be saved in the midst of such criminal propaganda he must be able to evolve an educational system of his own such as I have explained about the Jews.

SON: What a wicked world we are living in father!

FATHER: Wicked, my son! That is a mild characterisation of it. Although man is human, he is a devil. He cannot be trusted by anybody else but himself. He doesn't only lie to and deceive but he will kill his fellows just for a little benefit or profit to himself. To do this successfully he adopts every possible sinful means, and so when you deal with man you must realize immediately that you are not dealing with an angel. You must anticipate him at his worst. This is just what the Negro has not been able to do my boy. He is always taking other people by the face value. Even our religion we take at face value and so we are easily deceived. Our religion teaches us that all that is good is white and all that is bad is black, and without question we accept it as being true. So we think the Devil is like us and God is like the other fellow. Now if this is not propaganda I do not know what is. Yet our fathers never discovered it and so they have influenced us to accept the old order of Heaven with the white angels and Hell with the black imps. It is for you and your generation to correct these monumental errors.

SON: But, father, is religion as bad as that?

FATHER: Don't misunderstand me, boy. Religion is not bad. Religion is a good thing, but it is the way every man practises it. He has corrupted it to suit himself. Has he not slain nations and peoples and wiped out worlds, even in the name of religion, to attain his own selfish ends? If you were to go into the history of Christianity you will find terrible horrors committed in the name of the Lord. Yet there is nothing wrong with the Lord. He was indeed the Saviour of men, but the vile and evil ones who profess His name have corrupted the purity of His religion and the Negro has suffered and is suffering from its effects.

SON: So there must be a religious emancipation also father?

FATHER: Boy, there must be a universal emancipation. Religion is like politics. Politics is like industry, industry is like society. Everywhere the Negro is held down a captive and a slave and it will be so until he himself strikes the blow.

SON: Are we prepared to strike that blow, father?

FATHER: Not in ignorance, but after we are properly educated to the realization of the truth. When that day comes, Africa will stretch out her hands and her children will rush to her arms as to the arms of a loving mother. Indeed, then, "Princes shall come out of Egypt, Ethiopia shall stretch forth her hands unto God."

SOURCE NOTES

Printed in the *Black Man* (London) 1, no. 7 (June 1935): 10–12; 1, no. 8 (late July 1935): 13–16; 1, no. 9 (August–September 1935): 12–15; 1, no. 10 (late October 1935): 19–20; 1, no. 11 (late December 1935): 15–17.

SMILES FOR THE THOUGHTFUL

By the Imp

WHITE BOY: Say blackie, who made you so black?

BLACK BOY: Well, whitie, my father said he was sleeping in the sun when your father threw dust into his face.

WHITE BOY: Then what was your father doing sleeping?

BLACK BOY: He thought there were other honest men in the world and so he took a nap.

WHITE BOY: What do you mean by that?

BLACK BOY: I mean it is not so much my colour you object to as my condition, and my condition is due to the fact that somebody stole my father's heritage whilst he had his nap.

A BLACK BUM interrogating a WHITE PEDESTRIAN: Say boss, how is it you have so much and I have nothing?

WHITE PEDESTRIAN: Because I have been working whilst you have been sleeping.

BLACK BUM: But don't you sleep too?

WHITE PEDESTRIAN: Yes, I sleep, but on a normal stomach.

BLACK BUM: What do you mean by that?

WHITE PEDESTRIAN: I mean there is a difference between both of us.

BLACK BUM: What kind of a difference is it?

WHITE PEDESTRIAN: Whilst I sleep on a normal stomach you sleep on an abnormal one. That is to say you eat too much, which makes you sleep longer and dream more than I do.

BLACK BUM: So you would interfere with my eats, Mister!

WHITE PEDESTRIAN: If you did not want me to interfere

with your eats why did you interfere with me? The trouble with fellows like you is, you eat too much, sleep too long and dream all the time.

BLACK BUM: All right, boss, you have all the say, so let me have a quarter for another meal.

WHITE PEDESTRIAN: Here it is, but you must realise that you are keeping me where I am, whilst you are holding yourself back where you are.

WHITE LADY HECKLER, at Hyde Park: Say, nigger, you have been speaking long enough, why don't you go home?

NEGRO SPEAKER, from Platform: I can't because you have the front door key.

What do you say, Nigger? shouted the white lady.

NEGRO SPEAKER: I said you have the front door key and I believe it is in your closet.

WHITE LADY: Well, go home and get it.

NEGRO SPEAKER: If I should, you would get me lynched.

WHITE LADY: Yes, you may be smart at Hyde Park, but you surely wouldn't be smart in Johannesburg.

NEGRO SPEAKER: That is really why I can't go home, lady.

WHITE LADY, leaving the Embassy Theatre: Well, Jim, I really enjoyed the show "STEVEDORE."

JIM: What impressed you most?

WHITE LADY: The satisfaction of knowing through the play that I am so much better than a nigger.

JIM: I suppose others feel just like you.

WHITE LADY: There is no reason why they should not. Before I came I thought the niggers were somebody, but I realise now that white people need not have any respect for them.

JIM: I am afraid that you are wrong. It is only a Play and from what I can gather all the Negroes are not niggers. There are some who would make the best white man look ashamed if he did not conduct himself decently.

WHITE LADY: Is that so?

JIM: Yes, very much so. There is a difference between Negro and nigger, just as there is a difference between certain thoroughbred white people and others who are of no account.

WHITE LADY: I did not understand it that way.

JIM: Well, my dear, you better understand it correctly, because you are likely to meet a different kind of Negro one of these days, and your attitude toward a nigger may be very displeasing and the result may not be to your advantage.

WHITE LADY: But I saw Negroes at the Theatre in the audience; were they niggers?

JIM: I hardly believe you could call them niggers, because some of them were Doctors, Barristers, Professional and Business Men who were in England either on vacation or on business. Didn't you see how serious some of them looked and how dignified some of them walked? That was quite different from the humility of those who acted in the Play. Those are the Negroes with whom the world will have to deal sooner or later. Those are the men of thought and of action. They feel as noble, as able, and are as ambitious as the leaders of any other race.

WHITE LADY: I am afraid I have to learn more about the Negroes to be able to understand them.

JIM: That is very thoughtful of you. It may help to save a lot of trouble later on.

Two Negroes went to Brighton, England, to see the place, and to enjoy themselves with a summer splash as everybody was doing it. On arriving by train at 6 o'clock in the evening, they went about seeking seeking lodgings. The cabman drove them from hotel to hotel and boarding-house to boarding-house, but no accommodation was procurable. There was the usual excuse, "Sorry, all rooms are taken." At last the cabman drove them to a private home occupied by two sisters. The two sisters looked through a window at the two Negroes in the cab and had a conversation among themselves.

SISTER No. 1: Why, Ethel, we ought to take them in. They

look all right. They look like human beings.

SISTER No. 2: They may look like that but they may not feel or act like human beings.

SISTER No. 1: Why do you think so?

SISTER No. 2: Because I have seen dressed up monkeys looking just like them.

SISTER No. 1: Do you mean to call them monkeys?

SISTER No. 2: My child, haven't you seen the pictures and haven't you read in the books that these people do not know how to behave themselves, that they are cannibals and savages?

SISTER No. 1: But do you forget that our ancestors were also cannibals and savages and it is evolution that makes us what we are?

SISTER No. 2: That may be true, sister, but I am not prepared to have evolutionary theories practised on me in this house by those two Negroes.

After a conference, the Cab drove away, and the two persons left Brighton.

NATIVE CHRISTIAN, in Africa, speaking to WHITE MISSIONARY: How is it we take you into our huts in Africa and you refuse us accommodation in England?

MISSIONARY: That's because of prejudice.

NATIVE CHRISTIAN: Is prejudice a part of Christianity?

MISSIONARY: No.

NATIVE CHRISTIAN: Then your work of Christianizing men in England is not complete.

MISSIONARY (scratching his head): You see, there are sinners everywhere and men must be converted.

NATIVE CHRISTIAN: But I thought you told me according to Scriptures that charity begins at home.

MISSIONARY: That is true, but it must not be understood in the way you do.

NATIVE CHRISTIAN: I see, you mean to tell me that as far as religion is concerned there are two ways of thinking about it.

MISSIONARY: No, there is only one way to think about the

Christian religion.

NATIVE CHRISTIAN: Well, must I think my way or your way?

MISSIONARY (very much disturbed): My dear friend, let us leave all this to the Lord.

PROUD WHITE MAN: You blacks are a good-for-nothing race.

PROUD BLACK MAN: And you whites are a good-for-something race, aren't you?

WHITE MAN: What do you mean by that[?]

BLACK MAN: I mean that what you may be good for has no appeal to us.

WHITE MAN: And what is that?

BLACK MAN: Oh, you are good for everything that is roguish, you take people's lands, their lives, their everything and justify it by your peculiar philosophy.

WHITE MAN: How do you come to that conclusion[?]

BLACK MAN: Because when you are right you are right and when you are wrong you are right, according to your own arguments.

WHITE MAN: Have you proof of that?

BLACK MAN: Your politics, your religion, your literature, your everything are a convenient lie.

WHITE MAN: Whether you call it lie or not it puts us on top.

BLACK MAN: I admit that you are on top, but in view of the fact that the earth is round and revolves like a ball round its axis, one day you will find yourself in the reverse.

WHITE MAN: Do you mean to say I will not always be on top?

BLACK MAN: I never said so, but you may think it out. If you want you may think it from your own philosophy which I know is capable of even stopping the earth from going round.

WHITE PHILOSOPHER to NEGRO STUDENT: Why is it your race is so lazy?

NEGRO STUDENT: That is hard to explain, sir.

WHITE PHILOSOPHER: Well, I will explain it for you. It

is because you have no ambition. You take things too easily. You follow the line of least resistance.

NEGRO STUDENT: But if we do to the contrary, wouldn't we be displeasing you?

WHITE PHILOSOPHER: No, you would be admired.

NEGRO STUDENT: Are you sure that all of your race would admire us if we had self-initiative and ambition[?]

WHITE PHILOSOPHER: I do not know about all of the race, but I know the liberal minds would admire you much better than they do now.

NEGRO STUDENT: But I have often seen Negroes with ambition spurned and treated badly by white people.

WHITE PHILOSOPHER: That may be true, but that is generally due to the fact that you place your ambition in the wrong direction.

NEGRO STUDENT: Will you explain that, sir?

WHITE PHILOSOPHER: Yes, if you want me to be frank and brutal I will tell you the truth. Your coloured men, some of whom happen to be as capable as white men, instead of trying to maintain their own dignity, take a delight in running after the skirts of white women and watching their legs, and most of your blacks feel better straightening out your hair and bleaching your skins than to be proud of yourselves as you are.

NEGRO STUDENT: How do you come to that conclusion, sir?

WHITE PHILOSOPHER: Go round the streets of London and you will see coloured and black men hankering after white women. Go to the Colonies and you will see that the ambition of nearly every coloured man is to marry a white woman.

NEGRO STUDENT: Is that a fault?

WHITE PHILOSOPHER: It is more than a fault. It is a disgrace.

NEGRO STUDENT: But are you sure that the coloured men who are hankering after white women are not children of white fathers with black mothers?

WHITE PHILOSOPHER: White men do not run around with black women even though they have children by them, but you blacks and coloured take it as a delight to run around with white women.

NEGRO STUDENT: I see, sir, you do not object to the natural result, but you object to the demonstration.

WHITE PHILOSOPHER: Go on, you know too much.

NEGRO STUDENT: But you forget, sir, that I am a student of philosophy and psychology.

A COLOURED GIRL to a BLACK LOVER: Look here, Jim, I have been thinking about the presents you have been giving me, and those that are given by Mr. Brown to my friend, Janie.

BLACK LOVER: Well, what about it?

COLOURED GIRL: Janie is a black girl, and Mr. Brown is also a black man, but her presents are as good as mine and some even better.

BLACK LOVER: Well, what about that?

COLOURED GIRL: You seem to have no sense of appreciation.

BLACK LOVER: What do you mean by sense of appreciation?

COLOURED GIRL: Well, if I must tell you, it is this, you do not seem to appreciate my colour.

BLACK LOVER: Appreciate your colour?

COLOURED GIRL: Yes, you seem to think less of me than Mr. Brown thinks of Janie, who is a black.

BLACK LOVER: How do you come to that conclusion?

COLOURED GIRL: Because you have made no effort to reach up to me in appreciation of my colour.

BLACK LOVER: I see. Well, since I can't reach up I shall reach down. Please give me my hat. Goodbye, pretty.

PROFESSOR: Well, Jim, what do you think of the present political situation at Geneva?

NEGRO STUDENT: Rotten, sir, rotten.

PROFESSOR: Why do you say so?

NEGRO STUDENT: Because between Mussolini and the other fellows one is hardly able to tell the difference.

PROFESSOR: What difference are you looking for?

NEGRO STUDENT: Difference of character.

PROFESSOR: What do you expect to see?

NEGRO STUDENT: I and other people of decency expect, according to the platitudes of your political philosophy, something by way of decent behaviour among states-men when they are dealing with the destiny of nations and peoples.

PROFESSOR: Why, Jim, aren't you looking for something that is a kind of an extra?

NEGRO STUDENT: Yes sir, I have come to realize that this expectation of mine is really an extra, because the very people who have promulgated the ideals of politics seem not to expect anything of moral weight or value in return.

PROFESSOR: Are you offended because they have treated Abyssinia so badly?

NEGRO STUDENT: They have not only treated Abyssinia badly, but they have treated themselves badly, because the thoughts some of us have about them are not flattering to the nobility of their character.

PROFESSOR: What thought could that be?

NEGRO STUDENT: Well, I am not saying it Professor, but I heard it said not later than last night that the politicians are going on like prostitutes.

PROFESSOR: What do you mean by that?

NEGRO STUDENT: That they are selling themselves for whatever they can get, and not because they really represent any ideal.

PROFESSOR: How dare you say that?

NEGRO STUDENT: Well, do you not like to hear the truth, Professor?

PROFESSOR: Is that a truth?

NEGRO STUDENT: You ought to know Professor.

PROFESSOR: Well give me some proof of what you mean.

NEGRO STUDENT: Well, Professor, all that you have to do is to recast your mind over the entire Italo-Abyssinian affair, and you will find that from start to finish, very few, if any, of the Statesmen handling the matter have been able to look the world in the face. They are really ashamed of themselves. Compare this[,] Professor, with the action of certain women. When they know their conduct is bad and is watched or known they seldom look you in the face. In fact, they go dodging around the corner.

PROFESSOR: Do you mean to tell me that the statesmen have been dodging?

NEGRO STUDENT: I haven't to tell you that Professor. You ought to see.

PROFESSOR: Why should I?

NEGRO STUDENT: Because you are related, Professor. You ought to be interested.

PROFESSOR: Aren' t you impertinent[?]

NEGRO STUDENT: That is what they all say, Professor, when you tell them the truth.

PROFESSOR: If I knew you were going to be so insolent I never would have started this conversation with you.

NEGRO STUDENT: The statesmen use similar language at times, Professor, in explaining their conduct.

PROFESSOR: What do you mean by that?

NEGRO STUDENT: I mean that when they are discovered in their real tricks they generally do things that more clearly reveal them, as they are, and if you doubt it you can watch the reaction of Mussolini to the discovery of his original intent of fooling Abyssinia.

PROFESSOR: I shall never forget what you have said about European statesmen.

NEGRO STUDENT: And I hope, sir, you will never forget what they have done.

The following conversation took place between a West Indian Overseer (Busha) and a striking Native Labourer.

OVERSEER: Well, Joe, you gave me H—— yesterday, eh?

LABOURER: [G]ave you H——? You gave yourself H——.

OVERSEER: Didn't you all lick me down in the "strike," yesterday?

LABOURER: You playing smart to catch me, then hand me

over to the Police as rioter. You may be smart to rob my pay every week, and grow fat on it, but you are not smart enough to get me into trouble with the Police.

OVERSEER: You d—— brute, stop your freshness.

LABOURER: You left Miss [F]reshness at hom[e]. You better go back and look for her.

OVERSEER: If you insult my wife, I will kill you, you ugly beast.

LABOURER: I did not know your wife was fresh, but fresh or no, let me tell you that you will be well salted when she picks you up after I am through with you.

OVERSEER: Leave this estate at once.

LABOURER: I will leave when the owner dismisses me, but not for you. I have much I can tell him about you. You seem to forget that I know how many hundred bunches of Bananas you steal from the Estates every week.

OVERSEER: What do you say?

LABOURER: I know that you steal Bananas from the estate and sell them in your friend's name every week, so that when I leave, both of us will go together, but you will go to g[ao]l and I will go to another estate.

OVERSEER: Oh, go ahead to your work, Joe, you cannot even make a little fun.

Joe smiled and went his way.

AMERICAN WHITE MAN: Say, Nigger, why do you grin so much?

NEGRO: Because I want to please you, Boss.

WHITE MAN: Can't you please me otherwise?

NEGRO: I know you like cheerfulness because you are so sad by yourself.

WHITE MAN: How do you know that?

NEGRO: Boss, I have never seen a hangman who ever looked happy by himself.

WHITE MAN: But what has that to do with me?

NEGRO: You see, Boss, the Bible says that the sins of the Fathers shall visit the children even to the 3rd and 4th generations, and your fathers have murdered and done so much harm to people all over the world that I feel that you must be very sad.

WHITE MAN: My father never killed anybody.

NEGRO: Well, Boss, I have been looking for the Indians all over the place and somebody told me to ask you to show me the Burial Ground.

WHITE MAN: Get away from here, you Nigger, before I kick the devil out of you.

NEGRO (running): I told you so, Boss. You have murder in the blood. How can you really laugh?

SOURCE NOTES

Printed in the *Black Man* (London) 1, no. 7 (June 1935): 19–20; 1, no. 8 (late July 1935): 20; 1, no. 9 (August–September 1935); 18–19; 1, no. 11 (late December 1935): 17–18. Non-dialogue text omitted.

LESSONS
From the School of African Philosophy
THE NEW WAY TO EDUCATION

OATH OF THE SCHOOL
OF AFRICAN PHILOSOPHY

I ELINOR ROBINSON WHITE do solemnly swear before Almighty God that I have entered upon the instructions of the African School of Philosophy conducted by Marcus Garvey for no other purpose than to serve the Negro race through the Universal Negro Improvement Association and African Communities' League of which he is President-General and that I shall not use the knowledge so gained to promote or advance the interests of any other Organization. I shall confine myself always to the service of the Universal Negro Improvement Association and work within the frame-work of the Organization for any promotion I may desire for the improvement of my race. I shall never devulge or reveal any of these lessons I receive to anyone and shall never allow the lessons or records thereof to fall into the hands of anyone and shall safeguard the same with my life from falling into the hands of other races. I shall always use all my energy and ability to advance the interest of the Universal Negro Improvement Association and shall never be in rebellion against it. And to all this I swear myself, my honour, and sacred trust and should I fail this Oath may the just reward be meted out to me so help me God.

NAME OF STUDENT: / ELINOR WHITE /
ADDRESS: / 3841 State Street, Chicago, Ill., U.S./

DATE: / Sept. 23, 1937 /   PRINCIPAL: / MARCUS GARVEY/

LESSON 1

Intelligence, Education, Universal Knowledge and How to Get It

You must never stop learning. The world's greatest men and women were people who educated themselves outside of the university with all the knowledge that the university gives, as [and?] you have the opportunity of doing the same thing the university student does—read and study.

One must never stop reading. Read everything that you can that is of standard knowledge. Don't waste time reading trashy literature. That is to say, don't pay any attention to the ten cents novels, wild west stories and cheap sentimental books, but where there is a good plot and a good story in the form of a novel, read it. It is necessary to read it for the purpose of getting information on human nature. The idea is that personal experience is not enough for a human to get all the useful knowledge of life, because the individual life is too short, so we must feed on the experience of others. The literature we read should include the biography and autobiography of men and women who have accomplished greatness in their particular line. Whenever you can buy these books and own them and whilst you are reading them make pencil or pen notes of the striking sentences and paragraphs that you should like to remember, so that when you have to refer to the book for any thought that you would like to refresh your mind on, you will not have to read over the whole book.

You should also read the best poetry for inspiration. The standard poets have always been the most inspirational creators. From a good line of poetry, you may get the inspiration for the career of a life time. Many a great man and woman was first inspired by some attractive line or verse of poetry.

There are good poets and bad poets just like there are good novels and bad novels. Always select the best poets for your inspirational urge.

Read history incessantly until you master it. This means your own national history, the history of the world—social history, industrial history, and the history of the different sciences; but primarily the history of man. If you do not know what went on before you came here and what is happening at the time you live, but away from you, you will not know the world and will be ignorant of the world and mankind.

You can only make the best out of life by knowing and understanding it. To know, you must fall back on the intelligence of others who came before you and have left their records behi[n]d.

To be able to read intelligently, you must first be able to master the language of your country. To do this, you must be well acquainted with its grammar and the science of it. Every six months you should read over again the science of the language that you speak, so as not to forget its rules. People judge you by your writing and your speech. If you write badly and incorrectly they become prejudiced toward your intelligence, and if you speak badly and incorrectly those who hear you become disgusted and will not pay much attention to you but in their hearts laugh after you. A leader who is to teach men and present any fact of truth to man must first be learned in his subject.

Never write or speak on a subject you know nothing about, for there is always somebody who knows that particular subject to laugh at you or to ask you embarras[s]ing questions that may make others laugh at you. You can know about any subject under the sun by reading about it. If you cannot bu[y] the books outright and own them, go to your public libraries and read them there or borrow them, or join some circulating library in your district or town, so as to get the use of these books. You should do that as you may refer to them for information.

You should read at least four hours a day. The best time to read is in the evening after you have retired from your work and after you have rested and before sleeping hours but do so before morning, so that during your sleeping hours what you have read may become subconscious, that is to say, planted in your memory. Never go to bed without doing some reading[.]

Never keep the constant company of anybody who doesn't know as much as you or [isn't] as educated as you, and from whom you cannot learn something or reciprocate your learning, especially if that person is illiterate or ignorant because constant association with such a person will unconsciously cause you to drift into the peculiar culture or ignorance of that person. Always try to associate with people from whom you can learn something. Contact with cultured persons and with books is the best companionship you can have and keep.

By reading good books you keep the company of the authors of the book or the subjects of the book when otherwise you could not meet them in the social contact of life. NEVER GO DOWN IN INTELLIGENCE to those who are below you, but if possible help to lift them up to you and always try to ascend to those who are above you and be their equal with the hope of being their master.

Continue always in the application of the thing you desire educationally, culturally, or otherwise, and never give up until you reach the objective—and you can reach the objective if other[s] have done so before you, proving by their doing it that it is possible.

In your desire to accomplish greatness, you must first decide in your own mind in what direction you desire to seek that greatness, and when you have so decided in your own mind[,] work unceas[i]ngly toward it. The particular thing that you may want should be before you all the time, and whatsoever it takes to get it or make it possible should be undertaken. Use your faculties and persuasion to achieve all you set your mind on.

Try never to repeat yourself in any one discourse in saying the same thing over and over except you are making new points, because repetition is tiresome and it annoys those who hear the repetition. Therefore, try to possess as much universal knowledge as possible through reading so as to be able to be free of repetition in trying to drive home a point.

No one is ever too old to learn. Therefore, you should take advantage of every educational facility. If you should hear of a great man or woman who is to lecture or speak in your town on any given subject and the person is an authority on the subject, always make time to go and hear him. This is what is meant by learning from others. You should learn the two sides to every story, so as to be able to properly debate a question and hold your grounds with the side that you support. If you only know one side of a story, you cannot argue intelligently nor effectively. As for instance, to combat communism, you must know about it, otherwise people will take advantage of you and win a victory over your ignorance.

Anything that you are going to challenge, you must first know about it, so as to be able to defeat it. The moment you are ignorant about anything the person who has the intelligence of that thing will defeat you. Therefore, get knowledge, get it quickly, get it studiously, but get it anyway.

Knowledge is power. When you know a thing and can hold your ground on that thing and win over your opponents on that thing, those who hear you learn to have confidence in you and will trust your ability.

Never, therefore, attempt anything without being able to protect yourself on it, for every time you are defeated it takes away from your prestige and you are not as respected as before.

All the knowledge you want is in the world, and all that you have to do is to go seeking it and never stop until you have found it. You can find knowledge or the information about it in the public libraries, if it is not on your own bookshelf. Try to have a book and own it on every bit of knowledge you want. You may generally get these books at second hand book stores for sometimes one-fifth of the original value.

Always have a well equipped shelf of books. Nearly all information about mankind is to be found in the Encyclopedia Britannica. This is an expensive set of books, but try to get them. Buy a complete edition for yourself, and keep it at your home, and whenever you are in doubt about anything, go to it and you will find it there.

The value of knowledge is to use it. It is not humanly possible that a person can retain all knowledge of the world, but if a person knows how to search for all the knowledge of the world, he will find it when he wants it.

A doctor or a lawyer although he passed his examination in college does not know all the laws and does not know all the techniques of medicine but he has the fundamental knowledge. When he wants a particular kind of knowledge, he goes to the medical books or law books and refers to the particular law or how to use the recipe of medicine. You must, therefore, know where to find your facts and use them as you want them. No one will know where you got them, but you will have the facts and by using the facts correctly they will think you a wonderful person, a great gen[iu]s, and a trusted leader.

In reading it is not necessary or compulsory that you agree with everything you read. You must always use or apply your own reasoning to what you have read based upon what you already know as touching the facts on what you have read. Pass judgement on what you read based upon these facts. When I say facts I mean things that cannot be disputed. You may read thoughts that are old, and opinions that are old and have changed since they were written. You must always search to find out the latest facts on that p[a]rticular subject and only when these facts are consistently maintained in what you read should you agree with them, otherwise you are entitled to your own opinion.

Always have up-to-date knowledge. You can gather this from the latest books and the latest periodicals, journals and newspapers. Read your daily newspaper everyday. Read a standard monthly journal every month, a standard weekly magazine every week, a standard quarterly magazine every quarter and by this you will find the new knowledge of the whole year in addition to the books you read, whose facts have not altered in that year. Don't keep old ideas, bury them as new ones come.

How to Read

Use every spare minute you have in reading. If you are going on a journey that would take you an hour carry something with you to read for that hour until you have reached the place. If you are sitting down waiting for somebody, have something in your pocket to read until the person comes. Don't waste time. Any time you think you have to waste put it in reading something. Carry with you a small pocket dictionary and study words whilst waiting or travelling, or a small pocket volume on some particular subject. Read through at least one book every week separate and distinct from your newspapers and journals. It will mean that at the end of one year you will have read fifty-two different subjects. After five years you will have read over two hundred and fifty books. You may be considered then a well read man or a well read woman and there will be a great difference between you and the person who has not read one book. You will be considered intelligent and the other person be considered ignorant. You and that person therefore will be living in two different worlds; one the world of ignorance and the other the world of intelligence. Never forget that intelligence rules the world and ignorance carries the burden. Therefore, remove yourself as far as possible from ignorance and seek as far as possible to be intelligent.

Your language being English you should study the English language thoroughly. To know the English language thoroughly you ought to be acquainted with Latin, because most of the English words are of Latin origin. It is also advisable that you know the French language because most of the books that you read in English carry Latin and

French phrases and words. There is no use reading a page or paragraph of a book or even a sentence without understanding it.

If it has foreign words in it, before you pass over [them] you should go to the dictionary, if you don't know the meaning and find out the meanin[g]. Never pass over a word without knowing its meaning. The dictionary and the books on word building which can be secured from book sellers will help you greatly.

I know a boy who was ambitious to learn. He hadn't the opportunity of an early school education because he had to work ten hours a day, but he determined that he would learn and so he took with him to his work place every day a simplified grammar and he would read and me[m]orize passages and the rules of grammar whilst at work.

After one year he was almost an expert in the grammar of his language. He knew the differen[t] parts of speech, he could paraphrase, analyse and construct sentences. He also took with him a pocket dictionary and he would write out twenty-five new words with their meanings every day and study these words and their mords [forms?] and their meaning. After one year he had a speaking vocabulary of more than three thousand words. He continued this for several years and when he became a man he had a vocabulary at his command of over fifteen thousand words. He became an author because he could write in his language by having command of words. What he wrote was his experiences and he recorded his experiences in the best words of his language. He was not able to write properly at the same age and so he took with him to work what is called in school a copying book and he practised the copying of letters until he was able to write a very good hand. He naturally became acquainted with literature and so he continued reading extensively. When he died he was one of the greatest scholars the world ever knew. Apply the story to yourself.

There is nothing in the world that you want that you cannot have so long as it is possible in nature and men have achieved it before. The greatest men and women in the world burn the midnight lamp. That is to say, when their neighbours and household are gone to bed, they are reading, studying and thinking. When they rise in the morning they are always ahead of their neighbours and their household in the thing that they were studying[,] reading and thinking of. A daily repetition of that will carry them daily ahead and above their neighbours and household. Practise this rule. It is wise to study a couple of subjects at a time. As for instance—a little geography, a little psychology, a little ethics, a little theology, a little philosophy, a little mathematics, a little science on which a sound academic education is built. Doing this week after week, month after month, year after year will make you so learned in the liberal arts as to make you ready and fit for your place in the affairs of the world. If you know what others do not know, they will want to hear you. You will then become invaluable in your community and to your country, because men and women will want to hear you and see you everywhere.

As stated before, books are one's best companions. Try to get the[m] and keep them. A method of doing so is every time you have ten cents or twenty five cents or a dollar to spend foolishly[,] either on your friends or yourself [,] think how much more useful that ten or twenty five cents or dollar would be invested in a book and so invest it. It may be just the thing you have been looking for to give you a thought by which you may win the heart of the world. The ten cent, twenty five cent or a dollar, therefore, may turn out to be an investment of worth to the extent of a million dollars. Never lend anybody the book that you want. You will never get it back. Never allow anybody to go to your bookshelf in your absence because the very book that you may want most may be taken from the shelf and you may never be able to get one of the kind again.

If you have a library of your own, lock it when you are not at home. Spend most of your spare time in your library. If you have a radio keep it in your own library and use it exhaustively to listen to lectures, recitals, speeches and good music. You can learn a lot from the radio. You can be inspired a lot by good music [*lines repeated*]. Good music carries the sentiment of harmony and you may think many a good thought out of listening to good music.

Read a chapter from the Bible everyday, Old and New Testaments. The greatest wisdom of the age is to be found in the Scriptures. You can always quote from the Scriptures. It is the quickest way of winning approval.

TRAGEDY OF WHITE INJUSTICE

1. Read and study thoroughly the poe[m] "Tragedy of White Injustice" and apply its sentiment and statements in connection with the historic character and behaviour of the white man. Know it so well as always to be able to be on guard against any professions of the white man in his suggested friendship for the Negro.

The poem exposes the white man's behaviour in history and is intended to suggest distrust of him in every phase of life. Never allow it to get into the hands of a white man i[f] possible.

2. You can imp[ro]ve your English as you go along by reading critically the books of the language; that is to say, you must pay close attention to the construction of sentences and paragraphs as you see them in the books you read. Imitate the style.

Read with observation. Never read carelessly and recklessly.

3. In reading books written by white authors of whatsoever kind, be aware of the fact that they are [not] written for your particular benefit or for the benefit of your race. They always write from their own point of view and only in the interest of their own race.

Never swallow wholly what the white man writes or says without first critically analyzing it and investigating it. The white man's trick is to deceive other people for his own benefit and profit.

Always be on your guard against him with whatsoever he does or says. Never take chances with him. His school books in the elementary schools, in the high schools, in the colleges and universities are all fixed up to suit his own purposes, to put him on top and keep him on top of other people. Don't trust him. Beware! Beware!

You should study carefully the subject of ethnology. It is the subject that causes races to know the difference between one race and another.

Ethnic relationship is important as it reveals the characteristic of one people as different from another. There is no doubt that each race has different habits and manners of behaviour. You must know them so as to be able to deal with them. There are books on this subject in the library. In your reading and searching for truth always try to get that which is particularly helpful to the Negro. Every thought that strikes you, see how it fits in with the Negro, and to what extent you can use it to his benefit or in his behalf. Your entire obsession must be to see things from the Negro's point of view, remembering always that you are a Negro striving for Negro supremacy in every department of life, so that any truth you see or any facts you gather must be twisted to suit the Negro psychology of things.

The educational system of today hides the truth as far as the Negro is concerned. Therefore, you must searchingly scan everything you read[,] particularly history, to see what you can pick out for the good of the race. As for instance, you will read that the Egyptians were a great people, the Carthagenians, the Libyans, etc., but you will not be told that they were black people or Negroes. You should, therefore, go beyond the mere statement of these events to discover the truth that will be creditable to your race. You would, therefore, in a case like that ask where did the Libyans get their civilization from or the Carthagenians or the Egyptians.

Following that kind of an investigation you will come upon the truth that it was all original[ly] Negro and subsequently bec[a]me Negroid. That is to say, subsequent people were mixed with other people's blood, who were no doubt conquered by the Negro. As a fact, the original Egyptians were black men and women, and so the Carthagenians and

Libyans, but in the later centuries they became mixed in blood, just as how [now?] the blacks are being mixed in America and the West Indies by the infusion of white blood through the domination of the white man.

Never yield to any statement in history or made by any individual[,] caring not how great, that the Negro was nobody in history. Even if you cannot prove it always claim that the Negro was great. Read everything you can get written by Negroes and their ancestry, going back six thousand years. There are statements in the Bible in the Old and New Testaments to show that black was always an important colour among the races of men. Abraham had company with a black woman, even though he had his wife Sarah, by whom he had Ishmael.

All the original Pharaohs were black. Tutankumen, whose bones and body were dug up not very long ago at Luxor in Egypt, was a black Pharaoh. The sphinx, in Egypt which has stood through the millenniums, has black features. It is evident that as art it was portrayed to teach us of the greatness of men. When you are dealing with Jews let them know that they were once your slaves in Egypt if you have to say so. There is good ground to say that civilization started in Africa and passed from and through Northern Africa into Southern Europe, from which the Greeks and Romans and the People of Asia Minor made good copies. The swarthy colour of the Asiatics and the brunette colour of the South Europeans were due to the fact that the cultured and civilized blacks of Africa mixed their blood with them. Search all history and all literature and the Bible and find facts to support this argument but hold to it with a grip that will never loosen. Things that may not be true can be made if you repeat them long and often enough, therefore, always repeat statements that will give your race a status and an advantage. That is how the white man has built up his system of superiority. He is always telling you he is superior and he has written history and literature to prove it. You must do the same. One of the great backgrounds for your argument which cannot be disputed is that you are older than any other man as a race because you are black. Your argument is that in nature everything by way of age darkens. That you are darker than the rest of men, proves logically, that you are older than the rest of men. Another proof of that is that even among white people they grow darker in skin as they grow older in age in a lifetime.

If the one individual were to live for six thousand years he would surely be not white. If he were born white he would be as dark as the darkest man. Therefore, the old argument that the black man is black because as man he is older than the other man is good. Use it everywhere you go to defeat the white man in his belief that you sprung from something else. Use the argument that the white man is white because most of the time when the black man was great in Africa and had succeeded in running him across the Mediterranean into South Europe he had to hide himself in caves where there was very little light and air. He was almost covered up for most of the time in darkness. In natural creation the child in the womb of the mother is almost white even though it be a black child and it is almost born white and doesn't change colour until it comes in contact with light and air.

Living in caves for so many centuries the white man, therefore, became colourless and the length of time always made it so that he was born naturally white. You must interpret anthropology to suit yourself. The thing for you to do is to refute every pertinent statement of the white man which tends to degrade you and to elevate him. Turn the tables on him and search for all reasons in the world you can find to justify it. That is how new thoughts are given out by creation. Never yield to the statement of your inferiority.

In reading Christian literature and accepting the doctrine of Jesus Christ lay special claim to your association with Jesus and the Son of God. Show that whilst the white and yellow worlds, that is to say—the worlds of Europe and Asia Minor persecuted and crucified Jesus the Son of God, it was the black race through Simon the black C[y]renian who befriended the Son of God and took up the Cross and bore it alongside of Him up to the heights of Calv[a]ry. The Roman Catholics, therefore, have no rightful claim to the Cross nor is any other professing Christian before the Negro. The Cross is the property of the Negro in his religion, because it was he who bore it.

Never admit that Jesus Christ was a white man, otherwise he could not be the Son of God and God to redeem all mankind. Jesus Christ had the blood of all races in his veins, and tracing the Jewish race back to Abraham and to Moses, from which Jesus sprang through the line of Jesse, you will find Negro blood everywhere, so Jesus had much of Negro blood in him.

Read the genealogical tree of Jesus in the Bible and you will learn from where he sprang. It is a fact that the white man has borrowed his civilization from other peoples. The first civilization was the Negro's—black people. The second civilization was the brown people—Indians, the third civilization was the yellow people, Chinese or Mongols; the last civilization up to today is the white man and all civilization goes back to the black man in the Nile Valley of Africa. In your reading, therefore, search for all these facts. Never stop reading and never stop until you find the proof of them.

You must pay great attention to sociology. Get the best books on the subject that you can and read them thoroughly. Find out the social relationship among other races so [t]hat you may know how to advise your people in their social behaviour. Never admit that the Negro is more immoral than the white man but try to prove to the contrary. Socially the white man has debauched and debased all other races because of his dominant power. He is responsible for more illegitimacy among races than any other race. He has left bastard children everywhere he has been, therefore, he is not competent to say that he is socially and morally purer than any other race.

The mixed population among Neg[roe]s from slavery to the present in certain countries is due to [t]he white man's immorality. Therefore, if you should hear anyone talking about moral depravity of Negroes and the moral excellence of the whites, draw the above facts to their attention.

When through reading and research you have discovered any new fact helpful to the dignity and prestige, character and accomplishment of the Negro, always make a noise about it. You should keep always with you a note book and fountain pen or indelible pencil and make a note in that book of anything you hear or see that you would like to remember. Keep always at home a larger note book to which you must transfer the thought or experience, so that it will not be lost to your memory. Once at least every three months read over that book and as the book becomes more voluminous with facts, read it over at least once a year.

By the constant reading of these facts they will be planted on your subconscious mind and you will be able to use them without even knowing that you are doing so. By keeping your facts registered and your very important experiences, at the end of a full life you may have a volume of great value such as Elbert Hubbard's Scrap Book. Get a copy of this Scrap Book. Ask any publisher in your town to get it for you. It contains invaluable inspiration. Always have a thought. Make it always a beautiful thought. The world is attracted by beauty either in art or in expression. Therefore, try to read, think and speak beautiful things.

> Out of the night that covers me,
> Black as the Pit from pole to pole,
> I thank whatever Gods may be
> For my unconquerable soul.
>
> In the fell clutch of circumstance
> I have not winced nor cried aloud,
> Under the bludgeoning of chance
> My head is bloody, but unbowed.
>
> Beyond this place of wrath and tears
> Looms but the horror of the Shade,
> And yet the menace of the years
> Finds, and shall find, me unafraid.

It matters not how strait the gate,
How charged with punishments the scroll,
I am the master of my fate;
I am the captain of my soul.

"INVICTUS"
BY W. E. HENLEY

LESSON 2

Leadership

To lead suggests that you must have followers. For others to follow you, you must be superior to them in the things that they must follow you for.

You must have superior ability[;] in the particular, you must always be ahead by way of knowledge of all those you lead. The moment you fall down from the position of superior ability, you will automatically fail to lead and you will have to follow others. Therefore you must be ever vigilant in keeping ahead of those you lead by getting the latest and most correct information for which they are searching, because for it they are following you. People only respect leaders and follow them when there is something superior in them.

A leader must have personality; he must be clean cut in his appearance so as not to be criticized. An untidy leader is always a failure. He must be neatly dressed and his general appearance must be clean and presentable because people are supposed to follow him in his manner, in his behaviour, in his general conduct. A leader's hair should always be well kept; his teeth must also be in perfect order for people will criticize him for his unke[m]pt hair, and his bad teeth.

Your shoes and other garments must also be clean. If you look ragged, people will not trust you. They will critically say he has no clothing, his shoes are very poor, and it is logical that whatsoever money he gets hold of he will use it on himself rather than for the purpose for which he makes his appeal.

Never show your poverty to those you lead, that is[,]

personal poverty, they will never trust you. This does not mean that you should not reveal the poverty of the cause you represent because that cause is your cause and the people's cause in which both of you are interested. *Never tell lies* to those you lead, sooner or later they will find you out, and then your career will abruptly come to an end. NO MAN EVER TRUSTS A PERSON A SECOND TIME whom he disbelieves once and has proof for his disbelief.

A leader, under all circumstances, must carry himself with dignity. He must not be a snob but he must maintain his pride.

A leader cannot well afford to mix himself up with anything that is not dignified or self respected. If you have to do anything that you know [you] will be morally and socially ashamed of, if some one else knows, never do it, but if you have to do it, see to it carefully that nobody knows.

Don't carry your weakness on your face or in your eyes, somebody will detect it and you are ruined. If you have personal weaknesses try to conquer them and hide them as long as you can until you have conquered them, otherwise you are ruined.

Every man can conquer his vices by bringing his subconscious will to play upon and against such vices. In everything you do play the gentleman. Never be a hog, it doesn't pay. You lose a friend every time you play the hog. Keep smiling with the world even though your mother is dead. Smile with the world and the world will smile back at you; be vexed with the world, and the world will be vexed with you. Nobody is obligated to you to make you happy, so don't carry your sorrow to the world and on your sleeves. Keep them to yourself and get out of them the best way you can. Leaders are not children, they must not, therefore, act as children.

Leaders must be self possessed, confident, feeling self-reliant. When your followers see that self confidence they will believe in you and follow you. Always speak out right from your head and from your heart. If your heart is not in it, it is a lie. If your head is not in it, it is pure sentiment. Your head and heart must work together. People observing you can always tell when you are sincere and that is when you speak from your heart and your head. They can always tell when you are fooling them, by looking into your eyes and you cannot stand their gaze; at that time, indeed, you are lying. When your heart and head is in it, your whole body expresses the truth and you can hold any man's stare.

A leader must not be extravag[a]nt, he must not be flashy in the sense of being over sporty. People will not think you serious. Always make your followers believe you are serious. You can be serious without being sour. Always think before you speak or act. Don't write or speak just for hearing yourself. Speak or write only when you have something to say and never touch anything, by way of leadership, that you do not know about, because somebody who knows about it will have a joke at your expense. A leader must always have something to say, otherwise he forfeits his leadership and someone else who has something to say will supplant it.

A leader should always make effort to be known in his community. He must acquaint himself with everything that is happening. He must know the governor of the state or country, the secretary of his state or his colonial secretary. He must know the mayor of his city, and all the members of the legislature. He must know the bishops of his city, the administrative heads of all government departments, all the preachers and doctors and lawyers and prominent business men.

Don't be seen with Communists too often if you know them. Never take part in their meetings except you are to make a speech against their principles and always see that it is known by the public that that is your only cause for going among them. Never let them call you comrade to the hearing of anybody because you will be branded as a Communist, and your leadership will be destroyed.

You must seek to know all the people who you want to be in your organization. Visit them in their homes, their work places, and anywhere you can meet them and always extend to them a glad hand. Be always diplomatic in your approach. If a Negro is in company with a white man, never talk to him about the U.N.I.A. If he is in company with some one you think is not in sympathy with the U.N.I.A. don't talk to him about the U.N.I.A. but wait until he is alone. Never say anything in the presence of two or three people between whom may be sympathy with the organization except you know that the others are also sympathetic; because when you are gone the others may try to undo the good relationship.

But when you meet Negro strangers you may talk to all of them about the aims of the U.N.I.A. and try to win them over.

Never divide or create confusion between the different colours in the Negro race, but always try to prove that the standard Negro is the African and all Negroes should be proud of their black blood without insulting any colour within the race. This is very, very important.

The idea of the U.N.I.A. is to unite into one race all the grades of colour and build up a standard race. You should discourage intermarriage between white and black and black and other races. You should tell the people that it is an honour to be black and that nothing is wrong with the black skin but bad conditions. That a well-kept black woman or black man is as good as a well-kept white man or white woman. Never allow your followers to have their children play with white doll babies, because they will grow up to like white children and they will have them. Discourage the Negroes [from] having white pictures in their homes as those pictures will inspire them to becoming white in their ideas, but that they should have pictures of Negroes who have achieved greatness in their homes.

Tell Negro parents that they must teach their children in their homes Negro history, Negro pride and self-respect to counteract the elementary and high school education they get which holds up the superiority of the white race. Let the people know that God is not white nor is he black, but that God is a spirit and universal intelligence of which each and everyone is a part. All of us [are] part of that intelligence.

No man can have the full intelligence of God but only partial intelligence. No man, therefore, can be God, so neither the white man nor the black man is God, but a particle of God. Let the people know that in them and in themselves only is the power to rise. That God does not go out of his way to give people positions or jobs or to give them good conditions such as they desire; they must do that for themselves out of the fullness of nature that God has created for everybody. God does not build cities nor towns nor nations, nor homes, nor factories, men and peoples do that and all those who want them must work for themselves and pray to God to give them strength to do it.

SPECIAL NOTES O[N] INTERMARRIAGE AND RACE PURITY

For a rich Negro to marry a poor white is an unpardonable crime and sin because it simply means the transference of the wealth of the race to another, and the ultimate loss of that wealth to that race. It is logically evident that if the Negro is rich, he gained all or most of his wealth from his race. To ignore, therefore, the opposite sex of his race and intermarry with another race is to commit this crime or this sin for which he should never be pardoned by his race.

Teach the people to abhor such Negroes, and have nothing to do with them so long as they continue in that relationship. This must be done diplomatically, not to the hearing of the white race.

For safety, let the advice take the term [form?] of a whisper campaign, don't say it from the platform, but whisper it right through the neighbourhood and never stop until the burden of your campaign is felt by the individuals, so as to learn them a good lesson that others may not do the same thing with impunity.

For a Negro man to marry someone who does not look like his mother or not a member of his race is to insult his mother, insult nature and insult God who made his father. The best tribute a race can pay to nature and God is to preserve its species and when it does otherwise, it is in rebellion. Don't be in rebellion against God or nature or your parents who you know of, they came before you and should have known better.

Insist in a campaign of race purity, that is doing everything moral and social within the race and close ranks against all other races. It is natural that it is a disgrace to mix your race with other races. The splitting up of the race is unwholesome and doesn't tend to dignify morally the group. It will be a beautiful thing when we have a standard Negro race.

In preaching race purity, be very careful because it is a delicate subject, in that most of the people are ignorant of this idealism. You must never put colour within the race against colour, you must never insult any colour within the race. Whatsoever has happened in the past was without our consent and truly because slavery and the wicked damnation of the white man imposed upon us moral behaviour that we could not restrain. But now that we know better, it is for us to adjust these things within our own race.

Teach the people to respect all shades of their own race and never to have any prejudice against anyone whether he is black, brown, yellow or any shade that the white claims is not white.

Never allow any other race to preside over your affairs. If they come as visitors, they must conduct themselves as visitors. They must never have any executive control over you in your affairs because they will always say and do things to suit themselves as against your interest even though they profess the greatest amount of friendship.

If they swear on the Bible, don't believe them[;] if they swear in [on?] God, don't believe them—accept their friendship for all its worth to you and nothing more. Their interest as a race can never be yours whether they be Europeans, Asiatics[,] Jews or what not.

Never trust a Jew, don't let him know that. He is playing the odds against you all the time. He plays with loaded dice, his card is marked, you can never win against him. Make this a secret whispering propaganda in every community where you go into a Negro home. Whisper all the time that the Jew is bad. Flatter hi[m] as he flatters you, robs you, never give him a square deal because he is never going to give you one, but tell him how much you love and how kind and nice his people are. Get all you can from him and give him nothing back except good words and pleasant smiles, this is his policy.

The policy of the Jew is if he sees a Gentile dying on the pathway and a penny covers his eye, as a hope for recovery, he will take it off and let him die, but he will not do this to a Jew. You have your answer to this. Treat him similarly, always try to get something from the Jew because he has always robbed you and your fathers in that he believes he is the chosen of God and as such all other men must pay tribute to him. This is false and fictitious. It is Jewish propaganda, ignore it and let him pay tribute to you if tribute must be paid.

LESSON 3

Aims and Objects of the U.N.I.A.

1. To establish a universal confraternity among the race.

We mean by this that there must be a linking up of fraternal relationship with all the members of the Negro race to the exclusion of none.

Every Negro in the world must be a part of the confraternity. Every Negro's interest must come first in all things of humanity. Not until you have served every Negro in the world should you seek to be kind to others. Charity begins at home.

The home of the Negro race is all over the world. You /must/ attend to them first before you think of others. If you /have/ a shilling or twenty five cents to give away for charity, /before/ you give it to others['] charity see that all other Negro /char/ities are first attended to. So long as there is need in /your/ race attend to it first and always. Never deny help to your own race.

This is the meaning of confraternity. One for all and all for one. Never depart from this.

2. To prompt the Spirit of Pride and Love.

It must be the mission of all Negroes to have pride in their race. To think of the race in the highest terms of human living. To think that God made the race perfect, that there is no one better than you, that you have all the elements of human perfection and as such you must love yourselves.

Love yourselves better than anybody else. All beauty is in you and not outside of you, for God made you beautiful. Confine your affection, therefore, to your own race and God will bless you and men will honour you.

Never be unkind to your race. Never curse your race. If anything is being done that is wrong by a member of your race, try to put him right. Don't condemn him without hearing him. Give him a chance to do what is right before you denounce him. If he provokes you, try to put up with his ignorance and persuade him to be kind, to be good, to be gentle.

3. To reclaim the fallen.

Wherever a member of your race is down pick him up. Wh/enever/ he wants genuine help and you can help him do so. Never leave him stranded and friendless. If you cannot help him yourself, send him someone of the race who can help him, but put around him the arm of protection and keep him from going wrong and feeling absolutely friendless.

4. To administer and assist the needy.

Let it be your highest purpose in life to assist the needy members of your race. Use all your influence in your country, in your state, in your town to help the needy elements of your race.

Seek Government help for them, seek philanthropic help for them, seek help anywhere you can find it for them to improve their condition.

5. To assist in civilizing the backward tribes of Africa.

Africa is the motherland of all Negroes, from where all Negroes in slavery were taken against their will. It is the natural home of the race. One day all Negroes hope to look to Africa as the land of their vine and fig tree. It is necessary, therefore, to help the tribes who live in Africa to advance to a higher state of civilization. The white man is not conscientiously doing it, although he professes to do so, but this is only the method to deceive the world.

It is the Negro who must help the Negro. To help the African Negro to civilization is to prepare him for his place in a new African state that will be the home of all Negroes.

6. To assist in the development of independent Negro nati[ons] and Communities.

The Negro should not have but one nation, but work with the hope that these independent nations will become parts of [the] great racial empire. It is necessary, therefore, to strengthen the hand of every free and independent Negro state so that they may be able to continue their independence.

Every community where the Negro lives should be devel[oped] by him in his own section, so that he may control that section or part of the community.

He should segregate himself residentially in that community so as to have political power, economic power, and social power in that community.

If he should scatter himself about the community, if other people live in the community, he will be scattering his power and dividing it up with other people. If there are 10,000 Negroes in a town, they should live close to each other, and so if there are 1,000, 500, or a million, they will have the power of their numbers to do business, to appeal to the governor and to voice their rights as citizens—in this respect segregation is good, to do [o]therwise is bad.

7. To establish Commissionaries Or Agencies in The Princip[al] Countries And Cities Of The World For the Representation And Protection Of All Negroes Irrespective Of Nationalit[y].

This means that there must be someone in every city whose business it will be to look after the interest of Negroes who may come into that city or country. His position will be like that of an ambassador, consul, consular agent of a nation.

He will interest himself in all the things affecting the Negro race and see that no a[d]vantage or abuse is taken or made of a Negro who comes into the city or the country.

He is to report all happenings affecting the Negro and in which the Negro is interested to the U.N.I.A. This will not be necessary where Negroes have a community of their own but is applicable only to foreign countries such as Europe, Asia, and South America where the Negro may live in large numbers and have no contact with the government.

8. To Promote A Conscientious Spiritual Worship Among The Native Tribes of Africa.

This means, considering that there are so many different religious thoughts[, t]he Negro should be brought under the influence of one system of religion and the belief in one God, that an honest effort should be made to instruct him in his particular desires and not to exploit him by teaching him different religions.

There is to be no speculative idea behind his religion.

9. To Establish Universities, Colleges, Academies And Schools For The Racial Education And Culture Of The People.

This means that we are not to become satisfied with the educational system of the white man which has been devised by him for his own purpose, and to lead others to obedience to his system.

The Negro must have an e[d]ucational system of his own, based upon the history and tradition of his race. The text books, therefore, must be different to the white man's text books. The white man's books laud himself and outrages the Negro. /In such text books the Negro should substitute all that is bad affecting himself for that [which] is good relating to him./

The Negro, therefore, should not be satisfied with a college or university education from white schools, but should add to his schooling by going to his own schools and universities where possible or reading such text books that have [been] adopted by his schools and colleges, which must all glorify the Negro, for the white man's system glorifies the white man.

10. To Conduct a World-wide Commercial And Industrial Intercourse For the Good Of The People.

The economic life of the Negro is important. He is to live by eating, wearing clothes, and living in a home. These are essential. To get these things, he must work either with his hands or his brains.

The system of economy lays it down that commerce and industry are the feeding factors in the economic life. Hence, it is absolutely necessary that the Negro builds an economic structure suffic[ie]ntly strong enough to feed the arteries of his existence.

He should, therefore, indulge in every kind of business that is necessary for profit because it is by the worth that he may be able to obtain himself and his race.

11. To Work For Better Conditions In All Negro Communities.

There should be a ceaseless effort everywhere among Negroes to improve their conditions in every department of life and make their communities so prosperous as to compel the respect of their neighbour. No stone should be left unturned; go from one stage of development and progress to another. There is always work do in this respect.

APPLICATION

All the funds of the U.N.I.A. are supposed to be directed in these channels. The funds of the U.N.I.A. must be [us]ed for the race, and the race only, and belongs to no one individual or group of individuals, but is held in trust for the race, and all the profit it makes out of its investments through different companies which it controls must be ultimately used for the good and welfare of the Negro race at large.

Its property will be held in trust for the Negro race. Its wealth will be held in trust for the Negro race for serving generations yet unborn.

It shall go on eternally, one generation handing down to the next. No one person or persons can claim such wealth because it is for the race in perpetual existence. Stress this everywhere you go, so that people may know that what they contribute to the U.N.I.A. is not lost to them, in that their generations may benefit from the gift they give today.

NEGRO NATIONALISM

The culmination of all the efforts of the U.N.I.A. must end in Negro i[n]dependent nationalism on the continent of Africa. /Tha/t is to say, everything must contribute toward the final /obj/ective of having a powerful nation for the Negro race. /Negro/ nationalism is necessary. It is political power and /contro/l.

/No ra/ce is free until it has a strong nation of its own— its own system of government and its /own/ order of society. Never /give/ up this idea, let no one persuade you against it. It is the only protection of your generation and your race. Hold on to the idea, of an independent government and nation so long as other men have them.

Never be satisfied to always live under the government of other people because you shall ever be at their mercy. Visualize for yourself and your children and generations unborn of the race your own king, your own emperor, your own president, your own government officials and administrations who look like you.

God never could have intended to make you as you look and as you are, and to make your king, president, emperor, or ruler different to you in race.

This must not be a license for you to disobey the laws of kings of other races or rulers of other races while you live under their control, but you must always seek and work for a government of your own absolutely where you and your children will have a chance like anybody else in the state, to rise from the lowest to the highest position, which you may not attain under other governments, but while you will have under alien governments to get the best out of them, as your citizenship's right, but always have in view doing something to make it possible that your race can have a nation and a government of its own. Speak of this, dream of this, work unceasingly for this and never forget this, for this is the great task of the U.N.I.A.

Never confuse your ideas about Negro nationality with that of other peoples as to think that their nationality is good enough for you.

Never think that if Japan gains control of the worl[d] they will tre[a]t you better than Angl[o] Saxons, or the Latins. Don't think that if the Chinese get control of the world your position will be better, nor the Indians. All other races and nations will use you just the same as slaves, as under dogs.

Your only protection, therefore, is to have your own. Don't encourage Negroes to join Japanese movements, Chinese movements, Indian movements, or any other movement, with the hope of getting greater freedom. They will never get it because all peoples want all things for themselves.

Explain this thoroughly and sufficiently so as to discourage ignorant Negroes thinking otherwise. You should teach Negroes to have pride in their own nationality and not try to wear garments that typify membership in other nationalities—it is ridiculous and people laugh at them for so doing. Teach Negroes to look for honour in their own race and from their own nation and to serve their own race and nation to get such honours.

Any honours they can get from any other race for serving that race, they can get from their own for serving their own race. Don't waste time, therefore, in that. You can have your own king, your own emperor, your own pope, your own dukes, your own everything—therefore, don't bow down [to] other races for recognition.

When you have honoured your own men and women, recognise that honour before the whole world to let the world know that you honoured your own. If the world laughs at those you have honoured, ask them if you want them to laugh at those they honoured among themselves, for what is good for the goose is good for the gander. If they laugh, laugh at them.

A white king has no more right to drive in a golden coach than your king and sovereign. Their pope has no more right of putting on sacred robes than your pope. Their dukes and nobles have no more right to be dressed up in feathers than your dukes or nobles, therefore have pride in yourself and honour yourself.

Don't allow the other nations to get ahead of you in anything, follow the idea of the Japanese—every ship the ot/her/ races build, the Japanese build one, every university the oth/er/ races build for teaching men, the Japanese build one. Do the same. Always have your own because there will not be enough accom[m]odation for you later on. Create your own.

Every Japanese you see is working for the good of his nation, every white man you see is working for the good of his nation, teach every black man to work for the good of his nation. In conversation with him, never leave him until you have persuaded him to this line of thought.

Go to all your lawyers, doctors, ministers, and talk this into them. Argue with them until they perspire confession, go back and go back and talk till you get your man and let him work for a nation.

Always talk about a nation, always feel that you see the nation, use the object lessons of other nations to convince your people of the reality of a nation.

The sovereign of a people is in the nation. It is the result of a people, forming a society of their own to Govern themselves and to achieve their ends.

People with different outlooks and of different races never join together except they are subdued, they always find independent expression and action, and the highest is expressed in the sovereignty of a nation.

The flag of a nation is the emblem that signifies the existence of that nation. Have your flag—it is the red, black and green, and be proud of it as the emblem of your race. When other nations exhibit theirs, exhibit yours. Make songs about your nations and sing them, write poetry about your nation and read it and recite it. Glorify your nation in music and songs. Don't sing the songs of other races, don't recite the inspirational poems of othe[r] races, sing and recite your own.

Everything that inspires other races, turn into your own tune and fit it to suit your own inspiration and idealism. See only yourself in everything. Make your nation the highest expression of human idealism[,] the[n] live up to it.

LESSON 4

Elocution

Elocution means to speak out. That is to say, if you have a tale to tell, tell it and tell it well.

The idea of speaking is to convey information to others. You must, therefore, speak that they might hear you— to speak with dignity, with eloquence, with clearness and distinctiveness to be understood in the language you speak, to carry emphasis.

To be a good elocutionist you must embody in yourself clearness of thought, expression and action. You must first feel what you speak and as you feel it express it in like manner. If you feel the enthusiasm of a thing, express it with enthusiasm. Speech and truth should be just your feelings on all things. If you speak coldly or without emphasis it is because you feel coldly and not moved to action. Every man who is not tongue-tied by Nature can speak. God gave him a voice for that purpose, therefore if you have anything to say, say it out that others may hear you.

In addressing a crowd of people in a small room you must raise your voice to reach the farthest person in the room away from you. If you are addressing one hundred people you should raise your voice in expressing yourself loud enough for the person sitting farthest away from [you] to hear every word distinctly and in like manner if you have an audience of one thousand, two thousand or five thousand. If you stand up on a platform in front of an audience of a thousand and address them in the voice you would use for an audience of twelve feet by twelve feet, the people twelve feet away from you will not hear you and those farthes[t] away from you will have to strain their ears to hear and understand you. They will become disgusted and walk out on you. When you have an audience you must make effort for everybo[d]y in that audience to hear you distinctly. You must pronounce your words correctly for them to understand what you say. You must not run your words into each other but make them clear and distinct. You must not rush your sentences but speak in short sentences that carry clear thought[s] and everybody will be able to follow and understand what you say. The idea of listening is to hear. When an audience doesn't hear every word of the speaker[,] the speaker has failed to make a complete impression upon his audience. Probably the very thought he would like to leave is not suffficiently distinct and clear as to be heard, so the speech would be in vain.

Always speak in language of words that your audience understands. Never try to speak above your audienc[e]'s head because it would be a waste of time. Nobody would understand you. The important thing is to be understood in speaking. Always think first of what you are to say before you say it, otherwise you would be regarded as a fool for talking nonsense.

When you start a sentence in a speech always compl[e]te it. Never speak in long sentences because people cannot remember long sentences. When you are delivering a speech do so with emotion so that you feel what you are saying. Do not stand at one place like a mummy. People will think you are planted there. Put action behind your feelings and move as your feelings direct.

If you are honest in what you are saying you will feel it and it will move you. Always be enthusiastic over your subject. The way to do that is to know it well. Make your hands and feet and eyes give expression to your thoughts. Never express what is supposed to be an inspiration though without first giving expression to the thought. You can do that by the movement of your body according to the response of your own enthusiasm. You must hypnotise your audience by expression. Stare into their eyes and firmly express yourself. You must not shiver from their glare, you must make them shiver from yours. In that way you will subjugate them and make them do what you want, but this is first made possible by your honesty of purpose and confidence in yourself. If you are telling a lie you cannot subdue everybody or anybody that is looking straight at you, because he will see the lie in your eyes. If you have to tell a lie don't look at anybody. Your eyes will betray you. Whenever you see a speaker look away from the crowd into the c[ei]ling or at the walls, he is generally telling a lie. A person who is always facing his audience is never afraid of the truth.

Speak forcefully always and particularly at the beginning and middle and at the end of your speech. Start off in a little lower tone than five minutes after[,] then raise your vo[i]ce gradually until you have reached a convincing point in your speech then you may rest by lowering your tone to raise it again to get renewed interest, and continue the same way until you are about to reach the end, then redouble your efforts to win everybody over to you on what you were speaking. This is called your climax. Always sit down after you have made your speech with emphasis and then rise again to do anything else if you have more to do, such as raising a collection or asking for support. Don't let the people believe that all your efforts were just to get a collection. If you lift the collection the same time you make the speech they will think so, but make it immediately after the speech. That you made a good speech before, up to the end, they will listen to you even making a speech about the collection, but if the speech was no good you will have a no good collection.

To speak properly you must have sound and good teeth. You must have clear nostrils. Your lungs must be sound. You must have a healthy chest. Your stomach must not be over full and you must not be hungry. Never try to make a speech on a hungry stomach. You may faint and die before you are finished. If you have nasal obstruction go to the doctor and have it rectified. If you are suffering from lung trouble see the doctor. To be able to make a long speech for an hour or an hour and a half or two hours, you must treat and train your constitution. Your chest is the most serious part to be affected. If you haven't a strong chest you will feel exhausted in attempting to make a long speech. To prevent this, eat and suc[k] as many eggs as possible. You should eat eggs at least once a day, not hard but soft boiled or even raw if you can stand it. This will strengthen your chest and after a time it will become so hardened that you will speak five or six hours without feeling it. This must be done regularly and so long as you are going to indulge in public speaking you must eat eggs and use eggs. You should develop the disposition to drink water and sip it at intervals if your throat becomes th[ir]sty and dry. It is the most difficult thing to speak on a dry throat. All the straining you do will be of no effect because your words will be monotonous. There will be no harmony and rhythm, so soften your palate with water and bring back the music to your voice. You must never speak in a monotonous tone. Speaking is really music in another way. You must strike the different notes, play the different notes and let the people hear the sound and the harmony. This is done by giving each word its proper note, sound and emphasis. You must strike the right chord.

For goodness' sake, always speak out[.] Always speak loud enough for others to hear you except you have something to hide. The desire is to be heard, then let them hear you. Most preachers fail because their congregations do not hear them, especially Anglican Preachers. Negro Baptist Preachers, A.M.E. Preachers can raise more money than any other preachers because they talk loud enough to be heard and have more emotion in their expressions than other preachers. This is a hint. Such preachers are always fat, because they always have responsive congregations due to their ability to reach the congregation in telling them what they want. If you want anything told, tell it and tell it well that nobody will misunderstand so you must open your mouth and don't be afraid of [d]oing so except you have only gums and are afraid of people seeing the nakedness of your mouth.

Always try to avoid a cold because it is ruinous to any speaker. Whenever you catch one and have to speak[,] go to the drug store immediately and secure some speakers' tablets to clear away the phlegm. It is good to use eucalyptus for inhaling to keep the nostrils clear so as to give perfect sound to your words. Don't chew your words but talk them out plainly[;] otherwise no one will understand what you mean. Practice speaking to yourself in your room, in your own hall, drawing room or in any place where you are not disturbed. Go [to] the sea[,] beach or the woods and talk to yourself or to Nature to practise so as to command your expression and become accustomed. Never be afraid of your audience. If you know your subject well, you have no cause to be afraid. Always know your subject. Never make a long speech after ten o'clock at night. People will become restless and move away, because it is near bed time. If you are called upon to speak at ten o'clock or after take not more than fifteen minutes, but see to it if you are to speak anywhere that you are called not later than 9:30. At a certain hour of the night people are restless and tired and generally want to go home, they are never inclined to listen to speeches. Never apologise for any other speaker being better than you in an audience. Just rise to the occasion and try to beat the last man and let the audience judge. If you confess that any speaker is better than you, even though you are better the audience may still give the credit to the other man because you said so, by run[n]ing down your own ability.

Always see that your clothing is properly arranged before you get on a platform[;] otherwise people may see things to laugh at. Be careful not to make blu[n]ders in grammar because people may laugh loudly and expose you to others who are not thinking. You should not make any mistake in pronouncing your words because that also invites amusement for certain people and if they remember nothing else they may remember such mistakes and ever talk about them and create prejudice against you for it, so be careful.

When speaking you should always try to hold the people's interest in the best way you know. You may give a joke that is re[l]e[v]ant or logical in emphasizing your point. Never give vulgar jokes. To be a good speaker or elocutionist or orator is to hold a grand prize among men. If you can speak better than others you have a natural lead among them. Glory in this and strive after it, remembering that God gave you a mouth and a voice and you must use them for good results. Secure from any book seller a copy of a good book on elocution and study it.

LESSON 5

God

There is a God and we believe in Him. He is not a person nor a physical being. He is a spirit and He is universal intelligence. Never deny that there is a God. God being universal intelligence created the universe out of that intelligence. It is intelligence that creates. Man is a part of the creation of universal intelligence and man was created in the image and likeness of God only by his intelligence. It is the intelligence of man that is like God, but man's intelligence is only a unitary particle of God's universal intelligence.

God out of His universal intelligence made matter and made mind. That matter is made by God and man is matter as well as mind; then man must be in the image of God, because nothing could exist without God. As God made the universe out of His universal knowledge or intelligence so man in his unitary knowledge of intelligence can make a typewriter, an automobile or a chair, but cannot make the universe because his unitary intelligence is not as much or as great as universal intelligence. All the unitary intelligence of the universe goes to make God who is the embodiment of all intelligence, so no man can be as great as God because he is only a unit of God and God is the whole.

No man therefore can measure God nor ask God questions because he is not as intelligent as God and therefore cannot understand God. It is presumpt[u]ous therefore, when man questions God from his limited unitary intelligence.

Man never dies. Nothing dies. Man is made of body and spirit. The spirit is God. It is intelligence. The body of man is matter. It changes from living matter in the man to other matter in the soil. It is always the same matter. It doesn't die in the sense of how we understand death. It changes. When man sleeps and passes away in the flesh he goes to earth that lives on, out of which other men and things are formed. All matter is related so man is related to earth and the earth related to man. We eat ourselves over and over again. When we eat the apple, the banana, the fig, the cherry, the grape, when we drink the water, we are eating and drinking ourselves over and over again, so nothing is lost and nothing dies, so do not be afraid of death, because what you call death is only change and you are still in the universe either in the spirit of God to whom your spirit goes after the change or as matter which goes on forever.

You are related to the flower, to the beautiful rose, to the trees, to the fish and to the other animals just as you are related to God.

All of you sprung from God who is universal intelligence. Do not be more cowardly than the rose, the apple, the coconut, the sheep, the fish or the cow to do that which all must, and which we call death, to die. If you are going to weep to die then the ro[s]e should weep to die. If you weep you are a coward. Die like a man because you are not lost, you are still there. You only weep because you are a glutton, because you think you will not get any more to eat and drink and any more happy times[;] just as you have been feeding upon things, and other beings who came here before you, so someone else must feed on you to make creation true, otherwise God would not be fair to everybody and everything and God is fair and just and no respector of persons or things.

> It's everlasting, as we know—
> This THING we call Mysterious Life;
> It had no beginning some say,
> It's just a Constant Moving Flow;
> It goes from this, then back to that,
> And on it moves, in course well planned,
> That circles universe and all,
> Thus passing through each single lot.

Your life and mine is one long psalm,
In tune with that of other beings,
And everything that breathe[s] the Air,
In seasons rough and seasons calm;
One source they say contains the germ
That grows in range of Universe,
And all go back to this one Cause,
Whose life supplies the spreading sperm.

By being part of Source Divine
Each life has functions strictly drawn,
For all must bow to endless time,
In form and shape that mark each line;
So man must yield his flesh to dust,
With plants and weeds and birds and fish—
With rocks and mounts, and lilies too,
As trees break up in fibre crust.

Each one should like to hold his own,
And be a king in self alone,
But this IS NOT the way of LIFE,
That claims but ONE ALMIGHTY CROWN;
Thus disappointed, man grieves on,
For he should like his own strange way,
When suns and stars and steady moons
Would dance and change to suit his clan.

It's safer then to have one God,
Whose life is first and ever so,
And all the rest to live in Him,
With all the good they ever had.
For fleshy man would [r]uin things,
If he controlled the Source of Life;
The day would see an endless change
From slaves who crawl to haughty kings.

Live on good God of timeless Worth!
And keep man in his place to love,
That when he rises to the height,

He might perform his good on earth,
For life right here is sad today,
As lived by man in company,
If earth goes on, Thy grave should come,
To lead us all in goodness' way.

"THE EVERLASTING LIFE"
BY MARCUS GARVEY

LESSON 6

Christ

The doctrine of God carries with it the belief of the Father, Son and Holy Ghost. Christ is supposed to be the begotten Son of God. He had a special mission and that was to take on the form of man, to teach man how to lift himself back to God. For that reason Christ was born as man and came to the world.

If Christ as man never existed, but was only an assumption it would have been a glorious assumption to set man a spiritual high example of how he should live.

There is no cause to doubt that Christ lived, not because you did not see him yourself and feel him yourself or touch him yourself as Thomas did why should you doubt his existence, for if you can doubt that, you may as well doubt that your great grandfather ever lived, because you never saw him nor touched him, but logically there is fair assumption for you to believe that your grandfather whom you knew must have had a father, to be born must have had such a father, and he must have logically been your great grandfather.

You haven't to see everything to believe it, you must trust those who lived before you on good reason to believe that somebody or something existed before you came here, so never doubt that Christ lived and never doubt that God lived, because great things happened to prove that before you came into the world.

Deny that positively which you know of, and not that which you do not know of.

The New Testament reveals the life of Christ as an exemplary one. His life was faultless to a word. It is evident, therefore, that he must have been a superior creature.

If he had played the devil and behaved like the devil there would have been no example to lead us to the perfection of God. So that his life was perfect is evident and fair assumption that he was the begotten Son of God.

The greatest thing that Christ taught was love. Love thy neighbour as thyself, do unto others as you would have them do to you. In these statements are wrapt up the highest idealism of a Godhead in the relationship of a father with his children. There has been no greater philos[o]phy in the history of mankind. Support this philosophy and never change until God manifest[s] himself to the contrary, which is not likely[.]

It is evident that Christ had in his veins the blood of all mankind and belonged to no particular race. Christ was God in the perfect sense of his mind and soul. His spirit was truly God's spirit, his soul which acted on the advi[c]e of God's spirit was never corrupt.

Christ's soul was the free-will thought that is similar to the soul free-will thought of all men. Whilst other men with their free-will souls become corrupt and do evil even under the guidance of the Holy spirit of God, Christ with his free-will soul never disobeyed the Holy Spirit guide of God.

In every man there is the spirit of God, that is to say, that which is there to advise you and direct you to do good always, and in each man also is the free-will soul which is the mind. Each may accept the good guidance of the Holy Spirit or refuse to obey entirely.

Man generally disobeys the Holy Spirit of goodness and, therefore, becomes sinful. Christ never disobeyed the Holy Spirit of goodness, and that was why he was the Son of man with whom the spirit of God was well pleased, because he lived a life so perfect as was intended when God made Adam and Eve.

The mission of Christ, therefore, was to redeem man from sin and place him back on the pinnacle of goodness as God intended when he made the first two creatures.

The life of Christ is intended to show man that he could

lift himself by obedience to the highest soul expression in keeping with the Holy Spirit of God of which he is a part, but only with free-will. A free will can do as he likes. Man has a body, a soul which is hi[s] own identification of himself and the Holy Spirit of God.

In the vilest man, there is the Holy Spirit of God and that man cannot destroy the Holy Spirit of God because that spirit in him is the unit of God which cannot sin and cannot die because it is everlasting goodness.

The thing that sins in man is the man's individual soul which is his mind. When man corrupts this mind or soul, he is called bad, and is in rebellion against the Holy Spirit of God that is in him.

When he dies, as we know and call death, whether he dies a bad man or a good man, the Holy Spirit never dies, it goes right back to God, the everlasting goodness.

It is the soul of the man which identifies him as a unit of creation that passes away if it is bad and lives on like Christ if it is good. You can judge the truth of this philosophy from your own experience—try to remember how you think[,] if it is not a fact that sometimes there is something in you that tells you do this, and another something at the same time tells you do that, the Holy Spirit, which is goodness, is always telling you and advising you to do the right thing, but your free-will soul which is mind refuses to accept the instructions and advice of goodness.

There is always a debate with one's self to know what to do. You must analyze your system and your being so completely as to know when you are being advised by the Holy Spirit of goodness and follow that advice. If you can satisfactorily do that, then you can be like Christ and lift yourself to the highest plane of spirit and human life.

THE HOLY GHOST

The Holy Ghost is the spirit of God at large. It is everywhere. It is really what we call the spirit.

In everything that you see, there is the spirit of the Holy

Ghost, but man can be a complete manifestation of that spirit, for as a unit in him the spirit becomes responsible and lives and acts.

The Holy Ghost is the perfect spirit of God's intelligence which is distinct from matter as particles of creation. No particle can exist in nature without the knowledge of God because God created it, but a particle may not contain the spirit of the Holy Ghost. When life is given and thought is to be expressed there we have the spirit of the Holy Ghost.

A bit of iron may not have the spirit of the Holy Ghost, but in man there are the elements of iron as well as other elements, and the complete thoughtfulness of man is made up of all these elements which give existence to the spirit of the Holy Ghost, just as all things are related and man is related to all things in nature.

So God is everywhere in nature, but the spirit of the Holy Ghost is only in the higher thought life, and the highest thought life we know is man. The Holy Ghost spirit is always in man.

THE DOCTRINE OF THE TRINITY OF GOD THE FATHER, THE SON and the HOLY GHOST is not commonly understandable to the ordinary mind that will not think in the guiding spirit of God, but to the mind that thinks with the spirit of God it is very pleasingly understood that the Godhead is one in three parts all related and all doing good, you cannot separate them. This may be a mystery which the ordinary intelligence of man cannot explain because man is not God in intelligence, but nevertheless it explains the riddle of the universe. It is preposterous for man to say that he can analyze God in his completeness because man is only a finite and small unit of Divine and universal intelligence, hence his limited intelligence cannot ascend completely to universal intelligence. So whilst universal intelligence can analyze unitary intelligence, unitary intelligence cannot analyze universal intelligence.

So leave out trying to be like God by demanding from God in mental analysis why he does [or] why he does not do the other thing. You are not competent. No part is greater than the whole. The whole is always greater than any single part and man is only a single part of God, so he cannot be as great in mind as God.

There is a confusion of expression between mind, soul and heart. These expressions are used with laxity. In fact, they all mean the same thing. The soul of man is the mind of man and when we speak of the heart, not the physical thing, but the expressive thing, we mean the soul which is the mind, so remember always that you have the body which is a physical u-case [Eucharist?] for the soul which is the mind and which is the heart in the sentimental sense of the heart expressing itself.

The spirit is greater than all and it is the Holy Ghost and God in man. The spirit advises the soul, guides the soul and guards the soul and when it is disgusted with the behaviour of the soul, it leaves the physical body and the physical body does what we all call die, but in fact, the physical body does not die, it changes back to matter in a different form. It may become earth again from which flowers and vegetation grow and bloom and from which man eats back himself in the form of fruit and vegetable life; so nothing is lost in nature and nothing really dies because everything is God's that is eternal and everlasting.

A good soul may pass away in what you call death, like a bad soul, but that soul has also an everlasting identity that may pass into some higher realm of usefulness, probably to become an angel or to be used by God in some higher sphere.

The wicked soul never comes back, it goes out, and that is man's hell. Its going out is called "going to hell," because it never lives as a soul again. A good soul, therefore[,] lives forever. A bad [s]oul passes out when the spirit of God has left the body in which the soul is found, but the soul is judged before it completely disappears, and will recognize its punishment in the judgment before God, then is obliterated completely.

You can worship God by yourself. You are responsible to God by yourself. You have to live your own soul before God. Nobody but yourself can save your soul. Others may advise you because of your ignorance of life how to shape your soul.

Keep in communion with God. But none can save your soul but yourself in your soul relationship with God. Therefore, always worship with your own heart, soul and mind when you want to commune with God; make your heart, soul or mind your altar and express it in the following way:—

I've built a sacred place all mine,
To worship God, who is Divine,
I go there every day, in thought,
Right to my own, dear sacred heart—
MY ALTAR.

No one can change me in my mood,
For I do live on God's sweet food,
He feeds me every day, with love,
While angels look at it above—
MY ALTAR.

When all the world goes wrong without,
I never hold one single doubt,
For I do find a great relief,
When I do trust my own belief—
MY ALTAR.

I see the Saviour of the world,
Whose light to all has been unfurled,
He utters agonizing plea,
With shining eyes that surely see—
MY ALTAR.

I shall remain with faith of rock
To see the Shepherd lead His flock
And when He comes to claim each heart,
My yield shall be in wholesome part—
MY ALTAR.

"MY ALTAR"

Man was redeemed by Christ to reach the perfect state as man through his soul. The symbol of the Christ was the Cross in sentiment, therefore, man adores the Cross.

The black man has a greater claim to the Cross than all other men. If it is a symbol of Christ's triumph then the Negro should share in that triumph that Simon the Cyrenian who bore it, did. Every Negro, therefore, should claim the Cross as Simon the Cyrenian did. The shortest prayer we may give to God, even if we never pray otherwise, is by making the sign of the cross and by saying at the same time, in the name of the Father, the Son and the Holy Ghost. It is a powerful prayer. It supersedes all others, and if the words are repeated sincerely and earnestly from the heart, God answers that prayer. Do it always.

In going to bed you need not make a long prayer. Make the sign of the Cross and repeat the words the Catholics do. The Catholics appreciate the value of the Cross, and that is why they make the sign of the Cross as a part of their religion but they have no right to the Cross because they crucified Christ on the Cross.

The Cross is the heritage of the black man, don't give it up. This has nothing to do with the Roman Catholic religion. This is our religion and our interpretation of the significance of the Cross and Christ.

When it is said, "thou shalt not kill" it is meant thou shall not kill the soul because the soul is the personality of man. It does not mean flesh because the flesh is matter and passes from one stage to another. By change, it is always matter but the soul if it does wickedness and evil dies, it only lives when it is perfect in keeping with God's goodness. Therefore, when it is said "thou shalt not kill" it means you must not kill the soul of man.

This is how the warriors interpret it such as Napoleon and the Emperors and Pharaohs and the old religious warriors who fought battles among men. This is how the Israelites interpreted it when they fought against the Philistines. This is how Joshua interpreted it when he fought against the

Canaanites. This is how it shall ever be because man shall ever be at war with man in the fight of good against evi[l].

> Leaf after leaf drops off, flower
>   after flower,
> Some in the chill, some in the
>   warmer hour;
>
> Alive they flo[u]r[i]sh, and alive
>   they fall,
> And Earth who nourished them
>   receives them all.
> Should we, her wiser sons, be
>   less content
> To sink into her lap when life is
>   spent?

"LEAF AFTER LEAF DROPS OFF"
BY WALTER SAVAGE LANDOR

LESSON 7

Character

Men and women who want to be of use to themselves and humanity must have good character. Good character means that kind of behaviour and demonstration of it that will meet with the moral precepts of a civilization. The standard that is laid down by the society of the time in which you live, and which forms a part of and guides that very character.

If you do not live up to it in the highest sense, you will not be respected by that society. Your mission in that society for useful work will fall to pieces.

The greatest prop to character is honesty. Honesty is the best policy. Let no one believe that you are dishonest. If they believe you are dishonest, you are doomed and can never rise in any position of respect and trust except by some mere accident. You must live so clean that everybody can see the cleanliness of your life.

Never let people believe you are a liar, but the contrary. Let them believe you always speak the truth and live up to it.

Any conduct that your community or society condemns, be careful not to violate the rule or law because you will lose the respect of that community.

Never borrow money except you intend to pay it back, and do it as quickly as you can. If you give excuses when you should be paying, those you are obligated to will think you a trickster and even though you subsequently pay them, they will be loath to trust you a second time. Even if you have to make sacrifices, pay your debts because when you don't pay your debts, people talk about it and sooner or later everybody in the community knows about it and you are ruined.

It is a good policy to keep a good name and an honourable name. It is good credit, people will trust you on a good name; they will ask for the cash right on the spot and count it to the last farthing if your name is bad. People who trust you will almost take money from you without counting it. When you have lost that much confidence you are a marked object and you may as well move from that town or city or community to start life afresh somewhere else where nobody knows you, where you may practice the higher principles and retrieve your name.

Never move into a nearby nor adjoining community if you have lost your name. In the first place, go far away from it. No leader can hold his leadership who is dishonest. Nobody will follow him. Let your good character so shine that men will see it and talk of it.

Morality is upheld everywhere in civilization. Don't be immoral in your community, somebody will tell on you and expose you, and the homes of the community will be closed against you and respectable people will shun you.

If you have to be immoral because your nature is weak, then hide it—keep it within closed doors and be sure nobody knows about it.

If you read good books and think loftily, you will not be immoral. If you are intelligent, you will not be immoral because immorality leads to disease, to pain, to suffering and ultimately to premature death.

An immoral person cannot find good company because no good person wants to take the chance with immorality, so those who cater to your immorality must be people who have no character and who have nothing to lose. They must be either sick or diseased themselves and therefore, don't care.

No respectable woman or man who cares about his or her future is going to be indiscriminate because that is taking chances. Therefore, when you find a person of immoral habits, it is someone who has lost all proportions of decency and health and doesn't care. Such a person is a social danger.

Sensible people do not give themselves away for nothing, but sick people and diseased people, like a drowning man, catch at a straw. Never be seen with these people in your community or a person of bad character. You will be roped in and even though your character be good, it will also suffer because of your association with that person.

If you have to keep company with the opposite sex, let your companionship be consistent and steady with one person. Don't run around always with different people of the opposite sex. This does not mean that you must not associate socially with all the people of your class, it means if your name is to be linked up in the community as directly interested socially let it be that one person but don't run about with several.

As a leader, never flirt or indicate that you are a flirt[.] Never try to make love to two persons in the same organization, where both attend and you are a member at the same time, a fight will ensue and scandal will spread and you will lose your reputation. If you have to speculate with your love, keep the parties far apart, at least in different communities, but not in the same town, because it would leak out and be whispered and you would be called a bad person.

Mostly all the deformities in a community are the result of immoral and loose people cutting loose. Sick people never produce good children. Disease in man is destructive. It destroys the species and wrecks the mind of man. The first thought a healthy man has of a poor minded man is that his parents were immoral and stamped their immorality on him which he is to carry through the world by his particular affectation, be it in poor mentality or in nerve disability.

Don't be a public drunkard, don't drink inordinately, you may contract disease by so over drinking, and water your brain to that of deterioration. Don't take drugs or narcotics as a habit, they will have the same effect. Be temperate in everything you do. Learn in this respect self-control. By self-control you can conquer every bad habit. You can do so by concentrating on the thought always that the habit is bad and will ruin you, and say to yourself, "I shall not be ruined, I shall conquer you my bad habit." Say this and repeat it day after day, until you conquer the habit. Let the habit be your opponent and then fight your opponent and beat it. Never give up until you conquer. If you follow this rule, you will beat down every bad habit.

Always see the injury that the bad habit will do you, and if you don't want that injury done to your health, to mind and body to bring pain, worry and unhappiness, then fight it to the death. This is what is called "man mastering himself."

Anything that is not good rise above it and be its master. Don't be a public nuisance. Don't go out in public untidy or poorly dressed, keep always a good and clean personality.

Always bathe your skin and do so at least once a day, if not convenient, not less than three times a week. A dirty body emits bad odour, and causes people to shun you by drawing away from you. You yourself if you know you are dirty lose confidence in yourself, when you approach other people because you are always afraid that they are going to find out that you are not clean. It makes you nervous and lose your balance and sense of proportion.

When a man is clean in body, clean in appearance, clean in mind, he feels like a giant and a master and is afraid of nothing. Lacking these qualities he cringes, bows and hides. He is never himself.

Don't eat like a hog even in private, a custom or habit will develop on you and you will do it unconsciously. Observe good manners in eating and drinking when you go among company.

If you are invited to dine with friends and you are hungry, eat a little before you get to dinner, so as not to show how hungry you are, because if you eat up everything you[r] host will talk about you when you are gone. He or she and the rest of friends will talk about your gluttony and you may never be invited the second time.

Be courteous and gentlemanly everywhere. Be kind to and practice the respect for all children. Develop the habit of playing with children and treating them decently, the news will spread. Children will tell their parents and the parents will get to love you.

Never abuse a woman in public. Never abuse a man in

public. Never make a noise in your home. Never abuse your wife or your husband in public. Never make a fight where you are living or anywhere else in public.

If you are angry to the point of fighting, count ten and move off. If it is with your wife or family or relatives and friends, take your hat and go for a walk. In-hale the fresh air, look at the sky, look at the landscape, look at the flowers, look at the stars and new thoughts will come into your mind, and you will forget your anger—or go to your room, lock up yourself and take from your bookshelf a book of poetry and read the beautiful thoughts of the poet. You may even read the Bible for consolation, read the proverbs and the Psalms and you will come back to normal.

Never fall in love to the point of losing control over yourself, for if you do so, you will become somebody else's slave and that experience will surely take advantage of you and cause you to lose your best character.

Never love anybody for companionship except [that] person has the majority of qualities that you like and appreciate. Never love a person most for his or her physical appearance, or personality, investigate first the character, disposition, temperament and behaviour and thoughts of the person and when you find in that person along with good physical appearance such as you like all the qualities or as many of them as possible that would tend to satisfy you and make you happy through a lifetime, then love that person, but never love anybody better than yourself, for you are responsible for yourself to God. Only love God better than yourself.

Don't believe anybody loves you honestly in the truest sense of the word. It is something you have or something they can get from you generally why they love you or pretend to love you. When that something fails, you generally find that you were never loved which is always too late, so don't put your absolute Divine trust in human love, because man is bad and is susceptible to change.

If when you love one for qualities you think the person possesses and they are not fully developed, help the person to develop them for your own good happiness.

It is better you wait to find the person with the majority of qualities you like, than to rush into loving for a minimum of those qualities, for as soon as you get over your passion, you will still be searching for those other qualities and since that person has not got them, you will seek them otherwise and then break up your happiness.

It is best for people not to get married until they are about 30 or 35 when they have had enough time to see everything and understand everything. Don't try to get too many children, you will find it a burden and then your love will turn into misery and unhappiness.

Never wear clothes as if you were sleeping in them. In women it leaves a suspicion, in men it suggests untidiness. Never wear a dirty collar or a dirty pair of shoes; keep your finger nails clean and your teeth clean. Take salts or purgatives twice a week at least to keep your system clean. It helps to give you clear thought and vision and keeps your health in perfect state. A dirty breath is due to a foul stomach which is not clean. People will shun you if your breath is dirty. You may notice people drawing away from the faces of other people when they are talking immediately before them, and it is because such person[']s breath is foul. It betrays you to the person and to all who are observing.

Sometimes by keeping a foul breath, tiny flies hover around your mouth and everybody knows that your breath is foul. A Leader cannot be in that position because when he is addressing the crowd, they will be visible objects telling to [the?] audience how foul his breath is.

Remember a leader must be honest. You have your character to maintain. You can only mainain it by good conduct. Never try, therefore, to feel [fool?] anybody or deceive anybody.

Never fabricate nor falsify—if the thought should ever come to you, count the consequence and the risk—it may be your last chance, and it may be your first mistake. Most men suffer from their first mistake from which they never recover.

In working for the U.N.I.A. prefer death to stealing from the U.N.I.A. because if you steal from the U.N.I.A.

hundreds of millions of people will concentrate on you when they find it out, and you will be exposed if you are found out[.] They will have your picture before them to hate, to despise, curse and to damn; therefore play honest with the U.N.I.A. and its principles all the time because you are dealing with the destiny of a race.

As you will not steal from the U.N.I.A. do not encourage anyone to steal nor shield anyone in stealing—expose him. Life is too short to reform a thief. If he steals once, he will steal again; don't pardon him, therefore when he steals from the U.N.I.A. because we must speed up to get to the end. To waste time to correct a thief is to hold up the programme of the organisation. Get him out of the way and march along.

Before you steal from the U.N.I.A. beg the U.N.I.A. Ask for help from the U.N.I.A. but never, never steal.

Never make love to another man's wife, there is always bound to be trouble. It creates scandal which you will never be able to stop. It will ultimately ruin your reputation. Leave another man's wife alone, and a woman should do the same, in leaving another woman's husband alone. There has never been a case where doing such a thing has ever ended without a scandal. David was punished for it and nearly lost the Kingdom of God.

LESSON 8

The Social System

Society is an organisation of mankind to safeguard and protect its own interest. When society is organised and is made evident by regulations, rules, and laws, every member of that society must obey the said rules, regulations and laws.

Always, therefore, live up to the organised system of society of which you form a part. The only alternative to this is rebellion. You should never join rebellious movements against society except there is good reason and justification for it.

Society is intended to maintain the greatest good for the greatest number, and that is always uppermost so that in thought you may have to reform. Any society must be calculated to bring about the greatest good for the greatest number, and you must obey its laws, otherwise you are an evil genius living in the midst of that society and that society will seek to destroy you or compel you to obey its rules, regulations and laws.

You cannot live by yourself in a society, you must live upon the goodwill of your fellows. In that society, therefore, you must respect everything that tends to the good of all.

You should always seek to have something at stake in the community in which you live—property of some kind, so as to merit the regard and respect of the community, because society as organised into a community counts first its worthwhile citizens before it thinks of others.

Property in a community is an evidence of your status in the society of the community. If you have no property, have value of some kind to be considered substantial. The police, the officials and the government recognise property holders as the citizens of first claim in an organised society. They are generally recorded to be identified. You must, therefore, teach the people to own property and to be known and recognised members of the community.

Always adopt a friendly attitude to the police in your community, because the police is that civil body of officials who are supposed to protect the citizens and see that their right is not infringed upon. You should always welcome the police. The police are never the public enemy, but the public protector.

You should help the police to maintain order because if the community loses its peace, you will have riots and probably bloodshed. No peaceful citizen wants to be caught in such a dangerous state of public affairs.

Never join to incite public disorder. Keep away from it and be innocent to all that happens, by way of revolution. Never allow the U.N.I.A.'s name to be mentioned as among rioters, you will destroy the usefulness of the organisation in that community and may cause suspicion to be cast upon it in other communities.

Disavow always any attempt to label the U.N.I.A. with riotous behaviour. Whatsoever object is desired in a civilised community it can always be achieved by the approach of good reason and good judgment. Always use that good reason and good judgment.

You are not in a community to overthrow the law in that community, you are there to live under the law. The national aspiration of the race is to find expression not in revolution where you are established when you are under other people's government, but to accomplish the end in Africa. Therefore, never preach rebellion because you will disrupt the society in which you live and it will crush you.

The highest service a citizen can refer to in a community or organised society is to maintain and preserve peace. When the peace is disturbed, it is likely that anybody may get hurt and sometimes most innocently.

Never join the [m]ob, you will likely be shot or injured

even for curiosity. If you are once shot or injured in a riotous demonstration, it is almost evidence against you that you were one of the rioters, so keep away.

When the riot act or martial law is read or proclaimed in your community, keep indoors. Give this advice to the people.

Never join a mob in a foreign country under a foreign government or where you have very little political influence.

POLITICAL PULL

Politics is the science of government that protects those human rights that are not protected by law. Law is already established. Politics add to the laws or change the laws. You should play politics to get good government.

It is advisable that you become a tax payer of some kind or qualified under the statute to be a voter in your community.

To be a voter, you must have the franchise. To have the franchise you must register as a citizen. Always be a citizen of where you are. When you become a citizen seek to know all other citizens or as many as possible in your district, you may need them and they may need you for political action to insure good government.

The state, the nation or the community in which you live directly is always governed by politicians or statesmen. You should know them and become well acquainted with them for your own good. You need them in trouble and out of trouble.

Always try to know the Mayor of your city and the government of your state or island, or country and also other government officials. To know them before trouble is to get help when you are in trouble; not to know them is to be at a disadvantage when you are brought before them. Always treat them courteously and friendly even if you don't mean it, but let them always believe you are friendly.

If you are to be a leader in your community this makes it even more imperative that you should know everybody of political consequence, because you will have to approach them not only for yourself and for the organization, but, for the members of the race who look up to you as their leader.

You must never sell yourself to the politician, but you must get around him in the most skilful manner and get all your rights and the rights of others dependent on you out of him without selling yourself to him, to keep him in office, especially if he is not a good man in the community.

Always make your vote count for bringing about the reforms you and others think are right for your community. Never exchange it for money. You should see that every citizen who has a vote does vote on an election day, especially when you have reforms to be enacted.

Whatsoever may be the conditions that give you the suffrage, live up to those conditions to maintain and hold the suffrage, because just at the time when your vote may be most needed may be the time when you are not qualified because of carelessness.

In countries where as a race you are not allowed to vote, work always to get the vote by way of reform. Use the help of everybody, but have political power to bring about the change that will give you the vote, otherwise you would be governed without your consent.

To vote is to make the attempt to share in the government of the community with others. You should never be a political slave in a community because others will take advantage of you.

Always cast your ballot for good government. Never support a corrupt government.

APPROACH TO GOVERNMENT

Always make your government know about your presence. Never hide from the government. Whenever possible, seek an interview with the government on behalf of the people you lead.

Always impress government that your movement is not to controvert the established order of that government, but that your people seek a homeland in Africa which is not to be achieved by any revolution in the country in which you domicile as a citizen, but if possible with the co-operation of that government.

Leave all policies of an international character affecting the organization desired for a government in Africa to the international officers and don't complicate yourself with your government with anything revolutionary where you are. You will get the worst of it.

A constitutional political agitation is not a riot. If you are a citizen, you have the right of public assembly and the right to protest against anything that is politically wrong, but that does not suggest that you must riot because good government always puts down riots and always has a way to settle its political difficulties in the interest of society and the community of which you are a part, and in which you have a voice.

When you riot against your government, you are rioting against yourself because the government cannot exist without you. That is why there is a constitution. When the constitution is insufficient to give you all the protection you need change it by political action through voting for changes, not by rioting.

LESSON 9

Diplomacy

Diplomacy is a word used to express the peculiar relationship between nations in which they carry on or conduct their correspondence or approach in dealing with matters of state and affecting the relationship of a certain nature between them. In the broader sense, it means the thoughtful and careful consideration of thought expressed to reduce the expression and the thought to the minimum of offence, yet carrying with it force of what is desired to the maximum.

To be a diplomat, one has to be very careful in his expressions before indulging in them. He thinks seriously and calculatingly that his thoughts and words may have the desired effect without arousing suspicion or inviting hostility.

You must first be a very skillful thinker and psychologist to be a diplomat. A diplomat never reveals his true state of mind or his hand in dealing with the situation. He always keeps in reserve a line of defence for whatsoever he says or does.

A diplomat never talks before he thinks. He thinks over the things several times before he expresses it. The idea is that he must not be found wanting or on the wrong side of any question; if he does, his diplomacy fails. He must be able to read other people's minds and intentions and use that knowledge to safeguard and protect hi[m]self and the interest he represents.

A skillful diplomat is always master of the situation. He is able to fool others or deceive them to gain his point. He never exposes himself to be taken advantage of. He always leaves a loophole for escaping from any danger or trouble with which he is to deal.

His language is always couched in a manner to carry weight in the particular direction, but at the same time not to be so offensive or revealing as to cause the person dealt with to immediately jump at conclusions by the completeness of the thought expressed. In fact, a diplomat always gives out expressions that carry a double or more meanings, so that if the one interpretation is dangerous to effecting good relationship, he can always fall back and say it was not intended that way.

In diplomacy, if you mean to take advantage of the other person, never open a suggestion, but gauge your words most carefully to ultimately win that in view without expressing it in the raw.

A good way to get good results is to actually feed your opponent with good words that mean nothing and then when you come down to the business part, hold your ground but still use good and pleasant words to win.

Never approach anybody that you want to get anything out of or any good results from in an offensive manner, but to the contrary—win with the perfect smile in the most gentle of manner. Do this even to your enemy until your enemy has positively delivered himself and there is no other alternative, then show your hand but never show your hand at the start. The idea is to make friends and get results rather than to make enemies and lose results. This must be applied to all phases of organisation work dealing with the race and dealing with others of other races.

It is said that a kind word turneth away wrath. It is good diplomacy. Even if a man is going to kill you by threatening you, it is best to smile with him before he actually carries out the intention, so as to prevent him, by showing a smile rather than to suggest the gravity of your indignation to cause him to think that you are going to kill him first, because he will surely kill you in self-defense, even though he first threatened you. Many a man has been killed when his assailant did not really mean to kill him but only to bluff him, but in taking the matter too seriously and showing that he is going to do some killing too, he gets killed by the man, so as to protect himself following his threat from being killed.

Never lose your head in dealing with a problem because in doing so you are bound to blunder and ultimately lose. Even if you are in an accident where you are coming face to face with death, don't lose your head because you may need your calm and collective judgement to save your life. The moment you lose your head, you are taking chances— the odds are against you.

Morally a diplomat must be a scamp, in that he must be a mental twister. He could not deal with affairs with a very clean conscience because he is to anticipate the evil of other men's designs, in that the world and mankind are immoral and dishonest in their behaviour. He perforce has to adopt such a method as to safeguard himself or his interest from such designs.

You cannot be a true Christian before the act, but become so after by repentance which is personal.

If you are protecting the interest of others, you have to sink your own personality but still recognize the fact that you are responsible to those others, so you have to adopt all the methods of diplomacy to protect others, hence, you cannot do so on a very Christian soul because most of the soul[s] you are dealing with are corrupt.

After you have dealt with them and have won your point, if there was any act that was immoral or crooked which enabled you to win your point, then pray afterwards for forgiveness, but not before, but be sure that the act is done and leave the act where it is if it is in the interest of others, then square your conscience with God.

If the truth is going to affect your cause then never speak it but go around it in every kind of ambiguous way as to justify your lie to save the cause. But if you have won your cause by a lie, then as early as possible try to make the cause right. But only after you have won, for no cause can continue successfully without righteousness of the thing from all your imaginative experience.

Never give up in seeking support. If one logic fails,

use another until you have talked out your opponent by semblance of justification. You may say, "I don't mean so and so. It was not the way I intended it, I have a different idea entirely, you are misunderstanding me, you have a misconception of what I mean, probably you didn't hear when I said so and so, I may admit that I was not clear enough, but I didn't mean what you say." Then be able to build up a new argument on that and let the thing that you are arguing about take a back seat, so that they will forget what you were arguing about and take you up on the other things you have said and make that the debate; thereby leaving the situation where it was for another time.

Always try to lead the other fellow away from the true idea, if you are on the wrong side and build up a new argument and hold him on that until you have worn him out. Let him say that is not the argument, then still persist in something else.

Always profess friendship for your enemy so as to disarm him. Don't refer to him as Mr. Brown, say my good friend Mr. Brown. I cannot understand why my good friend is so opposed to me, I have always thought of him as a kindly disposed man and a very good fellow. But always watch him, don't take any chances.

Offer your enemy gifts that you can afford to lose, so as [t]o win him like the Greeks bringing gifts. Your words must be formed and be positive whe[n] you want to commit other people. As for instance "do you intend to pay my money?" "Have you made up your mind to answer my letter?" Let it always be a question with the answer *yes* or *no*.

Don't suggest to anybody long sentences. When you ought to commit yourself, do so in veiled language and never finally commit yourself until you are ready to close the matter.

Always try to escape giving yes or no to any question that is important. If you have to say yes or no, do so in long explanations, so that you may escape out of the explanation from the positive answer.

If trouble is involved it becomes your defence. Try always to leave in your remark or words room for controversy or denial of meaning as decided on by the other party.

When you want to protect yourself and trap the other fellow, let him write you short sentences by leading him up to such a manner of reply, but when you have to answer, make your sentences long and capable of taking many interpretations.

If you want to close the matter directly to your interest, then clinch it by accepting his argument in short sentences that cannot be misunderstood in law or arbitration.

When you are inviting explanations, make your sentences very short and to the point. When you are asked to give explanations, consider carefully if you should make your sentences long or short—use discretion.

Always allow the other fellow to talk first by leading him. Let him talk of everything in his manner, so that you may know your man.

Never let him lead you out. Always be reserved in a word; be a good listener, then when you have everything on the other fellow, decide the situation and take action.

To get a man to talk, offer him courtesy—like a drink, a cigar, "it is a beautiful day isn't it? How have you been keeping lately? Are you comfortable where you live? What do you think of so and so?["]

If he is reticent, you know you have a hard customer to deal with. Then find out his weakness by investigation and when you find it, invite him back again and cater to that weakness.

His weakness may be for ladies—invite him to meet your best friend and get your friend to pump him and tell you what you could not get from him yourself and if it is the opposite sex, do the same thing.

If he is addicted to drinking, give him a few extra glasses and let him talk, but you must not drink as much yourself otherwise you will be in the same position, but use your skill in letting him believe that you are drinking too, but don't drink.

If you cannot get him by himself, get his friend to tell you all he knows about him, but if the knowledge possessed by the person is important to you, never stop following him even if you have to go 6,000 miles, directly or indirectly, to get your information. You may get it through an agent, through a neighbour of his or business people he deals with, but follow every clue of an association until you get your information about the subject.

Never accept invitations from your enemies. Always find some excuse with kind thanks. If you have once injured a man, never trust him completely because he is always waiting his chance to get even with you.

Never talk your personal business or the business of your cause to a stranger whom you don't know. Tell him nothing until you know him sufficiently.

Don't accept complete friendship on first approach, but find out carefully if he or she is worthy of being a good and true friend, otherwise you may find yourself in the ditch.

Never give valuable papers or anything of value to a first acquaintance or a cordial friend or neighbour to keep. If the documents are very valuable, by way of information, don't allow even members of your own household to keep them.

Keep them secretly and privately because you don't know who may give you away—even innocently. There is always a *third person* in everybody's life. *Be careful* of that third person. [T]hat person may come in between man and wife, between brother and brother, between sister and sister, father and children, mother and children—*remember* there is always a *third person* and that third person may not like you very much, so *be careful* also of the *second person* because the third person always comes in through the second person.

You may quarrel, sometimes with the second person, and in the passion of revenge, which may be regretted afterwards, the second person may reveal your secrets, so keep your secrets to the grave and let only God know about them.

Never lose your head to divulge anything that would mean trouble for you with the law particularly because the person who has the secret may change his mind about you and give you up even after 20 years.

Many people get into trouble without knowing where

the trouble comes from. Sometimes it comes from right in their home by talking too much in your own home and by the circles in your own home not appreciating your position innocently giving the information out to other parties who are not interested in you, but probably interested to see that the one you have offended gets justice.

Therefore, the person prefers to see you hanged than to see his friend who you have injured go without justice because of what you might have done to that person in your secret.

LESSON 10

Economy

There are several kinds of economy, but this subject is specifically dealing with financial economy.

Economy is based upon good and sane judgment. The practice of it is that you must always be on the safe side of your bargains or your dealings; never to exhaust yourself but to have a reserve.

There should be always something left over which you may fall back on in the time of need. As far as money is concerned, which is the prop of life, in that it pays for all necessities and offers the security for all opportunities, one should never in his earnings of it spend at the same time all he earns, that is bad business.

Whatsoever is his earning capacity, he should always be thrifty enough to a[t] least save 15 to 20% storing it up for making better opportunities when they come and providing for the rainy day.

If you spend all you earn, you are keeping on the edge of bankruptcy all the time. If you spend more than you earn, you are not only a fool, but you are a very dishonest person, and you are bound to suffer without any other chance.

Make it always a policy, therefore, to save out of your earnings, caring not how small it is.

If you have better commercial ideas than your present jobs calls for and your present remuneration warrants, then save out of your present earnings to take advantage of the opportunity to improve yourself within a reasonable time in achieving these ideas.

Never engage yourself in living luxuriously when you can

only live ordinarily; ultimately you are bound to fail and be the laughing stock of your friends in the community by not being able to keep up your luxurious standard of living on a limited purse.

Never buy anything for more money than you have or positively expect to have within the time limited for the purchase.

Never give away money that you cannot spare. Never give away value that can be turned into money except you can spare it.

Never borrow on interest from anybody, if you can within a reasonable time pay your debts, for if you pay your own debts with your own money[, y]ou will save the interest for yourself that you paid to others.

The moment you start paying interest to others on money borrowed you become a slave working for somebody else. It is better to wait until you have the money yourself to do a thing before you borrow it to purchase that thing and pay interest on it.

At the same time you must use good judgment to find out whether it is to your advantage to seek an opportunity of doing something big—somebody else's money, even with interest to be paid, if that particular business will positively bring enough to meet the interest and give you sufficient profit to justify the risk you take in assuming the responsibility of paying interest to others may be of value.

The moment you are loaned money on interest to do anything, the person loaning you the money must be credited as being wise enough to know before hand if more money can be made out of the thing or investment, than only the interest. If it is so, it is likely that he himself will go into that business and not give you the chance to go into it with his money, but probably he may be a friend and want to help you, but few money lenders are friends. The[y] are lending for usury and have no souls, at least their souls are bad. So be careful in borrowing money to go into business.

It is better you save and wait until you are able to go into business on your own account before you take the risk. It is bad business to go into any business without enough capital to run that business—99 cases out of 100 will fail.

Always consider cost before you go into anything and in figuring out the cost be sure that there is a margin of profit before you do the thing, otherwise it is not worth while doing.

If you are going to address a meeting 100 miles away, first count the cost of railroad fare or transportation to and fro, the cost of the meeting, your living expenses whilst going and staying at the meeting and returning therefrom; the percentage to pay those who are looking after the meeting and the prospect of getting a crowd large enough that will meet all these expenses and leave you with a profit of at least 25%.

If there is no profit in it, you are taking a risk and when you are finished you will be sorry you went.

Always work out before hand the possible results financially of every transaction and be sure that your arrangements are of such as to bring profit at the end, otherwise you are wasting time.

As far as the U.N.I.A. is concerned, you should always calculate for profit for the association in everything you do. Profit comes in many ways to the association—as for instance, if you go to address a meeting 100 miles away, profit will come by the joining of new members to the association, the establishing of agencies there for the association; the leaving behind there of the association's sentiments may be an advantage to any money you receive for the expenses of the meeting, so long as you have converted and attached some permanently to the U.N.I.A. that may be considered as profit.

Always seek to get some profit, otherwise your work is a failure. When your work is to be judged, you will find that a balance sheet will be called for of how much you have received and how much you have disbursed as a representative of the association and how much net you have turned into the movement and how much morally you have helped the movement. If your balance sheet shows that for one month, three months, six months, one year you have not added anything net to the association, your importance in it is nil, you will not account for much. Your status will be far below that of others who have been more valuable to the movement.

A president or a representative who can show that for the year he or she has turned over $500., $1,000., $10,000. net to the association occupies a position of eminence that calls for the greatest recognition of service rendered and another president or representative may occupy no such position of recognition because of his failure.   Men and women are promoted on their record.

Their record must be profitable. If their record is that of failure, they remain failures until they can prove otherwise.

There is no other standard by which you can judge the ability of man. Always seek to get substantial value for their work—because you will never be able to re[ca]ll them, not as they move along.

Whenever you want to sell anything, except you meet somebody who is badly in need of that thing, you are always going to be offered less than the value of the thing. So never buy anything for its full value otherwise you will have it at a loss. It is better to buy things for cash or on short terms rather than on long terms.   A long term purchase carries a greater percentage of interest on the purchase. A thing that you purchase on terms can almost be bought at half of that price if bought for cash because people are also anxious to sell for cash even though they make a sacrifice of the thing because they want the cash.

When you buy on terms, you must bear the burden, not the seller.

When you buy for cash, the seller bears a burden in the loss to get cash. Always have cash and bargains will always show up.

Have no cash and when you see bargains and want them you pay twice the price for them, buying them on terms.

Never live above your income.   Never live up to your income.   Never assume responsibility when you are not prepared, it will burden you down.   Never marry broke.

Never marry before you are ready. Never allow anybody to force you to do anything against your will.

If you can see a thing and get good results from it at a cheaper price, don't pay a dearer price except you have money to throw away.

Don't lose your head in thinking that something is going to run away, therefore you must grab it now. Following that attitude you may find yourself to be a big fool because what you grab here thinking it is a wonder, you may find thrown away next door not worth anything.

Always look around first when you are in doubt. Try to find the duplicate. You may come back, but if a thing is in the neighborhood with one person, it is almost likely that a similar thing is also in the same neighbourhood. Search the neighborhood first before you decide to lay all on one thing.

Never think the one thing or the one person is the only peach in town, there may be better peaches on the tree. Try to curb your weakness for being a spendthrift. Every time you are tempted to spend 10¢ or $1.00 on a frivolous thing from which you will not get any direct profit or return, hold your hand, count ten before you do the thing and say to yourself "have I any other pressing need or use for this money, better than this frivolous thing?" because there is something else that you really need. You will, therefore, keep the money in your pocket.

Never give away your money outside of your race. If you are called upon to give it to God, ask yourself if God is really going to get it, and then only when you feel that it is going into a channel that God will really himself appreciate should you give it, because God himself doesn't want money, but a good cause in his name may need it and you should first find out if there is really a cause. To send a man touring around the world in the name of God for his own pleasure is not giving to God.

To give a man more worldly goods than he has already is not giving to God, but to give to carry on social service work in the community or to help the poor of the community, or to rescue the children of the community is giving to God.

If you have to be critical in giving to God, be even more so when you give to man, it must be for a good cause and the nearest cause to you is the cause of your own race.

Never fail to give charity where charity is needed within your own race, but don't allow yourself to be tricked.

If an old thing is good, don't buy a new one. Don't follow fashion for fashion's sake, but follow your own judgement for intelligence sake. If anything is wrong with your suit of clothes, don't buy a new one because someone else has done so; all it may need is attention and so with everything. You may badly need the money later on, that you may spend on a new suit.

It is better to have the money than the thing, because when trouble comes you can run with your money, but you may not be able to carry all the things, because the largest sum of money can be carried in your pocket-book; whilst the weight of other things may cause you to wait for the next train, and by waiting you may lose.

So put your values more in money than in things. Have those things only that are necessary.

If you have the ambition to be greater than you are and you have not the means to immediately do so, then practice rigid thrift in your present position by saving as much as you can so as to be able in a given period of time to change your position; be to the point you want to reach.

Never consume all you have and then expect to climb higher it cannot be done. Never go into anything you know nothing about by way of business. No fool can make a success of anything. Therefore, know your business before you go into it to make profit out of it.

Never live on the capital of your business, but on the profit.

If you start to live on the capital, there will soon be no capital and no business. If you mean to keep in that business, whatsoever the profit is, live only on it and not all of it, otherwise the time may come when you have to live on the capital by making no profit for that period.

Business is only successful when you are always making

profit and not spending all the profit.

Whenever any enemy or any person attempts to create prejudice against your organization with the government, take immediate steps to counteract the statement and reassure the government that you have no intention of doing anything not in keeping with the law.

Always watch for this because the government can easily outlaw your organization and curtail or prevent your activities. Therefore, don't join up with any movement that the government is not favourably inclined to tolerate, chiefly Communism.

Let the Communists fight their own battles. Let other people carry on their own discords, have nothing to do with them. The more they carry on discords and you keep away from it, the better it will be for you in that by keeping your head, you will be able to see more clearly and get an advantage.

Never let the government put you on the defensive, it will create prejudice against you.

Keep out of court as much as you can. Never go there if possible except to do social service work in helping others, but try never to be charged with crimes, or be on your trial. It will affect the association and affect you.

Always try first to settle racial disputes without going to law. Law is expensive and uncertain.

When you go to law, the lawyer burns up your money and you come out anyhow the loser, even if you win. All good citizens try to keep away from the law courts. Every busy person has no time to waste in sitting in law courts because you can never tell when the case will end.

When you go to law too often, you establish a bad record and when anybody wants to know anything about you and particularly government officials, they search the court record[. K]eep away as a defendant.

Encourage the people to keep away and not waste their money in litigation, if their litigation can be settled by you and any responsible representatives of the race.

The people pay too many fines in court. The money

they pay for fines could be used for their families and their own benefit.

Always counsel Negroes not to be anxious to start litigations or to persecute each other if it can be avoided.

Going to court too often gives the race a bad name and causes the Government to think badly of the race. Always try to impress the Government that you are law-abiding citizens, so that when you make a request of government, government may respect the request.

Always keep your good work before the government and acquaint the government of it[,] particularly social service work, charitable work, educational work—this does not mean racial education, your racial education is private like the Jews, but all public education tending toward good citizenship should be brought prominently to the attention of government.

LESSON II

Man

Man because of his sin which caused him to have fallen from his high estate of spiritual cleanliness to the level of a creature, who acts only for his own satisfaction by the gift of freewill, must be regarded as a dangerous creature of life. When he wants he can be good, otherwise he is generally bad. In dealing with him you must calculate for his vices and his damnable evils. He is apt to disappoint you at any time therefore you cannot wholly rely on him as an individual. Always try to touch him with the hope of bringing out that which is good, but be ever on your guard to experience the worst that is in him, because he is always in conflict with himself as between good and evil.

When he can profit from evil he will do it and forget goodness. This has been his behaviour ever since the first record of his existence and his first contact with his fellows.

Cain slew Abel for his success. Jacob robbed Esau of his birthright and down the ages of human history man has been robbing, exploiting and murdering man for gain.

Do not, therefore, completely trust him but watch him. When he is good try to keep him good although he may not always remain good. If he is bad avoid him. If you have no business with him to the extent of being too much in his company, always try to reform him and use good influence on him because the hope of life is to produce a better man. The passion of man is in evidence everywhere. It revolts against affection, kindness and even love when it has a personal object to attain.

We have heard and read of children murdering their

parents for gain and parents murdering their children in a similar manner and wives killing their husbands and the[ir] husbands killing them for gain. This reveals how wicked man can be. When we discuss man we discuss the creature and not the particular individual whom we know, whom we Love, whom we can trust. Man, therefore, is the abstract creature who is vile until we know him personally.

Seek first to know him then before you completely trust him, because you are apt to be disappointed. A man shakes your hand today and tomorrow he is chief witness against you for execution. What is it that has caused him to do that[?] It is his vileness. Know it then that he is vile, and only when you know him sufficiently may you trust him as far as your judgment would dictate. He is apt to change on you and probably at the psychological moment when you need his help most.

In dealing with man, therefore, trust your own character and your own judgment more than depending absolutely on his, for most of the time his advice to you is wrong and calculatingly so, so as to put you at a disadvantage.

Hear everything from man but do not believe everything until you have tested everything for yourself.

The history of the world shows that man has been the chief murderer or killer. He has killed more creatures than any other being. He plans his murders which he may execute on individuals or on large groups of men and he generally does this for profit—national profit, racial profit, political profit or economic profit.

He is so vile that he does no longer depend upon his physical strength to execute his vileness or to defend himself. He manufactures and makes the most deadly weapons to do the deed quickly, whilst seeking self-protection from a similar attack.

Contemplate the state of his mind therefore that he would calmly, cooly and collectively invent an instrument or chemical purposely designed to kill his fellows at a point where his fellow may not harm him to gain the property and possession of his fellows. Can anything be more diabolical[?]

No other animal sinks to this low level murdering, hence man must be stripped of his veneer to see the evil machinations of his mind. The mind that makes TNT (high explosives), the mind that makes mustard gas, the mind that invents the Krupp Gun, the Winchester Rifle, the fast proof calibre pistol, the poison—all calculated to kill his brother. Do you want anything more wicked? Can you realize then how bad man is? If you do then always be on guard because you know not when the evil genius cometh.

To be forewarned is to be forearmed, therefore know your man so that even though he comes with a smile find out what is behind the smile.

It is only a foolish man who accepts another at his word without finding out something about him.

Never then fall in love at first sight a[n]d marry at the first opportunity. Never then promise at the first request everything until you know the person is worthy of your promise.

If you prize your own good fortune never pledge it on the first approach of any man but follow him, investigate him, and when his conduct coincides with what he states and what he promises[,] you may take the chance of trusting him just so far. As proof of this there are more unhappy marriages than happy ones, although based upon the best of promise at the start. There are more unhappy relations between man than happy relations simply because the evil mind of man cannot keep always good.

It is generally evil, which gives you evidence sufficient that man is vile and only in remote instances good. If you know it then, why take the chance of always believing before seeing? The taste of the pudding is the proof of it. Know your man before you believe. Never believe before you know. Let your mission be always to make man good, therefore talk to man always from the loftiest pinnacle. You may convert someb[od]y, you may turn a vile man good, and if you succeed in doing this in even one instance you have accomplished a great work.

Leadership in good character must make sacrifice to raise

man from the lowest depths, but it is blind foolishness to sacrifice more than necessary; therefore redeem the man with the least amount of harm to yourself.

EDUCATION

The present system of education is calculated to subjugate the majority and elevate the minority. The system was devised and has been promulgated by agents of the minority. This system was carefully thought out by those who desire to control others for their benefit, and the disadvantage of others to the extent that the others would not immediately rise into happiness and enjoyment of life simultaneously and equally with them. It was never originally intended to make all the people equal at the same time, and more so was it not intended to elevate the darker races to the immediate standard of the white races from whom the minority sprung to establish the system of education[.] All text books and general literature therefore were coloured to suit the particular interest of those who established the system of education, and the group they represent as against the interest of others whom they did not want to immediately elevate to their standard.

There is always a limited process in the education of other races by the race that originates the system of education. As for instance, if a Negro attends a university with other students of the race that p[o]stulates or projects the educational system, whilst the Negro would have the privilege of the class room for general instructions to learn commonly, he may not have the privilege of his fellow students of the other race who may be admitted to certain club fraternities within the University from which he would be debarred. Such fraternities generally enjoy the privilege of special instructions and special discussions which convey a wider range of enlightment on the subjects taught than would be possible to the Negro. [H]ence when he graduates even from the same text books his technical knowledge is not as wide as that of others who have had fuller explanation in the technical interpretation of the particular text books and at the same time is only trained to reflect the system that props the intentions of the creators of the system, so that at his best he is making use of his education [a]s a slave of a system that was not intended for him but to which he renders service.

It is necessary, therefore, that the Negro be additionally educated or re-educated after he has imbibed the system of the present education. The best way to do this is to educate him racially in the home, in the meeting hall or in his own club where he will be put under the c[lo]sest scrutiny and analysis of what appears to be education, as coming from other people, because their system of education may not completely fit into the Negro's ideas of his own preservation.

By not being able to do this in the past, educated Negroes have not been able to assume proper leadership of their race, because their education was of the nature as to cause them to support the present system which is of no advantage to the Negro, except as a servant, serf and slave, for which purpose really the system was devised to a certain extent. This explains the behaviour of leading Negro intellectuals who are not able to dissect the educational system of others and use only that portion that would be helpful to the Negro race, and add to it for a complete curriculum that would be satisfactory as a complete education for the race. Do not swallow wholly the educational system of any other group except you have perfectly analysed it and found it practical and useful to your group. There is still room for the Negro educational system free from the prejudices that a present educational system upholds against him. Never fail to impress upon the Negro that he is never thoroughly educated until he has imbibed racial education.

It is by education that we become prepared for our duties and responsibilities in life. If one is badly educated he must naturally fail in the proper assumption and practice of his duties and responsibilities because the Negro has been badly educated. He has universally failed to measure up to his duties and responsibilities as a man and as a race. His education has been subversive. He must now make his education practical and real, hence he must re-arrange everything that affects him in his education to be of assistance to him in reaching out to his responsibilities and duties.

As you shouldn't expect another man to give you the clothing that you need to cover your own body so you should not expect another race to give you the education to challenge their rights to monop[o]ly and mastery to take for yourself that which they also want for themselves. If you are going to distrust the other man in his honesty because you know him to be dishonest, then you must maintain the attitude in every respect, for if he is dishonest in one[,] he may be dishonest in all. If he will rob you your wages he will also rob you your education that would enable you to know that he is robbing you of your wages. Trust only yourself and those you know, and those who look like you and are related to you ought to be known first before you know others. There may be good grounds for a common education of all groups in a community such a [as?] civic education and political education and social education, but this detail[ed] education that teaches man how to live to the highest and enjoy the best, is particular education and that particular education is always reserved particularly for those who want to gain an advantage, therefore if in no other way in particular secure education and have your own such as the Jews, who have outside of any common education a particular and peculiar education of theirs, which augments or adds to or modifies the common education that they have gathered in the community with others.

By view of the fact that the Jew gets a dual education, the education of the State and education of his race, he is always in a unique position to worsen or to better his compatriots of another race in the community, he is always making more out of everything than the Gentile, because he knows all about the Gentile while the Gentile knows nothing about him.

LESSON 12

The Purpose of Institutions

Organised society is always a mass of people, and as such cannot do anything explicit or by detail by themselves. Hence the organising of institutions to do the particular work that cannot be done by the masses as a whole.

There are different kinds of institutions in a society, but each institution has its particular function—whether it be the Church, the College or University, or School, Hospital, Academy, Chamber of Commerce, Fraternity, Trade Union, Literary Club, Sports Club, Athletic Club, or Gymnasium, Y.M.C.A. or Y.W.C.A., etc.

No society in our present civilisation would be considered functioning properly if such institutions did not exist. It is necessary, therefore, for the Negro to pay close attention to developing the appreciation for institutional life.

It is not necessary or binding that he copies completely the systems, methods, or manners of these institutions except in so far as they would go to help him to promote a higher life and in accomplishing the most out of this organised society, but it is incumbent upon him that he also have and control his own institutions, based upon his own cultural and civilised idealism. As for instance, he may have his own Church, but it is not necessary for him to adopt the peculiar articles of faith of the churches of alien races.

He is not a Hebrew, therefore he would not adopt the Hebrew faith. He is not by origin a Roman Catholic nor an Anglican be[c]ause these faiths or religions were founded by white men with an idea of their own.

But the Negro may safely, in his religious philosophy,

adopt articles of faith to link him to the Godhead of the Christian faith, and practice such as his particular religion and so likewise with all other institutions.

His universities, his colleges, and his schools may engage in the same process of education, but with an adopted curriculum necessary for the special benefit of the Negro.

His clubs, academies and unions should be modelled in the same way with the absolute objective of attaining the end that is particularly desired by the race.

The Negro should never completely surrender himself to the institutional life of other people, otherwise he will not be original but purely and merely a copyist. If this could be appreciated it shows the [*word missing?*] or reveals the wide fields which have remained untouched for Negro organisation and Negro activity.

It is through the institutions of a race that the civilisation and culture of the race are built. The Negro should occupy himself in cultivating his own culture and ultimately achieving his own civilised ends, so that in the comparison of racial achievements, he may be able to stand out distinctly on those achievements on his own account as others may do.

To live on the achievement of others is to really admit the superiority of others, and the inferiority of self. As a fact it is by such comparisons that the Negro is judged as an inferior being. Nothing should be sufficiently satisfactory to the Negro that is handed to him by somebody else; he should seek to surround it with originality and then claim it as his own.

He is justified in remodelling and reshaping the things to suit himself, in that there is nothing new under the sun, whatsoever other people have. The Negro himself was the father of civilisation when he constructed the first government in Africa and thereby taught others the way.

Seek always to improve on whatsoever you see fit to adopt. Never leave it at where you adopt it, because somebody else will claim it and prove their right to it, but when you have added to it or taken away from it, you can prove that it is not the same thing, therefore it is yours. Investigate always carefully and thoroughly the accomplishments of other races, and try to improve and beat them at those achievements and keep your achievements a secret from them. Never open up the facts of your achievements to others because they are too anxious to get the last word of anything that is worthwhile.

Always hide the secrets of your achievements whilst demonstrating those achievements; it must be like a chemist selling his preparation or demonstrating it without giving away his formula, because the moment he does so there will be many similar preparations on the market.

Each institution of a people has its special objects to attain, and may not fit in with the idealism of other peoples so the Negro should have his own. He is not to be a slave to other peoples' idealism.

In some detail or other each people's institution must differ from yours according to their particular idealisms. The Jew could never be a Negro in his institutional line, nor an Anglo Saxon a Latin, nor a Latin a Teuton, nor neither a Negro. Therefore, a Negro must not try to be either, but in his institutional line be himself, in that like the Jew whom nature made a Jew for a particular purpose, therefore he must be different both in his habits, in his way of living and in his idealisms. All peoples have separate and distinct functions and they should keep to those functions. The archangels in heaven have their functions, the cherubims have theirs, and the seraphims have theirs and so with humanity. Following God and heaven's example, there is no reason why the Negro should not have his and when he doesn't he is not living the proper life in accordance with the purpose for which nature made him.

Your entire physiognomy is different from other peoples. Your hair is wooly, your nose is broad, your lips are thick, and so this difference must also be intended in your outlook and in your viewpoints of life. Anyone who tells you the contrary is a liar and a fraud, in fact, an enemy to you and to nature.

Never let anyone tell you in this human world of confusion that although of different races, you are one. If you were one, God would have made you so because he is not a deceiver.

The Ethiopian is spoken of as being different. Even in the scripture it is said he cannot change his skin. Think what that means. It is fair assumption that others may change their skins but not the Ethiopian, who is the Negro, the blackman. So there must be something permanent and lasting and eternal about the blackman. God knows why he fixes it so. Don't try to change it by subterfuge or by inferential fraud. What a grand thing it is to know that whilst all other things change, you, because of your race, cannot change. Tell this to the world, how lasting you are and when they doubt it, send them to their Bibles, which you yourself never wrote, which emphasizes the greater truth that it may be so, because even those who wish otherwise have to acknowledge in this respect of virtue the black man evidently was the first man. Adam and Eve were black, their two children, Cain and Abel, were black. When Cain slew Abel and God appeared to ask him for his brother he was so shocked that he turned white, being the affliction of leprosy and as such, he became the progenitor of a new race out of double sin.

The white man is Cain transformed, hence his career of murder from Cain to Mussolini.

It is evident and fair assumption that when Cain ran away and disappeared from the neighbourhood of his parents and journeyed afar, he built up a new race, living in the same country but far away, and in the process of time in Africa, where all this happened, the Negro race, through Adam and Eve continued their multiplication and as it spread itself in the development of a civilisation, it came suddenly upon the settlement of Cain and knowing Cain's history of blood ran the entire race from that neighbourhood across the Mediterranean into Europe.

The white race of Cain hid in caves for centuries. Therefore, their white skin became fixed as most of the time they were hidden from the light. Hence, the white man as a European.

THE WORLD

The world is only part of the creation, an atom of universe. It is a complete entity of creation in relationship with other entities in the creation.

Man is made up of mind and matter. Matter is manifested through nature, and mind is the connecting link with the spirit of God.

The highest mind in the world is the mind of man in that behind it is the spirit of God giving the mind freewill to act through the soul. The soul is mind as well as the feeling of heart is soul and mind. The explanation of this is as intricate as the explanation of the Trinity, God the Father, God the Son and God the Holy Ghost.

As God rules the universe and all matter and mind, so man through his mind rules the world over which he is Lord. The whole world then belongs to man. Each man should get his appropriate or proportionate share.

When in a lifetime he fails to get this, he naturally fails to lift himself up to his Lordship. One man's dispossession of his [L]ordship enthrones another man's sovereignty over him; hence, a ruling man and a serving man, a ruling race and a serving race.

Never be a race of servers, but a race of sovereigns— Lords, control the world, because the world is your province.

The world will not yield more than you want it to yield, but if you know the world, you can make the world to yield much. What[s]oever you want, try always then to master the world.

To master the world, you must know the world, hence you must pass outside of your own district, of your county, of your own country, to know the world and possess it because all that is in it is yours for the getting, go out and get it.

There is no other rival but your fellowman. Never allow your fellowman to rise higher than you, otherwise he will make you his slave.

If you do not use the world well by understanding it, it will destroy you through its matter and through its mind. If you treat the world well by knowing it thoroughly the world will serve you obediently.

Dispute always the right of any other man's superiority over you in the world. Fear no other man but God, for God is your superior but man always your equal, so long as you rise to his attainments. You may rise to his attainments through the extraordinary use of your mind. *Mind is matter, mind is king, when it goes wrong,* it loses its sceptre. It remains right and wields the sceptre and sits upon a throne.

Always be on a throne, it is your prerogative, it is your right because you are the Lord and Master of the earth and all things therein.

In going through the world, hold your head and courage high for you must always remember that you are man and the ruler of the world and that you rule the world through your mind. Think high, think deeply, think in a way to make you know all around and about you, if you do not know you will fail, then be sure to know.

Knowledge is everywhere, it is hidden, search for it and when you discover it, and no one else knows about it, keep it and use it for the good of yourself and your race.

Your first duty in the world is to yourself, to your family, to your race and your racial nation, then worship God absolutely and thank him for all.

If you allow another man to know more than you, he will lead you up to the precipice and if it suits his purposes, he will let you fall in. Know as much as he does, therefore, and more that he may not lead you blindly. When you have to follow another man because you don't know, you are taking a dangerous risk. He may bury you, he may hide you away to suit his convenience. Therefore, while you walk through the world be always on guard.

Try not to lose your mind, try not to lose your mental balance, try not to lose your sense of perception because in losing these things you are doomed in the world.

There is nothing man cannot know except the Divine and almighty mysteries of God, but all that is possible to man, man may know by seeking knowledge which is in the world.

Always try to be self sufficient in yourself but where it is impossible seek that self sufficiency in your racial relations, comradeship, or in your race, but always see to it that your race is self sufficient—that means that everything you want must be obtainable in your race as far as human relationship will permit.

If you are not individually self sufficient or co-operative—in your racial relations or self sufficient in your race as a whole, you will have to go outside of yourself for that sufficiency which will make you absolutely dependent on the goodwill of others for your sufficiency.

No one will give away value that is wanted for self, so you will have to serve and become servants or slaves to sufficiency.

Never wait on another man's pocket-book. Use your own, for he may never show up, he may die on the way and your wait will be too long.

LESSON 13

The Universe

No man yet knows the riddle of the Universe. It has been the eternal puzzle, but men in their searching desires are aiming at unravelling the mysteries behind it. It contains universal knowledge beyond the knowledge of our world.

If man can succeed in ide[n]tifying the facts of the majority of units in the Universe, he approaches a greater degree of knowledge than those who confine themselves only to the investigation of things terrestrial.

The greater minds of our world have experimented and are experimenting in their desire to grapple with all the facts that sustain the Universe. No one knows if man will be permitted to enter into the mysterious realms of knowledge, but it is the duty of man to stretch his imagination afield, and gather for himself as much information as is naturally possible. Never rest therefore with your limited knowledge of the world, but seek to find other knowledge with which you may be able to lift yourself far above that which has been attained or accomplished by man.

In the Universe there are mysteries which may be mathematically or scientifically measured and reduced to the concept of the human mind. Let your mind reach out then to the grappling of these mysteries by an approach based upon reason. As man before you discovered many things, gravitation, the fixed positions of the stars, the regular movements of planets, and such heretofore hidden facts, you may in the search find out new truths upon which your race and civilisation might climb to the highest pinnacle. Carry, therefore, always an observant eye and an analytic mind.

You may suddenly stumble upon some truth for which your world is waiting.

It doesn't matter who the person is, when he has discovered a truth, for which mankind is in need or searching, he becomes a hero and an immortal.

Try to grasp at immortality in the leaving behind of a never dying name, because of the exceptional things you have been able to perceive and discover through the hidden mirror of universality. If you can see visions and dreams and make your visions and dreams true, you may focus the facts and the truths beyond your immediate reach by measuring them with your sublime knowledge.

Find the cause to justify the effect. The effect is visible everywhere, but the cause is generally hidden; but follow the line by the degrees until you approach the start, the beginning, the source. Never stop half way but go right through. If you have good grounds to believe that there is something beyond. If there is a mountain it is suggestive that there is a valley behind it. Don't rest with the mountain because you see it. Search for the valley because there may be much hidden there. Never cease studying the ideas or the facts that may lead you to a definite conclusion.

The things of this world have become common, because most of them have been revealed as far as we know but there are uncommon things even on this earth, and much so in the Universe, that we may search after and make use of as we make use of things today brought to us through the probing genius of other men who saw the need for more and searched for it and brought it to mankind. Edison saw the need for more light and he brought more brilliant electricity, Stephenson saw the need for more speed and he brought the rapid moving engine with its steam, Fulton saw the need for more river transportation and quicker speed and he brought his steamboat, Harvey saw the need for conquering the mystery of the human system and revealed the circulation.

Observe well and see what mankin[d n]eeds most in addition to what they have and try to bring it to them. That is the way you stand out in immortality, as these men do

stand out among us today even though they have been dead
and some for ages.

If I could lie down and dream out of my subconscious
mind the dream of life, and find its source in a more direct
way, how much more could I tell about life to astound and
convince men of what life is.

It is the dreamer, the subconscious manipulator who sees
things by looking through the mental darkness. See things
therefore for yourself, and see them in a way that [*words
missing?*] mysterious Universe.

It is said that God is behind the Universe. No man
has ever seen God. Suppose you, like Christ, could see
God. What a wonder and amazement! Christ saw God
behind the Universe as Man. Christ was an object lesson to
man's glorification and knowledge, therefore if you approach
thought with its deepest sublimity you may see as much as
Christ saw when he saw God.

It is thought that created the Universe. It is *thought*
that will master the Universe. Man must therefore use his
thoughts to be the limit to get the best results from the
Universe. No thinking, no knowledge. Proper thinking may
lead you suddenly into the conquest of that which heretofore
was mysterious.

If man can think most excellently, then he clim[b]s in that
excellence to the companionship of the *most excellent*. For as
he climbs in his excellence to *the most excellent* he shall not be
presuming, but he shall be taking to himself up to the most
excellent that which in other units was not excellent, and like
the dutiful servant who used his talents and used them well,
he shall be possessed of the talent of that servant who hid
his and was ultimately deprived of it for the benefit of that
servant who used his because he could appreciate the gift,
so man in his excellence lifts himself highest to God by his
mental industry, and the man who has not mental industry
forfeits that mentality to the useful servant who climbs in his
excellence to the *most* excellent.

Brush away the cobwebs of your mind, and see the
Universe as looking through a crystal, because beyond you

all is bright and beautiful.

The darkness is in you. See the light—see the light. We want knowledge to lighten our darkness. Bring down the light and knowledge into your soul and flash it through your mind like the spark from the thunderbolt, and all creation will ignite in one glorious illumination, and you will pass through the mysteries of the Universe with the knowledge and eyes of a God.

If I could dream my life into eternity, and come back, with wisdom should not I have the surpassing knowledge of my fellows? Then why not seek it since it is there for man to seek out, and to possess himself of it.

It is when you can reach up to it that you approach God's elevation. Not in rivalry of God, but as coming to God of whom you were always a part, but for the darkness of your own soul. Illumine the soul and God's brilliancy will be revealed as it was revealed to Christ[, w]hen the halo surrounded his head and He was declared the begotten Son of God in whom God was well pleased.

What a world of unfurlment. What a Universe of expectation to which man in his sublimity may climb. Why not be the first soul outside of Christ to climb in that sublimity to the *most excellent*.

The Greek Philos[o]phers suggested to the Greek youth that he should know himself. Across the temple of Delphi was written these words—"Man know t[h]yself," but I may add also "man know t[h]yself, and man know the Universe, and man know your God." In searching after this knowledge you may stumble upon the truth, a revelation that may lead you up to the heights of glory to be known as the greatest soul that fathoms the depths and reaches the heights.

LESSON 14

Self Initiative

Every man is on his own responsibility in life.

Nature never made anyone dually, but singly, therefore you have your sin[g]le responsibility.

The purpose of life is to live fully—hence the single life must be complete and in fact it is so with every man. Hence, it is the duty of every man to fall back on himself for what he wants.

The use of all the faculties of man is necessary for his own protection. He always has a reserve of self expression and self action upon which to fall to protect and defend himself. He must, therefore, develop his faculties to do things thoroughly for himself and first rely upon himself in initiating all these things that may conduce to his personal well being.

Whatsoever he wants to do should first come from himself, as he s[h]ould best know what is best for himself.

Advice may be helpful, but only to the extent that you have reason and jud[g]ement enough to see the value of the advice, otherwise it may be harmful. Very few persons, if any, who advi[s]e others—do so completely honestly, but generally with a motive for which the individual must pay the price, whatsoever that price may be.

The best individual policy, therefore, should be that the individual develop in himself or herself the courage to do things on his or her own account, counting always the cost in benefit or bad results.

The person who fails to be true to himself in taking the initiative to do things for himself will ultimately find out that he or she has been a "sucker" for others. Always surround yourself with the talent of being able to do by yourself, so as not to be too dependent. A person who has to depend on others, is not himself or herself, but the subject of others. A subject or a medium is apt to break under the influence of the controlling factor, as for instance a hypnotist who has a controlling factor may so hypnotise his subject as to cause the subject to lose his or her mind. Try, therefore, never to be the subject mentally of a factor, for a factor may destroy your opportunity of self-reliance and self-initiative.

Always maintain a strong will and emphasize that strong will the more, when from the first reasonable judgments you have come to the conclusion that you are right. To come to that conclusion, you must have the facts before you in your mind, and if your facts are as good as is known and can possibly be gathered on the particular thing on which a decision is to be based, then don't allow anyone but God Almighty to alter your will, because your will is your decision, and your decision is your intelligence, and your intelligence is your personality, and your personality is your self-confidence and your initiative.

Always try to help yourself, and only when you are completely satisfied that you have not the ability, the knowledge, the developed character and strength to do for yourself, should you call anyone to help you, and when you ask others to help you over anything, be sure that they are your very, very, very good friends or relatives because if the thing you ask them to help you out of, or what may be [of] value to you, and would be of value to others, they may take the value for themselves, and all that you will get for calling in someone else to do something for you that you should do for yourself is disappointment, and the sad experience of how bad man is to rob his fellows of his rights. Anything on earth that is of value to you is of interest to the other person, so if you have a good idea, try to develop it yourself and master it yourself, before you ask help, for you will have at least to share the results at the best with those who help you.

FEAR GOD AND KNOW NO OTHER FEAR

There is a God.

No man can say there is no God, because no man is like God. Man is limited in his intelligence at the most and man knows how insufficient he is between life and death—that he is born without his knowledge and dies without his will or wish; when his birth and death must logically and naturally be controlled by somebody else.

It could not be man because man is always man whether he be a big man or small man. So power that gives birth and causes death must be greater than man's power. Whatsoever that power is, it must be an absolute power.

Some men call it by different names but all mean the same thing and it is *God*. When man, therefore, says there is no God, he is a fool for he is not as great as God.

Join no man in saying there is no God, and join no man in saying he is God for it is blasphemy.

Fear God, but love God. If you love God, you need not fear God, for God is with you, and you are a part of him in your goodness.

You fear God only when you are conscious of being evil or wicked.

You love God and work with God whilst you are good. There is nothing in this world that you should fear otherwise, for everything in the world is subject to you as man. Never fear man but under[st]and man, so as to escape the wrath of man and master man. Man is vicious, man is wicked, but you must know that he is. By knowing that he is, you are able to handl[e] him without fearing him.

Meet the stare of man with your stare, never cringe before the stare of man, otherwise he masters you.

Develop courage enough, character enough, boldness enough, self-confidence enough, to look any man in the face and hold your ground; for the first time you take your eyes off him because of his stare, he conquers you because you are unprepared.

Look him straight in the eye; keep him covered with your eye, and let him bow and walk off, not you. This is the way man conquers the lion or a wild beast, by staring it in the eye; the moment he takes off his eye, the beast will spring upon him.

The daring look of man conquers man.   The self-confidence of man conquers man. The stron[g] character of man conquers man.

The conqueror is the fellow with the boldest and longest stare.   He hypnotises his victim and walks over him like a worm.

Never be a worm. To be in this position, try never to be obligated, for if you are obligated to a man, you cannot stare him to obedience; you will have to bow before him because he has a grip over you.

Try then to be free from all obligations to any man and thus be always yourself. God is pleased when man lifts himself to his true position in his kingdom of earth and Heaven.

Look to God, ask him for strength, ask him for courage in righteousness, and you will be able to battle in the world of men.

Don't ask him for wealth, but ask him for wisdom, as Solomon did, and he will open up to you the greater knowledge of goodness, if you are good in your approach to him through prayer for wisdom.

If you ask God for wisdom and understanding, you have everything else because with wisdom and understanding you will be able to take care of yourself. Therefore, never pray to [G]od for particular things[,] for individual things. He has already given all that is necessary for your existence in creation and has placed you as Lord and Master over them, then why worry him in further prayer and for these things?

It is a waste of time, it is annoying, it is disgusting to God, if God can be disgusted.   Seek ye first wisdom and understanding and all life will unfurl itself to you through God.

The mind and the soul are the receptacles of understanding and wisdom. Cleanse them with protection and approach the source who giveth them, and you shall be eternally blest.

The Angels of Heaven are the good spirits from earth and the other planets who have passed through their probation of original life.

No man on earth is an angel. The angels are spirits, not men.

LESSON 15

Personality

A thing to impress the world with is your own personality. Your make-up as a man or woman must be so cleancut as to leave nothing to suggest the incompleteness of a perfect person.

Man is always disposed to respect and honour those who show themselves observant of all the rules of manly dignity and character. It is said by some philosopher that cleanliness is next to Godliness.

Be, therefore, clean-cut in your appearance always, when you meet others and particularly the public. Never be slack in your appearance, at any time in meeting another person or persons, even in your own household, because the moment you throw off the reserve of your personality you invite disrespect for your person.

As far as your personal attire is concerned, always see that it is in style, in proper shape and presentable before you appear outside of yourself.

Always appear at your best, even though suffering under the greatest difficulties of strain, because by that very good appearance you may win support to enable you to get out of your difficulties.

Never let your difficulties weigh you down to such an extent as to forget the presentableness of your personality.

The world is always looking first for defects. Before they tabulate your virtues see to it that nothing is defective about your appearance from your shoes to your [c]ollar, from your toes to your head, from your nails to your mouth, for in search of this, they will strike upon the one defect.

If there is one defect, they will say that you are careless about yourself and, therefore, will be careless about other things.

To maintain a good personality, you must observe all the rules of hygiene. Personal sanitation adds to confidence in you and complete satisfaction. With your appearance, add also to your personal confidence. With this personal confidence you may face the world and win. With the personal defects you naturally lose confidence and lose generally.

Never let anybody persuade you to go anyhow, because you are not going very far; it may be just in that short distance that somebody of importance with deep scrutiny may observe you and conclude that you are a slack person and cause you to lose much.

A perfect personality, made through proper care of one's self is a passport to anywhere in the world, socially and otherwise.

Never go eating in the street. Never go into company and expose your bad manners in any direction; try to suppress those bad manners and leave them at home. Eating and talking are bad manners in public which are excusable and proper at the dining table.

Caring not how hungry you are, don't take your meals whilst walking and never eat as an individual at a public meeting before the audience; you will lose their respect immediately for not having regular meal hours and having your meals in an improper place which social regulations have established.

A public platform is not a restaurant nor a dining room. Don't go eating or even chewing gum in people's faces. It is always an ugly sight and shows gross disrespect for company. You may chew your gum in your home, but not on a public platform nor at a public meeting.

The man with good appearance walks down the street with pride, courage, self-confidence, and self-respect, but the man with a dirty shirt or dirty underwear and poorly kept clothes is self-consciously afraid of himself and is, therefore, afraid of company, hence he is without confidence in himself.

A dirty person on the street is bound to be affected by the heat. The heat betrays his dirt to the passer-by and everybody looks around to see who it is, and as you are spotted, you become marked and that odour you throw off as a result of the heat, may become your social undoing in that community. So be always clean in appearance and in body. It costs very little because even with one suit, you may keep it so clean as to be always presentable to the public.

It is better for the public to say, "that man has been wearing that suit for a year, but it has always been well kept," than for the public to say, "that man changes his clothes, but he is always dirty."

Never go on a platform with patched clothes because somebody will see the patch and surely come to the conclusion that you are patched up all around.

When you go before the public remember that they are looking at you scrutinisingly from head to foot, back and front. They are going right through you, searching for something that reveals your true character. Disappoint them always by giving them the best you have in character which is outwardly represented by your clean-cut appearance.

I looked at a man. He was a beggar. His shoes were broken in many places and very dirty. His clothes were ragged and torn in many places. His collar was swarthy, black and revealed dirt everywhere. His finger nails were black and dirty. His teeth were unkempt. His breath was foul. His shirt was black with dirt. He asked me for help. I gave him a penny and walked away, because I thought it was enough, for he could not appreciate the use of more.

I saw another beggar whose clothes were poor, but clean, whose pants revealed poverty, but were also clean. I gave him a sovereign because I thought he could appreciate the use of it—this is a moral. People will judge you by your appearance, whether you are rich or poor, and deal with you accordingly.

Never make it a custom to carry distress on your face or in your eyes or carry yourself as to suggest despondency and over burdening sorrow.

People will learn to shun you. Keep smiling, keep being

pleasant all the time even if you are dying. It is better to be a pleasant corpse than a hideous ugly looking one. Show distress only when you may win help from those you approach, but be sure that you have struck a right estimate of your sympathisers, for to show sorrow to those not interested is to drive them away from you. Never show it to those who are not interested.

When you are keeping an appointment always appear at your best to justify the particular mission. As for instance, if you are going to do big business, appear in a way as to suggest that you can maintain and live up to big business. If you are going to seek a job by an appointment modify your dress so as not to outdress your prospective employer.

If you are going begging for yourself, don't go flashily dressed or over-dressed, but dressed in keeping with the kind of impression you would like to make upon your benefactor— this is purely a question of judgment.

If you are going begging for a cause like the U.N.I.A., you must not go as a revealed personal beggar, you would cause the person to say to himself, "why should I give him money for a cause when he himself looks like someone who begs for himself, and cannot be trusted with such philanthropic responsibility for others."

Never go asking help for a cause, caring not how lofty it is, looking hungry, distressed and broken-hearted yourself; nobody will believe your story, you are likely to be jailed until you can prove your sincerity.

Win a good reputation in your community by being up-to-date in your personality. Let your individuality stand out clearly; every man has an individuality. He is known by that individuality. The background of that individuality should be his clean-cut personality.

Don't be lazy in whatsoever you have to do because that laziness will grow on you, and people will observe you and mark you as being lazy. If the news circulates, it will undo you.

If you find a thing to do as a job or occupation, do it well and show interest in it until you have decided to do something else, but whilst you are doing it, do it to the best of your ability, and put your personality and individuality behind it, for somebody observing or coming after you will say "this thing was well done by Jones or badly done by Jones," hence your reputation is at stake.

If you have the right of choice in employment or occupation, then choose only that employment or occupation that would give you complete satisfaction in its practi[c]e, so that you may put your whole heart and soul in it and behind it to achieve the greatest good or the greatest result.

To carelessly choose your occupation or employment, and find afterwards that it does not suit your nature, is a waste of time, for by disliking that employment or occupation, you will not concentrate on it and give the best results to your own benefit, for you will always be thinking of something else whilst mechanically doing what you are occupied with. Hence, to be your true self, always be sure to properly select the right occupation before you go into it.

Never be frivolous in the public eye or in the eye of company, because they will mark you down as a frivolous and irresponsible person. Try always to maintain the dignity of seriousness or at least a poise that would suggest you to be a person of dignified reserve. Going giggling, prancing and jumping about like a child stamps you as a clown. A man must be a man, a woman must be a woman, whilst a child must be a child. You are [a] child once and a man once, and a corpse once. In the three stages you must behave accordingly to nature. Prance and giggle as a child, be serious and dignified as a man, and rest peacefully as a corpse.

If you happen to make a mistake in getting into an employment or position that is not suited to your nature and disposition, whilst working at it, do the best you can to maintain your reputation, exercise your effort to find the occupation or employment you are best suited for, and see that you do not make a second mistake, but find your right place in life.

If you go on making mistakes of that kind, your life will end as a complete failure, because you will never be able to master anything, because your whole soul and hear[t] was never in anything.

Before you can impress others and get them to follow you or imitate you or accept your suggestion of anything higher in life, you yourself must show evidence of success in it. No man who is not successful can teach others how to succeed. It is impertinence for a man who has not succeeded through his personality to suggest to other people how they can succeed. Therefore, make yourself a success and other people will follow your advice, because they see success in you.

Never go among people better than yourself telling them how to succeed, but use your illustrations of success among others who have not succeeded and that illustration must be in your own personality and individuality.

To maintain a good personality and robust individuality, be sure to keep your body in proper physical condition. There is no better way to do this than at least once a week, taking some kind of effective purgative, which may so clean the system as to give you clear vision and healthy thought, with responsive body free of pain and ailments.

Doing this regularly may lengthen your life from ten to twenty years, as it keeps you in a state of hea[l]th to resist the germs of disease. If you follow this practice you may never have to see a doctor except on major physical matters.

Never try to make an important speech with a clogged system. The poison of your system will get upon your mind, and keep you so hazy in thought as not to reveal the mentality of your true self. When a person claims to feel bad and goes to a doctor, except it is an ailment resulting from a major cause, he always prescribes purgative. Why pay a dollar or two or ten to give you the same things you may take at a cost of five cents? A clear system is always a prevention against threatening diseases.

Keep your system clear at least once a week. If a motor car runs all the time without being cleaned or overhauled it will suddenly one day break down and it is iron, how much more will a human being not break down if he doesn't keep his system clear? All things he eats do not pass out voluntarily, they remain in the system to breed germs of disease which may affect you in all ways, so the greatest insurance against in[j]uring your health is to keep your system regularly cleansed.

A heavy stomach or disord[er]ed stomach affects the whole nervous system. All the nerves are related in the human body and they depend chiefly on the stomach as a main artery of supply. If the stomach grows sick it sends poison throughout the whole body. Keep your stomach clear. It is better to be half hungry than wholly filled.

LESSON 16

Propaganda

Propaganda means to propagate or to make know[n] extensively some particular phase of human intelligence. The desire be to convert or influence the people to the acceptance of the truth of the particular intelligence, that is sought to be spread in their midst.

Propaganda can be true o[r] false in its origin or intent, but is always directed at the public for the purpose of winning the support of that public to the sentiment expressed in the propaganda.

If you hat[e] a man, giving him a bad name well may e[x]plain one of the purposes of propaganda, without truth behind it.

Nearly all organised efforts have a system of propaganda to convert people to their principles and get them to support them even though there may be no merit behind it all.

Propaganda is all around you, to make you buy a special brand of cigarettes, although no good, advertised to be the best; to make you drink or use a certain brand of tea, telling of its wonderful qualities and its everlasting benefits when there is absolutely nothing to it, and so on.

Before the war of 1914–1918, the Germans were known to be the most cultured and scientific people in Europe. W[he]n the war started, the other nations, so as to discredit the Germans and hold them up to world ridicule, and to the contempt of civilisation, released the propaganda that classified the Germans as Huns and barbarians. This also reveals how organised intention can be carried to the public for the public acceptance without thought.

The press, the cinema, the pulpit, the schoolroom, are all propaganda agencies for one thing or the other. The pulpit carries on religious propaganda, the schoolroom carries on educational propaganda, the press carries on written propaganda, the platform carries on oral propaganda, the cinema carries on demonstrative propaganda. These methods have been devised by the white man to spread his ideas universally among men, that is why he is able, in a major sense, to control the minds of the people of the world.

The white man is a great propagandist. He realises fully and completely the value of propaganda. You must, therefore, organise your propaganda to undo the propaganda of other people, if their propaganda [a]ffects your interest. The Bible is religious propaganda, the school book is literary propaganda, the novels and books you read are also literary propaganda, all calculated to bring about certain results beneficial to the prop[ag]andists.

Never forget then that you are surrounded in a world of p[ro]paganda, all dressed up or cooped up to suit a doubtful public who is not careful with what it digests as coming from without.

The artist is also a propagandist. He paints pictures to convey the idea he wants to impress upon the non-thinking and doubtful public. The sculpt[o]r is also a propagandist. He chisels figures and portrays them to suit the aim or purpose he wants to achieve. The pictures of the Madonna, [of] Christ, and of the angels, is painted portraying a white race, so as to inflict upon the rest of the world that God, the angels and the Holy family are white as well as Adam and Eve. Adam and Eve were black.

They also paint the Devil and the imps of Hell black to impress the world that all that is black is evil and all that is white is good and holy.

Tear down from your walls all pictures, that [do not] glorify your race. Tear up and burn every bit of propaganda that does not carry your ideas of things. Treat it as trash.

When you go to the cinema and see the glorification of other [*word missing?*] in the pictures, don't accept it, don't believe it as true.   Visualise yourself inste[a]d as if achieving whatsoever is presented and if possible organise your propaganda to that effect.

You should always match propaganda with propaganda.

Have your own newspapers, have your own artists, have your own sculptors, have your own pulpits, have your own platforms, print your own books and show your own motion pictures, paint your own pictures and sculpture your own subjects.   Never accept your subjects as of another race, but glorify all the good in yourselves.

Keep your homes free and clear of alien objects, of other races on glorification, otherwise your children will grow up to adore and glorify other people.

Put in the places of others the heroes and noble characters of your own race.

Never allo[w] your children to play with and have white dolls, it will give them the idea of having white children themselves.   Give them the dolls of their own race to play with and they will grow up with the idea of race love and race purity.

Watch the newspapers daily, magazines and journals for propaganda against your race or your institutions, and particularly against the U.N.I.A. and rush into print immediately to defend your race institutions and organizations from any attack. Never allow an insult propagated to go unanswered by you. Be ever vigilant to down anything by way of propaganda that dishonours or discredits you. Don't help the other fellow to carry on propaganda against yourself or your race. All propaganda comes from the arranged desires of individuals and not from a race as a whole. It is the thinkers and leaders who originate propaganda, and by insisting on its wide distribution they get other people to think as they like.

Don't accept the thoughts of others through propaganda except it coincides with yours. Don't follow the band down the street because it plays sweet music to the propaganda of the circus manager, he may lead you into the circus tent and take away your pocket-book, that is to say, don't get on anybody's band wagon, because he may drive you to hell with his sweet music. Like the Pied Piper of Hamlin who played his sweet pipe and led the rats from out of the city into the sea and drowned them.

Propaganda organized by somebody else is always calculated to take advantage of you, don't help them to do so.

Always ask! ["]What is this about? What is the object of it? Who has sent this out? What is he aiming at? Will it hurt me and my race? Is he trying to get an advantage over me? Is it honesty? Is it true?"

If you ask these questions of every propaganda that comes up, before you swallow it, you will always be able to take care of yourself.

Don't sing the songs and repeat the praises that glorify other races, sing your own songs and r[e]cite your own praises that glorify your own race. As for instance, it is foolish for Negroes to sing or say "Britons never shall be slaves" when they themselves have been slaves and are likely to be slaves if they don't impress upon their own minds that they as Negroes shall never be slaves again.

Sing, therefore, "Negroes never shall be slaves." Be careful how you sing religious hymns, written, dished up and made popular by white writers to glorify the white race in the name of God, taking advantage of the silence of God to impress inferiority upon your race—such as "The great white wings of angels," "The white throne of God," "Wash me whiter than snow"—all these are damnably vicious propaganda against the black race. "Though my sins be as scarlet, they be whiter than wool." ["]Wash me in the blood and I shall be whiter than snow." All these things reflect the propaganda designed of the white man to glorify his skin and his race as against the black imps of hell, and the black devil and the black pall of gloom.

The idea of the white man making black a symbol of mourning and sadness is just to show the extreme of the purity of whiteness and its joy and happiness. Reverse it. If possible teach the Negro that when he is in mourning to wear white, and when he is in joy to wear black. This is meeting propaganda with propaganda, the hatchet with the hatchet, the stick with the stick, the stone with the stone. Everything on earth is man's creation and so out of man's propaganda and mind he has created his special systems of opinion to meet his designs.

Customs, therefore, are based upon the acceptance of propaganda skilfully engineered. Have your own propaganda and hand it down the ages. Write your own poetry and recite it. Compose your own songs and sing them. Write your own interpretation of scripture and history and teach them as far as the interpretation of others affects your race.

Challenge the thought of any book or literature that dishonours or discredits you in any particular, and give it the widest publicity so as to undo the harm intended, remembering always that an error not corrected ultimately becomes a fact.

Never allow false statements or allegations against your race to become current and pass into history, as if it were a fact.

War

War is the hellish passion of man let loose in opposition to man. It sums up the cruelty of man for man. It always aims at the stronger taking advantage of the weaker to gain that which could not have been acquired otherwise, because of failure to use human reason.

War comes with men after the failure of their reason to adjust their own differences.

Always be prepared for the exhibition of the vilest passions of men in war. Man has always warred against his fellowman. It started with Cain against Abel and has continued down the ages and shall ever be so, so long as man remains an unreasonable creature.

No generation has shown that man intends to become wholly reasonable; therefore, in the time of peace, prepare for war, so as not to be caught unprepared by your enemy who will naturally be the stronger, if he is prepared while you are not prepared in using the implements of warfare. War is not a good thing, but man is also not a very good being. From his disposition, therefore, you must expect war. All things are fair in war to win the advantage over your enemy.

When there is war, use all the implements at your disposal to defeat your enemy. Do not discuss terms while you are warring—discuss them after you are victorious.

When war comes, all resources of intelligence and wealth, all utilities are placed at the service of those who conduct the war to make it victorious on behalf of those of whom they are warring.

Have, therefore, in view the obtaining and controlling of all such resources, factors and utilities that may be necessary as ammunitions of war.

There may be righteous wars as well as unrighteous wars, depending entirely upon the civilization that makes the war or defends itself in war. It may be war to put down a human abuse in favour of the human virtue.

The war-makers have always justified war in some way or the other. If you become engaged in a war, always have a justification for your so engaging.

If the war is not yours, get something out of it before you go into it and complete it for the good of others.

Never go into war foolishly, to sacrifice your life [w]ithout good results for your cause. War is the best time to take advantage of your transgressor whoever he may be.

If, whenever he is engaged in war, he promises you nothing, you will never get anything from him in the time of peace. Therefore, during the time of war make your bargains before you help anybody else in a war. If you are suffering from the abuses of others and there should be a threat of [w]ar against them from some other source, encourage it because it will be your chance to force a square deal.

The more other people war among themselves, the stronger you become if you exercise good judgment.

Divide your enemies so as to gain your advantage. Keep them always divided so [a]s always to gain your advantage.

Your only hope of escaping the hate and prejudice of other people is to keep them severely occupied with other problems, for if they have nothing else to attend to, they will concentrate on you and your problems will be aggravated.

Whilst others are gone to war, try to be at peace among yourselves to gather in the spoils of war.

Never talk war openly to your enemies, but be prepared for war. If you talk it they will become prepared, waiting for you.

Keep the other races divided and fighting each other as much as you can so as to take advantage of yourselves.

If they have no other problems to occupy their time, they will turn to and on you, so keep them occupied otherwise. The more confused they are, worrying over their troubles, the more time you will have to get out of yours.

LESSON 17

Communism

Communism is a white man's creation, to solve his own [p]olitical and economic problems.

It suggests the enthronement of the white working-class over the capitalistic class of the race.

It was conceived by white men who were in sympathy with the economic struggles of their own white masses.

It was never conceived and originally intended for the economic or political emancipation of the blacks, but rather to raise the earning capacity of the lowest class of white workers.

It was founded principally on the theories of Karl Marx who knew very little of Negroes, and thought and wrote less of them. It is a dangerous theory of economic and political reformation because it seeks to put government in the hands of an ignorant white mass who have not been able to destroy their natural prejudice toward Negroes and non-white people.

Whilst it may be a good thing for them, it will be a bad thing for Negroes who will fall under the government of the most ignorant prejudice and cruel class of the white race.

The ignorant white man is cruel and prejudiced because of his very ignorance. You may see, therefore, how dangerous it would be to place in his hands, by the very strength of his numbers, a government dictated and controlled by him. Whilst the capitalistic system is ruthless and bad, it nevertheless gives the Negro a chance for employment competitive with the working classes of white men, for the purpose of extracting profit from labour, irrespective of the colour of labour.

The Negro being not an industrial employer shares,

therefore, the opportunity to labour in competition with the white worker only because the white capitalist is willing to use anybody irrespective of colour who can contribute the most profit to his industries.

The capitalist white man is an enemy of Communism for the preservation of his own interest, if nothing more.

If the Negro is not his own industrial employer, and loses the goodwill of the white capitalist employer, because he is a Communist, he will find himself unemployed, and that is just what the Communist wants, so as not to have a black competitor, which will enable him to dictate his terms to the white employer, and get him at the expense of the unemployed Negroes, because he too is a Communist.

The idea of the Communists inviting Negroes to join their ranks is to support the theory that Negroes are Communist too, so that if a white employer has to decide between a black Communist and a white Communist, by the appeal of race, the white Communist will get the consideration and advantage.

The scheme, therefore, to make Negroes Communists, is a vile and wicked one, as coming from the white communists. The Communists have created their own party and organization of which they are the international executive heads.

They alone as executives know the policy and designs of the Communist party which are kept from Negroes for the purpose of fooling them into a sense of false secu[rit]y.

When it is considered that a[ll] the outrages in war, in mob violence, and in extreme punishment have been administered to the Negro by the lowest class of white agents, as soldiers in war, and as sailors and as the mob, the Negro should have no doubt that his greatest enemy is the common white man who has not intelligence enough to know the injury that he is doing to a race even if paid to do so by his master.

All wars in Africa, the colonies where the natives have been shot down and punished, were carried out by the common white man in the ranks. In the lynchings that have occurred in the Southern section of the United States of

America, the mob has always been made up of the lowest class of the white race. No governor, no state official, no major, no aristocrat has ever been found in the mob or leading the mob. The mob has always been made up of the common, ignorant people from whom Communists are made up and whom the party is intended to give political power on economic advantages.

The threat to run Negroes out [of] Jamestown, Pa., the cotton fields of Mississippi, and other sections of the United States were threats that came from the common white people where notices were served "Niggers, don't let the sun go down on you in this town."

It was the common white people of Cardiff, Wales, who in 1923 stopped the funeral procession of a dead Negro seaman[,] smashed the coffin, cut off his head and made a football of it in the street as a protest of Negroes being employed as seamen in Cardiff whilst white men wanted [w]ork.

In South Africa, East Africa, and South West Africa, it is the poorer white colonists, who practice the most wicked discrimination and persecute the natives to rob them out of their rights. Everywhere it is the poor white colonist and the poor white man who carried out the dirty work of prejudice against Negroes, and those are the class of people for whom Communism is intended.

Consider that the socialist, the Communist and the Trade Unionist of the white race are all agitating for higher wages and better living conditions. It is evident that these economic improvements must only come at the expense of greater exploitation of weaker peoples.

The weaker peoples before were the Chinese, the East Indians and the Negroes. The Chinese have organized national resistance, the Indians have also organized national resistance, it is only the Negro, therefore, who is exposed to the most ru[t]hless exploitation in the future and surely the low class working white man will stop at nothing to raise his status even as controller of government through Communism, even though it crushes only the Negro.

Hence, the Negro must realize that he is being played for a "sucker."

What the Negro must do is to let the Communists fight their own battles, and stay off to see the fight, and take advantage of the opportunities presented during the fight, but not himself to join the fight as a Communist for he will be helping to bear the brunt of the battle with no guarantee that his condition will be better, but objectively worse, because he will help to transfer government from the more intelligent and cultured in behaviour, to that of ignorance, prejudice and cruelty.

The man who caught your forefathers in Africa was not the white Capitalist, but the white sailor who is a class of man from whom Communists are made. He is dangerous to the Negro's liberty as a common man and as an ignorant man, so never join him to destroy the intelligence that rules the civilization that has given you existence up to the present time.

Any time you are asked by your Communist associate or acquaintance to join the Communist party, tell him in answer "When you get to Russia, but not before nor until then."

READ STATEMENT ON COMMUNISM AND THE NEGRO IN PHILOSOPHY AND OPINIONS of Marcus Garvey.

LESSON 18

Commercial and Industrial Transactions

Commerce and industry are the feeding props of the economic life of the state, the community or society as a whole. On these two foundations [r]ests the universal system of exchange with its financial factors.

Every progressive people and nation indulge in some form of commerce and industry, manufacturing or agricultural industry. It is by such activities that the individuals find occupation within the normal life of the state.

You are either an employer or an employee, big or small. The employees are those who work for the employers. The employers are those who employ the employees and pay them salaries or wages. The employers pay themselves salaries out of their profits or dividends, so both employer and employee live off commerce and industry.

Those who do not work in this way are either wards of the state or recipients of charity or people who live off the earnings of others which flow from those who are industrious enough to work either as employers or employees.

Every self-respecting man finds an occupation, either as an employee or as an employer; according to his choice, his ability, his general fitness, he earns a livelihood.

All men try to earn as much as they possibl[y] can. To do so, they generally equip themselves for their occupation. A good labourer or worker quali[f]ies himself for his particular work, so as to demand the best reward or wages. The business man, proprietor or employer, generally goes into the most profitable business so as to secure the largest amount of profit.

The man without a business of his own or without training in perform[ing] a particular work is always at a disadvantage in making a living. Great wealth is made out of commerce and industry, not to say also of the professions which are dependent on commerce and industry.

Commercial enterprises are of different kinds as also industrial enterprises. In commerce we have the grocery business, the lumber business, the ironmonger's business, the mercantile business, or dry goods business, the clothing business, the tailoring business, retail and wholesale businesses of all kinds, and industrially we have the manufacturing businesses that manufacture the particular articles of commerce, whilst the farming industry produces such commodities that are necessary for human consumption.

The industrious man must find an occupation in one or the other of these enterprises or professions if he is to be a proprietor or employer. [H]e must have his own wholesale establishment or retail establishment. He must have his own factories or mills, either la[r]ge or small. His capital may be a million dollars or ten dollars, according to the size of his enterprise. One proprietor has a chain of grocery stores, another has a push cart with his wares carried on it, but both of them are proprietors.

One may make at the end of each week a profit of $10,000 on his investment, the other may make a profit of $10.00— this is due to the difference of the size of business.

So a man who is enterprising with little capital can start a business of his own equally or simultaneously with the man who has a large capital. One farmer may be proprietor of 10,000 acres of land, another may be a proprietor of one acre of land, but both of them are farmers and proprietors. Often it is a small proprietor who ultimately becomes a large proprietor, through the success of his small venture. Most of the successful business men in the world started with small capital. Rockefeller started with a dollar and so did Carnegie, Henry Ford started with less than $50.00 but they became great trust magnates in less than half a century, opening the way to enterprising men who are willing to start with a modest or small beginning and work steadily to the business of greater magnitude.

The examples of small men starting small businesses and building them up to massive concerns are common. In England, Joseph Lyons, a Jew, from a capital of less than £10/-/- built up the great Joseph Lyons & Company's tea room and restaurant syndicates that control the catering trade in that department of all Great Britain. This was also true of Thomas Lipton who afterwards became Sir Thomas Lipton, the great tea magnate of England.

This kind of enterprising success has its counterpart in nearly every country in the world, where small men have grown big by entering a business and sticking to a business until it becomes a colossal success.

Many an Italian millionaire started with a push cart selling oranges and bananas in the streets of New York and Chicago. Many a Greek also became a millionaire by starting with a small lunch counter at some side street corner with a capital of not more than $10.00. Many [an] Assyrian peddlar started peddling with a box slung across his shoulders containing assorted merchandise, not valued at more than $5.00, to become later a millionaire or Merchant Prince, proprietor of a dry goods establishment.

Many an enterprising boy started out with 35 cents to buy newspapers and sell them, morning and afternoon editions, and climbed up to be a great newspaper publisher or proprietor.

The fault with the Negro in business, commercial or industrial, has been his inability to appreciate starting at a given point and climbing steadily, whilst other races have been willing to start from the lowest down to climb higher up.

The Negro has always desired to start from the top, hence, he comes down. No success ever came from the top, it is always from the bottom up. The Negro must learn to climb from the bottom up. He will never be an industrial or commercial factor until he has learned the principles of commercial and industrial success, and these principles are as much open to him as to anybody else.

Find a particular kind of business that you would like to engage yourself in, because you can make it profitable, and start it with whatsoever capital you have. You can start selling newspapers with a capital of 25 cents, you can start selling oranges with a capital of $1.00, you can start selling bananas with a capital of $1.00, you can start selling stockings for ladies with a capital of $2.00, you can start selling ties for gentlemen with a capital of $2.00. Find out what your neighbors want most and are willing to buy, and start selling it to them, if not in a shop, by going from door to door.

If your capital is larger your opportunities become larger and easier. But no Negro need sit down at his door step and mourn his bad luck if he has 25 cents in his pocket to start business.

If you invest your 25 cents wisely at 9 o'clock in the morning, by 6 o'clock in the evening you may have 50 cents. If you eat 10 cents for that day and carry over 40 cents to the next day as its capital, from 9 [o]'clock to 6 o'clock on the next day you may have 75 cents. Eat 10 cents out of the 75 cents, which will leave you with a capital for the next day of 65 cents. Your 65 cents capital may bring you 90 cents. Eat 10 cents and carry over 80 cents to the following day and at 6 o'clock on that day you may have $1.20. Eat 10 cents and carry over the $1.10 to the business of the next day and at 6 o'clock on that next day you may have $1.50 and so you follow this method for one year and at the end of the year your capital in business may be $25.00 and your income may be $5.00 on that day, out of which you provide your food and still have a large capital to face the next day.

In five years your capital may be $1,000, in 10 years your capital may be $10,000, in 50 years you may be a millionaire, that is how Rockefeller did it, that is how Carnegie did it, and left their impression upon the world as self-made men.

If the Negro is going to look at Marshall Field in Chicago or Sears Roebuck and Company, and John Wannamaker in Philadelphia or Gordon Selfridge in London, England, and say I want to start like that, the dreamer will never start, because nothing starts that way. Wannamaker had to climb from the ground to the top of his skyscraper by perseverance and plodding and so did Selfridge and so did Marshall Field. They all started from the ground floor climbing up. The Negro must start from the ground floor of commerce and industry and climb up.

When he can make a good handkerchief, then later he will make a gross, and then a million gross with his factory going at top speed. When he can make a single tie successfully then he will make his gross, then hundreds of gross, then thousands of gross—his factory will hum and buzz with activity.

Businesses are necessary, shops, stores, wholesale and retail, and factories—these are the places where the majority of the people are employed outside of the farm.

The Negro to be employed then and to be his own employer must have his independent farms, stores, factories, and mills, but he must start them as the white man did, growing from the little single room of i[n]dustry to the mighty factory on the hillside of the plain.

Without commerce and industry, a people perish economically. The Negro is perishing because he has no economic system, no commerce, no industry.

There are tricks in every business. Never go into any business until you know all the tricks thereof, otherwise you are bound to fail.

If you like to indulge or engage yourself in a certain line of business, spend as much time as you possibly can investigating from your friends, acquaintances or whosoever you can approach who is already in that business or knows about that business, so as to have all the information necessary about it before you start in it.

It is the people who know of the tricks in trade that make the most profit out of the trade. If you are going to sell ripe bananas on a truck through the street, find out how long will a banana fully ripe last in handling, so that you may gauge the time of sale of the bananas that they may not spoil on your hands, so with oranges, with salt fish, with meat, with ribbons, with hats[,] with shoes, with anything that time and age will affect.

If you don't know about the particulars of these things and invest in them, you will find yourself losing money instead of making money.

No one goes into business just for fun or pleasure, but for profit and results. Study all the possible means of making profit and getting good results out of the business in which you are to engage yourself.

A democracy is the safest kind of government for persons of individual initiative who desire to go into business to live under, because it gives every man a chance to do business more safely.

As a fact the capitalist of today was the labourer or worker of yesterday. Most of the capitalists of our present age were workers, fifty, forty, thirty, twenty, ten or five years ago. Hence, the man who wants to go into business commercially, industrially or agriculturally and win a fortune for himself, to achieve the things he aims at, cannot and should not be a Communist because Communism robs the individual of his personal initiative and ambition or the result thereof. Democracy, therefore, is the kind of government that offers to the individual the opportunity to rise from a labourer to the status of a capitalist or employer.

PROPERTY

In acquiring property for commercial, ind[u]strial or personal purposes or use, always see that you get value for your money. The property market is regulated by the Real Estate brokers or agents and the Mortgaging and Trust Companies who take mortgages on property.

These people create the rise and fall in property values to suit their own conveniences and their own profits. When they can get the public to buy at high value, they induce the public to do so, when the public will not buy enough to insure their profit, they reduce the value of property and then encourage the buying of the same. And when the buying takes a gradual rise they inflate the values again to make the public pay more for what they have started again to buy.

As far as Negroes are concerned, the custom of the Real Estate brokers and Mortgaging Companies has been always to sell them property at 1/4[,] 1/3rd and sometimes 1/2 and other times 100% higher than the real value.

When the Negro is ready to sell, he never gets half of what he pays for his property, except in exceptional cases, in that it is always suggested that his ownership and particularly occupancy carries depreciation.

To be safe, therefore, when the Negro is purchasing property, he should first go to the official registry of property transfers in his community for a record of titles, to find out the price paid for the said property by the last purchaser, so that he will know how much he is being charged in excess of the last sales price[.] He should also go to the government registry where the particular property is assessed for taxation to find out the real value from the government point of view for the property.

Government assessed value on property is always about 2/3rds of its ordinary market commercial value. Add 1/3 to the government assessment and you will find the real market value of the property[.]

Never pay in excess of this value except you can afford to stand the loss, to suit you own convenience, because when you want to sell your property, that is the method others will adopt to find out its real value.

Always be careful and watch your mortgage or the person you have bought the property from to whom you owe balances after you have paid off the excess values of the property and started to pay on the real value.

The Mortgage or the seller of the property when he sells it to you in excess of its value, is always friendly and tolerant whilst you are paying off the excess value, because he realizes he is the one who is being benefited all the time, but when you start to pay on the real value of the property to have equity in it that will make it a marketable equity, he becomes nervous in the belief that you may pay off for the property and own it.

The more you pay off on the real value of the property, the more nervous he becomes, because he is always counting on your inability to pay for the property so as to foreclose on you to sell the property a second time, so as to make a double profit out of the excess value. That is to say, if he sells you the property originally at an excess value of $1,000 he will encourage you to pay off the $1,000 with tolerance because all that is gross profit, but he is always hoping to have the property to sell to another person at another excess value of $1,000. He can only have it when you have forfeited your regular payments on the real value to make it possible for him to foreclose.

Therefore, he may trick you into being off guard to pay your interest and sinking fund regularly, then in the first lapse of unpreparedness, he serves you by foreclosing and gets the property in his hands again for his second attempt.

This is the method of all usurers who take mortgages and property and who deal with property as a business. If you will investigate, you will find that the majority of Negroes in every country have lost their property in this way.

CHARITABLE INSTITUTIONS

Charity suggests the sympathy and goodwill of the fortunate for the unfortunate. The poor we should always have with us, and no one knows who shall be the poor, and so we become kindly in our behaviour and disposition towards those who are unable to help themselves through misfortune or bad circumstances of any kind.

To properly dispense kindness to those in need, society decide[s] on the establishment of institutions for charity. There may be hospitals, homes for the aged, and homes for the blind, foundling institutions, asylums, etc. All well organised races have such institutions for their own and contribute to and support them.

The Negro must also be interested in the foundling, and

keeping of such institutions for his own poor. In giving of charity to a worthy cause nothing is lost, in fact, it is like casting your bread upon the waters to come back to you after many days. You may help to do good to a member of your race without personally knowing the person and ten years hence some relative of that person may help some relative of yours without knowing them—it is the bread coming back on the waters.

To give charity outside of your race is probably sending it too far away, but to give it within your race is probably to be handing it to your own relative. In fact, charity begins at home, and your race is much nearer to you than a neighbouring one, so always find time to bestow charity upon your race at least first.

Every Negro helped from the ground to stand up is another man set on the journey of racial responsibility.

Always, when possible, seek to h[el]p your Negro brother. Never allow him to fall, because as low down as he goes, he may ultimately pull you down with him. As high up as you can send him, he might ultimately pull you up with him.

Let us then push everyone of the race up and not down. To help a Negro boy or girl to become a useful Negro man or woman, is probably to assist in giving to the world a great character who never would have found himself or herself but for the early help he got from you or your charitable institution. Try to educate your boys and girls who have no parents, try to assist those who have no one to depend on. Never let orphans go astray or fall into the hands of other races—they will only make servants of them. If you help them within your race, they may yet become the leaders of the race in some particular line of success.

Before you give to others not of your race, think first how much your race need[s] it and give it there. Never be unkind to your race. Never allow the Members of your race to die in poverty. It is your fault if they do. Always put yourself in the position of the other unfortunate fellow and ask, "how would I like to be in his stead," and if your feeling and conscience rebel against his condition, then help him out of it if you can, and as much as you do it unto him, so may others do unto you in your time or hour of need.

Whenever you find your own racial institutions worthy, support them. In any community in which you live, always seek to have your own charitable institutions. If the public funds are used for charity, then seek to get a proportion for your group, separately and distinctly from that of others. Because you yourself may not desire charity for the time being, why should you not support the appeal for charity for those of our race who need it.

One may be prosperous today on his own initiative and account and by misadventure lose the natural ability of self-initiative to become dependent upon charity. You may lose your eyes or arms or legs, you may lose your health without contributing to it personally, but purely by accident. In that case you would become a recipient of charity without your expecting it or contributing to the cause; so charity should always be maintained for its own good to benefit those who may be unfortunate enough to need it, and the next person to need it may be you. No one can tell, so never frown upon a worthy charity and never refuse to give and support if you can afford it.

WINNING MANKIND BY KINDNESS

A touch of kindness moves the heart of all men. To be kind is to be generous[,] to be pleasant, to be inviting in your manner. To be sympathetic and thoughtful of the other fellow's feelings may co[s]t you nothing, you should be kind, because sometimes you can extend it by a pleasant smile or pleasant salutation or a good wish. To say "I wish you well, I wish you everything that is prosperous, I hope you will succeed, I am so sorry to hear of your bad fortune, I wish things will turn for you successfully, I wish you long life and the joy and happiness of it," is a good turn. All these convey to your friend, acquaintance, or even your enemy, a beauty of thought and soul that wins appreciation and often gratitude.

If your friend comes to you for help and you cannot give it to him don't turn him away with cold words, but with the words of cheer and comfort. It may bring him joy in his disappointment, even though not getting the thing he had hoped for.

You can never tell who is sincere or who is honest, therefore you must always be on your guard not to loan your money, not to give away your money foolishly, because you may never get it back.

If you are in doubt that you will not get back a loan from a friend, then try never to loan a friend money, because he will become your enemy after. Offer him a drink of water, a piece of cake or a delicious fruit, and then express your sorrow in the kindliest of words of your inability to help him just at that time, and see that when he leaves the gate you smile with him and win his smile in return, which is an assurance of the parting of friendship which probably would not be otherwise if you had bluntly refused his original request.

Win the world to you with a smile, with the hearty shake of the hand, with the glad welcome. It costs very little, it costs less than the ugly stare, the fixed hand of unwelcome.

In the organisation life of the U.N.I.A. always give to those you want to win. Give to the poor in the neighbourhood and win them over to you. Give them from the charitable funds of the organisation, give them fruit, if they are sick give them flowers, give them the little niceties and necessities that they need and cannot buy. Be kind to the little children of the neighbourhood. Give them candies from the charitable fund, give them pennies to buy candies and these little ones will carry the name of the U.N.I.A. through the neighbourhood.

Then visit the neighbourhood from house to house. Leave a word of cheer everywhere you go and then persuade them to join the U.N.I.A. If they are in trouble, console them.

If the organisation can help them with advice, give it to them. If you cannot go, recommend some officer of the organization who has been well trained for such a work, to go there and give advice, but make your good work be seen and known in the neighbourhood and in the community, so that they will always come to you for organisation help, remembering that the organisation is for the purpose of helping the needy, the distressed, and assist all members of the race who need the race's help. It is by these methods that the Catholic Church has won the hearts of the people by the charit[y] of its sisterhood and the priesthood, helping the sick, the distressed, restoring them to health.

When people have recovered from their bad condition, their gratitude becomes the pillar on which the church rests. Let the gratitude of the Negro people in your community be the pillar on which the organisation rests in that community.

There should always be a charitable fund in every division of the U.N.I.A. and an amount placed at the disposal of responsible representatives of the Association for the dispensing of the charity of the neighbourhood in which they live. As a representative of the association the charity should be disclosed in the name of the organisation to maintain its reputation in the community.

Let the tender touch of kindness be everywhere as going from the U.N.I.A. to the people in the community.

When men will remember you for nothing else, they will remember you for the kindly deed, the touch of sympathy that seldom comes from others, but which is the duty of every representative of the U.N.I.A. and of the Association.

LESSON 19

Living for Something

Life is an important function. It was given for the purpose of expression. The flower expresses itself through the beauty of its bloom. The vine expresses itself through its rambling search in settling its own peculiar natur[e]. The tree expresses itself in its smiling green leaves, shaking branches and sometimes hanging fruits. The lark expresses itself in its laughter and song.

The river expresses itself in its gentle meandering unto the sea and man expresses himself according to the idealistic visions of his nature. There is a scope for each life. Let yours find its scope and fully express itself.

Man should have a purpose and that purpose he should always keep in view, with the hope of achieving it in the fullest satisfaction to himself. Be not aimless, drifting and floating with the tide that doesn't go your way.

To find your purpose, you must search yourself and with the knowledge of what is good and what is bad, select your course, steering toward the particular object of your dream or desire.

Never enter upon life's serious journey without a programme. Simpleton as you may be, you can have a programme. No ship ever reaches port without a positive destination beforehand, otherwise it will drift on the mighty ocean to be overtaken by the storm or the ill wind that blows.

The sensible captain goes to sea with a chart to map out his course so as to reach his harbour of safety. Your programme is your chart through life. Everything you do, do it by method, nothing succeeds continuously or repeatedly by chance. You may get success in a particular direction by accident, but it was chiefly because that accident was the correct method in achieving that particular thing, and you happened to have struck upon the right method by chance. But trying chances that way a second time may bring you failure, as it generally does.

To follow the correct method will give you the same result all the time. Therefore, make your life a methodical one. Rise at a certain hour, work up to a certain hour, retire at a certain hour. Do everything on time so that your entire system becomes methodical. If you have something to do, and it ought to be done, do it with proper method or system to get the best result. Study it first, then go after doing it.

If a thing is worth while doing, it is worth while doing well.

How pitiful it is to see a man living without a programme without knowing how he is going to use his todays and his tomorrows. If you follow him long enough you will find him going down the ditch of failure, because he has been travelling without a programme.

Observe the other man who has his programme, and see him go from one step to the next with success. If you have a programme, you know what comes next. If you have none, you have to improvise one and then it is too late to do it properly, and so you fail.

If you want to be 5,000 miles away in December and it costs $500.00, because you may be disappointed at the last mo[m]e[n]t[, s]tart from January thinking about your trip and making arrangements for it, so that when the time comes you will be perfectly ready. Make this a practice in everything, don't wait until time arrives, think ahead.

Always try to look through by calling upon your experience when you are looking to that future that is ahead of you. Analyse it, arrange it to suit your needs, so that when things come upon you, you will be ready. Don't let things come upon you suddenly.

The man who lives in the present, preparing for the future[,] always enjoys a better future than the man who doesn't visualise it, but who goes right into it unprepared. Future seeing is a worthy object.

Always try to look down the future. You make slight mistakes here and there but if you gauge it properly, with the experience of the past and the conditions of the present, you may strike an even or accurate estimate of what it ought to be, so when it comes, you will be able to welcome it with some kind of satisfaction.

To live for something doesn't only mean something for yourself, but something for your kith and kin and something for your race. If a father lives for something, he ought to be able to see his children through that something, so that what he does not accomplish for himself might be accomplished for his children. As for instance, an industrious father lives with the hope of improving his social condition and economic condition. He would like to live in a beautiful mansion on the hill, from which he could see the country places around, the valleys, the dales and the lofty mountains, but he is working in the valley, living in a small cottage[.] He is growing older without his dreams realised, but he looks to his son and says "if I cannot enjoy this desire of mine, because I may be too old, when the time comes, I shall make it possible for my son to live on that hilltop or my grandson[." T]hat is living in the future. That is living for something, because when the old man dies, the son inherits and when the son dies, the grandson inherits. Inherits what? That which the grandfather lived for.

This should be the policy of every Negro, to live for something to hand down to a son, to a grandson, that they may have life a little easier than their fathers before them. This is the way successful and great families have come into the world and great races too.

No Negro should be objectless or purposeless in life. Always have a purpose. To waste time in non-essentials is to be purposeless. Playing bone dice is purposeless. There is nothing achieved in the time wasted in doing it. No great fortune is guaranteed, no great art is accomplished, no structure is built because it is a game of chance. Playing pool is waste, because like playing the dice it is a game of chance. Sitting around and going from place to place without an occupation is waste, valuable time is going and nothing is being registered by way of achievement; but when one settles down upon a given and worthy idea or occupation, such as an architect, an engineer, a builder, a farmer, a poet, a teacher, he or she is working on something that may become tangible in results. It is from such tangible assets that we build fortunes. Find something tangible to do, then, and use your time in doing it well. It is better that you be dead than having no purpose in life.

Ella Wheeler Wilcox says:—

> Have a purpose, and that purpose keep in view,
> Have a purpose, and that purpose keep in view,
> For drifting like a helmless vessel,
> Thou can'st ne'er to self be true.

The ship without a helm must flounder on the rock. Why be such a ship? Why not sail through life like the barque whose helm is perfect? Be a captain with chart in hand seeing his port as he sails steadily on. See your port, visualise it, and as the time comes, anchor in it.

THE DIGNITY AND PRICE [PRIDE?] OF RACE

God made man as a complete and finished being. [No] flaws in him but his sin. The race of man, therefore, must be perfect in its physical origin. Hence there is nothing to be ashamed of as far as [the] species is concerned.

The black man's origin is as true as the sun. He needs not therefore, to apologise for his existence. His place in the world is fixed as a star and as such it is incumbent on him to maintain the dignity and pride of his own manhood.

There is nothing unusual about the Negro other than he is himself as man. He is beautiful in himself and why not so? The Anglo-Saxon sees beauty through himself, the Teuton sees beauty through himself, and [the] Mongol sees beauty through himself and so naturally and logically the Negro ought to see beauty through himself. When the Negro attempts to see beauty through aquiline features of an Anglo-Saxon then he images the homeliness and ugliness of his own features because his features are [d]ifferent to those of the Anglo-Saxon.

Beauty must be reflected out of your own eyes. A Negro must be beautiful to a Negro, as an Anglo-Saxon is to an Anglo-Saxon. The highest standard of beauty, therefore, for a Negro, is the Negro. Never allow any race to say that your race is not beautiful. If there is ugliness in race, it is in the other race, not in yours, because the other race looks different to you. To the Anglo-Saxon the Mongol is ugly; to the Mongol the Anglo-Saxon is ugly. Compare the Anglo-Saxon and the Negro, it is the Anglo-Saxon who is ugly, not the Negro. The long sharp nose of the European cannot be considered beautiful against a strong, healthy, air-free nasal passage of the black man who is free from those nasal defects that make health difficult. The thin lip of the European could not be beautiful compared with the strong, healthy and developed lips of the African. These are the ways self-respecting people see themselves. The round healthy face of the African is much more beautiful than the straight, sickly looking face of the European. Then why surrender all that is good in you and discount it for that which doesn't reach a standard comparable to yours and others.

Always think yourself a perfect being, and be satisfied with yourself except you are a jelly fish.

Never allow anyone to convince you of your inferiority as a man. Rise in your dignity to justify all that is noble in your manhood as a race.

> My race is mine and I belong to it.
> It climbs with me and I shall climb with it,
> My pride is mine and I shall surely honour it,
> It is the height on which I daily sit.

THE SOCIAL CONFUSION

Man at his best in his society is always quarrelling. He is never satisfied. Don't ex[pec]t that you will find in your lifetime the solution for all his problems and ills, attend only to those that concern you and your group. If you can solve your own group problems in your community you have done well. Let others solve theirs. The time you waste running around with others and helping them in their problems, you are robbing your group of that much time to help them solve their problems.

Whether a man is sober or drunk, he is a disagreeable beast—you will find it so in every community. So search out for your man, and tame the beast; he is never of the same mood all the time—at one time you think you can like him, at another time you think you could kill him. Tame him toward the end of your own social satisfaction for dabbling in the confusion of others will only make you more confused and your divided energy will only tend to defeat the special purpose which you should have in solving the problems of your race.

Never forget that all other groups in the society of your community are looking after their own individual group interest, and your interest except from the community point of view, is never theirs. Therefore, theirs should never be yours as far as the particular group interest is concerned. Don't be disappointed if other people shock you by their behaviour, because man is made that way, and he acts that way chiefly because he is racially different.

The White man may compliment you today and abuse you tomorrow, simply because of your race. Don't trust the whole community then if it is made up of different groups, because it is apt to disappoint you by being selfish at any moment, as far as the division of particular interest is concerned.

Always pick out your interest in the community and conserve it because others are doing the same. It is only when you tread on the heels of others eve[n] by accident, that you find out that there are differences between you and others, but your mistake doesn't prove a fact—the fact was there before your mistake, and it is always a fact that each group have their own individual and collected racial problems.

The white man never can be the Negro, and the Negro can never be the white man, except after eternity and you do not live so long.

You may be the same in soul but you cannot see soul, so that similarity is beyond you. What you see is yourself, physically, and there is no doubt that there is physical difference between you and the other man, so watch your step in the social confusion of life.

Always remember that another person is not you, for that other person knows too well that you are different to him, and is always on guard to divide the line of interest. This applies everywhere all around—in your home, in your office, in your workshop, in the street, in the community. Your wife will grab the article and say "This is mine["] and will refuse to give it up, although you thought you were one and what was yours was hers and hers yours[.] She always has a time to claim her own either in peace or confusion.

So always have your own in the social confusion of life, because even you and your partner may have to run in different directions to save your skins, and if one person is gone with what is yours in another direction, you may lose your life following what you should have been carrying with you. Never forget this, it is of great importance to you for your own safety, you should always have your own fare to pay the conductor. You may have to walk whilst the other person rides, because you can never tell where a confusion springs up. It may be in the street near the neighbourhood, it may be 100 miles from town, and that will be a long walk if the car moves off, because of the confusion between you and the driver.

Always expect confusion in the dividing line in the social contact of life.

LESSON 20

History of the U.N.I.A.

The U.N.I.A. and African Communities' League was conceived as an organization, for the purpose of raising the status of the Negro to national expression and general freedom in the year 1913, during the visit of Marcus Garvey to Europe, after completing an adventurous visit to the Central American Republics.

The conception continued to impress itself until the conceiver was compelled to make it practical, during his stay in England during the same period. To make it practical he sailed from England, foregoing a course of law which he had undertaken for the purpose of a profession in June of 1914, for Jamaica, B.W.I.[,] his native home.

In July of the year 1914 he got together a group of men and women in the city of Kingston, and there organized the association. Meetings, in the name of the association— U.N.I.A. and African Communities' League, were held regularly, after the organization of the same, at a place called the Collegiate Hall, in the Central part of the city of Kingston, Jamaica.

A set of officers was elected and the first organization came into substantial existence. Many meetings were held in different parts of Jamaica in the name of the organization, and it co[n]tinued to exist in that island as an organization until the year 1917 [1916] when the founder sailed for America, and on his arrival there he visited Tuskegee Institute on an outstanding invitation from the late Dr. Booker T. Washington. He met at the Institute the then Principal, Dr. Robert R. Moton and Professor E. J. Scott, the Secretary-Treasurer. He discussed with them the purposes of the Organization which were similar to the present aims and objects in the constitution.

He received very little encouragement and left Tuskegee in continuation of a trip throughout the United States. On his return to New York he visited Dr. E. B. Dubois at the office of the National Association for the Advancement of Coloured People, and discussed with him the aims and objects of the association, and the possibility of organizing the movement in the United States. He was very much discouraged by Dr. Dubois. He undertook to organize on his own account in Harlem, by first speaking on the streets, principally Lennox Avenue, during week evenings and inviting his hearers to attend Sunday meetings at the Lafayette Hall at 129 Street and Seventh avenue. The meetings at Lafayette Hall grew rapidly in membership, with occasional overflowing mass meetings held at the Palace Casino at 135th Street and Fifth Avenue. After the Lafayette Hall became too small to accommodate the growing membership, the Palace Casino was secure[d] for regular membership, the Palace Casino was secure[d] for regu[la]r Mass meetings with offices established at premises above what was then known as the Crescent Theatre at 135th Street.

From the Crescent Theatre building to the Palace Casino, the movement grew with such rapidity that premises were secured at 148th Street between Lennox and Seventh Avenue to be known as Liberty Hall.

All this progress took place within 18 months of the founding of the organization in Harlem, New York.

From Liberty Hall, the movement spread all over the United States and all over the world culminating in the calling and holding of the first International Convention of the Negro peoples of the world in August 1920 at New York, at which Convention Marcus Garvey was elected President General with 20 other persons as an Executive Council for guiding the destiny of the organization that had become international.

For further information on this history, read first

and second volumes of "Philosophy & Opinions of Marcus Garvey[.]"

HOW TO TEACH THE U.N.I.A.

To know what the U.N.I.A. is, you must first read its Constitution and Books of Laws, from cover to cover and all the literature written by the founder bearing on the activities of the organization.

The preamble of the Constitution is vitally important to those who are to interpret its supreme object.

Whenever the purpose of the organization is challenged by foes particularly, quote the preamble of the Constitution. This should be done particularly where its enemies assail it before a Court of Law or before Governmental Authorities.

This preamble was written particularly for the purpose of winning the sympathy and support of alien races where the other objects of the association were being threatened through hostility.

The U.N.I.A. and African Communities League were intended as one organization to carry out all the aims and objects of the Constitution, but the Law of States where the organization operates separate the functions of friendly and fraternal organizations from those of business organization[s], hence in the incorporation of the name of the Association in the State of New York in 1918, the two organizations were incorporated separately.

The organizations had to be incorporated—the Universal Negro Improvement Association, Incorporated and the African Communities' League, Incorporated. The U.N.I.A. as a fraternal organization and the African Commun[i]ties' League as a business organization, but the Convention of 1920 accepting the original idea, *linked the two organizations, together as the U.N.I.A.* and African Communities' League to hold the principles that were intended so that the two organizations would not go apart as if they were not related.

Whenever the U.N.I.A. is going to do business, it will do business as the African Communities' League or as some other business organization, as was evidence[d] in the Incorporation of the Black Star Line, the Black Cross Navigation and Trading Company, The Negro Factories Incorporated, etc., with all its interest of [or?] capital held by the U.N.I.A.

No private individuals were intended to own the capit[a]l of any of these enterprises, because these enterprises were organized as future ones will be organized, only for the purpose of supplying funds by way of profit to the U.N.I.A. to carry out its aims and objects as laid out in the Constitution in the interest of the race.

All subordinate companies of a business nature must be controlled by the U.N.I.A. to enable it to carry out the aims and objects of the U.N.I.A. and to comply with the law of the respective states.

Membership in the U.N.I.A. is divided into two kinds— the active member who joins a division or branch of the association and pays the regular dues according to the Constitution and By-laws of the organization, who has first claim through his or her division to all benefit[s], and any Negro who is considered an ordinary member by virtue of his race to whom charity may be dispensed if available and if he can prove his need.

The association is supposed to maintain an interest in every Negro, irrespective of his nationality or his condition, so long as he has not been proved a traitor to the race and outlawed as such. *All the properties of the U.N.I.A.* and associate business corporations or companies or enterprises *are held in trust* for the Negro race in the relationship of the race through the ac[ti]ve membership in the organization as above explained.

The accumulated wealth and property of the organization must be handed down from generation to generation as the property of the Negro race through the U.N.I.A., because it is held in trust to be given back to those who need it as the occasion may demand.

Always give a receipt for money of value received in connection with the U.N.I.A.

Always keep proper records and always have a duplicate for your protection. If you receive money from people in the name of the organization and do not give a receipt, you can bet they will investigate for the purpose of trapping you, and then your name will be dead if there is any delinquency.

When you attend a meeting of the U.N.I.A. as a representative, and you are to receive money for the Parent Body, always let that money be received first on the records of the local division, through its officers, from whom you are raising it for the Parent Body of the particular purpose, so that when an account is to be made, the local records will support your report to the Parent Body.

Whenever you officially visit a division of the organization, you are then the Superior Officer, if you are a representative of the Parent Body. You shall then see that all things are conducted in the proper way in your presence in accordance with the Constitution.

In visiting a division always make your visit profitable both to the division and to the Parent Body. Never create a loss or tax on the local division by your visit. Every visit you make to a division should be an opportunity for you to enroll new members for that division and increase the enth[u]siasm of the local members for the organization.

In planning a visit to a division, whether it be a regular visit or otherwise, *always acquaint the President and the Secretary* respectively and get them to make the necessary local announcements, so as to give you an extraordinary attendance of people and members, so that you may have an opportunity of increasing the local membership.

If your visits are always an asset to the division they will always invite you outside of your regular periodic visitation to come among them. The expenses of your trip should be well figured out before you make it. Railroad fare to and fro or bus fare to and fro, accommodation, etc., hence you should see that the meetings are worked up to such magnitude as to cover these expenses when they are held.

When you visit a division in your territory your financial returns should not be only from the Division, but you should seek to use the time that you are in the community to get support from individuals and to do work for the association, killing two birds with the same stone.

You should observe always the proper form of opening and closing as well as conducting the meetings of the association, as follows:—

(1). Opening hymn, "From Greenland's Icy Mountains."

(2). Reading of the prayers in the ritual or hymn sheet of the association. When your programme is not too crowded and the time for meeting is lengthy, you may go through the whole form of prayers, but if there is not sufficient time, read only such parts of the prayers as would enable you to go through the programme without length.

(3). After the prayers, sing either "Shine on Eternal Light" or "O Africa Awaken," then go into the rest of the programme, and when you are closing, close with the prayers of the association for that purpose and sing the African National Anthem.

Whenever your object is to raise financial assistance or collection for the Parent Body or for the local division, let the raising of the same come in the middle of the programme, after your most emphatic speech of the day is delivered, whether it is to be delivered by yourself or somebody else.

If you have things to dispose of for the association or other help to get, this must come after the main collection. If you are the person appealing for the collection you must do so with steady emphasis and proper worded appeal. This must never be done half-heartedly as it will bring half-hearted results.

If you have raised a collection for the Parent Body at a meeting, see to it that it has been properly accounted for, after it is taken up, and not mixed up with the funds of the local division in any way.

In visiting a division, you are always the guest of that division, and the President presides and then introduces you. If it is a special business meeting where you have been called in to regulate the affairs of the division, you will take the chair as a representative of the Parent Body and conduct the meeting accordingly and restore order and hand it back to the President or the responsible officer of the division afterwards.

Where a President has been removed and you have been called in, you may appoint someone temporarily, such as the Vice-President to act until you have reported the matter to the Parent Body and the Parent Body carries out an appointment.

If there happens to be factions in a division and you are called in to straighten out their affairs, *never take up residence at the home of EITHER side of the faction,* but seek independent lodging until you have disposed of the matter, otherwise you will have the prejudice against you of taking sides.

Never listen to one side without hearing the other side. Never give a decision on one side without hearing the other side.

Always try to pacify, always try to bring factions together in keeping with the principles of the association, always try to compromise the faction toward keeping the peace. Whenever you make your official visit to the division as a representative of the Parent Body, always call for the records and go through them and see that they are properly kept and make a report to the Parent Body.

Whenever you see mistakes that can be corrected, see that they are corrected and don't allow them to continue.

Never allow any division to have individuals owning the property of the division in their names, except in cases where proper documents have been passed, where the organization is not registered, as between the persons and the organization, showing that they are only holding such in trust for the organization.

But all this should be discouraged and immediate steps taken to register the organization in the particular state or community, so that its property may be held in its name.

When property is bought in the name of the organization,

the organization's name must be mentioned AND only the names of the officers of it at that time must appear *as officers, not as individuals.* As for instance, Brooklyn Division of the U.N.I.A., John Brown, President, Henry Jones, Secretary. In law the names are taken as being officers of an organization. Hence the individuals can make no separate claim as individuals, but only as officers of the organization.

Should they not continue to be officers of the organization those who may be then officers of the organization would have their names substituted as such officers without affecting the ownership of the property of the organization.

Pay careful attention to this, so that the association may not be defrauded of its property or its rights. Always look out for self-seeking officers and individuals in a division, and see that they do nothing detrimental to the interest of the organization.

Always confine yourself to your own designated territory and never go beyond it except authorized. Always respect the Charter rights of every division, chapter, branch or affiliated organization. Never use one against the other, so long as they are chartered.

Have no special favourite division except the one that you may be a member of. Always hold an even balance. Always encourage co-operation between the divisions. Always seek to put down antagonisms between the divisions. If a member cannot get on in one division, before his membership is lost, advise him to join another division.

Wherever there are no divisions or chapters and there are Negroes in the community, encourage the organizing of a branch, a chapter or a division. Over 1,000 Negroes in a community ought to have a division or a chapter, so in a community where you have 200,000 Negroes, you may have many divisions according to the district and location because all those 200,000 Negroes could belong to one or two divisions. You should approach ministers of the gospel in the community and ask them to organize chapters in their churches of which they will be Presidents, so as to get their church members to be U.N.I.A. members. Do the same with lodges and other fraternities, they can also be chapters of the U.N.I.A. although independent lodges and fraternities.

ARGUMENT TO CONVINCE FOR THE U.N.I.A.

Its Work in Twenty Years

(1). Activities from 1917 to 1937 of the U.N.I.A. have stirred the entire world of Negroes to a consciousness of race pride which never existed before.

(2). It has broken down the barriers of racial nationality among Negr[oe]s and caused American, African, West Indian, Canadian, A[us]tralian and South and Central American Negroes to realize that they have a common interest.

(3). It has given the Negro throughout the world a program of racial nationalism which never existed before.

(4). It has caused all Negroes to recognize their common origin as Africans or of African descent.

(5). It has caused all the other races to recognize the national aspiration of the Negro. It has placed the Negro's cause before the League of Nations and Versailles Peace Conference.

(6). It placed before the Disarma[m]ent Conference in Washington in 1924, the national aspiration of the Negro.

(7). It has caused the French, English, and European governments with colonies in Africa and the West Indies to extend greater privileges to the native races and to offer them more secure positions in the respective civil service, diplomatic service, and political life of the country.

(8). Negro justices, magistrates, and heads of government departments were appointed because of the activities of the U.N.I.A. in different countries.

(9). The economic status of Negroes was raised in different countries because of the association.

(10). It taught the Negro how to go into big business.

(11). It taught the Negro how to secure his own business enterprises through which tens of thousands of Negro business[es] have been started all over the world.

(12). It taught Negroes how to support their own professional men, doctors, lawyers, etc.

(13). It taught the Negro how to support his own church.

(14). It taught the Negro how to use his political power from which he has benefited in the United States, in the West Indies, in Africa and other countries.

(15). It gave the Negro a national flag and a national hymn.

(16). It cause[d] the other races to spell the word Negro with a capital "N."

(17). It taught Negroes self-respect for their race.

(18). It brought courage to the Negro race throughout the world.

(19). It caused the Negro to search for a new type of leadership.

(20). It taught the Negro preparedness against adversity.

(21). It has been the most outstanding Negro organization throughout the world.

(22). It is the most recognized international organization among Negroes.

(23). It is known in all parts of the world.

(24). It has taught the Negro to follow only Negro leadership.

(25). It has saved the Negro from the hypocritical, dishonest leadership of other people which never brought him any good results.

(26). It taught the Negro that the cats don't lead the rats nor the lions the sheep, nor the wolves the foxes and so Negroes should lead Negroes.

(27). It has taught the Negro never to rely upon the sweet sounding words of others and promises, but to rely on his words and his own promises if he is to be led safely.

(28). It has taught the Negro to believe in himself and not to believe that what another man seeks for himself he is going to give away freely.

(29). It has taught the Negro to have his own labour organizations and not to expect other labourers who are competing with him for the same employment, to give honest leadership to compete with them for the same job.

(30). It is the only organization that gave the Negro an international outlook.

(31). It gave the Negro press a wider point of view.

(32). It has kept the Negro from going Red for the convenience of others.

(33). For twenty years it has changed the attitude of the Negro and has set him on the way to a new hope. Give the U.N.I.A. the second twenty years of support for its new programme.

(34). One of the fundamental desire[s] of the U.N.I.A. is to approach every Negro with the attitude of friendship, brotherhood, and sympathy. Therefore, every representative of the association must adopt an attitude tending to bring about the realization of such a desire.

It may be necessary to use a great amount of tolerance to reach the end aimed at, but whatsoever is necessary must be done to bring about such a state of affairs.

The policy is that you cannot drive away a Negro from the organization and still want to organize all the Negroes. Every Negro that is lost presents [prevents] the ultimate achievement of the aims of the organization. So never try to drive a member out of the organization, but hold him and convert him.

Always appreciate the fact that the majority of Negroes are ignorant, and you must exercise a great amount of tolerance to educate them up to your point of view. This is your missionary work. As other people were willing to sacrifice their time, and even lives, to Christianize our race, so we must exercise patience and time to civilize our people.

The attitude of expelling members and suspending members is not accepted with good grace, and should be resorted to only under the most extreme circumstances. The attitude should be adopted to find [*words missing*].

The best way to prevent dissatisfaction in a division is to live up to the Constitution and By-Laws, because it is only on the Constitution and By-Laws that you can discipline a member, so that if a member violates the Constitution and By-Laws you can reasonably draw the violation to his or her attention.

You cannot show partiality in a division of the association or in the work of the association. You must be impartial to maintain the principles of the association as the attraction for those who do not know anything about the association.

Never cease your effort to influence a Negro to join the association until he has joined, because so long as he keeps out, the work of uniting all the Negroes cannot be accomplished.

Remember always that you are a missionary for the cause of the Association so lose no opportunity that may present itself to make converts for the Association.

A splendid way of proselyting for the association is to interest all your friends and acquaintances in its movements, and whenever you go among them to tell them of anything done and accomplished by the association.

Always find some work for the association. During the time you are not actually attending a meeting of the association or doing any special work of the association devote you time in calling upon your acquaintances in the neighbourhood in your community to talk them into becoming members and supporters of the association.

You should know all the people of your race in your street, in your neighbourhood and in your town, and approach them in your leisure hours, one by one, to convert them to the organization and in getting support from them for the organization.

Where you come across responsible people of the race, take their names, professions and addresses after talking to them about the association, and send the same in a weekly report or monthly report to the President-General's office at Headquarters, and ask him to communicate with such persons in the manner you think would best help to clinch the support of such persons for the organization.

In your own town secure the names and addresses and professions of all the responsible people—doctors, lawyers, merchants, preachers, etc., and send such names to Headquarters with comments against each name for Headquarters to help influence such persons to support the organization.

Always keep in touch with the newspapers published in your community and get them to publish favourable news about the activities of the organization.

See to it that every intelligent person in the community, of the race, subscribes to or purchases the 'Black Man' in its regular publication, so that they may keep up with the activities of the movement.

Read the 'Black Man' regularly yourself, so that others may not have information you have not got.

In attending meetings of divisions, as an official, always carry yourself with dignity and always be impartial in dealing with the affairs of the divisions. If you take sides, not based on the Constitution, you are only destroying your own usefulness in that division and to the Parent Body.

Your honour must always be uppermost in dealing with matters affecting the divisions when you visit them. If you are an official of the Parent Body, always see that the dignity of the Parent Body is maintained through you, because any bad behaviour of yours will reflect against the judgment of the Parent Body in appointing you.

If you are a representative of the Parent Body with proper credentials you must observe the agreement entered into between you and the Parent Body for dealing with the affairs of the association. For any violation of the agreement may cause you to lose your office as a representative of the Parent Body.

Never overstep your authority in dealing with a division as a representative of the Parent Body. Never attempt to show your grand superiority to the displeasure of members of the division or officers of the division, but be as modest, yet as firm as you can be, in your dealings. There is nothing to invite antagonism more than arrogant and unreasonable display of power. The most powerful people in the world are the most modest, when dealing with others, whose goodwill they have to depend on, because they know how much immodesty offends others. Never try to be offensive. Never threaten others but reason with them. To threaten an officer or a member is to invite antagonism and fight and make your task more difficult. Never enter into any unworthy arrangement with officers of divisions or members, because ultimately they will expose you when you do not do things to suit them. The moment you enter into any dishonourable arrangement the person you have done so with holds it as a club over your head, and will place you in a false position. So as not to have yourself exposed, don't do it, therefore, you don't want to be exposed.

When working as a representative in a community to get results for the association, you should divide that community into zones or districts. You may even reduce the districts to the streets or blocks of streets and appoint some responsible and enthusiastic member in that zone, district or street to be a kind of captain or lieutenant to keep the spirit of the people in that district, zone or street, regulated to the principles of the organization. The captain or lieutenant must be all active members of the division. Since they live in the street, they would likely know all the people in the street and could help greatly in organizing them as members of the organization.

Your chief aim must be to organize every man, woman and child. If with all this material and possibilities you cannot make the U.N.I.A. succeed in that community, you yourself are a colossal failure and not the people.

The greatest recognition of your merit and ability will be reflected by the number of people who are members of the association in your community, district, town or state, because their activities will testify to your greater activity in their midst.

You should not expect promotion from the Parent Body except you have something to recommend you in your community for such promotion, otherwise your promotion will not be fair to somebody else who has done his or her work. Don't complain, do the job. Get results. The moment you start to complain, you are stating that the thing cannot be done. If you cannot do it at one place, you cannot do it at another, you are a failure, you are no good.

Let your pride be in winning over an adversary. It gives good satisfaction. You have enough material in the U.N.I.A. to use as an argument against any man who is a member of the race, caring not how destructive he is. Don't leave him, therefore, until you have converted him, talk him out. In this respect, bring all your diplomacy to bear, all the experience you have had in dealing with men, and enlarge on and explain every good point of the U.N.I.A. Carry your Constitution and read to him the preamble and the aims and objects, and explain them as you have been taught and then when he makes up his mind, get him right there.

If you have approached him to become a member, let him join then. If you have approached him for support, get him to write or give his support right there, and immediately thank him by correspondence for joining or supporting, to give him an impression of your business-like ability.

The best time to call on people is immediately after meals, not before, because when people are hungry, they are in no good mood. Call immediately after the breakfast hour, the dinner hour and the supper hour. If you are calling at the office never call an hour before lunch or an hour before dinner. Always go smiling or pleasant. Don't carry a long face.

If you have been abruptly received and abruptly talked to, reply by pleasant remarks and smile your subject into changing his or her mood.

Even a savage will admit defeat when met by a smile. If a person has a frown on the face say, "I hope you are well Mr. Jones." That will put him off his guard immediately. If he states that he is unwell, sympathise with him and tell him about some remedy you know. This is good psychology to win your subject; or you may say, "you have a very pretty picture here Mr. Jones," or some other thing, though not pretty to flatter his vanity, but to take him off his sullen mood.

If he is a smoker, offer him a cigarette, telling him something that you think he ought to be interested in—you may strike at that something looking at the things around him. "Have you seen the latest picture?" "Have you heard the latest news?" Then go into your subject, after you have changed his attitude, but don't start talking to a sullen man on the subject you are approaching him on until you have won him over to a pleasant mood.

It would be better to go back a second time.

Always point out to him the trusteeship of the U.N.I.A. for the race, and the benefit each Negro will get through success of the organisation.

In arguing for support for the U.N.I.A. draw extensively upon your imagination and find an argument to support you. You have the argument of the success of a nation, the success of other race groups, and always use the Jew as argument.

Among the first persons to be approached for help for the U.N.I.A. are professional men and business men of the race. A better organised race will mean better business for them. Tell them that is the work of the U.N.I.A., therefore they should support it.

Let them realise the power you have in your hand to direct patronage one way or the other as an organisation.

To win over your new prospect, tell him that Mr. So and So has done so and so for the organisation, but *it must be a fact not a lie,* and then he will not want to be left out and will support you.

This must not be done for personal racket, because if you are found out using this method for personal gain, you will be struck off the roll of students and be disqualified as a representative because the moment the person finds out that you have used the approach for personal purposes, you have damaged the association and your own reputation. Hence, you are of no use, either to the association or to anybody else.

The first international convention of the U.N.I.A. held in New York, from the 1st to the 31st of August, 1920, formulated and adopted the Declaration of Rights of the Negro peoples of the world, to which the organisation is committed until the objects of the said Declaration are fully realised.

The Declaration must be studied by each leader of the race. It is to be found on page 135 in the second volume of the "Philosophy and Opinions of Marcus Garvey." In seeking financial aid for the U.N.I.A. always do so with confidence. The high and lofty aims of the association and the universal objects to be achieved which can only be done through the support of each and every member of the race, calls for the support of every man.

For gaining such support, always impress upon the Negro that heretofore he has supported white organisations, such as the churches, and contributed to their institutions, without getting any direct benefit. He has even supported the Salvation Army. Therefore, there is no reason why he should not support a movement of his own that calculates to bestow upon him and his generations untold benefits.

Contributions to the U.N.I.A. should be generally accepted from Negroes, but where other people of other races can be approached and are willing to give help, such help may be accepted, but without any strings tied to it, or promises made, that would in any way compromise the clear cut intelligence of the policy of the U.N.I.A. *Such contributions will not entitle the donors to any privileges of membership* or to any right to attend the *meetings of the U.N.I.A.* except public meetings as guests, but shall never entitle them to attend or take part in any of the business meetings of the organisation. Their donations may be accepted in the same way as Negroes give to white organisations, without having any claim on those organisations.

Whenever donations are accepted from white or other races the names of such persons when registered on the same account of donations as Negroes, must be *marked with a cross,* and when such donations are being forwarded to the Parent Body, an *explanation must be given* stating that such a person is a member of the white race or of whatsoever race the person may be, other than a Negro, so that no communication of a private nature would be sent to that person revealing the business of the U.N.I.A. This is very important, because by not distinguishing between the donors such persons may be written to as if they were members of the U.N.I.A. and may be sent communications which they should have no right to receive.

In approaching other people of other races for help, your argument must be different to that of an approach to members of your race. Your appeal should be based on humanity, good citizenship, or helping a worthy cause, *but never* explain the objects that are uppermost to which they would naturally react with unfriendliness and suspicion.

Never believe another race is so friendly as to know your objects and not try to hinder you from succeeding ultimately.

Whenever you make an appeal to the individual or individuals for financial help for the organization, and you have failed in getting a response, the failure is not due to the person or persons you have addressed yourself to, but may be due to your inability to properly interpret to them the objects and the aims and the reasons why they should support the associations, so be always in a position to so interpret those aims and objects as to always gain support, because people are always willing to respond to a thing that is to benefit them, even in a remote way.

Never approach anyone for help for the association with doubt in your mind. It is better you wait until you are in a frame of mind to talk conscientiously so as to carry conviction, rather than try to do so when your spirit is low.

Let every day, every hour, and every minute count in your life for something done, something accomplished.

Don't waste time, it is a sin, for time wasted can never be recalled or regained. Try to be always the best advocate of the cause of the U.N.I.A. Try to let no one surpass you in doing that. There is something in you that is individual, that nobody else has; try to bring it out and let that be your individuality and personality, for which people will remember you and talk about you. There is nothing that someone else has done in the triumph of a cause that you cannot do if you go about it in the right way.

Always try to find the right way. Never hang around people who are always discouraged, despondent, poverty stricken, poor and never-do-well, you will ultimately become like them. Try to get around cheery people, happy people, prosperous people, and you will unconsciously take on their prosperity and their happiness, just as you may be around sorrowful and poverty stricken people, and then take on their sorrow and their poverty.

Never live in a house with or keep company with people who are always having bad luck stories, their sins will come upon you for the same evil spirit that is following them may also be near you. Always appear bright when you are seeking help for the U.N.I.A.

DEALING WITH DIVISIONS

In dealing with a division of the U.N.I.A. always recognize the Division itself as a chartered body, as the representative body. The units of a division, according to the Constitution, are all subordinate to the division. The division officers are the only responsible officers in a division. *No auxiliary then has the status of the Division*.

In dealing with the Division, first recognize the officers of the division, according to the Constitution. The Legion, the Black Cross Nurse[s], the Motor Corps and all other auxiliaries *must be obedient* to the officers of the division.

Great care must be taken in watching and controlling the activities of the Legions, because they are apt in ignorance to get the division or organization in trouble, by trying to exercise authority whilst they are only members of an organization registered by the state.

Their function is more physical culture and discipline than anything else. Any hostile demonstration by them to the danger of the community or the peace thereof or even among the members, must be quickly put down and if necessary, their unit suspended to prevent such trouble. The Legions have no control over the Black Cross Nurses. The Black

Cross Nurses are a separate unit. The only relationship may be that someone from the Legions with the ability to train may give them physical exercise and proper discipline, but *they fall entirely under their own head nurse,* who is to seek for them through the officers of the division, first aid training from some medical institution or individual.

The Motor Corps are also an independent body of women who may be trained by a competent Legion officer, but with no direct affiliation. See to it that divisional officers *do not allow members of the Legion to appoint themselves* to any office as lieutenants, captains, majors, colonels or what not *without the authority of the President* who is the ranking officer of the Legion in his division as set out in the Constitution. See to it that divisions do not allow Tom, Dick and Harry to go into the division *to speak to and lecture* to them *without authority* from the *Parent Body,* and that they do not allow anybody to use the meetings of the U.N.I.A. to put over their own propaganda tending to distract from the U.N.I.A.

See to it that no fake lecturer or wild cat scheme representative gets into any meeting of the U.N.I.A. through any individual influence.

Keep a close eye on African princes, African chiefs, princesses and all such fake personalities from coming into the meetings of the U.N.I.A. No prince, chief or princess allows such methods of going around begging and exploiting. Princes and princesses are royal personalities who keep at home or only make State visits to other countries and are generally accommodated by the head of the nation.

Any time such fake princes or chiefs come among you expose them and drive them out. *Never entertain anyone* who claims to be Christ, God, John the Baptist or such presumptive titles.

Never allow divisions to take the words of persons as representing Mr. Garvey or sent by Mr. Garvey. Let them *produce the letter.* If they can't, drive them away. Whenever you find such fakers, hand them over to the police and make an example of them, and have it announced in the newspapers to scare others.

Whenever anyone is called upon to sit in a U.N.I.A. meeting and speak in your presence and say things not in keeping with the policy or membership training of the association, after they have finished you should rise immediately and correct them, for the good of the membership, and instruct all Presidents and Presiding officers to do the same.

Whenever you think something is said detrimental to the organization and its policy, never fail to correct it immediately, so that the people may not get the wrong impression. Always defend the organization and protect its name in the public press or otherwise. If you find an opportunity to debate with other people to maintain the principles of the organization, do so by challenging them, but before you debate, always read up on the point of view or subject, so as to be able to handle the same in keeping with the principles and objects of the U.N.I.A.

Whenever you are in doubt about anything in the U.N.I.A. write to headquarters. Never take upon yourself to settle the question decisively if you are in doubt. Always say "pending the ruling of my superior officers, this is my opinion" and leave it at that, but this is only when you are in doubt.

Encourage the divisions to use only programmes at meetings, regular and public, that express the sentiment of Negroes. As for instance, all recitations should be from Negro poets and authors. Songs[,] hymns and choruses should be sung from Negro composers.

Encourage the juveniles to study Negro poems and songs. Encourage local divisions to have a reader who must be educated to read striking articles from the "Black Man" each week. Encourage some bright juvenile in each division to study and recite the "Tragedy of White Injustice." *Never have them recite this poem when white people are present*. Encourage some bright boy or girl to study and recite "African Fundamentalism."

Keep these two major bits of literature always before the people until they almost come to know them by heart.

Lesson 21

Five-Year Plan of the U.N.I.A.

At the International Convention of the U.N.I.A. held at Edelweiss Park, Cross Roads, St. Andrew, Jamaica, B.W.I., the President-General of the Association presented to the Convention in session, the Five-Year Plan scheme, as the most possible and p[ra]ctical scheme through which the Association could rehabilitate itself, and carry out as far as possible, the major objects of the organisation.

The scheme was thoroughly discussed and adopted by resolutions, properly moved and seconded and carried unanimously, as set out in the reprint circular from the "Black Man" magazine, August–September, 1935 herewith incorporated (secure a copy of this circular).

Explanation of the Five-Year Plan

The Five-Year Plan is a scheme of colossal magnitude[.] Should the amount budgeted for be fully subscribed, it would enable the organisation to, in a most practical and efficient manner, carry out, not only the industrial, commercial and other phases of the Convention programme, but to a great extent encourage and carry out many of the major objects for racial development. The idea is to get every Negro in the world to pledge to contribute voluntarily a sum of money for five years and pay the same within five years to the Plan.

The amount to be contributed is to be left entirely to the financial ability of the Individual person. It was sugge[st]ed that no person could be so poor as not to, within five years, be able to contribute at least $5.00 to such a fund to assist in the general development of the race. Hence, nobody should be left out, whilst the majority of people would be in a better position to contribute larger sums within the five years, according to their financial ability.

As for instance, some may be able to contribute for the five years $10.00, $20.00, $100.00, $500.00, $1000.00, as the case might be.

There is every reason why every Negro should contribute to this fund, and voluntarily, for it would s[u]pply the organisation with the financial resources to work, without prejudice, in the complete interest of the Race, and to have all its objects realised, from which each and every Negro would benefit.

The method of contributing to the fund is as follows:— A person desirous of contributing makes a voluntary pledge for the amount to be contributed within five years, to be paid in instalments, monthly, quarterly, half-yearly or yearly, until paid, or according to circumstance pay the amount at one time.

The pledge must be sent to the headquarters of the organisation, The Parent Body, 2200 E. 40th Street, Cleveland, Ohio. The person pledging must give his or her full name, correct address and profession. The person may send the first instalment with the pledge. On receipt of the first payment on the pledge, a pledge card is issued from headquarters to the subscriber or don[o]r with the amount pledged written on the card and the amount of instalment paid also entered.

The card is returned to the donor with the request that whenever other instalments are to be paid that the card be forwarded with the instalment for the amount to be entered on the card and in the ledger at headquarters and returned to the donor.

After the pledge is fully paid up, a certificate is issued by the Parent Body to show that the particular person paid the pledge in contributing to the Five Year Plan of the organisation.

At the close of the period for the Five Year Plan a record will be published in which each donor who has paid up to the pledge will have his or her name recorded for the information of all concerned.

The amounts of money collected on the Plan will be appropri[ated] for carrying out the many schemes authorised by the Convention of 1934 as set out in the circular above referred to. In explaining the Five Year Plan great stress must be laid on the fact that for the Negro to realise the objective of a nation and government of his own, he must first have financial security. Whilst no individual person can create a nation or government for the race, in that each individual is looking after his own personal and private business, there must be an organised co-operative effort toward this en[d,] hence the effort is represented by the U.N.I.A. to which all Negroes must com[muni]cate and with which they must cooperate.

Established nations and governments get their revenue from taxes levied on the citizens. The [N]egro having no government cannot raise revenue for such a purpose in that way, hence those who desire such a thing must be voluntary contributors.

The establishment of the different enterprises which will help to find employment for Negroes, and the profit of which will go to help the organisation to carry out its nationalistic programme, is in keeping with the principles of the organisation to hold all its properties and wealth in hereditary trust for the Negro race, so that a contribution to the fund simply means assisting to place the race, through organisation, in a position of financial security, through which it can march on to the realization of nationhood and government.

If everybody contributed just the amount of money that would be thrown away on non-essentials, in five years it would turn out that the very amount that would have been lost in waste becomes the actual resource to establish that which is most needed by every Negro in the world.

It is a patriotic duty, therefore, for every Negro to contribute to the fund to make the Plan a success. The many enterprises we undertake in America, in Canada, in the

West Indies, in South and Central America and in Africa will be instrumental in finding employment, if the Plan is fully supported, for countless thousands of Negroes who never would have been employed otherwise. The very "magnitude" of the Plan would give it a status that would compel respect by all races and all the aims of the organisation by all parties. The Five Year Plan has been seen as the most thoughtful, economic scheme that could be undertaken as a solution of the economic, industrial[,] political, and other problems of the Negro Race. No Negro should be left out of an interview on the subject without fully convincing him that he should contribute and to have him contribute to such a Plan.

How to Get Results

It is no use trying to represent the U.N.I.A. without first having in mind the getting of good results. The most important results are financial, active and moral support.

Financial support means to get as much money as possible to help finance the programme. In getting such money you must do so at the least cost, so that the amount received will produce a net that can be used for the purpose for which it was obtained.

Active results mean enrolling persons as active members of the Association, people who will always work as members to help put the programme over.

Moral results mean to secure that sympathy and co-operation from individuals that would enable the organization to always count on such persons doing their best for the movement.

The Way to Get Money

There are many ways to get money for the U.N.I.A. To approach and interview the most substantial members of the race in your community or your jurisdiction, such as the ministers of the gospel, doctors, lawyers, business men, and substantial tradesmen and persons of important occupations.

Meet them at their homes or at their offices or places of business and seriously talk to them about the programme of the organization, explaining all its details, aims and objects, and after doing so, ask them to contribute to the assistance of the Association. Whatsoever they contribute must be always recorded with their names, occupations, addresses and the names of such persons must be always transmitted to the Parent Body for record, and all remarks that may be necessary to explain the character and disposition of the person must be added to the report of each person, so that the Parent Body can be well advised as to the disposition and nature of the person to help the cause, so that communications to the persons may be couched in language consistent with the person's disposition and intentions. It must be taken for granted that people of this class will be sceptical at the first, and have to be convinced by proper arguments. If you can win over the support of such people who are the natural representative class of the race in the community, you have achieved a great deal in winning the kind of support that will enable the organization to speak with authority as having the best class of people supporting it.

In approaching ministers of the gospel, be always diplomatic enough to convince them of the Christian policy of the organization [and t]he willingness of the organization to support the cause of the Christian religion[.] If the preacher is won over and himself contributes, you may get further assistance from him by seeking permission to speak to his congregation to raise funds for the organisation. In doing so always arrange with him that a percentage of what is raised is given to the Church, so that he may feel interested and satisfied to assist that way. No preacher should be left until he has consented to help in some way, as there is no greater way of the Church showing its willingness to expand the functions of the Church than by helping a cause like that of the U.N.I.A. If a preacher refuses it is evident that he has not been in touch with the proper argument or that he is positively selfish.

One of the arguments to be used with the preacher is

that the association by preaching unity, is assisting the Church by getting Negroes to support their own religion as their own everything else.

In approaching a doctor you should point out that by the Association preaching unity, self-support and self-reliance, you are helping to increase his practice in the community; the same argument should be used for Negro lawyers and Negro business men.

The argument for those who are in good positions employed as they may be to white people, is that the white people will not always employ Negroes, but only do so until they have been approached or forced by influencing [influence of?] their own race to substitute white employees for Negroes, and that the Association is seeking to establish such economic and industrial independence for the ra[ce] as to be able, through its success, to find substantial employment for its own men and women of quality and ability as evidenc[ed] by the programme of the Five Year Plan.

A general approach should also be made to all other Negroes in their homes, or at any place that you may convenient[ly] meet them and get them by argument to contribute individually.

The argument for the common people is that there is no economic security for the race depending always on the white man's employment. Therefore, by supporting the U.N.I.A. to the point of success, opportunities of employment will be created in the establishment of factories, mills, commercial enterprises, farming enterprises, shipping enterprises, etc., which may offer them employment according to their sphere of lab[or].

You can explain to all of them, professional and common people, that contributing to the funds of the U.N.I.A. is no different to contributing to the funds of white organisations, which so many of them have done, for so many centuries but the point is that whilst contributing to white organisations they are supplying the club to break their own heads economically and politically. In contributing to the U.N.I.A. they will be supplying the ammunition that will be used to fight their enemies and to establish their own security, that there is as much need for self-denial even to the poorest person of the race to help the U.N.I.A., as the self-denial to help other causes with which they are not directly identified. There should be a proper method of approach in acquiring funds for the organisation. If you are a representative you will be supplied with the necessary credentials and the necessary account forms to submit for the gathering of such support.

No one is supposed to make any appeal for the U.N.I.A. who is not authorised to do so, for it will mean trouble and fraud and would be unworthy of anyone who has secured these lessons.

This method of approach must not be used for personal purposes[,] but only for the purposes of the U.N.I.A.

One of the major ways of raising funds for the U.N.I.A. is by public meetings advertised for the U.N.I.A. to explain its objects and to speak on its general programme. Such meetings may be arranged through the agency of divisions of the association or an affiliated one or through agents in a community and where there is no branch of an association through friendly Churches.

In organising such meetings, an agent should be first appoin[ted,] a place secured and proper advertisement prepared and distributed in the community before the date of the meeting.

In a community of 2,000 people, at least 1,000 handbills should be printed, in a community of 10,000 or more, 2,000 or 3,000 handbills should be printed and widely distributed among the coloured population. All agents should be written to and asked to see that this is carried out so that on going to the place to address the meeting, you will not go where no one knows about i[t.]

Always word your handbills in the most attractive manner so as to create general interest among Negroes.

You should mention yourself as a graduate of the School of African Philosophy to suggest to the public that you have rare, important knowledge and not commonly known, which would attract their curiosity. In going to speak at such a meeting you should be at your best on the subject that you are going to discuss. If you have made your speech, sit down for a couple of minutes, then rise again and make your financial appeal.

Except you are addressing a Division, don't make an appeal for money in the speech that you make, as people will think that you are only speaking for money, but immediately after the speech get up and make another short speech for funds to support the organisation.

Always have your meeting well organised inside by arranging for ushers to take up the collection after you have asked for special contributions, which would be brought up to a table immediately in front of the platform.

After you have made the appeal for special contributions of large amounts then get the ushers to take up the small amounts in a collection. Never ask for extraordinary amounts in special contributions, considering the pockets of the people. You may ask for $5.00, $3.00, $2.00 or $1.00 who can give that much for such a cause; then after you have exhausted that, you may even ask for special contributions of 50 cents and then take up a collection from those who may not be able to give more than 25 cents or 10 cents.

When you go into a strange community where the people are not members of the U.N.I.A. then make your first public meeting a meeting for obtaining members and all members who are to join must pay $1.00—35 cents of which will be their first Monthly Dues, 25 cents Joining Fee, 25 cents for their Constitution and 15 cents for their Button and Certificate.

Each person must be given a receipt for the $1.00 and the person's name, occupation, address and age registered in the book.

If you have secured seven or more as members, you have enough to start a division, then after the meeting, call those who have joined to appoint a President, and have them elect a Vice-President and a Treasurer and Secretary.

Leave a Constitution and tell them they must control the organisation in keeping with the Constitution, that they will be privileged to hold regular meetings, suggestive twice a week, but particularly on Sunday at 3 P.M. or at 8 o'clock at night, and instruct them to work to secure more members and then apply to the Parent Body for a Charter, the cost of which is $25.00; that they will be privileged to collect money in their community from others who are sympathetic to the association to secure the Charter money.

You should keep in constant touch with the Secretary you have elected and find out when they are ready to apply for their Charter and recommend accordingly the Parent Body for the Charter.

When they receive their Charter they should be advised to have a special meeting for the dedication of the Charter and invite all the Negroes of the Community to attend in which they should try to make more members.

If you remain in town the second night, call for Members also and make appeal for funds for the Associations, but always see that you secure your expenses and to have money as a net to forward to the Parent Body in whose name you may be representing. If you remain in town for one, two or three days, working up a division or visiting a division, you should take the time to interview all the possible people in the community to get support financially for the organisation, so that the expense of the trip would not only be on the meeting but on the community from whom you may get financial support.

In joining members in a division and electing officers, you should leave with them that portion of the first Month's Dues that is the division's by Constitutional law, and such portion of the proceeds as will enable them to start out with something in their treasury.

In setting up a new division, you should always advise them to rent a hall of their own where they will be able to hold their meetings without being disturbed. Suggest to them that they should not only depend on the regular Monthy Dues and the collections to support the division, but that they should organise entertainments of an innocent nature, including dances, concert[s], beauty contests, popularity contests, or any kind of a social regularly, to assist to bear the cost of the rental of the place. You should explain to them that they must make from the very first month the regular Monthly reports to the Parent Body according to the Constitution.

You should mark and point out to them those important sections of the Constitution that make a Division related to the Parent Body. If you are a representative of the U.N.I.A. with credentials such as a Commissioner in a State, you should raise funds in the following ways also for the Parent Body which you represent: By bazaars within the State, picnics, garden parties, concerts, or any general amusement that the public is accustomed to, and would likely patronise particularly for a cause. Flower days, rose days, tag days, or self-denial days, if these functions are to take the arrangement of a State nature, then ask all friends and Divisions within the State to co-operate. When it takes on the form in a special community, then ask all friends or Divisions in that particular community to co-operate. This must only be done with the previous arrangement of the Parent Body and the report must accompany every such function to the Parent Body, to show the results. All these functions must be held in the name of the organisation. You may also have groups of people in your jurisdiction to organise house parties, and give public entertainments for the benefit of the organisation. A way to do this is to approach some responsible person in a street or in a neighbourhood and ask him or her friends at his or her house and if possible always be present, but it is not necessary for you to be present if the person you have asked to do so is a responsible and honest person who is in sympathy with the organisation.

If you arrange a tag day or flower day, this should be of a private organisation nature, as if made public would be in conflict with particular municipal or State laws for charity.

These things are to be organised within the organisation and among its friends and you could appoint members of the organisation such as units of the Black Cross Nurses to go into people's homes and offices and ask them to buy the tag, or the flower or the rose to help the cause, but not to have them do that publicly on the street except where in commun[i]ties you are privileged to do so.

In organising these things always try to get interesting parties who will take part in them for the love of the cause and not for the payment. You can arrange with Churches in your jurisdiction to stage plays at their Church halls or in the Church on a percentage basis, and then get local talent in your jurisdiction to contribute to the programme free of cost. In this way you will find yourself continuously active, and after you have done this thoroughly for a year, you will become acquainted with all the parties and it would then be very easy for you to do the same thing annually. In such work let every minute count, because if you appreciate all this, you will have no time for being idle. As far as the white people are concerned, we do not specialise in seeking contributions from them, but where you think it on your own judgment wise to arrange lectures among them, revealing only the humanitarian part of the work, you may conduct such lectures and raise a collection or ask for help only on those humanitarian grounds, but not to commit yourself in any statement that would lead them to think that they could become Members of your association, or be affiliated with it or have any part in it, as this would be a direct violation of the Constitution and against the association.

This applie[s] to individual persons of the opposite races that you may ask to contribute to any special fund, but wherever such contributions have been made, a record should be kept of the person's name and address, and a report should be given to headquarters and remarks made to show the race for the purpose of guiding the Parent Body in communication with such a person, then and in the future.

COLLEGE YELL
SCHOOL OF AFRICAN PHILOSOPHY

(1) We must win, we shall win, we will win,

CHORUS— Win, yes win, and win to win:

(2) You and I shall win to win,
For Africa, for Africa we win
We must win, we shall win, we will win:

UNITED CHORUS

Win, yes win, and win to win:
For Africa, for Africa, we'll win to win.

THE CREED OF GOODNESS

To pass the time in doing good,
To count the evils we put down,
To have our deeds so understood,
Is nobler than to wear a crown,
To bless the people as we go,
To scatter seeds that grow to life,
To strike all sin a deadly blow,
Is better than to stir up strife.

Just think how happy all would be,
If kindness was the usual deed!
Just think what that would mean to me
If that was man's accepted creed:
The world would be more satisfied
If all the people felt to love;
Good souls would not be crucified,
But all would look to God above.

Let every day that comes your way
Count for some goodness fully done,
Let every act of every day
Shine out as brilliant as the sun:
Let others call you by the name
That represents a crown of joy,
For this of all, is greatest fame,
That none on earth can e'er destroy.

BY MARCUS GARVEY

SOURCE NOTES

Lessons 1–20, James Stewart papers, Monrovia, Liberia. Oath and Lesson 21, Elinor Robinson White papers, Chicago. Typed documents with some autograph insertions. Portion of Lesson 8 autograph copy from Mason Hargrave papers, Cleveland.

GLOSSARY
of Names and Terms

This annotated index covers names and subjects referred to by Marcus Garvey in the speeches and writings collected in this volume. Cross-references to other entries in the glossary appear in small capital letters. References to the Universal Negro Improvement Association (UNIA) appear frequently and are not indicated as cross-references. In keeping with the editorial policies of the Marcus Garvey and Universal Negro Improvement Association Papers, members of the UNIA, black historical figures, and issues dealing with the status of minorities receive more detailed descriptions than do more commonly documented persons and events. Source notes are included for only the more detailed entries. Abbreviations specific to single entries appear in parentheses after the initial citations and are used thereafter within the entries. Page numbers are not included in references to *Garvey Papers* volumes; consult the index of the volume cited for pages concerning the entry subject. Volume 6 of the *Garvey Papers* is forthcoming. The names of individuals who signed the UNIA Declaration of Rights in 1920 have not been included unless additional biographical information has been located.

Frequently Cited Sources:

BA	*Baltimore Afro-American*
Black Moses	E. D. Cronon, *Black Moses: The Story of Marcus Garvey and the UNIA*
BM	*Black Man* (London)
Bm	*Blackman* (Kingston)
CD	*Chicago Defender*
DAHB	M. R. Lipschutz and R. K. Rasmussen, *Dictionary of African Historical Biography*
DANB	*Dictionary of American Negro Biography*
DB	J. McKenzie, *Dictionary of the Bible*
DG	*Daily Gleaner* (Kingston)

DW	*Daily Worker*
G&G	A. Jacques Garvey, *Garvey and Garveyism*
Garvey Papers	*The Marcus Garvey and UNIA Papers*
MG v.U.S.	*Marcus Garvey* v. *United States,* no.8317, Ct. App., 2d Cir., 2 February 1925
NW	*Negro World*
NYA	*New York Age*
NYAN	*New York Amsterdam News*
NYT	*New York Times*
NYW	*New York World*
PC	*Pittsburgh Courier*
P&O	*Philosophy and Opinions of Marcus Garvey*
WWCA	*Who's Who of Colored America*
WWCR	*Who's Who of the Colored Race*
WWW	*Who Was Who*

ABBOTT, ROBERT S. (1870–1940), was the founder and editor of the *Chicago Defender*. He was born in Simmons Island, Ga., the son of former slaves. He graduated from Hampton Institute, Hampton, Va., in 1896 and received his LL.B degree from Kent College of Law in Chicago in 1899. He founded the *Chicago Defender* as a four-page handbill in May 1905; twelve years later the thriving weekly had a circulation of nearly 250,000 copies. Abbott and Garvey were frequently critical of one another's editorial opinions, and their differences led them into court on more than one occassion. Abbott successfully sued Garvey over a NEGRO WORLD article in 1919. After Abbott published negative coverage of the BLACK STAR LINE in the 6 September and 13 September 1919 issues of the *Chicago Defender*, Garvey countered with his own libel suits. The case of the *Black Star Line* v. *Chicago Defender*, heard in the U.S. District Court in New York in June 1920, ended with the jury awarding Garvey's corporation damages of six cents. Three years later, Abbott joined several other black business and political leaders in instigating the "Garvey Must Go" campaign (Mertz T. P. Lockhard, "Robert S. Abbott—Race Leader," *Phylon*, 1947: 124–128; *P&O*; *Garvey Papers* 2, 5).

ABD EL-KRIM (1885?–1963) was leader of the Rif rebellion against Spanish rule in Morocco. An administrator for the Spanish until 1920, Abd El-Krim led a three-year war of independence culminating in the defeat of Spanish troops and establishment of the Rif Republic. He was captured in 1926 by a joint expedition of Spanish and French troops and was subsequently exiled. He escaped from French custody in 1947. Although he never returned to Morocco, in 1958 he was awarded the title of national hero by King Muhammad V of Morocco.

ABEL. See CAIN.

ABORIGINAL AUSTRALIANS were the indigenous inhabitants of Australia before European colonization of the continent in the eighteenth century. Traditional aboriginal communities, of which there were over five hundred in 1788, were made up of semi-nomadic hunters and gatherers whose communal economies and religious interpretation of the landscape conflicted with British practices of private ownership and pastoralism. British policy toward the aborigines was characterized by dispossession, forced relocation, and efforts to secure cultural assimilation of European models of dress, behavior, and religious belief. As British settlers encroached farther into the interior in the nineteenth century, they were met with aboriginal armed resistance. Over the next few decades, warfare, massacres, epidemic disease, and the disruption of traditional food and kinship patterns resulted in aboriginal depopulation, even to the point of extinction of tribes in some areas by the time of the second generation of contact. The Queensland Act of 1897 resulted in the restriction of approximately half the remaining aboriginal peoples to controlled reserves, where they had few civil rights and were subjected to contract labor. By the early 1900s the aboriginal population had been reduced by over 75 percent in relation to its numbers at the beginning of colonization in the 1780s (Richard Broome, *Aboriginal Australians: Black Response to White Dominance, 1788–1980* [Sydney, London, and Boston: George Allen & Unwin, 1982]).

ABRAHAM, a herdsman and ancestor of the Israelites, was the first biblical figure to receive divine revelation. Abraham was the husband of SARAH and the father of ISAAC. He was also the father of ISHMAEL, who was born to Sarah's slave, Hagar, an Egyptian whom Sarah gave to Abraham as a wife when she was unable to bear children. When Hagar bore Ishmael, Sarah expelled her and the child from Canaan. The vindicationist, or revisionist, school of black religious thinkers has identified Abraham—in addition to Joseph, MOSES, Judah, Samson, and others—as among those who married or had children with black women and as descendants of Ham, ancestor of the Canaanites, Ethiopians, and Egyptians (Gen. 12, 15, 16, 21, 22; W. L. Hunter, *Jesus Christ Had Negro Blood in His Veins* [1901; reprint, Brooklyn: author, 1910]; Alonzo Potter Burgess Holly, *God and the Negro: Synopsis of God and the Negro; or, The Biblical Record of the Race of Ham* [Nashville: National Baptist Publishing Board, 1937]; *DB*, pp. 5–6).

ABYSINNIA was the name Ethiopia was widely known by outside Africa up to the mid–twentieth century. The name derives from the Arab word "habesh," or "mixed breed," a reference to the Habeshat people, a migratory group that settled the northeastern coast of Africa in the seventh century B.C. The name *Abysinnia* is also a geographical designation, referring to the large plateau that extends from the NILE RIVER to the Red Sea. The term *Abysinnians* is still in use for the northern Christian-Amharic ethnic group that traditionally people the highlands. *Ethiopia* is another name for the same region of ancient northeastern Africa, bounded on the north by Egypt and on the east by the Red Sea. This name is Greek in origin and comes from the word *ethiops*—or *aethiopes,* featured in the Homeric poems as the peoples who inhabit the lands of the rising and setting sun; it can be translated as "black face." While the name Abysinnia was commonly used in the Middle East, Europe, and most of the Western world in the late nineteenth and early twentieth centuries, Ethiopian leaders preferred the alternate title (Fred Halliday and Maxine Molyneux, *The Ethiopian Revolution* [London: Thetford Press, 1981], p. 51 n. 1; A. H. M. Jones and Elizabeth Monroe, *A History of Ethiopia* [1935; reprint, London: Oxford University Press, 1955], p. 10; Robert W. July, *A History of the African People* [New York: Charles Scribner's Sons, 1974], p. 49; Chris Prouty and Eugene Rosenfeld, *Historical Dictionary of Ethiopia* [Metuchen, N.J.: Scarecrow Press, 1981], p. 3).

ACL. See AFRICAN COMMUNITIES LEAGUE.

ADAM and EVE were, according to biblical tradition, inhabitants of the paradise of Eden until their sin and their expulsion by God, and they were parents of CAIN, ABEL, and SETH. According to Garvey, Adam and Eve were black, and the white race began with the banishment of their son Cain, the first murderer (Gen. 2–4).

AFRICAN COMMUNITIES LEAGUE (ACL) was the commercial and political wing of the UNIA. The full title of the UNIA when founded in 1914 was the Universal Negro Improvement and Conservation Association and African Communities (Imperial) League. The UNIA was conceived as the fraternal, benevolent section of the organization. The ACL was designed to fortify political and economic connections between blacks of different nationalities, just as the Imperial Federation League of Great Britain—the model on which the ACL may have been based—was dedicated to strengthening the imperial bonds between England and the self-governing portions of her colonial empire. The ACL was the umbrella wing of the organization under whose auspices the BLACK STAR LINE, the NEGRO FACTORIES CORP., the *NEGRO WORLD*, the leasing of LIBERTY HALL and UNIA offices, and the establishment of other UNIA and ACL commercial endeavors (restaurants, laundries, hotels) officially operated. It was incorporated in New York in July 1918 (*Garvey Papers* 1–4).

AFRICAN DUTCH. See AFRIKANERS.

AFRICAN GUARDS (Universal African Legion) were the military auxiliary of the UNIA and ACL. Like the UNIA itself, the African Guards were composed of a number of local divisions or legions, with a local, regional, and national hierarchy of officers. Male members of the UNIA between the ages of eighteen and fifty-five were eligible to join, and thirteen- to sixteen-year-old members of JUVENILE DIVISIONS could be trained as cadets. (Female UNIA members were eligible to join the UNIA MOTOR CORPS, an auxiliary similar to the legion.)

Many legion members were veterans of WORLD WAR I who were attracted to the discipline and prestige of the paramilitary units. African Legion uniforms, drill procedures, officer titles, and oaths of allegiance were based on revised versions of U.S. Army regulations and protocol. The guards served a dress military function within the UNIA, appearing as marching units in parades, as attendants during ceremonies, and as peacekeepers or bodyguards at UNIA gatherings and conventions (*Garvey Papers* 2, 3).

AFRIKANERS, whom Garvey refers to as the "African Dutch," are Afrikaans-speaking white descendants of Dutch, French, and other European settlers in South Africa. Originally agricultural peoples primarily, Afrikaners have politically dominated South Africa (now the Republic of South Africa) since 1910. They make up approximately 60 percent of the minority white population of South Africa (Monica Wilson and Leonard Thompson, eds., *The Oxford History of South Africa*, 2 vols. [New York and Oxford: Oxford University Press, 1969], 1: 187–232, 424–446; T. Dunbar Moodie, *The Rise of Afrikanerdom: Power, Apartheid, and the Afrikaner Civil Religion* [Berkeley, Los Angeles and London: University of California Press, 1975]).

ALEXANDER THE GREAT (356–323 B.C.), king of Macedonia, established an immense empire through invasions of Egypt, Mesopotamia, Babylon, Persia, and parts of India.

ALEXANDRIA was an Egyptian seaport founded by ALEXANDER THE GREAT after he captured Egypt in 332 B.C. It became a center of trade and intellectual life characterized by the cross-influences of Arab, Jewish, and Greek cultures and ideas.

ALFRED (Alfred the Great) (849–899), King of the West Saxons and patron of scholarship, became overlord of all England in the 880s.

ALLEN, ISAAC B. (1884–?), was president of the UNIA between November 1917 and January 1918, when Marcus Garvey served as international organizer. Allen was born in Barbados, BWI, and worked as a longshoreman in New Jersey and as a real estate agent in Harlem after immigrating to the United States. Although Garvey accused Allen of joining SAMUEL DUNCAN in creating a faction that attempted to split the membership of the UNIA in January 1918 Allen appeared as one of the directors of the pro-Garvey wing of the organization on the certificate of incorporation that was filed the following July and continued to be an active leader, serving as a UNIA delegate to the National Liberty Congress of Colored Americans in 1918 and becoming the second vice president of the BLACK STAR LINE in 1919. Allen resigned from the UNIA in the summer of 1919. He was first vice president of the International League of Darker Peoples, a temporary coalition formed in January 1919 to prepare a united platform for black delegates elected to attend the Paris Peace Conference. He later became the secretary of William Monroe Trotter's National Equal Rights League (*Garvey Papers* 1).

S.S.*ANTONIO MACEO*. See *KANAWHA*.

ANTONY, MARC (Marcus Antonius, Mark Anthony) (83?–30 B.C.), Roman militarist, politician, and protegé of JULIUS CAESAR, formed a triumvirate after Caesar's death with Marcus Aemilius Lepidus and Octavius Caesar and ruled the Asian sector of the Roman empire (40–36 B.C.). Antony is best known for his love affair with CLEOPATRA.

ARGONNE, a rural wooded area of Champagne and Lorraine in northeastern France, was a major WORLD WAR I battleground during the Allied advance in the autumn of 1918. The black American 369th Infantry Regiment (93d Infantry Division) participated in the initial assault as part of the French 161st division.

ARMAGEDDON is the biblical name used to designate the final battlefield where the armies of the earth will fight at the end of the world (Rev. 16:16). The word is derived from the Hebrew name for the mountain of Megiddo, a major battleground in ancient Palestine (Judg. 5:19, 2 Kings 23:29).

ASHFORD, CARRIE M., a delegate to the 1920 UNIA convention and one of the signers of the 1920 UNIA Declaration of Rights, was a leader in the Atlantic City, N.J., division of the UNIA. She often presided over UNIA meetings in Atlantic City in the early 1920s. She also served as the Atlantic City delegate to the 1921 UNIA convention (*NW*, 30 April 1921; *Garvey Papers* 2, 3).

ASHWOOD, AMY (1897–1969), feminist, playwright, lecturer, and pan-Africanist, was one of the founding members of the UNIA in Jamaica, and the first wife of Marcus Garvey. Ashwood was born in Port Antonio, Jamaica, and spent several years of her childhood in Panama. She returned to Jamaica to attend high school and met Marcus Garvey at a debating society program in July 1914, when she was seventeen years old. Ashwood became the first secretary and a member of the board of management of the newly formed UNIA in 1914–1915. She worked with Garvey in organizing the inaugural meeting in COLLEGIATE HALL in Kingston, the weekly Tuesday night elocution meetings, and the office that was soon established in a house on Charles Street rented by the Ashwood family. She also helped establish the ladies' auxiliary wing of the movement and was involved in early plans to begin an industrial school. According to her memoirs, Ashwood was courted by Garvey during those early years with love letters referring to her as "My JOSEPHINE" and signed from "Your devoted NAPOLEON, Marcus." The two became secretly engaged; her parents, who did not approve of the match, arranged her return to Panama in 1916. Garvey traveled to the United States the same spring. Ashwood and Garvey were reunited in New York in September 1918 and she became, in the words of a Bureau of Investigation special agent, his "chief assistant, a kind of managing boss" (*Garvey Papers* 2: 15), working as she had in Jamaica to organize the movement in the United States. She became the general secretary of the organization in 1919 and was one of the first directors of the BLACK STAR LINE. She and May Clarke Roache helped shield Garvey when he was shot by George Tyler at the UNIA offices in October 1919. She and Garvey were married in a private Catholic church ceremony, followed by an elaborate public ceremony and reception at LIBERTY HALL on Christmas Day, 1919.

The marriage soon failed. Garvey sought an annulment in early March 1920 but dropped the charges one month later. Ashwood suffered a miscarriage in June soon after Garvey removed his personal affects from their household. He obtained a divorce (which Ashwood challenged in court and never recognized) in Missouri on 5 July 1922 and later the same month married AMY JACQUES—Ashwood's former friend and maid of honor at the Garveys' 1919 wedding and Ashwood's replacement as Garvey's companion and personal secretary since 1920. Ashwood became a world traveler in the years following her separation from Garvey and remained active in politics and the arts. Her musical *Hey, Hey,* a comedy set in the United States and Africa, was produced at the Lafayette Theatre in New York in 1926. She traveled to Europe and West Africa and lived in London in the mid- and late thirties, operating a restaurant that was a gathering place for African students and activists in the Pan-African movement. She was a strong supporter of Haile Selassie during the ITALO-ETHIOPIAN WAR and his subsequent exile in Britain. During World War II, she went to Jamaica, where she founded a domestic science institute for girls, worked for Jamaican self-government, and was a candidate for the legislature, hoping "to use her position to champion the rights of women" as well as those of labor (*NYAN,* 4 March 1944). She participated in UNIA memorial services for Garvey in ST. ANN'S BAY after his death in 1940. When she died she left two unpublished manuscript drafts of her memoirs of her life with Garvey and the UNIA (*NYAN,* 3 November and 10 November 1926, 21 September 1940; Amy Ashwood Garvey, "Portrait of a Liberator" [1969], Amy Ashwood Garvey papers, Lionel Yard collection, New York; *Garvey Papers* 1, 2, 6).

ATTILA (d. 453) was king of the Huns (445–453), a nomadic people sometimes referred to as Mongolians who originated in north central Asia and migrated to Europe during the fourth century. Attila was a feared warrior-ruler who threatened the Roman Empire, gaining concessions and control over a large portion of central and eastern Europe in a series of raids and treaties with Roman leaders.

ATTUCKS, CRISPUS (1725?–1770), legendary Afro-American hero, was one of five patriots killed by British troops in the Boston Massacre on 5 March 1770. The incident served as a symbolic precursor to the American Revolution. Attucks was described in the 12 March 1770 *Boston Gazette* as "a mulatto man . . . born in Framingham, but lately belonged to New Providence." Attucks, probably an ex-slave, may have been of mixed black and Native American heritage, possibly of the Natick tribe. Some historians place his birth in the West Indies rather than in the United States. Contemporary accounts describe him as a tall man of imposing presence (Hiller Zobel, *The Boston Massacre* [New York: W. W. Norton & Co., 1970]; Harry Hansen, *The Boston Massacre: An Episode of Dissent and Violence* [New York: Hastings House, 1970], pp. 52–62; Sidney Kaplan, *The Black Presence in the Era of the American Revolution, 1770–1800* [Washington, D.C.: New York Graphic Society and Smithsonian Institution Press, 1973]).

AUSTIN, REYNOLD FITZGERALD, signer of the August 1920 UNIA Declaration of Rights, was president of the Brooklyn division of the UNIA in the early 1920s (*NW*, 19 March 1921; *Garvey Papers* 2).

BAGLEY, THOMAS E., was a delegate to the 1920 UNIA convention from Stamford, Conn. He spoke from the floor during the 4 August 1920 session, addressing the issues of fair housing and the lack of race consciousness among blacks in Stamford. He was one of the signers of the 1920 UNIA Declaration of Rights (*NW*, 14 August 1920; *Garvey Papers* 2).

BAGNALL, ROBERT W. (b. 1883), was director of branches for the NAACP from 1920 until the early years of the Depression, when the organization suffered from financial cutbacks, and funding for his salaried position was no longer available. Bagnall was born in Norfolk, Va. The son of an Episcopal minister, he attended Bishop Payne Divinity School and became a rector of St. Matthew's Church in Detroit. He became active in the NAACP and served as secretary in Detroit and as principal speaker at the first session of the 1914 NAACP convention in Baltimore. In 1918 he became the district organizer of the Great Lakes district of the NAACP and was soon promoted to the executive leadership. He was chair of the national convention of the FRIENDS OF NEGRO FREEDOM in 1920 and joined in that organization's "Garvey Must Go" campaign in 1922, speaking on "The Madness of Marcus Garvey" at a 20 August meeting in Harlem and publishing an article with the same title (*BA*, 25 August 1922; Robert W. Bagnall, "The Madness of Marcus Garvey," *Messenger* 5, no. 3 [March 1923]: 638, 648; B. Joyce Ross, *J. E. Spingarn and the Rise of the NAACP* [New York: Atheneum, 1972], pp. 132–136; *WWCR*; *Garvey Papers* 4, 5).

BATSON, PETER EDWARD, one of the signers of the UNIA Declaration of Rights, was a pastor at the Community African Methodist Episcopal Church in New York. He reported to the 1920 UNIA convention that he had organized a division of the UNIA in Middletown, N.Y., which had begun with twenty members and had added twenty-six members in the previous six months. Batson was one of the five pastors who officiated at the 15 August 1920 Sunday service in Liberty Hall, at which the declaration of rights was read; he assisted in the religious services on the other Sundays during the convention period and appeared with UNIA officers and dignitaries in the closing convention parade (*NW*, 25 June 1921; *Garvey Papers* 2).

BAYNE, JOHN G., was a New York division member who sometimes presided over meetings at Liberty Hall in 1919. On 23 January 1920 Bayne joined William Ferris and Garvey in filing a certificate of incorporation for the NEGRO FACTORIES CORP. in New York City. The organization was incorporated in the state of Delaware one week later. Bayne was a delegate to the 1920 UNIA convention and, as a New York county clerk, registered the UNIA Declaration of Rights (*Garvey Papers* 2).

BELSHAZZAR, son of Nebuchadnezzar, was the last king of Babylon. The prophet DANIEL interpreted handwriting that appeared on the wall at his last feast as a portent of death; following the feast Belshazzar was murdered, and his kingdom fell to the Medes and the Persians (Dan. 5:1–31).

BENEDICT, SAINT (d. 547), of Italy, was the founder of the Benedictine order and author of *The Rule of St. Benedict,* which articulated the philosophy of monasticism.

BENIN, a city-state in southern Nigeria's Niger delta region, arose in the fifteenth century. One of the most advanced states of West Africa, it was a regional center of precolonial artwork and trade in ivory, spices, metals, and slaves. The kingdom began to decline when it became involved in wars with neighboring Yoruba states, and in 1897 it was invaded by the British, who placed it under colonial administration in 1899. Benin is also the modern-day name for the former French colony of Dahomey and a hundred-mile-long river in the Niger delta that flows into the Bight of Benin.

BINGA, JESSE (1865–1950), was a black businessman who had a meteoric career as a banker and real estate agent in Chicago. As one historian has written, his life "embodied the culmination of the Horatio Alger theme, . . . [he] had become the symbol of the Negro's bid for power via respectability." Cognizant of the similarities between the Horatio Alger myth and his own life story, Binga published a collection of "Benjamin Franklin–like aphorisms," *Certain Sayings of Jesse Binga,*" in which he shared "his secrets of success" (Carl R. Osthaus, "The Rise and Fall of Jesse Binga, Black Financier," *Journal of Negro History* 58, no. 1 [January 1973]: 39–60). Binga owned over twelve hundred leaseholds on Chicago's South Side. He specialized in opening previously white neighborhoods to black buyers at inflated prices. In a period when violence was directed against black residents by members of white homeowners' protective associations, Binga's own spacious home in an all-white area was bombed at least five times. Binga founded the Binga State Bank and offered mortgage loans to black customers who were unable to obtain them from larger white financial institutions. He also founded a black business association and constructed the landmark Binga Arcade building, a lavish architectural tribute to black capitalism. His terrific success was shattered in 1930 when the Binga State Bank collapsed, and examiners found strong evidence of mismanagement and fraud. Binga was imprisoned for embezzlement in 1933. Released in 1938, he died in poverty (*Chicago Whip,* 10 September 1921; *Crisis* 23, no. 6 [April 1922]: 253–254; 34, no. 10 [December 1927]: 329, 350–351; *Chicago Tribune,* 8 May 1927).

BIRKENHEAD, LORD. See FREDERICK EDWIN SMITH.

BLACK CROSS NAVIGATION AND TRADING CO., INC., founded in 1924, was the successor to the defunct BLACK STAR LINE, designed, as the previous stock corporation had been, to carry on trade and provide passage in the Caribbean, Central America, and the United States, with an eventual goal of maintaining a passenger and commercial route between the United States and Africa (*Black Moses,* pp. 121–124; *Garvey Papers* 6).

BLACK CROSS NURSES were a female auxiliary of the UNIA, modeled to some extent on the traditional Red Cross. The nursing auxiliaries, like the other auxiliaries of the UNIA divisions (the JUVENILE DIVISIONS, sometimes referred to as the girl guides and boy scouts, the AFRICAN GUARDS, and the MOTOR CORPS), were organized on the local level; the first Black Cross Nurse unit was established by members of the Philadelphia UNIA. HENRIETTA VINTON DAVIS was active in recruiting women to local Black Cross Nurse groups in the early 1920s, and the groups were formed in cities across the United States, Central America, and the Caribbean. The nursing corps grew in conjunction with the development of the paramilitary wing of the Garvey movement, and the Black Cross Nurses appeared in UNIA parades with the blue-uniformed female Motor Corps and marching male legion members. The nurses formed their own marching contingent, making a striking appearance in long cowled white robes or green nursing uniforms. Although some of the Black Cross Nurses had formal medical training in nursing and maternity care, most worked with practical training in first aid and nutrition. The auxiliary performed benevolent community work and provided public health services to black neighborhoods, specializing in infant health and home care and in some localities working in conjunction with established social service agencies (*Garvey Papers* 3).

BLACK MAN/BLACKMAN were titles used by Garvey for two different publications. Garvey began publishing a daily newspaper called the *Blackman* in Kingston in 1929. The paper became a weekly in 1930 and was published until February 1931. Garvey began publishing a monthly called the *Blackman,* subtitled *A Monthly Magazine of Negro Thought and Opinion,* in Kingston in December 1933. After the first six issues its name was changed to the *Black Man,* and Garvey moved its publication to London in June 1935. It was produced there until June 1939, when Garvey, in financial difficulties and suffering from failing health, discontinued its publication. A total of twenty-four issues were produced over a five-and-a-half-year period. Written mostly by Garvey but containing some essays by other writers, including Eric Walrond, the *Black Man* featured editorials, poems, Socratic dialogues, critical commentaries on current world events, news of the local divisions of the UNIA and the UNIA conventions in Canada in 1937 and 1938, and Garvey's opinions on world leaders, including MUSSOLINI, Hitler, Oswald Mosley, Haile Selassie, and other black leaders and editors, including George Schuyler and Father Divine (*NW,* 13 April and 20 April 1929, 5 April 1930; *Bm,* 14 February 1931; *BM*).

BLACK STAR LINE (BSL) was the black steamship line operated by Garvey and the UNIA from 1919 to 1922. The BSL was incorporated in Delaware on 23 June 1919 and was capitalized at a maximum of $500,000, divided into 100,000 shares at five dollars each. The S.S. *Yarmouth* was the first ship purchased for the line; it had its maiden BSL voyage in November 1919. The S.S. *Shadyside,* a Hudson River excursion boat, and the steam yacht *Kanawha* (renamed the S.S. *Antonio Maceo*) were added to the line in 1920. BSL stock was sold at UNIA meetings and conventions, by traveling agents, by mailed circulars, and through advertisements in the *Negro World*. The line—intended to display black pride and self-sufficiency and to foster black-operated enterprise and trade—was a propaganda success but a financial fiasco. Garvey announced its suspension shortly after his February 1922 indictment on mail fraud charges stemming from the sale of BSL stock. The original incorporators of the line were Garvey, EDGAR M. GREY, RICHARD E. WARNER, GEORGE TOBIAS, and JANIE JENKINS. The officers elected at the first board of directors meeting were Garvey, president; JEREMIAH CERTAIN, first vice president; HENRIETTA VINTON DAVIS, second vice president; George Tobias, treasurer; Richard Warner, secretary; Edgar Grey, assistant secretary; and Janie Jenkins, assistant treasurer (*Black Moses*, pp. 73–102; *Garvey Papers* 1).

BLACKSTON, IRENA MOORMAN, an active Socialist, was one of the early supporters of the UNIA in the United States. Blackston was among the small group of people who heard Garvey's first public lecture in New York. She was lady president of the New York division in 1917–1918 and chaired the meeting addressed by Mary Church Terell in October 1917. She was the first vice president of the short-lived faction of the UNIA headed by SAMUEL DUNCAN in January 1918 but continued with Garvey's group, signing the certificates of incorporation of the UNIA and the ACL as a director in July 1918, and becoming one of the first to purchase BLACK STAR LINE stock when the venture was launched in 1919. Blackston was the president of the Harlem branch of the Women's National Fraternal Business Association in 1919, and in 1931 she chaired the Colored Women's Organization of the State of New York. She became active in the African Blood Brotherhood in the early 1920s. According to a Bureau of Investigation informant, Blackston supported Garvey's decision to negotiate with the Ku Klux Klan in 1922 (*Garvey Papers* 1, 4).

BLENHEIM, a village on the Danube River in Bavaria (now West Germany), was the site of a major battle between Anglo-Austrian and Franco-Bavarian forces in the War of the Spanish Succession in 1704. The battle led to the defeat of the French and Bavarians.

BONAPARTE, JOSEPHINE (1763–1814), was born at Trois Ilets, Martinique, the daughter of slaveholding French Creole parents. She married NAPOLEON Bonaparte in 1796 and was divorced by him in 1809 after failing to produce an heir to his throne.

BOURNE, CLIFFORD (b. 1880?), UNIA commissioner of divisions in Guatemala in 1921, was elected high chancellor of the organization in 1922. He was one of the UNIA officers chosen by Garvey to oversee the international organization during Garvey's temporary incarceration in 1923 following conviction on mail fraud charges. Bourne was born in Barbados and worked in England and in Guatemala as an accountant for commercial firms. He became president of the Guatemala chapter of the UNIA in 1921 and soon moved into the international leadership of the organization. Bourne remained affiliated with the New York–based UNIA, Inc., when Garvey created a new wing of the movement in 1929; he served as president general of the UNIA, Inc., in 1931 (*Garvey Papers* 2).

BRAITHWAITE, ISAAC NEWTON, was coproprietor, with Cyril Crichlow, of the Crichlow-Braithwaite Shorthand School in New York (*NW*, 14 August 1920; *Garvey Papers* 2).

BRANCH, SARAH, of Liberia, was a UNIA activist who used her oratorical skills to organize for the movement. Journalist John E. Bruce praised Branch for her fund-raising ability, writing in unpublished notes for one of his "Bruce Grit" columns, "Sister Sarah Branch is a fine type of African womanhood and is a good organizer[,] an indefatigable worker [and] an enthusiastic speaker and can get more money for the association in a drive than almost any other woman speaker on the list of speakers" (Schomburg Center for Research in Black Culture, New York, papers of John E. Bruce). Branch appeared at the podium at LIBERTY HALL meetings in 1919–1921. She was elected one of the delegates from the New York division to attend the 1920 UNIA convention, where she shared the platform with Garvey and other UNIA officials. She told the convention audience that the term "Negro is simply a pet name that the white man, when he went to Africa and stole our foreparents, gave us" and urged the delegates to call themselves Africans (*Garvey Papers* 2: 517). Branch was president of the New York branch of the BLACK CROSS NURSES in 1921 (*Garvey Papers* 2, 4).

BRIGGS, CYRIL VALENTINE (1887–1966), journalist and Communist activist, was editor of the *CRUSADER* magazine and founder of the militant African Blood Brotherhood. Briggs was born in Nevis, one of the Leeward Islands of the West Indies, and immigrated to New York in 1905. He worked as a reporter and editor for the *New York Amsterdam News* (1911–1915, 1916–1918). He resigned from the *News* and began his own monthly, the *Crusader,* in September 1918. In 1919 the editorial offices of the *Crusader,* on Seventh Avenue in New York, became eastern headquarters of the Hamitic League of the World, founded by George Wells Parker, John Albert Williams, and John E. Bruce. The *Crusader*'s affiliation with the Hamitic League ended in 1920, and in 1921 Briggs began describing the journal as the organ of the African Blood Brotherhood (ABB), a secret revolutionary fraternal organization that had been formed in 1919. Members of the ABB included Claude McKay, Arthur Reid, Otto Huiswood, Grace Campbell, and former Garveyites W. A. DOMINGO, JAMES D. BROOKS, GEORGE ALEXANDER McGUIRE, JOSHUA COCKBURN, and CYRIL CRICHLOW. Like the UNIA, the ABB was organized through local divisions, or posts, and soon claimed to have members throughout the United States and the West Indies, reaching a dues-paying membership of some seven thousand at its peak in 1923. Like the UNIA, the ABB was highly ritualized, offered sick and death benefit insurance to its members, and planned to open black-owned businesses—plans that were short-lived because of lack of funds. Delegates from the ABB attended the 1921 UNIA convention and passed out literature critical of Garvey during the proceedings. The obvious rivalry that had grown up between Briggs and Garvey reached a crisis point in the autumn of 1921, when Garvey accused Briggs of being a "white man" and a "Negro for convenience" (*NW*, 8, 15, and 22 October 1921). Briggs sued Garvey for libel and won. Garvey withdrew his statement but publicized the fact of Briggs's illegitimacy in the process. After Briggs published a number of comments critical of Garvey in the October and November 1921 issues of the *Crusader,* Garvey sued Briggs for libel. The propaganda war between the two men was fueled by a Bureau of Investigation confidential informant, James Wormley Jones, agent "800," who infiltrated both the UNIA and the ABB; Jones reported that Briggs had furnished the government with evidence to support charges against Garvey for using the mails to defraud. The actual charges were brought against the UNIA leader in February 1922. Briggs became affiliated with Rose Pastor Stokes's wing of the (Communist) Workers Party of America in 1921, and the ABB became in effect the black wing of the Communist party in the United States by 1923. The organization was dissolved and replaced by the American Negro Labor Congress (ANLC) in 1925. Briggs was the national secretary of the ANLC and editor of its publication, the *Negro Champion.* In 1929 he was elected to the central executive committee of the Communist Party of the United States (CPUSA). In the following year the ANLC became the League of Struggle for Negro Rights. Briggs maintained his position on the national committee and edited the renamed organ of the group, the *Liberator.* He remained active in Communist politics until 1939, when he was expelled from the CPUSA because of his black nationalist leanings. He moved to California in 1944 and became the managing editor of Charlotta Bass's *California Eagle* (1945–1948). He rejoined the Communist party in 1948, became active in the Ella Mae Wiggins Club of the Los Angeles County Communist party and went underground during the McCarthy era of the 1950s (*Crusader* 5, no. 2 [October 1921]: 11, 29; *NW*, 26 November 1921; Robert A. Hill, ed., *The Crusader Magazine* [New York: Garland Publishing, 1987]; *Garvey Papers* 1–4).

BROOKS, JAMES D., an American-born pastor, was secretary-general of the UNIA in 1920–1921. He joined a group of other leading Garveyites, including GEORGE ALEXANDER McGUIRE and CYRIL CRICHLOW, in leaving the UNIA to join CYRIL BRIGGS's African Blood Brotherhood in 1921. Brooks began his career with the UNIA as an organizer, traveling to divisions in the South, West, and Northeast in 1920 to raise funds and increase membership in the organization. He went on a UNIA fund-raising tour of northern cities in the spring and early summer of 1921, speaking in Cleveland and Cincinnati in June. He ceased to report to the executive council of the UNIA in July 1921 and was charged with incompetence, embezzlement, and violation of the UNIA constitution at the August 1921 UNIA convention. His office was declared vacant after delegates testified to his misuse of organization funds. Brooks disappeared until detectives tracked him down in November 1921, arresting him on larceny charges brought by the National Surety Co., the company that held him on bond for the UNIA. He was interviewed by Bureau of Investigation agents in January 1922 in connection with Garvey's upcoming mail fraud trial. Garvey testified at his August 1922 larceny trial. He was acquitted of the larceny charges on 31 August 1922 (*New York News,* 3 December 1921; *People of New York* v. *James D. Brooks,* no. 34086, City Magistrates' Court of the City of New York, August 1922; *Garvey Papers* 1, 3, 4).

BRYAN, ARDEN A. (1893–1971), was traveling field secretary and chief stock salesperson for the BLACK STAR LINE from 1919 to 1921. Bryan was born in Barbados and worked in Panama before moving to the United States in 1914. He became an elevator operator in New York before he joined the UNIA. He traveled with Garvey on stock-selling trips to major cities in the northeast in 1918 and 1919, collecting money for the Liberian Construction Loan and the African Redemption Fund as well as for the shipping line. He was a delegate from Barbados to the 1921 UNIA convention; became UNIA commissioner of Connecticut from 1921 to 1922; and briefly served as foreign affairs editor of the *NEGRO WORLD.* Bryan resigned from the organization in 1922, after his request for a commissioner appointment over a field with a larger black population than Connecticut was refused by Garvey. He appeared as a witness for the defense at Garvey's mail fraud trial in the following year. In 1933 Bryan organized the Nationalist-Negro Movement and African Colonization Association and became its first president. The organization's goal was to obtain the former German colony of Kamerun (Cameroon) as a concession from the League of Nations, in order to begin a program of black American colonization (*NW,* 14 June 1919; *MG* v. *U.S.,* pp. 1,379–1,400; *Garvey Papers* 1, 3).

BSL. See BLACK STAR LINE.

BUNDY, LEROY (1883–1943), dentist and politician, was elected first assistant president general of the UNIA in 1922. Bundy was born in Hamilton, Ohio, to a prestigous black family. He made his home in East St. Louis, Ill., where he was involved in Republican party politics and on the board of supervisors for St. Clair County. In events leading up to the East St. Louis race riots of 1917, Bundy was alleged by the white press to be the leader in a conspiracy to bring black voters into the city to influence local elections. When two white detectives were killed during the ensuing riots, Bundy was arrested and tried on the charge that his leadership had inspired the violence. He was convicted by the lower court, but the Illinois Supreme Court reversed the conviction and ordered a new trial, which was never held, because of the weakness of the prosecution's evidence. Bundy turned to the NAACP for help with his trial, but differences arose, and the NAACP withdrew from his defense. After the reversal of his conviction, Bundy joined the UNIA. He was president of the Cleveland division of the UNIA in 1922 and was honored by Garvey as a knight commander of the Distinguished Service Order of Ethiopia at the 1922 UNIA convention (*Garvey Papers* 4).

BURRELL, BENJAMIN E. (1892–1959), poet, journalist, and political activist, was associate secretary of the UNIA in late 1917 and 1918. Born in Daviton, Manchester, Jamaica, Burrell was the son of a prosperous coffee grower. He was a rural correspondent for the *Jamaica Times* before moving to the United States in June 1917. He worked in an ammunition factory in the Carolinas before coming to New York and becoming active in the UNIA. He was the coauthor, with ARNOLD J. FORD, of the lyrics of the official UNIA hymn, the "Universal Ethiopian Anthem." Burrell soon split from the UNIA and became involved, along with his brother, Theophilus Burrell, in radical black politics. He was a contributing editor to the *Crusader* and worked with CYRIL BRIGGS's African Blood Brotherhood. He and three other African Blood Brotherhood delegates were expelled from the 1921 UNIA convention after being accused of distributing literature discrediting the work of the UNIA. Burrell helped to found the Amalgamated Garment Workers Union in 1931 and joined with W. A. DOMINGO, Ethelred Brown, and others to organize the Jamaica Progressive League (of New York) in 1936. He and Theophilus also ran the Gleaners, a black history study club for young blacks that met at the Harlem YMCA (*Garvey Papers* 1, 2).

BUSHA is a Jamaican word for "overseer," derived from the period of slavery. The word metamorphosed from *obisha* ("overseer") in the late 1700s, to *bersheer* or *busha* in the 1800s. Busha is still in usage in Jamaica.

CAESAR, JULIUS (102–44 B.C.), Roman statesman, orator, and military hero, was dictator of Rome from 49 B.C until his assassination by fellow statesmen in 44 B.C. His military conquests brought him to Gaul and Britain in the Gallic Wars (58–49 B.C.) and to Spain, Egypt, Syria, and parts of Africa in the Roman civil war, in which his forces clashed with those of Pompey (49–47 B.C.) and during which he formed a liaison with the Egyptian leader CLEOPATRA. He established a colony at CARTHAGE in 44 B.C.

CAIN and ABEL were the first and second sons of ADAM and EVE. Cain murdered Abel, a shepherd, out of envy and was condemned to a nomadic life in the land of Nod (an area somewhere east of Eden), where he became the eponymous ancestor of the Kenites, a non-Israelite nomadic clan. In a separate legend Cain is made the founder of early civilization, the inventor of metalworking, and the establisher of the first city, called Enoch, after his son. In the School of African Philosophy, Garvey describes Cain as the ancestor of white Europeans (Gen. 4; *DB*, pp. 2, 113–114, 471–472).

CAMPBELL, GWENDOLYN, was one of the initial members of the UNIA after it was founded in Kingston, Jamaica, in 1914. She worked as a private secretary for Marcus Garvey and was active in the affairs of the organization. She appeared in plays, debated such issues as women's rights in UNIA elocution contests, and served on special committees and as a member of the UNIA board of management in 1914–1915. After Garvey established the organization in the United States, he invited Campbell to come to work for the UNIA in New York City. In March 1920 she became head stenographer at the parent body headquarters. She was in charge of the secretarial pool that worked on UNIA, *NEGRO WORLD*, and BLACK STAR LINE projects. She also handled office accounts and performed Amy Jacques's usual office duties when Jacques accompanied Garvey out of town. She left her employment with the UNIA in the fall of 1921 and went to work in the office of a Harlem stockbroker. After Garvey was arrested on mail fraud charges in January 1922, Campbell voluntarily approached a Bureau of Investigation officer to discuss the case. She expressed her willingness to give a statement but declined to be called as a government witness, stating that she feared for her personal safety if she testified against Garvey. On 6 March 1922 she gave Special Agent Mortimer J. Davis a statement about the handling of accounts in the UNIA office, implying that both Garvey and Amy Jacques made improper and undocumented use of organization funds. She was eventually called as a witness for the defense in Garvey's mail fraud trial (May–June 1923), but her testimony indicates that she appeared under duress (*DG*, 11 February 1915; *MG* v. *U.S.*, pp. 1,241–1,275; *Garvey Papers* 1, 4).

CARDIFF, an industrial seaport, is the capital of Wales. Because seamen from throughout Britain's colonial empire were drafted into the British merchant marine during WORLD WAR I, a significant community of immigrant minorities developed in Cardiff in the late 1910s, including black West Indians, West Africans, and Somalis, as well as Arabs, East Indians, and Asians. Postwar unemployment in the dock areas and objection among some whites to the intermarriage of minority workers and white Britons increased racial tensions and discrimination. In June 1919 race riots occurred in Liverpool, Cardiff, and a number of other cities in southern Wales. White mobs set fire to black residences, and at least three black men were killed before troops were sent into Cardiff on 14 June 1919 to quell the violence. The local press reacted to the riots by calling for the deportation of blacks. Improvement of the status of black seamen and their families in Cardiff became a priority of Harold Moody's League of Colored Peoples in the 1930s (Roy May and Robin Cohen, "The Interaction Between Race and Colonialism: A Case Study of the Liverpool Race Riots of 1919," *Race and Class* 16, no. 2 [October 1974]: 111–126; P. Cecil Lewis, ed., *The Keys* (quarterly of the League of Coloured Peoples, London) 3, nos. 1–4 [1935]; Kenneth Little, *Negroes in Britain* [London: Routledge & Kegan Paul, 1948], pp. 79–82; *Garvey Papers* 2).

CARGILL, SCHUYLER (b. 1904), a solution maker for the National Chemical Co., lived in Roselle, N.J., in 1923. Cargill testified at Garvey's 1923 mail fraud trial that he was employed as an office worker at the BLACK STAR LINE (BSL) offices from 1919 to 1921; that his duties had included preparing mailings and taking mail to the post office; and that he remembered mailing the circular to BENNY DANCY upon which Garvey's conviction on mail fraud charges eventually rested. During his cross examination Garvey established that Cargill was incorrect in identifying his supervisor, could not remember other individuals he would have had daily contact with while working in the office, and could not adequately describe the method of delivering bulk mailings to the post office. Cargill also testified under cross-examination that MAXWELL MATTUCK had coached him to say he had been employed at the BSL offices during the time period in question and that just prior to his testimony Mattuck had shown him a copy of the circular he would be asked to identify to the court (*MG* v. *U.S.*, pp. 683–704).

CARNARVON, LORD. See GEORGE EDWARD STANHOPE MOLYNEUX.

CARNEGIE, ANDREW (1835–1919), a Scottish-born American industrialist and philanthropist, made his fortune as head of the Carnegie Steel Co., which, under the management of Henry Clay Frick, fostered a virulent anti-union policy in the steel industry. At the turn of the century the Carnegie Steel Co. controlled a multimillion-dollar conglomerate of railroads, ships, coke ovens, and mines. Carnegie's "The Gospel of Wealth," first published in the *North American Review* (June and December 1889), is a seminal manifesto of free enterprise and the self-made man.

CARTHAGE, an ancient city-state on the Mediterranean Sea in north Africa, was located in the peninsula area near modern Tunis, Tunisia. Founded by the Phoenicians in the eighth century B.C., Carthage developed into an empire with control over major Mediterranean trade routes and colonies in Spain. Its commercial power and wide political influence made it the rival of both the Greeks and the Romans. Roman armies destroyed the city at the end of the Third Punic War (147 B.C.).

CATHERINE, SAINT (Catherine Benincasa) (1347–1380), of Siena, Italy, was an Italian spiritual leader and visionary. She was a member of the Dominican order and served as a papal ambassador to Florence, drawing a large following for her teachings, which focused on the principle of love. Her *Dialogue of Saint Catherine; or, A Treatise on Divine Providence* was recognized as a major mystic work in the Middle Ages.

CERTAIN, JEREMIAH M., was born in Florida. He was the first vice president of the UNIA, in 1918–1919, and a member of the board of directors of the BLACK STAR LINE in 1918–1920. He was a cigar manufacturer in Passaic, N.J., when he moved to New York to join the Black Star Line staff; he later founded the Gold Dollar Cigar Manufacturing Co., in 1921. When Certain resigned in 1920, Garvey asked him to reconsider the decision. He appeared as a witness for the defense during Garvey's 1923 mail fraud trial (*NW,* 30 November 1918, 1 January, 21 June, and 19 July 1919; *MG* v. *U.S.*, pp. 1,290–1,311; *Garvey Papers* 1, 2).

CERVANTES, MIGUEL DE (1547–1616), Spanish poet, playwright, and novelist, is most famous for his satiric picaresque, *Don Quixote de la Mancha,* written between 1605 and 1615. Garvey frequently paraphrased Cervantes in his speeches and writings, including the lessons from the School of African Philosophy.

CHARLEMAGNE (Charles the Great) (742?–814), conqueror of the Saxons, the Avars, and the Slavs, was king of the Franks from 768 to his death. He was crowned emperor over the Carolingian (formerly Roman) empire by Pope Leo III in 800. He has been hailed as a champion of Christendom and a guardian of learning and was legendized in *Chanson de Roland* as a romantic hero.

CHATHAM, LORD. See WILLIAM PITT.

CLAYTON, NETTIE, was a delegate from Pittsburgh to the 1920 UNIA convention. She spoke from the floor on the issue of racial discrimination in urban housing and was one of the signers of the UNIA Declaration of Rights (*Garvey Papers* 2).

CLEOPATRA (69–30 B.C.), powerful queen of Egypt, reigned with her younger brother and husband, Ptolemy XII. She was aided in a revolt against him by JULIUS CAESAR, who became her lover, and she gained sole possession of the throne. Cleopatra traveled to Rome with Caesar, where she bore a son. She returned to Egypt after Caesar was assassinated and formed a personal and political alliance with MARC ANTONY (42 B.C.). After their combined forces were defeated by Octavian in the battle of Actium, in 31 B.C., they retreated to ALEXANDRIA, where they committed suicide after Octavian's occupation of the city.

COCKBURN, JOSHUA (Cockbourne) (1877–1942), was the first captain employed by the BLACK STAR LINE. Cockburn was born in Nassau, Bahamas. Educated in England, he served as a seaman and officer in the Royal Navy, studied navigation, and had over two decades of nautical experience in different areas of the world, including West Africa, when he approached Garvey in 1919 about service for the Black Star Line. Cockburn received a $1,600 commission as a broker in the negotiations for the S.S. *YARMOUTH*. He traveled with Garvey on a promotional tour for the sale of stock in the line, and on 1 November 1919 he was appointed commander of the newly acquired ship on its maiden voyage. In the summer of 1920 Garvey dismissed Cockburn, charging him with reckless handling of the ship and citing numerous complaints about its operation. Cockburn remained in Harlem as a shipping agent and became a highly successful real estate broker in the decade preceding the Depression (*NW*, 18 December 1927; *PC*, 13 February 1937; *NYT*, 10 February 1937; *BM* 2, no. 7 [August 1937]: 1; *NYAN*, 13 July 1940; *MG* v. *U.S.*, pp. 292–423; *WWCA*; *Garvey Papers* 1, 2).

COLEMAN, JULIA P., a pharmacologist, was one of the signers of the January 1923 "Garvey Must Go" letter to Attorney General HARRY M. DAUGHERTY. Coleman was born in North Carolina and graduated from Scotia Seminary in Concord, N.C. She received a degree in pharmacology from Howard University in 1897 and completed postgraduate work at the Pennsylvania College of Pharmacy in Philadelphia. She worked in the drug industry in Philadelphia for ten years, then became the president and manager of the Hair-Vim Chemical Co. in Washington, D.C., a firm specializing in beauty preparations for blacks. Coleman was involved in a NAACP desegregation suit in 1918, when the organization, represented by WILLIAM ASHBIE HAWKINS, presented her suit against the Washington, Baltimore, and Indianapolis Railroad for the line's Jim Crow seating policies. The court ruled in favor of Coleman, and the company stopped rigorously enforcing its separate car regulations (Charles Flint Kellogg, *NAACP: A History of the National Association for the Advancement of Colored People* [Baltimore and London: Johns Hopkins University Press, 1967], p. 204; *WWCR*; *Garvey Papers* 5).

COLLEGIATE HALL in Kingston, Jamaica, was the meeting place for the nascent UNIA in 1914–1915. Weekly public meetings were held in the hall on Tuesday evenings, featuring lectures, debates, recitations, elocution contests, concerts, and dramatic performances. The early UNIA also held events at the Ward Theater (*DG*, 14 September and 17 September 1914; *Garvey Papers* 1).

COLUMBUS, CHRISTOPHER (1451–1506), Italian explorer, is traditionally credited with discovering America. He established a colony on Hispaniola (now the Dominican Republic and Haiti) in 1492. He favored the creation of a slave trade between the Caribbean islands and Spain, and in the spring of 1494 he shipped the first of many human consignments, a cargo of five hundred enslaved Amerindians, for sale by auction in Seville. Only a small percentage of the indigenous people who lived on Hispaniola upon his discovery of the island survived the first decade of colonization, since the population was decimated by the conditions of forced labor and disease.

CONGO RIVER (Zaire River) in west central Africa is one of the longest rivers in the world. The Congo River basin is heavily forested; the Congo and its tributaries have long formed the geographical basis of a network of trade. The river forms much of the current boundary between the People's Republic of the Congo and Zaire. In the 1930s the river formed the boundary between the Belgian Congo and French Equatorial Africa and between the Belgian Congo and Portuguese West Africa (Angola).

CONSTANTINE (288?–337), emperor of Rome (310–337), was a Christian convert who used Christianity to bring a measure of political unity to the empire. In 325 he presided over the first ecumenical council at Nicaea, attended by bishops from both East and West. He re-established the capital of the empire at Byzantium, which was renamed Constantinople (now Istanbul).

CONWAY, WALTER J. (1880–1920), was first vice president of the UNIA in 1917–1918 and one of the six directors of the organization listed on the 1918 certificate of incorporation. He worked as an attorney and as a clerk in the general post office in New York City from 1902 until his death (*Garvey Papers* 1).

COOLIDGE, CALVIN (1872–1933), was a leading Republican politician and president of the United States (1923–1929). Coolidge was vice president of the United States when WARREN G. HARDING died in office, whereupon he succeeded to the presidency. He was elected to a full term in 1924, heading a conservative pro-business administration that encouraged the 1924 land concession arrangement between the Firestone Rubber Co. and the Liberian government, an arrangement that impeded negotiations between President C. D. B. King and the UNIA over the UNIA's Liberian colonization plan. Many black leaders were dismayed when he chose C. Bascom Slemp as his personal secretary, because Slemp was an avowed segregationist who had advocated that blacks be barred from the Republican party in his home state of Virginia. After Garvey was convicted on mail fraud charges in 1923, UNIA members began organizing appeals to Coolidge for a pardon. Garvey's formal appeals to the president in 1925–1926 were rejected as premature, but his 1927 reapplication was accepted. Coolidge commuted the remainder of Garvey's five-year sentence on 18 November 1927, and Garvey was released from Atlanta penitentiary subject to immediate deportation (*Garvey Papers* 5, 6).

COOLIE is a derogatory or slang term for an immigrant Chinese laborer. The first wave of Chinese immigration to the western United States occurred in the mid–nineteenth century, when a majority of Chinese workers entered the mining industry in California. In the 1870s and '80s most were employed in other forms of low-wage manual labor and menial trades, including construction, agriculture, domestic service, and urban sweatshops. Chinese people made up one-quarter to one-fifth of California's wage work force in those decades. Chinese workers also migrated to live and work in the eastern and southern sections of the United States. They were subjected to residential segregation and expulsion, racial harassment, and a series of discriminatory laws that denied them citizenship and limited their civil rights and rights of entry, culminating in comprehensive exclusion in 1902. The Chinese exclusion acts were not repealed until 1943 (Cheng-Tsu Wu, ed., *Chink!: A Documentary History of Anti-Chinese Prejudice in America* [New York: World Publishing/Straight Arrow Books, 1972]; Alexander Saxton, *The Indispensable Enemy: Labor and the Anti-Chinese Movement in California* [Berkeley, Los Angeles, London: University of California Press, 1971]; Lucy M. Cohen, *Chinese in the Post–Civil War South* [Baton Rouge and London: Louisiana State University Press, 1984]).

CORTEZ (Cortes), HERNANDO (1485–1547), was a Spanish mercenary who invaded and destroyed the Aztec empire of Mexico in 1519–1521.

CRANSTON, JOSEPH JOSIAH, a pastor in the Universal Ethiopian church, was president of the Baltimore division of the UNIA in 1920–1921. He spoke along with Rev. JAMES D. BROOKS at a UNIA fund-raising meeting at the Mount Carmel Baptist Church in Washington, D.C., in July 1920, praising the international character of the Garvey movement and comparing Garvey himself to leaders of the past, including MOSES and Frederick Douglass. He also compared the aims of the UNIA with those of the Irish independence movement. The militancy of his rhetoric on that occassion was matched by his statement to his fellow delegates at the 1920 UNIA convention: "I hope that as we marched along in this great procession today, the time will not be far distant when we shall congregate ourselves as a mighty army marching to the conquest of our motherland, Africa" (*Garvey Papers* 2: 496). Cranston was ordained by GEORGE ALEXANDER MCGUIRE in April 1921. He resigned from the presidency of the Baltimore division in the spring of 1921 and worked for the UNIA in Pittsburgh. He was a candidate for the newly created post of second assistant president general at the 1921 UNIA convention but lost the election to Robert Lincoln Poston (*NW,* 19 June 1920, 7 May 1921; *Garvey Papers* 2).

CRAWFORD, ANTHONY, was the freight agent for the S.S. *GENERAL GOETHALS* in 1925–1926. Crawford was the president of the Overseas Navigation and Trading Co., 80 Wall Street, New York City. In March 1926 Garvey claimed that WILLIAM SHERRILL had appointed Crawford and CYRIL BRIGGS (who was at the time an employee of Crawford's Overseas Navigation and Trading Co.) operating agents of the BLACK CROSS NAVIGATION AND TRADING CO. Crawford wrote to Garvey on 27 January 1926 to inform him that the S.S. *Goethals,* then harbored in New York, "must carry out its contract by discharging cargo at Miami, otherwise there will be breach of contact suits to the extent of several hundred thousand dollars" (text of letter quoted in the *NEGRO WORLD,* 20 March 1926). He also told Garvey that the skeleton crew had deserted the ship for lack of payment and that thousands of dollars of wharfage fees were accumulating monthly (*DW,* 29 October 1930).

CRAWFORD, LEE (1875–1942), was a black activist who belonged to many black fraternal and benevolent organizations before joining the UNIA in the early 1920s. Crawford was born in Alabama and migrated to New York. He was the grand chancellor of the New York State chapter of the Knights of Pythias from 1906 to 1941 and president of the local branch of the NAACP in New Rochelle, N.Y. (*NYT,* 2 May 1942; *NYAN,* 9 May 1942; *Garvey Papers* 2).

CREESE, GEORGE D., was the delegate representing Nova Scotia and eastern Canada at the 1920 UNIA convention, where he reported on labor conditions experienced by blacks in the iron and steel industries. Creese was an active member of the Sydney–New Aberdeen, Nova Scotia, division. He was appointed commissioner to Canada at the 1921 UNIA convention and was active on the floor of the convention in 1922. He recommended in 1922 that the convention consider ways to improve relations between the local divisions and the parent body in New York (*NW,* 16 July and 10 September 1921; *Garvey Papers* 2, 3).

CRESCENT THEATRE was located at 36–38 West 135th Street in Harlem. It was used as a meeting hall of the New York division of the UNIA in 1919 for its regular Sunday evening meetings (*Garvey Papers* 1).

CRICHLOW, CYRIL A., a stenographer and accountant, was the secretary of the UNIA commission to Liberia in February 1921 and served on the UNIA high executive council. He was a delegate to the 1920 UNIA convention and one of the signers of the UNIA Declaration of Rights. Crichlow resigned from the UNIA while in Liberia in June 1921, after a dispute arose between him and the UNIA potentate GABRIEL M. JOHNSON over the proper administration of funds and distribution of authority. Although the executive council refused to accept the resignation and cabled money to Crichlow to enable him to return to New York, Crichlow persisted in withdrawing from the association. He filed a report on the UNIA activities in Monrovia, in which he expressed little optimism for the success of the organization's colonization goals. He joined the rival African Blood Brotherhood and published an article critical of Garvey in the December 1921 issue of the *CRUSADER* (*Garvey Papers* 1, 3, 4).

CROMWELL, OLIVER (1599–1658), was the leader of the primarily middle-class Puritan/parliamentarian forces opposing the English monarchy in the first and second civil wars of the 1640s and early 1650s. After the execution of Charles I and the establishment of the commonwealth (1649), he led military expeditions against royalists in Ireland and Scotland, instigating a policy of land dispossession against the Irish. He became lord protector of England in 1653, exercising virtually dictatorial powers.

CRUSADER was a monthly magazine edited and published by CYRIL BRIGGS from September 1918 until early 1922. The *Crusader* became the organ of Briggs's African Blood Brotherhood. Briggs also operated the Crusader News Agency press service (1932–1938) and a mimeographed weekly called *Crusader Service* (1923) (Robert A. Hill, ed., *The Crusader Magazine* [New York: Garland Publishing, 1987]; *Garvey Papers* 1).

CUNNING, ARNOLD S., one of the signers of the August 1920 UNIA Declaration of Rights, was secretary to GEORGE ALEXANDER MCGUIRE, UNIA chaplain general, in 1921. He accompanied McGuire on his 1921 tour of Cuba (*NW,* 23 April and 16 July 1921; *Garvey Papers* 2).

DANCY, BENNY, was a janitor at Pennsylvania Station in New York who bought fifty-three shares of BLACK STAR LINE stock and was on UNIA, Black Star Line, and NEGRO FACTORIES CORP. mailing lists. Dancy was not a UNIA member but had heard Garvey speak and was an occasional reader of the *NEGRO WORLD*. A hand-addressed envelope with a stamped Black Star Line return address that had been mailed to Dancy at his Brooklyn residence was entered into evidence by the prosecution at Garvey's mail fraud trial. Dancy testified that he had turned over his mail to be used as evidence at the request of government agents, that he received many mailings from the UNIA but did not necessarily read them, and that he had no recollection of what had been in the particular envelope entered into evidence (*MG* v. *U.S.*, pp. 860–865; *Garvey Papers* 5).

DANIEL was a Judahite taken into the household of Nebuchadnezzar, king of Babylon. When Nebuchadnezzar dreamed of a statue of a beast, Daniel interpreted the dream as a vision of four kingdoms, including the otherwordly kingdom of God, which would destroy the kingdoms of the world and be everlasting (Dan. 2:1–49).

DARWIN, CHARLES (1809–1882), English naturalist, is best known for his formulation of the theory of natural selection articulated in *The Origin of Species* and *The Descent of Man*.

DAUGHERTY, HARRY M. (1860–1941), was U.S. attorney general under the HARDING presidency. Daugherty received the appointment in 1921 as a political reward for his management of Harding's bid for nomination at the 1920 Republican convention. The appointment was widely opposed by public officials and members of the press, who charged Daugherty with corruption. Harding's successor, CALVIN COOLIDGE, asked Daugherty to resign in March 1924 after a Senate investigatory committee disclosed Daugherty's close ties with organized crime. Daugherty was charged with fraud as a result of the Senate investigation, and was tried before Judge JULIAN MACK in 1926.

The trial resulted in a hung jury, and Daugherty was retried and acquitted in 1927.

DAVID, the successor of Saul as king of Israel, is most famous as the Israelite hero who slew the giant Goliath and as the reputed author of the Psalms. David, a polygamist, married many wives before he seduced Bathsheba, the wife of one of his military officers. When she became pregnant by him, he arranged her husband's death and married her as well. As one religious historian has put it, "from this point his life [was] one unbroken series of misfortunes" (John L. McKenzie, *Dictionary of the Bible* [Milwaukee: Bruce Publishing Co., 1965], p. 178; 1 Sam. 17, 18, 25; 2 Sam. 3, 5, 6, 11).

DAVIS, GERTRUDE, was the president of the Ladies' Division of the UNIA in Cleveland in 1921 (*NW*, 19 March 1921; *Garvey Papers* 2).

DAVIS, HENRIETTA VINTON (1860–1941), dramatic actress and lecturer, was one of the stalwart leaders of the UNIA for some twenty years. She was born in Baltimore and educated in Washington, D.C. She was a public school teacher and later became a copyist at the Office of the Recorder of Deeds, where she was an assistant to Frederick Douglass. Douglass encouraged her in her dramatic career, and she made her professional debut in a one-woman show in Washington, D.C., in 1883. Her success in Washington was followed by a tour of several eastern cities. She supported the Populist cause in 1892 and lectured on the party's behalf. She established her own dramatic company in Chicago in 1893, where she produced the black playwright William Edgar Easton's play *Dessalines*. In the spring of 1912 she toured Jamaica with contralto Nonie Bailey Hardy and became the manager of the Covent Garden Theatre in Kingston. While in Jamaica she organized a benevolent society called the Loyal Knights and Ladies of Malachite. She continued her tour with Hardy, performing in Central America before returning to the United States, where she raised funds to begin a school for girls in Jamaica. She joined the UNIA in New York in 1919 and was one of the original directors, as well as the second vice president of the BLACK STAR LINE. She presided over the dedication of LIBERTY HALL in August 1919 and chaired the UNIA meeting at Carnegie Hall in the same month, as well as the November 1919 mass meeting at MADISON SQUARE GARDEN and sessions of the 1920 UNIA convention. She traveled aboard the S.S. *YARMOUTH* to the Caribbean and Central America as international organizer in 1919–1920 and 1921. Garvey referred to her at that time as "the greatest woman of the Negro race today" (*Garvey Papers* 2: 311). In 1920 she embarked on a nationwide organizing tour, visiting and reorganizing divisions in several states. Garvey made Davis a lady commander of the Sublime Order of the Nile at the 1921 UNIA convention and nominated her when she was elected fourth assistant president general in 1922. She was a member of the UNIA delegation to Liberia in December 1923–March 1924, meeting with President C. D. B. King in February 1924. Davis represented the UNIA with M. L. T. DE MENA and George Emonei Carter during S.S. *GENERAL GOETHALS*'s trip to the Caribbean in 1925. Her relations with Garvey became strained in the late 1920s.

She became closely involved with the New York division during his incarceration in Atlanta penitentiary, serving as lady president of the division in 1926 and assistant president general of the UNIA in 1928–1929. When the pro-Garvey wing of the UNIA split off from the UNIA, Inc., of New York at the 1929 UNIA convention in Jamaica, Davis was sworn in as secretary general of the new UNIA (August 1929) of the World, although she and Garvey had been openly in conflict during the convention proceedings. Despite her election to office in the pro-Garvey faction, she remained affiliated with the rival UNIA, Inc., of New York and in the early 1930s was its first assistant president general, second in command to LIONEL FRANCIS (*Garvey Papers* 1–6).

DAVIS, JAMES J. (1873–1947), was U.S. secretary of labor during the HARDING, COOLIDGE, and Hoover administrations (1921–1930).

DE BOURG, JOHN SYDNEY, West Indian labor leader and reformer, was the delegate from Trinidad at the 1920 UNIA convention and was elected UNIA provincial leader of blacks in the West Indies, Central America, and South America at that convention. De Bourg was born in Grenada and taught school there before moving to Trinidad, where he became a leader of the Trinidad Workingmen's Association. He was elected secretary of the association in July 1914 and led a major strike in 1919 that was successful in temporarily disrupting colonial rule on the island. His role in the labor revolt led to charges of sedition, and he was deported back to Grenada in 1919. He first met Garvey in New York in 1920, and the UNIA leader encouraged him to serve as a delegate at the organization's international convention. After his election to office in the UNIA, de Bourg made an organizing tour of the West Indies with HENRIETTA VINTON DAVIS, speaking at public meetings and selling stock in the BLACK STAR LINE. He joined Garvey on his speaking tour of Jamaica in 1921. He resigned his office at the 1922 UNIA convention and subsequently sued Garvey for $8,000 in back salary, claiming he had not been paid for his twenty-two months of service to the organization. He appeared as a witness for the prosecution at Garvey's mail fraud trial (W. F. Elkins, "Black Power in the British West Indies: The Trinidad Longshoremen's Strike of 1919," *Science and Society* 33 [winter 1969]: 71–75; *MG* v. *U.S.*, pp. 917–953; *Garvey Papers* 2).

DE MENA, MAYMIE LEONA TURPEAU (1891–1953), was a leader in the Garvey movement from the early 1920s through the 1940s. Born in San Carlos, Nicaragua, De Mena was educated in Nicaragua and the United States. She joined George Emonei Carter and HENRIETTA VINTON DAVIS as an organizer, translator, and secretary aboard the ill-fated Caribbean tour of the S.S. GENERAL GOETHALS in 1925. She moved to the forefront of the movement during the years of Garvey's imprisonment in Atlanta penitentiary. She worked as Garvey's representative, speaking and organizing in communities throughout the United States in 1925, becoming assistant international organizer in 1926 and fourth assistant president general in 1927. Her daughter, Berniza, became active in the UNIA in New York in the 1920s. In

1928 De Mena married Milton Ebimber of Cameroon, West Africa, in a LIBERTY HALL wedding ceremony. Ebimber was a linguist and medical doctor who had studied in Berlin. De Mena appeared beside Garvey on the speaker's platform at the 1929 UNIA convention in Jamaica and led the convention parade through the streets of Kingston on horseback. She was elected international organizer at that convention and was a central figure in Garvey's reorganization of his wing of the movement as the UNIA (August 1929) of the World. She became the officer in charge of the American field in 1930 and conducted speaking tours of the Caribbean and Central America in 1930–1932. She briefly assumed the directorship of the *NEGRO WORLD* in 1933, later moving to Jamaica to live with her third husband, Percival Aiken, who was also involved in the UNIA. She became a social worker and was active in local charities, women's groups, and political organizations in Kingston, where she was also the owner-editor of the *Ethiopian World*. She continued to be active in the Harmony Division of the UNIA in Kingston in the 1940s (*NW*, 11 July and 5 September 1925, 27 March and 11 December 1926, 19 March 1927, 14 January and 21 January 1928, 15 April and 17 October 1933; *DG*, 2 August and 3 September 1929, 3 August 1937; *Minutes of the Harmony Division Conference of August 1942*, S.U. Smith papers, Kingston; *Garvey Papers* 6).

DE VALERA, EAMON (1882–1975), Irish nationalist and statesman, was born in New York and immigrated to Ireland in 1885. He joined the Irish Volunteers in 1913 and commanded the third battalion of the volunteers' Dublin Brigade in the Easter Rebellion of 1916. He was sentenced to death by the English after the uprising but was released under a general amnesty after a brief imprisonment. He returned to Ireland in 1917, where he was elected to the provisional parliament and became president of Sinn Fein and of the Irish Volunteers. After leading an anticonscription campaign, he was again imprisoned by the English but escaped in 1919. He was elected president of the Irish Republic in 1919 and was reelected in 1921. He traveled to the United States in 1919–1920 to raise money and political support for the recognition of the republic. He resigned as president in 1922 after a treaty was signed between Great Britain and Ireland which established the Irish Free State but excluded northern Ireland from the agreement. In 1926 he formed his own party, Fianna Fail, which gained control of the government in 1932. De Valera served as prime minister in 1932–1948, 1951–1954, and 1957–1959 and as president from 1959 to 1973. Under his leadership Ireland suspended oaths of allegiance to the British Crown and the payment of land annuities to Britain; it also maintained a neutral position throughout World War II.

DISRAELI, BENJAMIN (1804–1881), was prime minister of England in 1868 and again in 1874–1880, and one of the founders of Britain's Conservative party. His terms as prime minister saw the strengthening of the British imperial system, including the annexation of the Fiji Islands (1874) and the Transvaal (1877), the purchase of a controlling portion of stock in the Suez Canal (1875), the ceding of Cyprus to Great

Britain by Turkey during the Russo-Turkish War (1877–1878), and the attack on the Zulu in South Africa in 1879. A close confidant of Queen Victoria, he was instrumental in securing the title of empress of India for her in 1876. Garvey spoke of NAPOLEON's and Disraeli's ability to build empire in a March 1920 speech at LIBERTY HALL. He urged his audience to think of them as role models for a black leadership who would create "a free and redeemed Africa," acting as these men had "done for their race, for their nation, for their empire" (*Garvey Papers* 2: 255, 256). Disraeli was also a prolific novelist and essayist; his works include *Vivian Grey* (1826), *Vindication of the English Constitution* (1835), *Venetia* (1837), and *Sybil* (1845).

DOMINGO, W. ADOLPHUS (1889–1968), was the first editor of the *NEGRO WORLD*, beginning in August 1918. Domingo was born in Kingston, Jamaica, and was raised in Garvey's hometown of SAINT ANN'S BAY. He met Garvey in Kingston, where Garvey had gone to work as a printer and Domingo had become an apprentice tailor. The two young men were officers in S. A. G. Cox's National Club, and in 1910 they collaborated in writing a pamphlet about Cox's political efforts called *The Struggling Mass*. Domingo introduced Garvey to the work of Edward Wilmot Blyden, whose writings had a profound effect upon Garvey's perspective of race. Domingo immigrated to the United States in August 1910, with plans to study medicine in Boston. He moved to New York in 1912, where he continued to be involved in working for Jamaican labor and political reforms. Garvey and Domingo remained in correspondence, and Garvey wrote to Domingo about his plans to come to the States to meet with BOOKER T. WASHINGTON in 1915. He joined Domingo in New York in 1916, and Domingo introduced him to black leaders in the city. Domingo assisted with the establishment of the UNIA in New York but never became an official member. Meanwhile, he established close ties with A. Philip Randolph, CHANDLER OWEN, and other leading black Socialists and became a member of the Socialist party's speaking bureau in Harlem. His expression of radical political viewpoints in the *Negro World* caused a deep rift between him and his former friend, who had him tried before the executive committee of the UNIA on charges of writing editorials inconsistent with the expressed goals of the organization. Domingo resigned from the *Negro World* staff in July 1919, stating that he disagreed with Garvey's authoritarian methods and felt his business dealings were backward and dishonest. He became one of the most outspoken critics of Garvey through the pages of his *Emancipator* weekly newspaper and as a contributing editor for the *MESSENGER* and the *CRUSADER*. Domingo was a member of the African Blood Brotherhood and remained a central activist in the Jamaican self-government movement. He was one of the founders of the Jamaica Progressive League in 1936 and worked with the People's National party, headed by Norman Manley, in the 1940s (*NW*, August 1918–July 1919; *Garvey Papers* 1).

DRAKE, FRANCIS (1540?–1596), English navigator and privateer, was the first Englishman to sail around the world (1577–1580). Drake began his naval experience by serving aboard slaving ships that captured blacks in West Africa and sold them as slaves on the Spanish main. He headed a series of expeditions raiding Spanish possessions in the New World in the 1570s and '80s. In 1581 he was knighted by Queen Elizabeth following his lucrative circumnavigation of the world. He was vice admiral of the English fleet that defeated the Spanish Armada in 1588 and died at sea during a 1595–1596 raid on the West Indies.

DU BOIS, WILLIAM EDWARD BURGHARDT (1868–1963), was an editor, historian, sociologist, novelist, civil rights leader, socialist, and pan-Africanist. Born in Great Barrington, Mass., Du Bois studied at Fisk University, Nashville, Harvard University (B.A. 1890, M.A. 1891, Ph.D. 1896), and the University of Berlin. He began teaching at Atlanta University in 1897. His experience in the South caused him to reject the accommodationist methods of BOOKER T. WASHINGTON and to advocate public protest against racial violence and discrimination. He put forward the ideas of a "talented tenth," or the development of race leadership through an intellectual elite, and the aggressive demand for black integration into American political and economic life. He was cofounder of the Niagara movement and of the NAACP in 1910. He was the editor of the NAACP's publication, the *Crisis*, for some twenty-four years. He organized the first Pan-African congress in Paris in 1919 and helped coordinate other congresses in 1921, 1923, and 1927. Du Bois moved increasingly to the left in his political thinking, embracing a Marxist analysis of black labor and eventually advocating a "nation within a nation" form of black economic separatism or cooperation. In the 1940s he became increasingly involved in work on behalf of world peace. He was dismissed from the NAACP in 1948 and became the vice chair of the Council on African Affairs, which monitored political events in Africa and supported African liberation movements. He was a delegate to the World Congress for Peace in Paris in 1949 and supported the abolition of atomic weapons. In the 1950s Du Bois was subjected to increasing governmental restrictions. In 1961 he officially joined the American Communist party, then moved to Ghana, which had gained independence in 1957. He became a Ghanaian citizen and died there. Personal and political antagonism between Garvey and Du Bois was formidable and longstanding. The ideological differences between the two men are often interpreted as a split along integration/separatism and elite/working-class lines (although the latter dichotomy is somewhat obscured by Garvey's pro-capitalist outlook and Du Bois's Marxism); but both in their lifetimes supported the ideas of economic nationalism, pan-Africanism, and the preservation of a black cultural heritage (W. E. B. Du Bois, "Marcus Garvey," *Crisis* 21, no. 2 [December 1920]: 58–60; idem, "Back to Africa," *Century* 105 [February 1923]: 539–548; "A Symposium on Garvey," *Messenger* 4 [December 1922]: 551; *NW*, 18 February 1928; *BM* 1 [November 1934]: 9–10; Herbert Aptheker, ed., *The Correspondence of W. E. B. Du Bois*, 3 vols. [Amherst: University of Massachusetts Press, 1973–1978]; *The Autobiography of W. E. B. Du Bois* [New York: International Publishers, 1968]; Bernard K. Johnpoll and Harvey Klehr,

Biographical Dictionary of the American Left [New York: Greenwood Press, 1986], pp. 117–121; Elliott Rudwick, *W. E. B. Du Bois: Voice of the Black Protest Movement* [1960; reprint, Urbana: University of Illinois Press, 1982]; *Garvey Papers* 1–6).

DUCHATERLIER, MARIE, an elocutionist and advocate of black nationalism, was the lady president of the Bocas del Toro, Panama, division of the UNIA in 1919–1920. Duchaterlier was a popular Panamanian lecturer on race issues in the 1890s and a member of the Negro Society for Historical Research in 1911. She became an active organizer for the UNIA and toured Panama in 1920 raising funds for the BLACK STAR LINE. She was a delegate to the 1920 UNIA convention in New York and one of the signers of the UNIA Declaration of Rights (Tony Martin, *Race First* [Westport, Conn.: Greenwood Press, 1976], pp. 82, 100, 182; *Garvey Papers* 2).

DUNCAN, SAMUEL A. (b. 1880), was third vice president of the UNIA in 1917 and president of the rival wing (sometimes referred to as the Negro Universal Improvement League) that challenged Garvey's authority in New York in 1918. Duncan was born in St. Kitts and was a resident of Bermuda before he immigrated to the United States in May 1900. He gained employment in Harlem as a porter and was editor of the Harlem *Pilot-Gazette* before he joined Garvey's organization. He founded the West Indian Protective Society of America in October 1916. Duncan briefly seized control of the UNIA from Garvey in early 1918. His fellow officers included John E. Bruce, Elizabeth Jackson, LOUIS LAVELLE, and IRENA MOORMAN BLACKSTON. Although Garvey mentions ISAAC ALLEN as one of Duncan's colleagues in this intraorganizational coup, Allen's involvement has not been documented. Articles in the Harlem *Home News* in 1918 reported that Garvey's wing of the movement was meeting in the Odd Fellows Hall in Harlem, while Duncan's group had control over the Lafayette Hall meetings, where it also maintained its headquarters. Duncan's group was soon eclipsed, however, whereupon he returned to his role as head of the West Indian Protective Society, which came to be known by a number of UNIA-like names (e.g., Universal Improvement and Cooperative Association, and Universal Negro Protective Association, Universal Negro Protective and Co-operative Association). Duncan's organization worked to aid West Indian immigrants to New York and volunteered to form a separate American–West Indian regiment under joint British–U.S. control to go into combat in WORLD WAR I. In 1920 Duncan wrote to British colonial officials, charging Garvey with anti-British propaganda and responsibility for inciting labor unrest in the Caribbean (*Home News*, 16 January, 20 January, 23 January, 27 January, and 30 January 1918; *PC*, 22 February 1930; *Garvey Papers* 1, 2).

DYER, CONSTANTINE FREDERICK (b. 1881), was a Jamaican longshoreman working in New Orleans. He was arrested along with WILLIAM SHAKESPEARE for the murder of J. W. H. EASON in January 1923. Dyer was identified by witnesses as the man who fired the gun; Shakespeare, as an accomplice. Dyer was apparently an active member of the UNIA. A UNIA police badge was found on Dyer's person at the time of his arrest, as was a newspaper clipping of a photograph of the UNIA delegation to the League of Nations. Shakespeare was also identified by witnesses as a Garveyite. The UNIA organized a defense fund for the two murder defendants soon after their arrest. In March 1923 both Shakespeare and Dyer were found guilty of manslaughter in connection with Eason's death. They were sentenced to the Louisiana state penitentiary for a term of eighteen to twenty years. However, the Louisiana Supreme Court remanded the case for retrial, and at the new trial in 1924, both men were found innocent and acquitted (*NW,* 20 January 1923 and 9 August 1924; *CD,* 16 August 1924; *Garvey Papers* 5).

DYETT, BENJAMIN, a resident of Bermuda, was a delegate to the 1920 UNIA convention in New York. He addressed the issues of discrimination in governmental hiring practices and the relegation of black workers to menial positions in factory labor when he reported to the convention. He was one of the signers of the UNIA Declaration of Rights (*Garvey Papers* 2).

EASON, JAMES W. H. (1886–1923), was an African Methodist Episcopal Zion clergyman who became a prominent leader in the UNIA. Eason was born in North Carolina and graduated from Livingstone College and Hood Theological Seminary in Salisbury, N.C. He was pastor of the People's Metropolitan AME Zion Church in Philadelphia. Eason and other black ministers organized the Colored Protective Association as a response to the Philadelphia race riot of July 1918. He also joined the NAACP but became disillusioned with the organization and turned instead to Garvey and the UNIA. He was soon elected as the first UNIA chaplain general (1919) and later as "leader of American Negroes" at the 1920 UNIA convention. In the same year he was nominated as the presidential candidate of the Harlem-based Liberty party, organized by William Bridges, Hubert Harrison, and former UNIA general secretary EDGAR GREY. Eason was described as "tall and of splendid physique," "brilliant," and "noble looking" in a 3 September 1921 *NEGRO WORLD* article. He was one of the signers of the UNIA petition to the League of Nations in July 1922. He spoke and traveled as an organizer for the UNIA, and his great charisma soon attracted a following. He and Garvey parted ways during the UNIA convention in August 1922, when Garvey had Eason impeached for alleged irregularities in the handling of UNIA revenues, disloyalty, and moral conduct unbecoming a UNIA officer. Eason was found guilty on all charges and expelled from the UNIA. He countered the expulsion by impeaching Garvey on charges of incompetency, violations of the UNIA constitution, and affiliation with the KU KLUX KLAN. A vote of confidence in Garvey's leadership was taken, and Eason's charges against him were rescinded without a hearing. Eason reacted to these events by forming a rival organization, the Universal Negro Alliance, in September 1922. On New Year's Day, 1923, Eason was shot as he was leaving a church where he had held a meeting in New Orleans. It was publicly known that he had been subpoenaed to appear as a government witness in Garvey's mail fraud trial in New York in the coming week. Severely wounded, he gave a statement to police from his hospital bed that he suspected that the assassination attempt had been carried out by members of the UNIA and that he had been physically threatened by UNIA members on other occasions before the fatal attack took place. He did not identify his assailants by name. He died of his injuries on 4 January 1923, and two Garveyites, CONSTANTINE "FRED" DYER and WILLIAM SHAKESPEARE, were arrested in connection with the killing (Randall K. Burkett, *Black Redemption: Churchmen Speak for the Garvey Movement* [Philadelphia: Temple University Press, 1978], pp. 51–63; *Garvey Papers* 1, 3–5).

EDELWEISS PARK was located at 67 Slipe Road, Cross Roads, St. Andrew, Jamaica. Garvey purchased the property from C. A. Benjamin in January 1929 and set up offices and international headquarters for the UNIA there. The park served as the venue of a number of businesses, including the Edelweiss Amusement Co. (which featured evening concerts, plays, dances, and vaudeville shows), a daily newspaper, the *BLACKMAN* (produced by the Black Man Printing and Publishing Co., with its head office at Edelweiss Park and its press at 5–7 Peters Lane in Kingston), and Marcus Garvey and Co. (an auctioneering and real estate company). In 1931 a "Coney Island" section featuring games and sporting contests was added, open from 7:30 to 12:00 each night for a small admission fee. Ceremonies and business sessions of the international UNIA conventions of 1929 and 1934 were also accommodated there. Garvey's businesses failed during the Depression, and the mortgagee foreclosed on Edelweiss Park in December 1934. The park was sold at public auction, but Garvey remained a tenant there until his move to London in 1935 (*NW,* 12 January and 10 April 1929; *Bm,* 13 May and 8 August 1929, 1 February, 31 June, 9 August, 16 August 1930, 3 January 1931; *DG,* 9 August 1929, 4 April 1930, 15 February, 1 July, and 5 July 1932; *G&G,* p. 218).

EDISON, THOMAS (1847–1931), was a self-taught scientific genius and inventor who established research laboratories in Menlo Park (1876) and West Orange, N.J. (1887) and patented over one thousand inventions, including the microphone, the phonograph, the incandescent electric lamp, and the alkaline battery.

ELLEGOR, FRANCIS WILCOLM (1877–1928), commissioner general of the UNIA in 1921–1922, was born in Demerara, British Guiana, and educated at Durham University, Durham, England. In 1910 he was ordained as a priest in the Protestant Episcopal church in Monrovia, Liberia, where he taught at Liberia College. He immigrated to the United States in 1916 and lived in Yonkers, New York. He became active in the UNIA and served as a delegate to the 1920, 1921, 1922, and 1924 conventions. He announced his resignation as high commissioner at the 1922 convention but continued to serve as a chaplain at meetings and as a member on key UNIA committees. At the beginning of the 1922 convention he was elected as a member of the UNIA delegation to the League of Nations (*Garvey Papers* 2, 4, 5).

ESAU and JACOB were twin sons of Rebecca and Isaac. According to biblical tradition the two infants struggled in the womb, and the Lord told Rebekah that "Two nations are in your womb, Two peoples shall be separated from your body; One people shall be stronger than the other, And the older shall serve the younger." The firstborn was Esau, who became a hunter. The second born was Jacob, a pastoral herdsman. Esau sold his birthright of primogeniture to Jacob. Later, when Isaac was blind and dying, Rebekah urged Jacob to impersonate his brother in order to receive his father's blessing and become his brother's master. When the deceit was discovered, Isaac blessed Esau also, promising him that he would someday break his brother's yoke from his neck (Gen. 26:22–34, 27:5–40).

ETHIOPIA. See ABYSSINIA; see also ITALO-ETHIOPIAN WAR.

FELIX, REYNOLD RANDOLPH, of St. Lucia, BWI, was a delegate to the 1920 UNIA convention. He spoke on the status of labor in St. Lucia, describing long hours and depressed wages in the cane and cocoa fields and the difficulties faced by black women occupied as coal carriers. He was one of the signers of the UNIA Declaration of Rights (*Garvey Papers* 2).

FIELD, MARSHALL (1834–1906), one of Garvey's frequently cited exemplars of success, began his career as a clerk in a Massachusetts dry goods store in the 1850s and ended up the wealthy head of Marshall Field and Co., the largest wholesale and retail mercantile establishment in the world in the 1880s and '90s.

FORD, ARNOLD JOSIAH (1877–1935), composer, and religious scholar, was musical director for the UNIA at LIBERTY HALL in the early twenties. Ford was born in Barbados and was a member of the musical corps of the British Royal Navy during WORLD WAR I. He moved to Harlem in the postwar years and was attracted to the UNIA because of its concern with African repatriation. He wrote many UNIA hymns, including the "Universal Ethiopian Anthem" and "Shine on Eternal Light," and authored the *Universal Ethiopian Hymnal*. Ford was affiliated with his own synagogue, Beth B'nai Abraham, and with the Commandment Keepers congregation, another black Hebrew temple located in Harlem. Always interested in African colonization, Ford traveled to Ethiopia in the early thirties to consider the possibility of his congregation sponsoring a settlement there. He attended the coronation of Haile Selassie and received a land grant from the Ethiopian ruler for the establishment of a colony. Ford encouraged members of his congregation to emigrate, and more than fifty came to settle in Ethiopia. Internal factionalism and hostility from external forces caused the small colony to fail, and most of the emigrants returned to the United States. Ford died in Addis Ababa one year after the community's dissolution (K. J. King, "Some Notes on Arnold J. Ford and New World Black Attitudes to Ethiopia," *Journal of Ethiopian Studies* 10, no. 1 [January 1972]: 81–87; William R. Scott, "Rabbi Arnold Ford's Back-to-Ethiopia Movement: A Study of Black Emigration, 1930–1935," *Pan-African Journal* 7 [summer 1975]: 191–202; *WWCA; Garvey Papers* 2).

FORD, HARRY E., one of the signers of the UNIA Declaration of Rights, was from Rahway, N.J. (*Garvey Papers* 2).

FORD, HENRY (1863–1947), American industrialist and automobile manufacturer, was the founder of the Ford Motor Co. and a pioneer in mass production techniques. Ford's Dearborn Publishing Co. produced a compilation of four pamphlets first published in 1921–1922 under the title *The International Jew,* which became a best-seller in Germany and brought Ford to the notice of Adolf Hitler. Ford's publications were also distributed by the KU KLUX KLAN in the United States. Hitler praised Ford in *Mein Kampf,* and a *New York Times* correspondent who interviewed the Nazi leader reported that he had a large picture of Ford on the wall beside his desk and several translations of Ford's book on display in his antechamber. A second series of anti-Semitic articles was launched in the *Independent* (which had a circulation of over one million) in 1924. After becoming embroiled in legal controversy over the articles, Ford publicly apologized for their content in 1927. In 1938, however, he accepted the Supreme Order of the German Eagle award from Hitler in recognition of his technological advances in assembly-line production. Ford was an isolationist before both world wars, but his plant was converted to wartime military production in 1915 and again in 1941 (Carol Gelderman, *Henry Ford: The Wayward Capitalist* [New York: Dial Press, 1981]).

FRANCIS, LIONEL A. (b. 1881), was an active UNIA member for many years and eventually became a rival of Garvey. Francis was born in Trinidad and graduated from Howard University Medical School and the University of Edinburgh. He practiced medicine in London before he came to the United States in 1920 to attend the first UNIA convention. He became one of Garvey's key lieutenants in the early 1920s, taking charge of the Philadelphia division, one of the largest of local UNIA branches, in 1921. In that year William Ferris described Francis as a "brilliant, magnetic, energetic, and ambitious" man, who promised to "evolve into a real racial leader" (*NW,* 16 July 1921). Francis and Garvey parted ways in the mid-twenties, and Francis temporarily resigned from the movement. He rejoined the UNIA after Garvey's deportation from the United States, and in 1931 he became the president general of the New York–based UNIA, Inc. (the original parent body of the UNIA in the United States, incorporated in 1918, with which Garvey and his reincorporated UNIA [August 1929] of the World in Jamaica vied for recognition as the official group of the international UNIA movement). Francis and Garvey challenged each other in court as rightful heirs to the lucrative Isaiah Morter estate, and Francis was eventually victorious. Francis went to British Honduras (Belize) in 1939 to administer the estate on behalf of the American-based wing of the movement and became active in local politics there. He served on the Belize city council, was president of the People's Group of British Honduras, and served as an adviser to Belizean labor unions (*Philadelphia Tribune,* 16 August 1924; *BA,* 20 July 1932; *NW,* 6 May 1933; *NYA,* 7 April and 14 April 1934, 18 November 1939; *Public Opinion,* 6 September 1947; *Garvey Papers* 2, 6).

FRANCIS, NAPOLEON J., was a UNIA organizer and BLACK STAR LINE stock salesperson in Port-au-Prince, Haiti. He was a delegate to the 1920 UNIA convention and signed the UNIA Delaration of Rights. He told the 1920 convention audience that when the American members crossed "the ocean to Africa we shall send you every available officer of the Haitian army" to assist in the cause (*Negro World Convention Bulletin,* 3 August 1920). He was president of the UNIA chapter in Haiti in 1921 and traveled again to the United States to attend an April meeting of international officers in New York and the second UNIA convention (*NW,* 8 September 1921; *Garvey Papers* 2, 3).

S.S. *FREDERICK DOUGLASS.* See S.S. *YARMOUTH.*

FRIENDS OF NEGRO FREEDOM was a radical political organization formed by A. Philip Randolph and CHANDLER OWEN. One of many similar organizations begun by Randolph and Owen, this group was founded in May 1920 and envisioned as an association with local chapters much on the model of the UNIA. It was largely a paper organization until 1922, when the "Garvey Must Go" campaign was launched under its auspices. The Friends evolved into a small intellectual forum and study group that gathered to discuss political issues and occasionally organized public lectures in Harlem, inviting black historians, psychologists, editors, and leading Socialists to speak. Regular members included ROBERT BAGNALL, Frank Crosswaith, WILLIAM PICKENS, George Schuyler, Joel A. Rogers, and Theophilus Lewis. The association began to disband after the death of Owen's brother, Toussaint, in March 1923, caused the disillusioned Owen to leave New York (Jervis Anderson, *A. Philip Randolph: A Biographical Portrait* [New York: Harcourt Brace Jovanovich, 1972], pp. 139–143).

FULTON, ROBERT (1765–1815), American artist, inventor, and engineer, is usually credited with the invention of the steamboat. Paddlewheel steamboats had been in existence in Europe since the late 1600s, and several Americans had already demonstrated workable models when Fulton was commissioned in 1807 to build a boat that could be used for commercial purposes on the Hudson River. The result was Fulton's *Clermont,* which became a symbol of the steamboat commerce that revolutionized the American economy in the early national period.

GANDHI, MOHANDAS K. (1869–1948), Indian nationalist leader and philosopher, was given the religious title Mahatma ("great soul") by his followers in the 1920s. Gandhi was educated in India and England and practiced law in South Africa, where he became a leader in the effort to end anti-Indian discrimination and advocated nonviolent civil disobedience against unjust laws. A devout Hindu, Gandhi also taught the principles of asceticism and simplicity, including the denial of materialism. Fasting was one of his primary tools of dissent. In 1915 he returned to India, where he led demonstrations for labor and agrarian reform and voiced his hope for an independent and united Indian nation. His nationalism included an economic policy favoring cottage industries, especially the home production of cloth combined with the boycotting of imported British fabrics. In 1930 he led a long march to the ocean to protest the British salt tax and was imprisoned for this display of noncooperation with British rule. He was freed from prison in 1931 to attend the London Round Table Conference on India as the delegate of the Indian National Congress. He was imprisoned again during World War II but figured largely in the postwar nego- tiations with British, Sikh, and Muslim leaders that resulted in Indian independence in 1947. Gandhi personally opposed the terms of that independence, which divided India into separate Hindu and Muslim (Pakistani) states. He was assassinated on his way to a prayer meeting in New Delhi by a Hindu who opposed his efforts to accommodate Muslims and Sikhs in a unified India (M. K. Gandhi, *An Autobiography* 2 vols. [1927–1929; reprint, Ahmedabad, India: Navajivan Press, 1940]; Dhananjay Keer, *Mahatma Gandhi: Political Saint and Unarmed Prophet* [Bombay: Popular Prakashan Press, 1973]; Louis Fischer, *The Life of Mahatma Gandhi* [New York: Harper & Row, 1950]; George Woodcock, *Mohandas Gandhi* [New York: Viking Press, 1971]).

GARCIA, ELIE, was indicted along with Marcus Garvey, ORLANDO THOMPSON, and GEORGE TOBIAS on mail fraud charges in February 1922. In the spring and summer of 1920, Garcia carried out an information-gathering visit to Liberia on behalf of the UNIA. He was born in Haiti and educated in Haiti and France. He visited the United States in 1916 and immigrated to New York in 1917. He moved to West Virginia, where he worked with UNIA member Eliezer Cadet at a federal laboratory in Nitro during the war. Garcia became a stock salesperson for the BLACK STAR LINE in Philadelphia in August 1919 and was secretary of the Philadelphia division from June 1919 to April 1920. He was promoted to a field position for the Black Star Line before becoming one of its directors and secretary in September 1920. He was also appointed auditor of the UNIA in August 1920, receiv- ing the appointment while he was still in Liberia. Garvey had Garcia prosecuted for theft and fraud in two cases heard in March 1923. The first case, which was reviewed at the Washington Heights Court in New York City, was dismissed for lack of evidence; at the second, Garcia was convicted of forging a check, but his attorney won an ap- peal on the grounds that the evidence introduced was circumstantial. Garcia was defended in the mail fraud trial by Henry Lincoln Johnson. He, Thompson, and Tobias were acquitted on all charges (*NW,* 21 August 1920, 24 March 1923; *Garvey Papers* 2, 4, 5).

GARVEY, AMY ASHWOOD. See AMY ASHWOOD.

GARVEY, AMY JACQUES. See AMY JACQUES.

S.S. *GENERAL GOETHALS*, originally named the *Grunewald*, was built in Germany in 1911. It was purchased by the BLACK CROSS NAVIGATION AND TRADING CO., INC., in October 1924 and unofficially renamed the S.S. *Booker T. Washington*. The four-thousand-ton vessel was bought from the Panama Railroad Co. for a purchase price of $100,000— $75,000 of which had been paid by the time the UNIA's shipping line took possession in October. The remainder of the payments were made after repeated delays, and the Black Cross Navigation and Trading Co. received clear title in January 1925. The ship had accommodations for 175 passengers and was equipped to carry freight. The *Goethals* was launched on 18 January 1925. It proceeded on a voyage that was plagued with problems and took four and a half months, rather than the scheduled one month, to complete. The ship was captained by a Norwegian, Jacob de Rytter Hiorth. It sailed from New York to Norfolk, Va., and from Virginia to Cuba, Jamaica, and Panama, then returned via Miami and Jacksonville, Fla., and Charleston, N.C., arriving in New York on 31 May 1925. UNIA officials George Emonei Carter, HENRIETTA VINTON DAVIS, and M. L. T. DE MENA were aboard throughout the tour as organizers and fund-raisers for the organization. The crew grew increasingly disgruntled as the trip proceeded because of lack of provisions and the failure of the officers to disburse scheduled advances on their salaries. Funds raised through local UNIA efforts failed to meet the expenses of the ship, which was in need of frequent repairs, and emergency monies were forwarded from the New York office. In both Kingston and Havana, the *Goethals* was detained by municipal authorities in the interest of the creditors of the BLACK STAR LINE, so that old debts had to be paid before the ship could continue. The white officers requested discharge when the ship was docked in Kingston because of the lack of payment of their own salaries and fear of bodily harm from the crew. The ship nevertheless continued to Panama, where Hiorth quit the vessel and was replaced by another white officer, Capt. Charles V. Vaughan. When it returned to the United States, the *Goethals* was boarded by members of the KU KLUX KLAN while in port in Jacksonville. It proceeded to Charleston, where it was subjected to fines for violation of U.S. maritime regulations. It also rammed a pier twice but successfully returned to New York without further misadventure. The *Goethals* was sold at auction in March 1926 for $25,000 (*NW,* 23 August 1924, 17 January, 8 August, 15 August, 5, and 12, 19, and 26 September 1925; *Jacksonville Times-Union,* 8 May, 9 May, and 17 May 1925; *Dawn of Tomorrow* [Montreal], 6 June 1925; *BA,* 31 March 1926; *DG,* 14 August 1929; *DW,* 12 September, 28 October, 30 October, 8 November 1930; *Garvey Papers* 5).

GENGHIS KHAN (1167?–1227), a Mongol chieftain, led Mongolian troops in conquering large areas of northern China, Turkistan, Afghanistan, Persia, and eastern Europe.

GIBSON, JOSEPH D. (1880?–1963), was the first president of the Boston division of the UNIA (formed in November 1920) and the surgeon general of the UNIA in 1920–1922. Gibson was born in St. Pierre, Martinique, and attended schools in Grenada before he immigrated to the United States in 1909. He attended Holmes Institute in Atlanta and in 1915 received his medical degree from the Boston College of Physicians and Surgeons. He failed his first attempts to qualify for a medical license and served as a ship's surgeon before finally obtaining his license to practice medicine in West Virginia in 1922. Garvey had Gibson impeached at the 1922 UNIA convention for alleged disloyalty and incompetency, based on his failure to obtain a license to practice medicine in the state of New York and his criticism of Garvey's autocratic methods in administering the organization. During the

impeachment proceedings, Gibson testified that he had loaned the
BLACK STAR LINE money for the purchase of ships, that he had not
been repaid for these loans, and that he had been paid only a fraction
of his salary while a UNIA officer. In January 1923 he contacted the
U.S. SHIPPING BOARD in an effort to receive a rebate of the monies
he had invested in the Black Star Line. He moved to Logan, W.Va.,
where he worked as a physician for the United Mine Workers. He was
a candidate for the U.S. Congress in 1933 and was active in Republican
party politics throughout the 1940s and 1950s (*NW*, 8 May 1920, 12
August 1922; *NYT*, 16 November 1963; *Garvey Papers* 2, 4, 5).

GIDEON was one of the judges of Israel when the Israelites were attacked in
a number of Midianite raids. He received a series of visions that guided
him and his clan in a military victory over the Midianites, whereby he
was offered the crown, which he refused on the grounds that God was
the only true ruler of Israel (Judg. 6–8; *DB*, p. 308).

GORDON, GEORGE WILLIAM (1818?–1865), nineteenth-century Jamaican
reformer, was the son of a landed white proprietor and a black female
slave. A member of the Jamaican house of assembly in the 1840s,
he was reelected as a representative from St. Thomas in 1863 and
became an outspoken opponent of the policies of Gov. Edward John
Eyre. Gordon championed the issues of prison reform, unemployment,
provisions for the poor, and other concerns of lower-class blacks,
as well as the separation of church and state. Eyre blamed public
unrest on these rebellious criticisms of social inequities. After a protest
demonstration by black settlers was violently repressed by the militia
at Morant Bay on 11 October 1865, precipitating mass rioting, Gordon,
a civilian, was taken into custody in Kingston, which was not subject
to martial law. Charged with treason, he was taken to Morant Bay,
where he was quickly court-martialed and condemned to death. He
was executed on 23 October. Many hundreds of persons were killed
by government troops or by order of the courts during the existence
of martial law in the Morant Bay region. Eyre was later charged
before an English grand jury for the murder of Gordon (Marcus
Garvey, "The British West Indies in the Mirror of Civilization: History
Making by Colonial Negroes," *African Times and Orient Review* 2 [mid-
October 1913]: 158–160; Ansell Hart, *The Life of George William Gordon*
[Kingston: Institute of Jamaica, 1972]; Douglas Hall, *Free Jamaica:
1838–1865, An Economic History* [New Haven, Conn.: Yale University
Press, 1959], pp. 244–248).

GORDON, JOHN D., was assistant president general of the UNIA in 1920–
1921. He was born in La Grange, Ga., and attended Morehouse
College in Atlanta. He was pastor of the Mt. Olive Baptist Church
in Atlanta before he moved to California in 1903. He became a
community leader in Los Angeles, where he founded the Tabernacle
Baptist Church. He was delegate to the National Equal Rights League
meeting in Chicago in September 1918. He traveled as an evangelist
and became involved in the UNIA while in New York in 1919. He
was a major participant in the 1920 UNIA convention and was elected
to the executive council at its close. The founding ceremony of the

Los Angeles division of the UNIA took place in his Tabernacle Baptist Church in January 1921. He was one of Garvey's closest aides and confidants during the year between the 1920 and 1921 conventions, but he resigned from the organization at the 1921 convention after Garvey accused him of mismanaging UNIA funds. Gordon sued the UNIA for back payment of salary and returned to Los Angeles, where he became involved in the Pacific Coast Negro Improvement Association, a faction of the UNIA that was opposed to Garvey's methods of leadership. Garvey temporarily reconciled his differences with Gordon during a peacemaking tour of California in June 1922, and Gordon rejoined the UNIA, remaining a member until November 1923 (*NW*, 14 August 1920, 27 August 1921; Emory J. Tolbert, *The UNIA and Black Los Angeles* [Los Angeles: Center for Afro-American Studies, University of California, Los Angeles, 1980], pp. 42–44, 51, 53, 59–62; *Garvey Papers* 2, 3).

GREEN, WALTER, a railway mechanic from Portsmouth, Va., was a delegate to the 1920 UNIA convention and one of the signers of the UNIA Declaration of Rights. A regular reader of the *NEGRO WORLD*, he joined the UNIA in 1919 after experiencing disillusionment with the discriminatory policies of the American Federation of Labor (AFL), with which he had been active for five years. He introduced a resolution to support black organizers in the field at the AFL convention in Buffalo in November 1917, only to see the resolution die in committee. He then became involved in the National Brotherhood Workers of America, a black industrial union for both men and women that was chartered in Washington, D.C., in March 1919 (*NW*, 19 July 1919; *Garvey Papers* 1, 2).

GREY, EDGAR M. (b. 1890), was general secretary of the UNIA and one of the incorporators of the BLACK STAR LINE in 1919. Although Garvey maintained that Grey was born in Antigua, BWI, documentation of Grey's life indicates his birthplace was Sierra Leone, West Africa. Grey was evidently educated in Freetown before immigrating to the West Indies, where he attended school in St. Johns, Antigua; later he was a student at Aberdeen University in Scotland. He became an interpreter for the U.S. government in Puerto Rico and worked as a secretary to Don Juan Moncastro, the president of the Dominican Republic. He immigrated to the United States in 1911 and worked as a postal clerk and bookkeeper before meeting Garvey in Harlem in May 1917. Grey served in the U.S. Army during WORLD WAR I and became a naturalized U.S. citizen. He organized the Foreign Born Citizens Political Alliance in 1919 and became the general secretary of the UNIA in May of the same year. He was also the secretary of the New York local division, business manager of the *NEGRO WORLD*, secretary of the AFRICAN COMMUNITIES LEAGUE, and a director and assistant secretary of the Black Star Line. He left the UNIA in July 1919 after only a few months on the job and was formally expelled by official order on 2 August 1919. Garvey accused him of theft and corruption and claimed that District Attorney EDWIN P. KILROE had prevented charges from being filed against him in exchange for information from

Grey about UNIA financial practices. Kilroe sued Garvey for libel in connection with the allegation, but Grey did supply government officials with information about Garvey and his business dealings. He helped organize the Harlem Liberty League in 1920 with his close friend Hubert H. Harrison and was its secretary in 1921. He also joined the African Blood Brotherhood. He became a chiropractor in 1921 and later in the twenties served as associate editor of the *New York News* and contributing editor to the *New York Amsterdam News* and the *American and West Indian News*. In 1921 a Bureau of Investigation agent described him as "very intelligent . . . talkative, but very truthful and reliable" and passionate in his loyalties (reports by Agent P-138, Bureau of Investigation, New York, 22 June and 31 August 1921, National Archives, Department of Justice, Federal Bureau of Investigation, files 198940, 202680-667). He appeared as a witness for the prosecution at Garvey's 1923 mail fraud trial (*NW*, 2 August 1919, 23 June 1923; *MG* v. *U.S.*, pp. 61–119; *WWCA*; *Garvey Papers* 1, 3).

HAMILCAR BARCA (d. 229 BC.), a Carthaginian general and statesman, defended Sicily during the First Punic War and subdued a revolt of mercenaries following the war, becoming virtual dictator of CARTHAGE. He then led the conquest of Spain, winning territory there as a base from which to confront the Romans. He was the father of HANNIBAL.

HAMILTON, ALEXANDER (1755–1804), member of the Continental Congress and first U.S. secretary of the treasury (1784–1795), was born on Nevis, one of the Leeward Islands east of St. Croix. He immigrated to the United States in 1772. The details of Hamilton's early life in the West Indies are still open to historical debate. While most biographers have focused their descriptions of his youth on the fact of his illegitimacy, the question of his racial heritage has also been raised. The idea that Hamilton, as biographer Marie Hecht put it, "had Negro blood," was dismissed with repugnance by some historians, including Gertrude Atherton, who, when told on a research trip to the West Indies in 1902 that Hamilton was a mulatto "was almost taken ill" and confessed that "were it the truth" she would be unable to write the biography, since "both enthusiasm and imagination would shrivel" (Gertrude Atherton, "The Hunt for Hamilton's Mother," *North American Review* 175, no. 549 [August 1902]: 229–242). Atherton subsequently discovered that all persons still living on Nevis with the surname of Hamilton's maternal grandfather (Fawcett) were black. She recovered Hamilton's mother's name (Rachel Lavien or Levine) from probate records in which three slaves were deeded to Lavien by her mother (Mary Fawcett) but did not trace the intricacies of the racial relationships inherent in Hamilton's family background. Hamilton's grandson is among those who have rejected the idea of Hamilton's black heritage, but others, including W. E. B. DU BOIS, accepted it. The topic was not only one of historical debate but of popular appeal as well. In 1933 a correspondent to the *New York Age* wrote that "it is generally believed by the colored people of Washington, D.C., that in the popular sense this illustrious one [Hamilton] was one racially with themselves" (Louis G. Gregory to *NYA*, 20 May 1933; Harold Larsen, "Alexander Hamilton: The Facts and Fiction of His Early Years," *William and Mary Quarterly* 9, no. 2 [April 1952]: 139–151; Marie B. Hecht, *Odd Destiny: The Life of Alexander Hamilton* [New York: Macmillan, 1982], p. 14; Allan McLane Hamilton, *The Intimate Life of Alexander Hamilton* [New York: Charles Scribner, 1911], p. 29; Elliott M. Rudwick, *W. E. B. Du Bois* [New York: Atheneum, 1969], p. 279).

HAMILTON, VENTURE, was one of the early members of the UNIA in Jamaica when it met in COLLEGIATE HALL in 1915. He attended the 1920 UNIA convention and signed the UNIA Declaration of Rights (*DG*, 4 February 1915; *Garvey Papers* 1).

HANNIBAL (247–183 B.C.), was a Carthaginian general and powerful enemy of Rome during the Second Punic War (218–201 B.C.), wherein he commanded a large army of Libyan and Spanish mercenaries. He is renowned as a tactical military genius, perhaps best known for his feat of crossing the Alps with elephants as a prelude to his invasion of Italy. Hannibal was frequently mentioned as a laudable black hero in UNIA speeches, including addresses by Garvey, EDWARD SMITH-GREEN, RICHARD HILTON TOBITT, and others (*Garvey Papers* 2).

HARDING, WARREN G. (1865–1923), a leading Republican politician, was president of the United States from 1921 to 1923. Born in Ohio, Harding was a member of that state's legislature as well as lieutenant governor and U.S. senator. During Harding's presidential campaign the Republican party made a major effort to capture the votes of white southerners. Harding refused to take a stand against LYNCHING or the violent activities of the KU KLUX KLAN; his failure to address these issues, which were so central to blacks, led many of them to end their allegiance to the Republican party. His administration was distinguished by high-level corruption (including the Teapot Dome scandal and the impeachment of his appointee Attorney General HARRY M. DAUGHERTY), much of which was revealed after his sudden death in San Francisco in August 1923. After Harding's death, Garvey wrote a message to the new president, CALVIN COOLIDGE, offering lamentations, referring to Harding "as one of America's truest and most devoted sons," and proclaiming, on the part of "two and a half million members" of the UNIA, "Long live President Coolidge!" (Francis Russell, *The Shadow of Blooming Grove: Warren G. Harding in His Times* [New York: McGraw-Hill, 1968]; Richard B. Sherman, *The Republican Party and Black America* [Charlottesville: University Press of Virginia, 1973]; *Garvey Papers* 5).

HARRIS, GEORGE WESLEY (1884–1948), Republican politician and editor and publisher of the *New York News*, was born in Topeka, Kans., and attended Tufts College, Medford, Mass., and Harvard University Law School. He had a long career in publishing; he edited the *New York Age* in 1909 and was part owner of the *New York Amsterdam News*. He was a Republican alderman in Harlem in the early 1920s and served as a delegate to the Republican National Convention in 1924. Harris was a vocal critic of the KU KLUX KLAN. After Garvey met with the acting imperial wizard of the Klan in June 1922, Harris published an editorial stating that Garvey's error in judgment in agreeing to the meeting stemmed from his West Indian origins, which prevented him from fully appreciating the Klan's history of violence against blacks and the extent of blacks' attachment to their country and their desire to achieve full civil rights in the United States. Garvey responded by reading the article aloud to a LIBERTY HALL audience at a 16 July 1922 meeting, lambasting Harris and elaborating upon his reasons for dealing directly with the Klan (*NYW*, 16 July 1922; *NW*, 22 July 1922; *NYT*, 28 March 1948; *WWCR*; *Garvey Papers* 2, 4).

HARVEY, WILLIAM (1578–1657), English physician and student of Galileo, was the first to describe the function of the heart and the way in which blood circulates through the human body. His theories on circulation, published in *On the Movement of the Heart and Blood in Animals* (1628), were not fully accepted until the nineteenth century.

HAWKINS, WILLIAM ASHBIE (1862–1941), was an editor and attorney in Baltimore. He was born in Lynchburg, Va., and attended the University of Maryland Law School until 1890, when he and another black student were forced out of the university by an antiblack petition signed by a majority of the student body. He continued his education at Howard University Law School, graduated in 1892, and established a law practice in Baltimore. He edited the *Cambridge Advance* while a student in 1887; after earning his law degree he edited the *Baltimore Spokesman* (1893–1895) and the *Baltimore Lancet* (1902–1905). He was a candidate for the U.S. Senate in 1920 (*NYT*, 15 September 1890; *Baltimore News-Post*, 7 April 1941; *Garvey Papers* 5).

HAYWARD, WILLIAM (1877–1944), was a white New York attorney who recruited and trained the much-honored all-black New York Fifteenth Regiment, 369th U.S. Infantry (the "Buffaloes"), which served in France during WORLD WAR I. Hayward was the colonel of the regiment, which received a collective citation of the croix de guerre for its heroic conduct in battle as well as numerous other awards. Hayward was born in Nebraska City, Nebr., and began a law practice in New York in 1910. He became an assistant to District Attorney Charles S. Whitman in 1913 and managed Whitman's campaigns for governor in 1914 and 1916. After World War I he was appointed chair of the New York State Republican Convention (1920) and U.S. attorney for the Southern District of New York (1921–1925). In September 1921 an agent for the military intelligence division reported that U.S. Attorney Hayward had confiscated the records of the UNIA. He was involved in the government's effort to develop a mail fraud case against Garvey, and he supported Judge JULIAN MACK in the sentencing phase of the trial when he requested that Garvey be sent to the federal penitentiary at Leavenworth, Kans., rather than to Atlanta where he might be subjected to greater racial discrimination. Hayward was among many prominent New Yorkers who responded favorably to an exposé on the KU KLUX KLAN printed by the *New York World* in September 1921 (Arthur W. Little, *From Harlem to the Rhine: The Story of New York's*

Colored Volunteers [n.d., ca. 1920; reprint, New York: Haskell House Publishers, 1974], pp. ix–xi, 370; *Garvey Papers* 4, 5).

HEMMINGS, PHILIP, a Jamaican immigrant to Philadelphia was a delegate to the 1920 UNIA convention from the Philadelphia division. Hemmings praised the work of FRED A. TOOTE and Rev. J.W.H. EASON from the floor of the convention, crediting the two men with the success of the Philadelphia division. In 1916 Hemmings was among a group of Jamaican residents of the United States who wrote to the editor of the *Jamaica Times* (7 October 1916), reporting that Garvey's lectures in the United States had been "pernicious, misleading, and derogatory to the prestige of the [Jamaican] government and the people." The letter went on to question Garvey's assertions that poverty and vice in Jamaica were the results of low wage scales, that education was not extended to the lower classes, that racial intermarriage was not beneficial to black people, and that Anglo-Jamaicans were prejudiced against blacks. Hemmings apparently changed his opinion of Garvey in the ensuing years; he was one of the signers of the UNIA Declaration of Rights in 1920 (*Garvey Papers* 1, 2).

HENLEY, WILLIAM ERNEST (1849–1903), was a British poet and playwright as well as an editor and scholar. He edited collections of poetry by Burns and Byron and published numerous other scholarly works in the field of English literature. Henley's poem "Invictus," published in the collection *Echoes* in 1888, was his best-known work. It was one of Garvey's favorite works of poetry, and he often quoted lines from the poem in his speeches and writings.

HILLS, PARTHERIA, one of the signers of the 1920 UNIA Declaration of Rights, was one of many Garveyites who petitioned for executive clemency for Garvey after he was incarcerated in Atlanta penitentiary (*Garvey Papers* 2).

HOBBS, ALLEN, was an agent of the BLACK STAR LINE in Norfolk, Va., in 1920 and president of the Norfolk division of the UNIA in 1921. He was a delegate to the 1920 and 1921 UNIA conventions, and he signed the 1920 UNIA Declaration of Rights (*NW,* 19 February 1921; *Garvey Papers* 2, 3).

HORSFORD, INNIS ABEL, was president of the New Haven, Conn., division of the UNIA in 1920 and 1921. He represented New Haven at the 1920 UNIA convention, where he addressed the issues of discrimination against blacks in Connecticut hospitals, the underpayment of black women in the labor force, and the need for trade schools to educate black youth. He was one of the signers of the UNIA Declaration of Rights (*NW,* 3 December and 31 December 1921; *Garvey Papers* 2).

HOUSTON, MARIE BARRIER, of New York, was an active UNIA member and musician. She was the director of the Salem Methodist Episcopal Church Choral Society. Houston appeared regularly as a soloist at UNIA meetings in LIBERTY HALL in 1919–1922, helped to direct the Liberty Hall choir, and appeared as a central figure in musical programs during the 1920, 1921, and 1922 UNIA conventions. She also accompanied Garvey and AMY JACQUES on organizational tours in the United States. She participated in Women's Day events at the

1922 convention and signed the UNIA Declaration of Rights (*Garvey Papers* 2, 3).

HOWARD UNIVERSITY was founded in Washington, D.C., in 1867. Originally called the Howard Normal and Theological Institute, it was first envisioned as an institution for the training of teachers and ministers but was soon expanded into a liberal arts and sciences college for the general and professional education of blacks (Rayford W. Logan, *Howard University: The First Hundred Years, 1867–1967* [New York: New York University Press, 1969]).

HUBBARD, ELBERT (1856–1915), was a New York commonsense philosopher and printer who wrote and edited the monthly magazine, the *Philistine* (1895–1915). He also compiled over fourteen volumes of biographical essays on persons who "changed the course of empire and marked the destiny of civilization," called *Little Journeys to the Homes of the Great* (1894–1908). *Elbert Hubbard's Scrap Book* was a popular book of quotations containing hundreds of sayings attributed to famous persons or excerpted from poetry, prose fiction, and political and historical works. The *Scrap Book* was a favorite of Garvey, who quoted from it and recommended it to his students in the School of African Philosophy. He used a THEODORE ROOSEVELT quotation taken from it in his 31 May 1930 *Pittsburgh Courier* article. The topics covered in Hubbard's book of quotations range from philosophical questions of enlightenment or truth to more pragmatic issues, such as success in business, self-confidence, and the relations of labor and capital (*Outlook* 135, no. 15 [12 December 1923]: 609; Elbert Hubbard, ed. and comp., *Elbert Hubbard's Scrap Book* [New York: William H. Wise and Co., 1923]; Felix Shay, *Elbert Hubbard of East Aurora* [New York: William H. Wise and Co., 1926]).

HUDSPETH, J. W., one of the signers of the 1920 UNIA Declaration of Rights, was still active in the UNIA in 1922. He contributed to the fund to raise monies for the 1922 UNIA convention (*NW*, 6 May 1922; *Garvey Papers* 2).

HUGHES, CHARLES EVANS (1862–1948), secretary of state during the WARREN G. HARDING administration (1921–1925), was involved in the state department's monitoring of Garvey's activities in the Caribbean during the UNIA leader's organizing tour of that area in 1921, including efforts to deny him a visa to reenter the country. He was governor of the state of New York (1907–1910), associate justice of the U.S. Supreme Court (1910–1916), and a candidate for president of the United States (1916). After serving on international tribunals in the late 1920s, he was appointed chief justice of the U.S. Supreme Court and served in that capacity until his retirement in 1941 (*NYT*, 28 August 1948; *Garvey Papers* 3, 4–6).

HYDE PARK, London, a 361-acre landscaped park located in Westminster borough, is famous for its Speakers' Corner, an area near the Marble Arch which serves as a gathering place for soapbox orators and their audiences. Garvey often spoke at Speakers' Corner in the late 1930s. In her memoirs AMY ASHWOOD Garvey reported last seeing him on his way to Speakers' Corner, and the 18 May 1940 *Boston Guardian* reported that "in 1937 African students in London once almost mobbed Garvey because of his reactionary position regarding Ethiopia, and his anti-labor bias caused him to be hissed off the platforms of Hyde Park, to which he never returned." George Padmore, the political organizer of the pan-African lobby in England, confirmed that Garvey was heckled for his views on the ITALO-ETHIOPIAN WAR, but he attributed Garvey's withdrawal from Hyde Park to his increasingly severe asthma, not to this verbal opposition (*CD*, 18 May 1940; Amy Ashwood Garvey, "Portrait of a Liberator" [unpub. ms., 1969], pp. 29–30, Amy Ashwood Garvey papers, New York, Lionel Yard, executor).

INDIANS. See NATIVE AMERICANS.

INTERNATIONAL CONFERENCE ON THE LIMITATION OF ARMAMENTS was held in Washington, D.C., in November 1921. Garvey traveled to Washington during the conference and noted the lack of representation of Africa among the world powers. He sent a telegram to the conference organizers "as the elected spokesman of the Negro peoples of the world," reminding the delegates from Japan, the United States and Europe that "there are four hundred million Negroes in the world who demand Africa as their rightful heritage, even as the European claims Europe, and the Asiatic, Asia" (*Garvey Papers* 4: 168–169). He went on to encourage the representatives to go beyond the issue of disarmament in their deliberations and to consider the implications of colonial occupation as an impediment to long-lasting world peace. At the end of the conference a treaty was signed between Great Britain, France, Japan, and the United States which signaled Japan's growing influence in international affairs (*NW*, 17 December 1921; *Garvey Papers* 4).

ISAAC. See ABRAHAM.

ISLES, WILLIAM, was a member of the New York UNIA local and director of the thirty-piece BLACK STAR LINE band, which performed at LIBERTY HALL and on fund-raising tours in the early 1920s. Isles's Black Star Line band combined with ARNOLD FORD's UNIA band to play at the opening of the 1920 UNIA convention; he also led the band at conventions in 1921 and 1922. After Garvey's arrest on mail fraud charges in January 1922, Isles joined other New York division members in signing an open letter of confidence in the UNIA leader. He was among a number of New York Garveyites who allied with George Weston and WILLIAM SHERRILL when a major split occurred in the movement in 1926 (*Garvey Papers* 2, 4, 6).

ISHMAEL, the son of ABRAHAM and Hagar, an Egyptian slave, was banished into the desert with his mother. He became a nomad and the ancestor to a number of Arabian tribes (Gen. 16:15, 21:8–21, 25:12–18).

ITALO-ETHIOPIAN WAR. Italian troops invaded Ethiopia in October 1935, and MUSSOLINI's forces began supplementing conventional bombing raids with chemical warfare in December 1935. Haile Selassie went into exile on 2 May 1936, and Addis Ababa, the capital of Ethiopia, was occupied by Italian troops on 5 May 1936. The Ethiopian cause was supported by many Afro-American organizations, including the New York division of the UNIA, headed by Capt. A. L. King, who was one of the organizers of the Harlem-based Provisional Committee for the Defense of Ethiopia. Although Garvey was originally sympathetic to the Ethiopian cause, his editorials in the BLACK MAN became increasingly critical of Haile Selassie, whom he characterized as naively reliant on the willingness of the League of Nations to impose sanctions against Italy for its aggressions in Ethiopia; as a weak ruler; and as one who identified with whites rather than with fellow blacks. This animosity may have stemmed in part from Garvey's feeling of being slighted by the Ethiopian emperor. When Haile Selassie was forced into exile and arrived in London in June 1936, he declined to meet with a greeting party composed of representatives, including Garvey, from several black organizations active in Britain. Haile Selassie began petitioning the League of Nations to censure Italy following the Wal Wal incident of December 1934. League action on his appeals was forestalled by British and French policies of appeasement toward Mussolini; meanwhile both Britain and France boycotted the sale of arms to Ethiopia. Haile Selassie appealed directly to the league in a 30 June 1936 speech, but to little avail; economic sanctions against Italy were lifted on 6 July 1936. Haile Selassie was in exile in Britain until 1941, when he returned to Ethiopia with British expeditionary troops and joined forces with the still-active Ethiopian resistance movement. On 5 May 1941 his forces reoccupied Addis Ababa, and he returned to power (*BM,* June 1935, July–August 1936, January 1937, March–April 1937; *BA,* 10 April 1937; William R. Scott, "Black Nationalism and the Italo-Ethiopian Conflict, 1934–1936," *Journal of Negro History* [April 1978]: 123–124; Frank Hardie, *The Abyssinian Crisis* [London: B. T. Batsford, 1974]; Thomas M. Coffey, *Lion by the Tail: The Story of the Italian-Ethiopian War* [New York: Viking Press, 1974]; George Baer, *The Coming of the Italian-Ethiopian War* [Cambridge, Mass.: Harvard University Press, 1967]).

IVEY, JOHN EDWARD, of Costa Rica, was one of several delegates representing Central America at the 1920 UNIA convention. He signed the declaration of rights (*Garvey Papers* 2).

JACK, RATFORD E. M., was one of the signers of the 1920 UNIA Declaration of Rights. He was ordained as a deacon in the African Orthodox church by GEORGE ALEXANDER McGUIRE in 1921. Jack had previously organized several chapters of the UNIA in St. Vincent in the West Indies; he moved to Chaparro, Cuba, in 1921 (*NW,* 7 May 1921; *Garvey Papers* 2).

JACOB was the son of Isaac and Rebecca, and the twin brother of ESAU. While traveling to Bethel, Jacob had a visionary dream of a ladder to heaven, with God appearing at its top. The elements of this vision became important symbols of deliverance and faith and can be found in the lyrics of Negro spirituals (Gen. 25:19–34, 27:6–29, 28:10–22).

JACQUES, AMY, editor, feminist, race activist, (1896–1973), was Garvey's second wife and his principal lieutenant during his incarceration in Atlanta penitentiary in 1925–1927. Jacques was born in Jamaica; she moved to the United States in 1917 and became involved in the UNIA

after hearing Garvey speak in 1918. She became Garvey's personal
secretary and traveling companion, as well as the office manager at
UNIA headquarters and secretary of the NEGRO FACTORIES CORP.
She and Garvey married in July 1922, and she emerged as a major
propagandist for him during the period of his trial, conviction, and
imprisonment on mail fraud charges (1923–1927). In an effort to
improve Garvey's reputation and raise funds to pay for his defense,
Jacques published two volumes of his speeches and writings as
Philosophy and Opinions. She acted as his personal representative while
he was in prison, traveling to speak at local UNIA divisions throughout
the country, meeting with public officials and UNIA officers to carry
out his directions, and organizing UNIA conferences and affairs. She
became the associate editor of the *NEGRO WORLD* (1924–1927), and
introduced a new page, called "Our Women and What They Think,"
which carried international news about the status of women, poetry,
profiles of leading black women and black female historical figures,
and columns by and about members of the women's auxiliaries. She
continued as a contributing editor of the UNIA paper in 1927–1928.
She and Garvey toured England, France, and Germany in the spring
and summer of 1928, and she wrote articles for the *Negro World* about
her impressions. She gave birth to Marcus Mosiah Garvey, Jr., and
Julius Winston Garvey in 1930 and 1933. She stayed behind in Jamaica
when Garvey moved to England in 1934; she took the children to
join him there in 1937, but because of the failing health of Marcus
Garvey, Jr., she returned to Jamaica while Garvey was away at the 1938
convention in Canada. After Garvey's death in 1940, Jacques became a
contributing editor to a black nationalist journal, the *African,* published
in Harlem in the 1940s, and established the African Study Circle of the
World in Jamaica in the late 1940s. She published *Garvey and Garveyism*
in 1963 (*DG*, 26 July 1973; *Garvey Papers* 1–6).

JENKINS, FLORIDA LEE, attended the 1920 UNIA convention and signed
the UNIA Declaration of Rights. Jenkins remained active in the
organization; she contributed to the African Redemption Fund in
September 1921 (*Garvey Papers* 2, 4).

JENKINS, JANIE (1879–1926), an early Garvey loyalist, was born in Baltimore.
She met Garvey in 1917 and became active in the UNIA. In 1918 she was
second vice president of the organization and one of the incorporators
of the AFRICAN COMMUNITIES LEAGUE. In 1919 she was assistant
treasurer of the UNIA, president of the Ladies' Division, and one of
the incorporators and first directors of the BLACK STAR LINE. She was
reelected to the Black Star Line board in 1920 and 1921. In June she was
elected as a delegate to represent the New York division at the 1920
UNIA convention; she signed the UNIA Declaration of Rights in that
capacity in August. Jenkins appeared as a witness for the defense at
Garvey's mail fraud trial in 1923, and Garvey praised her testimony in
his closing address to the jury. She was unmarried and employed as a
domestic worker when she died in February 1926 (*NW*, 3 July 1920, 20
February 1926; *MG* v. *U.S.*, pp. 1,336–1,340; *Garvey Papers* 1–3, 5).

JERICHO was a city in the Jordan valley of ancient Palestine the Israelites conquered the Canaanites circa 1250 B.C. (Josh. 6).

JEROME, SAINT (342?–420), a classical scholar and secretary to Pope Damasus I, prepared a new Latin translation of the Bible.

JESSE, a native of Bethlehem, was the father of DAVID (Ruth 18:22; 1 Sam. 16:1–12, 17:18).

JOAN OF ARC (1412–1431), martyred French national heroine, was tried as a witch and a heretic and burned at the stake after claiming she had received divine inspiration to lead Charles VII's forces in a successful defense of Orleans against the English.

JOHANNESBURG, the largest city in southern Africa, is located in the Transvaal, South Africa. It was founded in 1886 after the discovery of gold and became a major manufacturing and mining center.

JOHNSON, ADRIAN, was a colonel in the New York African Legion (see AFRICAN GUARDS). Probably the son of West Indian immigrants, he grew up in Panama, and served in the British army in WORLD WAR I. He was a delegate to the 1920 UNIA convention, where he occupied a seat on the platform with Garvey. One of the signers of the declaration of rights, he worked closely with Garvey in the months following the convention and traveled to divisions outside New York to speak on behalf of the organization. In July 1921 Garvey reported that Johnson had brought over two thousand new members into the New Orleans division during an organizing tour of Louisiana. Johnson organized in the Northeast as well as in the South and Southwest and was a frequent speaker at LIBERTY HALL. He and E. L. Gaines led the African Legion on horseback in the opening parade of the 1921 UNIA convention. He was nominated to be West Indian leader of the Eastern Province during the convention proceedings, and was chosen as speaker in convention for the next convention. However, during the 1922 convention, Garvey had him impeached for not paying his UNIA dues. Although Johnson protested that the other officers shared his failure to pay dues, he was successfully impeached by a majority of the delegates present. Attendance at the convention fell off after his impeachment, apparently in response to Garvey's autocratic handling of the matter. Although he was stripped of his office, Johnson remained active at the convention as a delegate. When Garvey was criticized for his alleged alliance with the KU KLUX KLAN, Johnson brought a motion that a vote of confidence be taken, and Garvey successfully won the endorsement of the delegates. In 1951 Johnson was secretary general of the wing of the UNIA affiliated with LIONEL FRANCIS (*Garvey Papers* 2, 3).

JOHNSON, GABRIEL M. (b. 1871), mayor of Monrovia, Liberia, and president of the Monrovia division of the UNIA, was elected UNIA potentate at the 1920 convention. Johnson was a member of a prominent Americo-Liberian family that migrated to Liberia in the nineteenth century. His father, Hilary Johnson, was elected president of Liberia in 1884, and his brother, F. E. R. Johnson, was a member of the Liberian supreme court. Gabriel Johnson was a building contractor and worked in his family's commercial establishment; he was also involved in the recruitment of labor for contract work in Fernando Po. The UNIA paid his passage to attend the 1920 UNIA convention, where he delivered one of the major addresses, encouraging the UNIA's proposed colonization plans. He was the liaison person with Liberian officials during the UNIA delegation's visit to Liberia in 1921. He saw the UNIA as an alternative source of investment and development to the U.S. government, whose financial intervention in Liberian affairs he opposed. After he lost his bid for reelection as mayor of Monrovia in 1921, President King appointed him consul general to Fernando Po. Johnson addressed both the 1921 and 1922 UNIA conventions (*Garvey Papers* 2–4).

JOHNSON, MARY E., one of the signers of the 1920 UNIA Declaration of Rights, was president of the UNIA Ladies' Division in Hartford, Conn., in 1921. She was executive secretary of the Women's Industrial Exhibit at the August 1921 UNIA convention (*NW,* 23 April and 16 July 1921; *Garvey Papers* 2).

JONES, ALPHONSO A., one of the signers of the 1920 UNIA Declaration of Rights, was director of the UNIA's trucking and delivery service in 1921 (*NW,* 26 February 1921; *Garvey Papers* 2).

JONES, E. J., was a pastor who attended the 1920 UNIA convention and signed the UNIA Declaration of Rights (*Garvey Papers* 2).

JOSEPHINE. See JOSEPHINE BONAPARTE.

JOSHUA was an assistant and successor to MOSES and was the military leader of the Israelites in the conquest of the Canaanites (Josh. 1:1–2; 6:2, 21; 8:1, 24–26).

JUVENILE DIVISIONS, the youth corps of the Garvey movement, were affiliated with local UNIA divisions and divided into classes according to age. The infant class (ages one through seven) studied the Bible, the doctrine of the UNIA, and the history of Africa. After the age of seven, the children were segregated by sex. Girls were taught sewing, boys woodcraft, and both received further instruction in black history and in etiquette. After the age of thirteen, boys received military training to prepare them for membership in the African Legion (see AFRICAN GUARDS), while girls learned hygiene and domestic science in order to prepare them to be BLACK CROSS NURSES. The superintendent of each local juvenile division was the lady vice president of the division at large, and teachers were chosen from the adult auxiliaries. The juvenile divisions took part in UNIA parades, the boys marching in blue uniforms and the girls in green dresses (*Garvey Papers* 3).

KANAWHA was a steam yacht purchased by the BLACK STAR LINE (BSL) in April 1920. The 227-foot boat, which the UNIA renamed the S.S. *Antonio Maceo,* was bought for $60,000; another $25,000 was spent refitting it for passenger service. The vessel had formerly been owned by oil magnate HENRY H. ROGERS. The BSL intended it to be used to provide service between the larger ships in the line; however, the *Kanawha* was as ill-fated as other BSL purchases. Before the ship was taken out to sea, a boiler burst on a public relations excursion of New York Harbor, scalding a crew member to death. The outdated boilers continued to cause problems when the *Kanawha* attempted a trip to Cuba; over $40,000 was spent in repairs without the vessel ever reaching farther south than Virginia. The ship, captained by Adrian Richardson, finally sailed successfully from New York to Cuba in the spring of 1921, but it continued to require extensive repairs in order to operate. After being used intermittently during Garvey's 1921 tour of the Caribbean and Central America, the disabled ship was eventually abandoned in port at Antilla, Cuba, where it decayed. In just over a year, the *Kanawha* cost the Black Star Line over $130,000 in repairs, operating costs, and harbor fees (*Black Moses,* pp. 58–59, 85–92).

KILROE, EDWIN P. (1883–1953), was assistant district attorney of the state of New York in 1916–1923. An Irish-Catholic Democrat, he was affiliated with Tammany Hall. Kilroe and Garvey became adversaries in 1919, when Kilroe repeatedly attempted to constrain the UNIA leader in his business ventures. After Garvey published an article attacking Kilroe in the 2 August 1919 *Negro World,* Kilroe sued for criminal libel. The case reached trial in August of the following year, and Garvey publicly retracted his allegations (*NYT,* 10 July 1953; *Garvey Papers* 1).

KINCH, EMILY CHRISTMAS (d. 1932), was an Afro-American missionary to Africa, an educator, and a UNIA activist. Kinch was born in Orange, N.J., and was raised within the African Methodist Episcopal church, in which her father, Rev. Jordan C. H. Christmas, was a prominent pastor. She became the first president of the AME New Jersey Conference's Sunday School Institute before she became a missionary. She traveled to West Africa from 1908 to 1910 and did missionary work in Sierra Leone and Liberia, where she organized the Eliza Turner Primary School. She returned to the United States and wrote a pamphlet, *West Africa: An Open Door,* based on her missionary experience; she also became a recruiter of Afro-American missionaries to Africa. Kinch spoke to a UNIA meeting at LIBERTY HALL in June 1920, lauding the UNIA's repatriation program, telling her audience that the time was ripe for "going back to Africa and possessing the land . . . Africa never was in a more susceptible, receptive mood for the UNIA than today" (*NW,* 26 June 1920). Kinch was a delegate to the 1920 UNIA convention and one of the signers of the UNIA Declaration of Rights. UNIA Potentate GABRIEL JOHNSON visited her in Philadelphia when he came to the United States in July 1921, and she contributed to the African Redemption Fund in September of that year (Randall K. Burkett, *Black Redemption: Churchmen Speak for the Garvey Movement* [Philadelphia: Temple University Press, 1978], pp. 43–46; *Garvey Papers* 2, 4).

KIRBY, HARRY WALTERS, was the president of the Washington, D.C., division of the UNIA in 1921. He was a delegate to the 1920 UNIA convention and one of the signers of the declaration of rights. He presided over a series of UNIA mass meetings in Washington, D.C., in September 1920, in which Garvey gave the main addresses (*NW,* 4 June 1921; *Garvey Papers* 2, 3).

KRUPP GUN, the first mild-steel gun without welds, was designed at the Friedrich Krupp Steel Foundry of Essen, Prussia (now in West Germany), in 1851. The new design of the Krupp gun improved velocity and range while reducing the weight of guns. The Krupp company flourished after the introduction of the design; in the 1930s it was at the center of German rearmament.

Ku Klux Klan (KKK) is a white supremacist fraternal society that first emerged among Confederate veterans in the Reconstruction period and was later revived, garnering a nationwide following in the 1920s. Membership—which cut across class lines, and included many civic leaders and politicians as well as farmers and lower-class whites—reached a peak of between three and five million in the mid-1920s and declined rapidly to some thirty thousand by the beginning of the Depression. In a move that brought him severe criticism from other leading blacks and many UNIA members, Garvey met with Acting Imperial Wizard Edward Young Clarke in Atlanta on 25 June 1922. He reported that Clarke was sympathetic to the UNIA's Africa repatriation goals and agreed with his own antimiscegenationist stance. The minutes of the interview were never published, but a KKK memorandum on the meeting reportedly stated that the two men had agreed that the KKK would offer protection to UNIA members selling Black Star Line stock in exchange for the UNIA's continued opposition to the NAACP, whose crusade against Lynching constituted a threat to Klan operations. Garvey's meeting with the Klan came not long after the *New York World* published an extended exposé on the racist actions of the secret society (September 1921) which sparked an ineffectual U.S. House of Representatives investigation of Klan atrocities. Garvey defended his action by pointing out that the publicity given the Klan in the *New York World* exposé, which had been syndicated in numerous newspapers nationwide, had actually caused a boost in the racist organization's membership. Garvey also told a Liberty Hall audience that he considered the KKK "the invisible government of the United States of America" and that it "expresses to a great extent the feeling of every real white American," reminding them that the UNIA, as a separatist organization, "is in a way similar to the Ku Klux Klan. Whilst the Ku Klux Klan desires to make America absolutely a white man's country, the Universal Negro Improvement Association wants to make Africa absolutely a black man's country" (*NW*, 15 July 1922). The parallels between the UNIA and the KKK as race-conscious fraternal organizations caused one reporter in the 1920s to describe Garvey as "the African wizard," a play on the title given to the leader of the Klan (*Brooklyn Informer* [Jamaica, N.Y.], 8 January 1921; *NYW*, 7 September 1921; *NW*, 6 September 1924; *Southern Exposure* 8, no. 2 [summer 1980]; David M. Chalmers, *Hooded Americanism: The First Century of the Ku Klux Klan, 1865–1965* [Garden City, N.Y.: Doubleday and Co., 1965]; Kenneth T. Jackson, *The Ku Klux Klan in the City, 1915–1930* [New York: Oxford University Press, 1967]; *Hearings on the Ku Klux Klan, 1921* [New York: Arno Press, 1969]; *Garvey Papers* 4, 5).

Lafayette Hall consisted of meeting rooms located at the corner of 131st Street and Seventh Avenue in Harlem. Garvey led UNIA meetings at the hall on Sunday afternoons from July 1917 to January 1918, when the building began to be used as a headquarters and meeting place for the rival wing of the UNIA, headed by SAMUEL DUNCAN (*NYAN*, 10 November 1926; Jervis Anderson, *This Was Harlem: A Cultural Portrait, 1900–1950* [New York: Farrar Straus Giroux, 1982], pp. 110–113; *Garvey Papers* 1).

LaMOTTE, WILLIAM MUSGRAVE, of Brooklyn, was a delegate to the 1920 UNIA convention. He addressed the convention audience on housing conditions in Brooklyn, the need for more business enterprises owned and operated by blacks, and the discrimination faced by black patrons of white-owned establishments. He was one of the signers of the UNIA Declaration of Rights (*Garvey Papers* 2).

LANDOR, WALTER SAVAGE (1775–1864), English poet, playwright, and pamphleteer, was a friend of Charles Dickens, who created a caricature of him in the figure of Boythorn in *Bleak House* (1852). Garvey quotes one of Landor's poems in lesson 6 of the School of African Philosophy but changes lines three and four slightly. The original reads: "Alike they flourish and alike they fall, / And Earth, who nourisht them receives them all" (Geoffrey Grigson, comp., *Poems by Walter Savage Landor* [London: Centaur Press, 1964], p. 193).

LAVELLE, LOUIS A. (b. 1877), was a lawyer who became involved in the UNIA in its formative stages in Harlem. He was elected sergeant-at-arms of the rival UNIA headed by SAMUEL DUNCAN at a 20 January 1918 meeting at LAFAYETTE HALL. He was born in Lancaster, Ky., and established a law practice in New York in 1904. He was also president and general manager of the Thunderer Printing-Publishing Co. Garvey's allegations that Lavelle was interested in forming the UNIA into a political club are supported by Lavelle's own political ambitions. In 1914 he was an unsuccessful Progressive candidate for a seat in the New York assembly from the twenty-first district; and in 1922 and 1924 he was a Democratic nominee for U.S. Congress from the Third Congressional District in the Bronx. He maintained law offices in New York until 1944 (*NYT*, 27 August 1922, 24 August 1924; *WWCA*; *Garvey Papers* 1).

LEADETT, CARRIE MERO, was associate secretary of the Ladies' Division of the UNIA in 1917–1918. She was born in Woodstock, Vt. As a clerk-stenographer at the UNIA headquarters on 135th Street in 1918–1921, she worked alongside EDGAR M. GREY and RICHARD WARNER on BLACK STAR LINE and UNIA business and was one of the original incorporators of the UNIA, Inc. She testified as a witness for the defense at Garvey's 1923 mail fraud trial (*MG* v. *U.S.*, pp. 1,211–1,241; *Garvey Papers* 1, 2).

LEWIS, D. D., was president of the Montreal division of the UNIA in 1920. Lewis was a medical doctor who practiced at a sanitarium on Peel Street in Montreal. He was a delegate to the 1920 UNIA convention, which he addressed in the afternoon session of the opening day. He also spoke on the afternoon that the declaration of rights, which he signed, was first read to the convention at large. He was sworn in as surgeon general at the end of the convention (*NW*, 7 May 1921; *Garvey Papers* 2).

LEWIS, J. A., was a pastor who attended the 1920 UNIA convention and signed the UNIA Declaration of Rights (*Garvey Papers* 2).

LIBERTY HALL was the spiritual cradle and main meeting place of the UNIA in New York from 1919 onward. The hall, located at 120 West 138th Street between Lenox and Seventh avenues, was formerly owned by the Metropolitan Baptist Church. W. E. B. DU BOIS described the building, much of which was below ground level, as "a long, low, unfinished church basement, roofed over . . . a rambling basement of brick and rough stone" (W. E. B. Du Bois, "Back to Africa," *Century* 105 [February 1923]: 539, 548). Garvey gave a clue to the origin of the hall's new name when he referred to the Irish nationalist movement during dedication ceremonies on 2 August 1919. Liberty Hall was also the name of the headquarters of the Irish Transport and General Workers' Union in Dublin, which served as a center for militant nationalist politics in Ireland and the site from which was launched the Easter Rebellion in 1916. Local liberty halls were established by the various UNIA divisions; as AMY JACQUES Garvey noted in her memoirs, they were used for "Sunday morning worship, afternoon Sunday Schools, Public meetings at nights, concerts and dances . . . notice boards . . . for a room, a job . . . [and] soup kitchens" (*G&G*, p. 91; see also *Garvey Papers* 1–6).

LIPTON, SIR THOMAS (1850–1931), was frequently cited by Garvey as a model of personal success. Born into humble beginnings in Clones, northern Ireland, Lipton went to work while still a child. As a young man he opened a provisions shop in Glasgow. He used innovative advertising techniques and parlayed his initial small investment into a string of Lipton tea shops throughout the British Isles. In 1889 he purchased a number of large agricultural estates in Ceylon and began the international tea import business for which he is best known.

LOUIS, like Charles, is a name common to a succession of emperors and kings. Louis I (778–840), the son of CHARLEMAGNE, was emperor of the West in 814–840.

L'OUVERTURE, TOUSSAINT (1744–1803), was a Haitian hero and martyr of the slave insurrection and war of rebellion against colonialism in the 1790s and early 1800s. Born a slave and self-educated, he joined the anti-French liberation forces in 1791 and quickly revealed a tactical and organizational genius. When the British occupied the coastal sections of the island, Toussaint and military leaders Dessalines and Christophe mounted an offensive against them, forcing their withdrawal in 1798. Toussaint's soldiers also occupied SANTO DOMINGO, which had passed from Spanish to French colonial hands, and thus governed both parts of the island of Hispaniola. In 1802 NAPOLEON sent French forces to counter this condition of independence from colonial rule; although a peace treaty was negotiated, Toussaint was seized by the French and brought to France, where he was imprisoned and died (Wendell Phillips, "Toussaint L'Ouverture," in *Wendell Phillips on Civil Rights and Freedom,* ed. Louis Filler [New York: Hill and Wang, 1965], pp. 163–184; James Redpath, *Toussaint L'Ouverture: A Biography and Autobiography* [1863; reprint, New York: Books for Libraries Press, 1971]).

LOVELL, C.B., one of the signers of the 1920 UNIA Declaration of Rights, was a real estate agent in Brooklyn and president of the Home Progressive Association, a black real estate venture (*NW,* 28 August 1920; *Garvey Papers* 2).

LUCK, JESSE W., a pastor from Newark, N.J., was a delegate to the 1920 UNIA convention. He reported that he had participated in laying the claims of the UNIA before the Ministers' Conference in Newark and that the ministers of the city had expressed their willingness to cooperate with the movement. He also addressed the issue of racial segregation in New Jersey, describing discrimination against black working women in that state's factories and public places and he expressed his own bitterness as a veteran of WORLD WAR I who had fought with whites abroad only to be denigrated by them at home. He signed the UNIA Declaration of Rights (*Garvey Papers* 2).

LYNCHING was a common means of mob execution used against blacks in the Reconstruction and post-Reconstruction eras, mainly in the South. Over three thousand lynchings of American blacks were recorded between 1889 and 1929. Efforts to secure antilynching legislation became a focal point for many black organizations in the 1920s. The UNIA joined these groups in supporting the Dyer antilynching bill introduced in Congress in 1922. Although the bill was passed by the U.S. House of Representatives, it was allowed to die in the Senate (*NW,* 12 July 1924; Robert Zandgrando, *The NAACP Crusade Against Lynching, 1909–1950* [Philadelphia: Temple University Press, 1980]; Ida B. Wells-Barnett, *On Lynchings* [1892–1894; reprint ed. New York: Arno Press, 1969]; *Thirty Years of Lynching in the United States, 1889–1918* [New York: NAACP, 1919]; *Garvey Papers* 4).

LYONS, JOSEPH (1870–1947), was a wealthy entrepreneur born into a middle-class south London family. Lyons founded Joseph Lyons & Co. in 1894. The success of the first tea shop, located in Piccadilly, made it the prototype for a chain of over two hundred such shops established throughout London. Lyons invested much of his profits in real estate and amassed a huge personal fortune.

McCONNEY, PRINCE ALFRED, sometimes referred to as Prince Alfred McConnery, was a delegate to the 1920 and 1921 UNIA conventions. He was one of the signers of the UNIA Declaration of Rights in 1920 (*Garvey Papers* 2, 3).

McGUIRE, GEORGE ALEXANDER (1866–1934), chaplain general of the UNIA in 1920, was born in Antigua, BWI, and educated at Mico College and the Nisky Theological Seminary, St. Thomas, Virgin Islands. He immigrated to the United States in 1894 and became a priest in the Protestant Episcopal church. In 1904 he took up his own parish at the Church of St. Thomas in Philadelphia, and in 1905 he became the first black to be appointed archdeacon, moving to take up duties in the diocese of Arkansas. Disillusioned with the racism he encountered within the white Episcopal church hierarchy, McGuire made a decision to change careers. He attended Jefferson Medical College in Boston, and in 1913 he returned to Antigua to practice medicine and work for the Church of England. In 1919 he moved back to the United States following a rift with the Anglican bishop of Antigua and shortly after became involved in the Garvey movement. His experience as an Episcopal priest had led him to a belief in the necessity of a separate black church, and he began to promote the idea among UNIA members. He presided over Episcopal services at the 1920 UNIA convention, and in 1921 he drafted the UNIA's *Universal Negro Ritual* and *Universal Negro Catechism*. His use of UNIA membership lists brought him into conflict with Garvey. He resigned from the UNIA and threw his support to the competing African Blood Brotherhood, led by CYRIL BRIGGS. He organized the independent African Orthodox church in September 1921. He returned to the UNIA fold at the August 1924 convention, at which he promulgated the worship of the Black Madonna and Jesus as the Black Man of Sorrows (*NW*, 6 November 1920, 6 August 1921; *NYT*, 12 November 1934; Randall K. Burkett, *Black Redemption: Churchmen Speak for the Garvey Movement* [Philadelphia: Temple University Press, 1978], pp. 157–180; *Garvey Papers* 2, 4).

MCINTYRE, SAMUEL, a pastor, was a delegate to the 1920 and 1921 UNIA conventions, and his signature appears on the 1920 UNIA Declaration of Rights (*Garvey Papers* 2, 3).

MACK, JULIAN (1866–1943), was the federal judge in Garvey's 1923 mail fraud trial. After holding a number of judicial appointments in Illinois, he became a member of the U.S. Circuit Court of Appeals (Second Circuit) for New York in 1913 and served in that capacity until his retirement in 1941. Mack worked with Jane Addams in Chicago in the establishment of the Maxwell Street Settlement (later affiliated with Addams's Hull House), which served Jewish immigrants living on Chicago's West Side. He succeeded Addams as president of the National Conference of Social Workers in 1911. He supported the coalition movement of immigrants, radicals, and progressives who opposed the execution of Nicola Sacco and Bartolomeo Vanzetti in 1927. He was also a prominent leader in the American Zionist movement, serving as president of the National Conference of Jewish Charities (1904–1906), the Young Men's and Young Women's Hebrew associations (1917), the Zionist Organization of America (1918–1921), the American Jewish Congress (1919), and numerous other Jewish associations, political organizations, and charities. He chaired the committee of Jewish delegations at the Paris Peace Conference in 1919 ("Judge Julian W. Mack," *Maccabaean* [August 1918]: 242–243; *The National Cyclopaedia of American Biography*, 32: 73–74; *Dictionary of American Biography*; Harry Barnard, *The Forging of an American Jew: The Life and Times of Judge Julian W. Mack* [New York: Herzl Press, 1974]; *Garvey Papers* 5).

MADISON SQUARE GARDEN is the name given to four sports and entertainment auditoriums in New York City. The UNIA held convention

sessions in the second garden, an elaborate Renaissance-style terra-
cotta structure designed by Stanford White, built on the site of the
original garden on Madison Square in 1890. The main amphitheater
of the magnificent complex seated over nine thousand people. In 1925
a new building, in use until 1968, was erected at Eighth Avenue and
50th Street. As Garvey mentions, the *New York World* carried a feature
article in 1924 on memorable events in the old garden on Madison
Square, including the 1920 UNIA convention, along with William
Jennings Bryan's speech during the 1896 presidential campaign, the
evangelist meetings of Dwight Moody and Ira Sankey, Buffalo Bill's
Wild West Show, and the murder of Stanford White by Harry K.
Thaw (*NYW*, 22 June 1924; Joseph Durso, *Madison Square Garden:
One Hundred Years of History* [New York: Simon & Schuster, 1979]).

MALONE, ANNIE (ca. 1875–post 1930), was the president of a large cosmetic
manufacturing firm that she began as a one-room enterprise in 1900
and the president of Poro College in St. Louis, an institute that trained
black women for independent pink-collar positions as saleswomen and
technicians. The "Poro system" of beauty products was dispensed
door-to-door by saleswomen trained at the college, which had a
hospital, a community center, a regular schedule of literary and musical
programs, and a monthly newspaper, the *Poro Purpose*, as well as
technical facilities. By the 1930s Malone's system had spread nationwide
and had branches and agents in many major cities, including a Poro
school on Seventh Avenue in New York and a new headquarters in
Chicago. Malone's Poro system, like C. J. WALKER's enterprise, was
an important means to independent paraprofessional jobs for black
women. The Poro company, unlike many other cosmetic retailers
advertising in black periodicals, did not overly stress white ideals of
beauty, although it did present a long-haired classical image in one
of its longest-running advertisements. More typical ads stressed the
educational aspects of a Poro career by featuring a drawing of the
school, or placed emphasis on the acquisition of modern, marketable
skills. "In your two hands is the power to succeed" read one ad;
"let Poro of New York train them" (*NYAN*, 11 September 1937).
This emphasis on the economic self-sufficiency of black women was
heightened during the war years, when ads read, "Uncle Sam needs
our men—Let the Poro System take care of you" (*BA*, 31 January 1918).
A millionaire from the proceeds of her system, Malone used her funds
to endow many black colleges, medical schools, churches, orphanages
and community organizations. In 1923 she was reported to have paid
the highest income tax of any black American (*Philadelphia Tribune*, 15
November 1924; *PC*, 6 December 1924; *BA*, 4 January 1930; *WWCA*).

MARATHON, a settlement and plain near Athens in ancient Greece, was the
site of the battle in which the Athenians and Plataeans defeated the
Persians in 490 B.C.

MARKE, GEORGE O. (1867–1929), supreme deputy potentate of the UNIA,
1920–1926, was born in Freetown, Sierra Leone. Marke's father,
Charles Marke, was a Methodist minister and a follower of the
philosophy of Edward Wilmot Blyden. George Marke attended

Wesleyan Boys' High School in Freetown and studied medicine at Aberdeen University, Scotland, and the University of Edinburgh. He returned to Freetown and was employed as a government clerk there when he attended the 1920 UNIA convention as a delegate from the Freetown division. In February 1921 Marke accompanied the UNIA delegation to Liberia. While in Monrovia, he established a newspaper called the *Liberian Patriot*. He returned to New York in July 1922 and was appointed minister plenipotentiary to the UNIA delegation to the League of Nations, which petitioned the league to turn over former German colonies in Africa to black settlement under the direction of the UNIA. Marke eventually fell out of favor with Garvey and was removed from office at a pro-Garvey emergency convention called in Detroit in March 1926, while the UNIA president general was in prison. In August 1926 Marke joined WILLIAM SHERRILL, George Weston and other New York division officers at a rival convention at LIBERTY HALL which elected a separate slate of "official" UNIA leaders. The following year he sued the UNIA for back payment of salary and was awarded a judgment against the then-insolvent parent body in New York. After Garvey's deportation, Marke levied payment through the Jamaican courts against UNIA property in Kingston, embroiling Garvey in yet another lawsuit, in this case resulting in the UNIA leader's serving a short sentence for contempt of court. Marke died in Brooklyn in October 1929 (*NYAN*, 4 August 1926; *BA*, 7 August 1926; *NYT*, 30 August 1926; Rina L. Okonkwo, "The Garvey Movement in British West Africa," *Journal of African History* 21 [1980]: 105–117; *Garvey Papers* 2, 6).

MARNE, a region surrounding the Marne River in northern France, was the site of major battles during WORLD WAR I. The first battle of the Marne took place in September 1914, when Allied troops halted a German advance against Paris and forced a retreat. The black American 93d Infantry Division, fighting as part of the French 161st division, took part in the second battle of the Marne, which repelled the final German offensive of the war, in July 1918.

MARX, KARL (1818–1883), German socialist and political theorist, was coauthor, with Frederick Engels, of the *Communist Manifesto* (1847) and author of *Capital* (3 vols. 1867, 1885, 1895). Garvey's claim in the lessons from the School of African Philosophy that Marx "thought and wrote less about [Negroes]" is open to debate. Marx specifically endorsed the abolition of slavery during the American Civil War and linked the fate of white members of the working class with that of blacks. He wrote in *Capital*: "Labor cannot emancipate itself in the white skin where in the black it is branded" (*Capital* [Chicago: Charles H. Kerr and Co., 1915], 1: 329). His position on European imperialism in Africa was more ambivalent. While he criticized the atrocities committed by colonial administrations, he also saw colonialism as a transitory political stage that would eventually result in more positive sociopolitical transformations. Marx also had personal reason to think about the issue of the status of blacks. His daughter Eleanor married Paul Lafargue, a Cuban-born mulatto (Earl Ofari, "Marxism,

Nationalism, and Black Liberation," *Monthly Review* 22, no. 10 [March 1971]: 18–25; Saul K. Padover, *Karl Marx: An Intimate Biography* [New York: McGraw-Hill, 1978]; Jerrold Seigel, *Marx's Fate: The Shape of a Life* [Princeton, N.J.: Princeton University Press, 1978]; Yvonne Kapp, *Eleanor Marx* [New York: Pantheon, 1972]).

MARY of Nazareth was the mother of Jesus. The UNIA convention of August 1924 ended with ceremonies for the canonization of the Virgin Mary as a black woman. In presenting the idea to the convention, Garvey attacked the acceptance of white ideals in conceiving of the deity. Rt. Rev. Bishop J. D. Barber told the audience that "the Virgin Mary was of Ethiopian extraction, descendant of Tamar and of Rahab." In 1925 the UNIA produced a motion picture called *Black Man of Sorrows*. It starred members of the New York local division, who depicted "The Mother of Our Lord as a Black woman and Jesus as the 'Black Man of Sorrows.'" The film was made available to other divisions by mail order. In 1926 a reader of the *NEGRO WORLD* wrote to tell of a church in Algiers which represented "the Holy Mother as a black African Woman," and one of the editors commented that "When Negroes can think of the Saviour and His holy mother as being 'in their own image and likeness,' our cause is half won" (*NW,* 6 September 1924, 5 September 1925, 16 March 1926; Matt. 1:18–25, Luke 2:1–20; W. L. Hunter, *Jesus Christ Had Negro Blood in His Veins* [Brooklyn: author, 1910]; *Garvey Papers* 5).

MATTHEWS, WILLIAM C. (1877–1928), Boston lawyer and colleague of BOOKER T. WASHINGTON, was a UNIA attorney in the early twenties. Matthews was born in Alabama and educated at TUSKEGEE INSTITUTE and Philips Andover Academy, Andover, Mass. A prominent athlete at Andover, Matthews excelled in football and baseball at Harvard University. After graduating in 1905 he briefly pursued a professional baseball career, then attended law school at Boston University. He opened a law practice in Boston with William H. Lewis in 1907. Lewis was a supporter of Booker T. Washington, and Matthews soon became a member of the Tuskegee political machine. His political connections won him a patronage appointment as a special assistant to the U.S. district attorney in Boston. He served in France during WORLD WAR I and became a supporter of Garvey in the years following the war. He continued to be involved in Republican party politics and received an appointment as special assistant to the attorney general of the United States as a political reward for his support of CALVIN COOLIDGE in the 1924 presidential campaign (*WWCR*; *Garvey Papers* 2).

MATTUCK, MAXWELL S. (1893–1957), was the assistant U.S. attorney who headed the criminal division of the U.S. district attorney's office in the postwar years. A graduate of Harvard University Law School, Mattuck successfully prosecuted Marcus Garvey for mail fraud in 1923. He later became head of the commercial fraud division of the U.S. district attorney's office (*NYT,* 8 November 1957; *Garvey Papers* 4, 5).

MENELIK II (1844–1913), emperor of Ethiopia, was king of Shoa (central Ethiopia) until he seized power, with Italian support, in 1889 and declared Addis Ababa the capital of Ethiopia. Italian troops invaded Ethiopia after Menelik protested Italy's claim on Ethiopia as a protectorate, and this Italian encroachment helped Menelik unify his own people. In 1896 the Ethiopians defeated the Italians in a decisive military victory at the battle of Adowa, the old capital of Tigre. Italy was forced to renounce its claims on Ethiopian territory and to make indemnity payments to the African nation (R. H. Kofi Darkwah, *Shewa, Menilek, and the Ethiopian Empire, 1813–1889* [London and Nairobi: Heinemann, 1975]; George Baer, *The Coming of the Italian-Ethiopian War* [Cambridge, Mass.: Harvard University Press, 1967], pp. 1–24; Harold G. Marcus, *The Life and Times of Menelik II: Ethiopia, 1844–1913* [Oxford: Clarendon Press, 1975]).

MESSENGER, a black socialist periodical founded and edited by A. Philip Randolph and CHANDLER OWEN, was published from 1917 to 1928. It became a major forum for anti-Garvey criticism in 1922–1923, featuring articles by participants in the "Garvey Must Go" campaign. Theophilus Lewis, Joel A. Rogers, and Langston Hughes were among the black writers who contributed to the *Messenger*. W. A. Domingo, George Frazier Miller, and others served on the journal's editorial staff. The periodical reached its peak of circulation in the immediate postwar years, dwindling from some twenty-six thousand copies in 1919 to less than five thousand just prior to its demise. George Schuyler operated the magazine from 1925 to 1928, after Owen left New York and Randolph became increasingly involved in the organization of the Brotherhood of Sleeping Car Porters (Theodore Kornweibel, Jr., *No Crystal Stair: Black Life and the Messenger, 1917–1928* [Westport, Conn.: Greenwood Press, 1975; *Garvey Papers* 4).

MILLER, KELLY (1863–1939), author, educator, and sociologist, was born in Winnsboro, S.C. His mother was a slave, and his father, a free black, was a soldier in the Confederate army. He graduated from HOWARD UNIVERSITY (1886) and did graduate work in mathematics at Johns Hopkins University before becoming a member of the faculty at Howard (1890), where he taught until his retirement in 1934. He was dean of the College of Arts and Sciences at Howard from 1907 until 1919 and had a profound effect upon the college curriculum, which steered a middle course between the industrial-technical mode of education advocated by BOOKER T. WASHINGTON, and the intellectual-collegiate educational methods favored by DU BOIS. He was demoted to the post of dean of the junior college in 1919 by Howard's last white president, J. Stanley Durkee. Durkee abolished the junior division entirely in 1925, further limiting Miller's power within the university. In the 1920s Miller wrote a syndicated column that appeared weekly in over one hundred black newspapers nationwide, including the *Baltimore Afro-American* and the *New York Age*. He began publishing *Kelly Miller's Monographic Magazine* in 1913, reprinting articles on race and politics, and he compiled the essays into books in 1914 and 1924. In 1923–1924 Miller was the chair of the committee of arrangements for the Negro Sanhedrin, or All-Race Assembly, a conference held in Chicago and attended by representatives from a coalition of black organizations, including Miller's National Race Congress, CYRIL BRIGGS's African Blood Brotherhood, the FRIENDS OF NEGRO FREEDOM, William Monroe Trotter's National Equal Rights League, the NAACP, and others. The UNIA was invited to participate but declined to send delegates, and Garvey lambasted both the conference and its organizers in the pages of the NEGRO WORLD. Miller took an increasingly conservative political stance in the mid-thirties. He attacked Communist and union organizations, deplored the decline of religious instruction in schools, and opposed the movement of blacks from an agricultural economic base to an industrial and urban one (NW, 28 July 1923; NYT, 30 December 1939; WWCA; DANB; Garvey Papers 5).

MOHAMMED (Muhammad, Mahomet) (570–632) was the prophet of Islam, the principal religion of much of Asia, the Middle East, and northern Africa and one of the three major monotheistic religions of the world. Mohammed was born in Mecca (Saudi Arabia); his revelations form the basis of the Koran.

MOLYNEUX, GEORGE EDWARD STANHOPE (1866–1923), the fifth earl of Carnarvon, was an Egyptologist who joined Howard Carter in the excavation of tombs of Egyptian royalty, including that of TUTANKUMEN.

MONTGOMERY, JOHN W., was a delegate to the 1920 UNIA convention from Grand Bassa, a seaport southeast of Monrovia, Liberia, now known as Buchanan. Montgomery was one of the signers of the UNIA Declaration of Rights (Garvey Papers 2).

MOORE, JAMES H., of Kansas City, Kans., was a member of the UNIA in the early 1920s. He contributed one dollar to Garvey's defense fund in November 1922 (NW, 11 November 1922).

MORRIS, CHARLES S., was a pastor at the Abyssinian Baptist Church in New York City when it moved from Waverly Place to 40th Street. Morris preached at evangelistic tent meetings held in the summers of 1920 and 1921 on a lot next door to LIBERTY HALL (Garvey Papers 5).

MORSE DRY DOCK was a Staten Island, N.Y., shipbuilding and repair company. It attached the funds of the BLACK STAR LINE for debts incurred in 1921, unpaid bills for the storage and repair of the S.S. YARMOUTH, which was held at the dry dock in 1921–1922, unseaworthy and in need of extensive renovation. In 1922 the company refused to work upon the yacht KANAWHA without prepayment, whereupon the directors of the Black Star Line tried to arrange the suspension of mortgage payments on the ship in order to have the cash to make necessary repairs. After a repair contract of $45,000 was established, the company worked on the Kanawha, which broke down again immediately after sailing out of New York (Garvey Papers 4, 5).

MOSES was the Hebrew prophet who led his people out of bondage in Egypt. At the 1924 UNIA convention, Rt. Rev. Bishop J. D. Barber reportedly stated that Moses "was a black man, and recounted the incident where Moses was told to thrust his hand to his bosom" (NW, 16 August 1924). Barber's reference is to Exodus 4: 6–7: "Furthermore the Lord said to him, 'Now put your hand in your bosom.' And he put his hand in his bosom, and when he took it out, behold, his hand was leprous, like snow. And He said, 'Put your hand in your bosom again.' So he put his hand in his bosom again, and drew it out of his bosom, and behold, it was restored like his other flesh."

MOTON, ROBERT R. (1867–1940), succeeded BOOKER T. WASHINGTON in 1915 as principal of TUSKEGEE INSTITUTE in Alabama. Moton was born in Virginia and attended Hampton Normal and Agricultural Institute in Hampton, Va. He was employed as a commandant of cadets at Hampton for twenty-four years before receiving the appointment as head of Tuskegee, where he carried on policies in accordance with his predecessor's beliefs. He became president of the National Negro Business League in 1919 and helped organize the National Negro Finance Corp. in 1924. He served as a director of the American Bible Society in 1921 and as a trustee for Fisk University, Nashville. He was chair of a number of commissions dealing with education, finance, and international interracial relations, including U.S. commissions on education in Haiti and Liberia. He was also a leader in publicizing statistics on LYNCHING in the United States. He received the NAACP's Spingarn Medal in 1932 and retired as head of Tuskegee in 1935. Garvey corresponded with Moton in 1916 concerning Moton's impending visit to Jamaica, Garvey's plans to establish an industrial school on the model of Tuskegee in Jamaica, and his own impending trip to the United States (*NYT*, 1 June 1940; *WWCA; Garvey Papers* 1).

MOTOR CORPS (Universal African Motor Corps) was a female auxiliary of the UNIA with chapters affiliated with local divisions and associated with the paramilitary African Legions (see AFRICAN GUARDS) the membership of which was exclusively male. While the head of the motor corps, who was given the title brigadier general, was a woman, the officers and commanders of the units were male. Members were trained in military discipline and automobile driving and repair (*Garvey Papers* 3).

MUSSOLINI, BENITO (1883–1945) Italian dictator, was premier of Italy (1922–1943), and leader of the National Fascist party.

MUSTARD GAS, a poisonous chemical compound first employed as a weapon in WORLD WAR I, was used extensively by the Italians during the ITALO-ETHIOPIAN War. Dispersed as an aerosol by a bursting shell, the gas causes severe blistering and eye irritation; dropped in liquid form, it can cause disfiguring burns, pulmonary edema or suffocation, blindness, and death, while contaminating water supplies and destroying plant life.

NAACP. See NATIONAL ASSOCIATION FOR THE ADVANCEMENT OF COLORED PEOPLE.

NAIL, JOHN E. (1883–1947), was a prominent black real estate entrepreneur in Harlem and a member of the board of directors of the NAACP and the National Urban League. Nail was born in New London, Conn., and was raised in New York City, where his father operated a restaurant and hotel. In 1907 he founded the realty company of Nail and Parker with a partner, Henry G. Parker, and became a leader in the development of Harlem as a center for black housing and businesses and facilitating the movement of middle-class blacks into the area. Nail became the first black member of the Real Estate Board of New York, and by the 1920s his firm had an annual income of $1 million. The Depression, however, brought the firm into bankruptcy in 1933, and Nail opened a new company that year. He worked without success during the 1930s to secure New Deal federal funding for the renovation of deteriorating housing in Harlem. Nail socialized with the literary and business elites of Harlem, including the wealthy MME C. J. WALKER and NAACP Secretary James Weldon Johnson, who married Nail's sister, Grace E. Nail, in 1910. He was elected to the board of directors of the NAACP in January 1926 (*NYT*, 5 January 1926, 6 March 1947; Langston Hughes, *Fight for Freedom: The Story of the NAACP* [New York: W. W. Norton, 1962], p. 132; *WWCA; DANB; WWCR*).

NAPOLEON BONAPARTE (1769–1821), French emperor and military genius, was one of Garvey's favorite historical figures and a man with whom he identified.

NATIONAL ASSOCIATION FOR THE ADVANCEMENT OF COLORED PEOPLE (NAACP), was founded in 1909–1910 as an outgrowth of the 1905 Niagara movement and the 1909 National Negro Committee. Morefield Storey was the first president of the multiracial progressive organization, and W. E. B. DU BOIS was editor of its monthly publication, the *Crisis*. Other founders and backers of the NAACP included Mary White Ovington, Frances Blascoer, Jane Addams, Ida B. Wells-Barnett, William English Walling, and Oswald Garrison Villard. James Weldon Johnson became field secretary in 1916 and, with Walter White, became one of the organization's investigators of LYNCHING in the South. By 1919 the NAACP had over three hundred branches in the United States and some ninety thousand members. The NAACP vigorously worked on a range of civil rights issues, including fair employment, mob violence, residential and educational desegregation, equal treatment under the laws, and voting rights; its legal committee was eventually involved in providing the defense in many highly publicized and precedent-setting trials, including the Scottsboro "Boys" cases in Alabama and the Sweet trial in Detroit (Mary White Ovington, *The Walls Came Tumbling Down* [New York: Schocken Books, 1947]; Charles Flint Kellogg, *NAACP: A History of the National Association for the Advancement of Colored People* [Baltimore and London: Johns Hopkins University Press, 1967]; Langston Hughes, *Fight for Freedom: The Story of the NAACP* [New York: Berkley Medallion Books, 1962]; B. Joyce Ross, *J. W. Spingarn and the Rise of the NAACP* [New York: Atheneum, 1972]).

NATIVE AMERICANS. As Garvey implies in both "Dialogues" and *The Tragedy of White Injustice,* colonial and Anglo-American policies toward Native Americans resulted in gradual genocide through disease, warfare, forced relocation, and slavery. Official efforts were also made to modify or destroy Native American culture through the forcible prevention of the practice of ceremonial rituals; the occupation of traditional lands; the modification of dress, food ways, and hunting and gathering patterns; the introduction of Christianity and federally operated schools; and the individualized distribution of land, which helped weaken communal social systems and the authority of tribal governments (Gary B. Nash, *Red, White, and Black: The Peoples of Early America*, 2d ed. [Englewood Cliffs, N.J.: Prentice-Hall, 1982]; Jack D. Forbes, ed., *The Indian in America's Past* [Englewood Cliffs, N.J.: Prentice-Hall, 1964]; Ronald T. Takaki, *Iron Cages: Race and Culture in Nineteenth-Century America* [Seattle: University of Washington Press, 1979]).

NEGRO FACTORIES CORP., business wing of the UNIA, was incorporated in the state of Delaware on 30 January 1920 by Garvey, William Ferris, and JOHN G. BAYNE. AMY JACQUES GARVEY was secretary of the corporation in 1920, and Cyril Henry was its treasurer. The stock corporation was created with the goal of constructing factories that would employ blacks and produce goods to be sold to black consumers. In May 1920 Garvey reported that the company had taken over the management of a Harlem steam laundry and was opening a millinery and a hat factory. By June 1920 the Negro Factories Corp. had opened the Universal Steam Laundry, with a Universal Tailoring and Dressmaking department, at 62 West 142d Street. The laundry continued to operate until 1921, when the corporation became insolvent. The Negro Factories Corp. sponsored a fashion show at the 1922 UNIA convention that featured clothing made by UNIA dressmakers. The UNIA also operated three grocery stores, one on 135th Street and two on Lenox Avenue, and two restaurants, one on 135th Street and the other at LIBERTY HALL (*Garvey Papers* 2, 4).

NEGRO TIMES was a short-lived daily newspaper published by the UNIA and ACL from August to October 1922. Marcus Garvey was the daily's editor in chief; T. Thomas Fortune, who joined the editorial staff of the *NEGRO WORLD* in 1923, was its managing editor; and John E. Bruce, a contributing editor of the *Negro World* from 1921 until his death in 1924, was associate editor. The daily sold for five cents and was designed, as Garvey put it, to "compete with the big white dailies, furnishing all the news which the latter furnish" (*NW*, 8 July and 2 September 1922; *Messenger* 4, no. 12 [December 1922]: 546–547; *Garvey Papers* 4).

NEGRO WORLD, a weekly newspaper with worldwide circulation created by Marcus Garvey, was the official organ of the UNIA and ACL. Garvey first planned to produce the newspaper in Kingston, Jamaica, in 1914, but did not actually begin to publish issues until after his move to the United States. The paper was produced in New York beginning in August 1918. It was initially financed by the New York local division of the UNIA, which owned the ACL stock corporation under which the periodical operated. As membership in the UNIA grew and the circulation of the *Negro World* increased to between sixty and sixty-five thousand, the New York local sold its interest in the paper to the parent body of the UNIA, also headquartered in New York. The weekly paper was issued on Saturdays, and was printed by the Henri Rogowski Co., which also printed the Socialist *New*

York Call. It featured a front-page editorial letter by Garvey; news items covering current events concerning politics and the status of blacks in the United States and abroad; reports on UNIA enterprises, such as the BLACK STAR LINE; descriptions of the activities of local divisions and of UNIA leaders and organizers; and advertisements. A Spanish language section was begun in 1923, a French language section in 1924. AMY JACQUES Garvey added a page called "Our Women and What They Think" during her tenure as associate editor, from 1924 to 1927. Marcus Garvey was managing editor from the paper's inception on his birthday, 17 August 1918, until his split from the New York division leadership in the early 1930s. He disavowed responsibility for the editorials that appeared under his name in 1932, and from 31 July 1932 to 15 April 1933, no issues of the *Negro World* were published. The paper was briefly revived under the management of M. L. T. DE MENA from April through October 1933 (no issues of the paper published after 17 October 1933 have been found). Eminent black writers and editors who contributed to the *Negro World* during its heyday included Zora Neale Hurston, W. A. Domingo, Hubert Harrison, T. Thomas Fortune, John E. Bruce, William H. Ferris, Norton G. G. Thomas, and Eric Walrond. The UNIA organ had an international distribution—reaching the Caribbean, Central America, Canada, Europe, and Africa—with a circulation of two hundred thousand at its peak. Preaching the philosophy of black consciousness, self-help, and economic independence, it was banned as seditious in many areas still ruled by colonial powers in Africa and the Caribbean (*NW,* 1918–1933; *Garvey Papers* 1–6).

NELSON, HORATIO (1758–1805), was a British naval hero. In 1798 forces under his command destroyed the French fleet at Aboukir, stranding NAPOLEON's army in Egypt. In 1805 his forces defeated the combined French and Spanish fleets off Cape Trafalgar.

NERO (Nero Claudius Caesar) (37–68), despotic emperor of Rome and self-styled poet, instigated the first Roman persecution (A.D. 64).

NILE RIVER, of eastern and northeastern Africa, is one of the longest rivers in the world; the size of its basin is estimated at over one million square miles. It originates in Ethiopia and the Great Lakes area of East Africa and flows into the Mediterranean.

NOBLE, RICHARD C., of Norfolk, Va., was a delegate to the 1920 UNIA convention. He reported that conditions in Norfolk were better than those in most southern cities and addressed the issue of the reactions of black ministers to the Garvey movement, saying that while some pastors took a conservative view of racial organization, others had done the association good by preaching in accordance with its aims (*Garvey Papers* 2).

NORRIS, J. AUSTIN (1893–1976), a prominent black Philadelphia attorney, served as defense counsel at the trials of Dr. J. D. GIBSON and Rev. J. W. EASON at the 1922 UNIA convention. Norris was born in Chambersburg, Pa., and attended Lincoln University, Pennsylvania, and Yale University Law School. He was the founder and editor of a black weekly periodical, the *Philadelphia American,* in 1919–1920. Norris

415

was elected as a member of the UNIA delegation to the League of Nations in 1922. He was also the attorney for the powerful Philadelphia division of the UNIA in the early twenties. A close friend of Eason's, Norris gave information about UNIA activities to CHANDLER OWEN after Eason's murder. The information subsequently made its way into Bureau of Investigation reports. Norris later gave evidence to Assistant U.S. Attorney MAXWELL MATTUCK, helping the federal authorities locate Esau Ramus, a suspect in the case (*NYT*, 5 March 1976; *Garvey Papers* 4, 5).

O'BRIEN, GEORGIANA ("Georgie") L., one of the signers of the 1920 UNIA Declaration of Rights, was ladies' president of the Montreal UNIA division in the early twenties. She continued to represent Canada at the international UNIA conventions, appearing as a delegate and a member of various convention committees in 1921 and 1922. She participated in the discussion of male-female relations within the black race during Women's Day sessions in August 1922 (*NW*, 7 May 1921; *Garvey Papers* 2–4).

OGILVIE, F. O., one of the signers of the 1920 UNIA Declaration of Rights, was president of the Meron, Camaguey, Cuba, division of the UNIA in the early 1920s (*NW*, 15 October 1921; *Garvey Papers* 2).

OWEN, CHANDLER (1889–1967), was cofounder and coeditor, with A. Philip Randolph, of the Socialist periodical the *MESSENGER*. Born in Warrenton, N.C., Owen graduated from Virginia Union University and Columbia University's New York School of Philanthropy. He became friends with Randolph in 1915. In 1916 the two organized the Independent Political Council, an activist organization that supported the campaigns of black political candidates in Harlem. Later in the same year the pair joined the Socialist party and began editing the *Hotel Messenger*, the newsletter of the Headwaiters and Sidewaiters Society. They began their own *Messenger* in August 1917. Like other leading Socialists in the WORLD WAR I era, they were arrested and charged with sedition in the fall of 1918. Both were acquitted, and Owen was drafted into the U.S. Army. In 1920 he and Randolph became contributing editors to W. A. DOMINGO's short-lived *Emancipator*; in the same year they founded the FRIENDS OF NEGRO FREEDOM. After Garvey met with the head of the KU KLUX KLAN in June 1922, Owen and Randolph joined with WILLIAM PICKENS, Robert Bagnall, and others in launching a "Garvey Must Go" campaign, holding public meetings in New York to denounce the UNIA president general. Owen became increasingly conservative in his political beliefs after his brother, Toussaint Owen, a tailor who had been denied admission to the Socialist needle trade unions in New York and had suffered from frequent unemployment, died impoverished in 1923. Although he remained friends with Randolph, Owen moved away from New York and began work as a reporter in Chicago. He stopped contributing to the *Messenger* in 1925 and became involved in Democratic and Republican ward politics. He worked for the U.S. Office of War Information in Washington, D.C., during World War II (A. Philip Randolph and Chandler Owen, "The Garvey Movement: A Promise or a Menace to Negroes?" *Messenger* 2 [October 1920]: 114–115; Jervis Anderson, *A. Philip Randolph: A Biographical Portrait* [New York: Harcourt Brace Jovanovich, 1972], pp. 142–143; Theodore Kornweibel, Jr. *No Crystal Stair: Black Life and the Messenger, 1917–1928* [Westport, Conn.: Greenwood Press, 1975]; Bruce Kellner, ed., *The Harlem Renaissance: A Historical Dictionary for the Era* [Westport, Conn.: Greenwood Press, 1984], pp. 275–276; *Garvey Papers* 1, 2, 4, 5).

PACE, HARRY H. (1884–1943), musician, writer, and entrepreneur, was the president of the Black Swan Phonograph Co., which produced classical and popular music by black musicians. Pace was born in Covington, Ga., and received his A.B. from Atlanta University in 1903. In 1905 he became the managing editor of W. E. B. DU BOIS's first newspaper, the *Moon*, in Memphis. He taught classics at the Lincoln Institute in Jefferson City, Mo., from 1906 to 1908, then returned to Memphis and held a number of business positions with financial institutions there. He organized the Colored Citizens Association, which worked for better schools, safer streets, and fairer treatment of blacks by police and the criminal court system. In 1912 he served as assistant secretary to the Tennessee State Republican Convention and became the only black delegate-at-large to the national convention in Chicago in that year. In 1907 he cofounded the Pace and Handy Music Co., one of the first black music publishing enterprises in the United States, with composer W. C. Handy, and collaborated with Handy as a lyricist for such songs as "St. Louis Blues" and "Memphis Blues." In 1918 the two moved their company to New York; in 1921 Pace dissolved the partnership and began his own Pace Phonograph Corporation, soon renamed the Black Swan Phonograph Co., the first black-owned recording company in the country. Fletcher Henderson was the recording director of the company, which introduced Ethel Waters, Alberta Hunter, and others. Both JOHN NAIL and W. E. B. Du Bois were on the Black Swan board of directors. The company slogan, which appeared on the label of each disk, was: "The Only Genuine Colored Record. Others Are Only Passing for Colored." The marketing success of the Black Swan company led white-owned recording corporations that had earlier refused to carry black artists on their labels to reverse their policy, widening opportunities for black performers. Black Swan merged with Paramount Co. in 1924. Pace moved to New Jersey and went into the life insurance business. He was president of the National Negro Insurance Association in 1928–1929 and became active in Democratic politics in the 1930s (*NYA*, 15 March 1924; "Biggest Northern Business," *Ebony*, August 1946, p. 43; Bruce Kellner, *The Harlem Renaissance: A Historical Dictionary for the Era* [Westport, Conn.: Greenwood Press, 1984], pp. 39, 277; David Levering Lewis, *When Harlem Was in Vogue* [New York: A. A. Knopf, 1981], pp. 174–175; *WWCR; WWCA*).

PALACE CASINO was used by the early UNIA as a meeting place in Harlem before the organization moved to LIBERTY HALL in July 1919. The white-owned Palace Casino, located at 135th Street and Madison Avenue, was used for other types of UNIA meetings—

including Sunday afternoon ladies' auxiliary meetings and Tuesday evening elocution contests—as early as 1917. Mary Church Terrell, one of the founding members of the NAACP, spoke at a UNIA ladies' auxiliary meeting there in October 1917, and Nicholas Murray Butler, president of Columbia University, judged an elocution contest at the casino in December. It was used for regular mass meetings beginning in early 1918 (*Garvey Papers* 1, 2).

PAN is the mythological Greek god of pastures and woodlands.

PANAMA RAILROAD CO. See S.S. *GENERAL GOETHALS*.

PANKEN, JACOB (1879–1968), justice of New York's Seventh District Court, was presiding judge in the civil suits brought against Garvey for fraud and nonpayment of wages by JAMES B. BROOKS and Edward Orr, a BLACK STAR LINE stockholder who sued Garvey in April 1922 for nonpayment of dividends. Panken suspended decision on Orr's charges and found in favor of Brooks's claim for $750 in back wages. He severely reprimanded Garvey in delivering judgment in the case, reportedly accusing him of "preying upon the gullibility of your own people," investing unwisely, granting officers inflated salaries, and mismanaging accounts. He also questioned Garvey's psychological health, stating that he manifested a "form of paranoia" in believing himself to be a great man (*Garvey Papers* 4: 620–622). Panken was a leading Socialist and an activist in labor reform and the trade union movement. He was one of the founders of the Ladies' Garment Workers Union and the Amalgamated Clothing Workers' Union. He was elected to his municipal court post in 1917 and held the position until 1937 (*NYT,* 5 February 1968; *Garvey Papers* 4).

PETIONI, CHARLES (1885–1951), West Indian journalist and physician, was one of the signers of the 1920 UNIA Declaration of Rights. Petioni was born in Trinidad and moved to New York in 1918. He studied at the City College of New York and HOWARD UNIVERSITY Medical School, receiving his medical degree in 1925. He practiced in the out-patient department of Harlem Hospital, New York, in 1926. He edited a Spanish-English newspaper in Port of Spain in 1917–1918 and was associate editor of Hubert H. Harrison's *New Negro* in 1918 and a reporter for the *NEGRO WORLD* while a medical student in 1921–1925. Petioni became a leading advocate of West Indian political rights. He organized a number of activist associations in New York, including the Trinidad Benevolent Association and the West India Committee in America (later called the Caribbean Union). He worked for Caribbean independence and West Indian economic autonomy throughout the 1930s and 1940s (*WWCA; Garvey Papers* 2).

PHILLIPS, WENDELL (1811–1884), Boston abolitionist, orator, and writer, became president of the American Anti-Slavery Society in 1865. He was well known as an orator, ranking with Daniel Webster as one of the leading public speakers of his time. His oration on TOUSSAINT L'OUVERTURE, first delivered in New York and Boston in 1861 and published as a pamphlet in 1863, was a favorite of Garvey's. GEORGE TOBIAS delivered the oration at a UNIA meeting at the PALACE CASINO in June 1919 (Wendell Phillips, *Speeches, Lectures, and Letters*

[Boston: Walker, Wise and Co., 1864]; Louis Filler, ed., *Wendell Phillips on Civil Rights and Freedom* [New York: Hill and Wang, 1965], pp. 163–184; *Garvey Papers* 1).

PICKENS, WILLIAM (1881–1954), a black educator, was field secretary of the NAACP in 1920. A graduate of Talladega College, Talladega, Ala. (B.A., 1902), Yale University (B.A., 1904), and Fisk University (M.A., 1908), Pickens became dean of Morgan College, a black institution in Baltimore, in 1915, and vice president of the college in 1918. He was an active member of the Baltimore branch of the NAACP and was elected to the NAACP's Committee of One Hundred in 1910. His work made him a candidate for field secretary of the organization in 1916, but he was bypassed for the position, which went to James Weldon Johnson. Pickens publicly defended Garvey's right to reenter the United States during the Department of State's efforts to exclude him in 1921. Writing for the 22 April 1921 *New York Dispatch,* Pickens urged blacks to unite in support of Garvey and said that when the issue came down to "the question of common rights, we are all inseparably linked with Garvey and he with us." He followed that article with another for the *Nation* which offered an opinion generally favorable of Garvey but critical of his stand on the issue of segregation. Garvey requested that Pickens attend the UNIA convention in August 1922 as a delegate and apparently met with him to discuss his becoming a member of the UNIA executive council. Pickens decided to remain with the NAACP after its executive board raised his salary and expanded his responsibilities. He was bitterly opposed to Garvey's meeting with the KU KLUX KLAN in June 1922, and he became a leader in the "Garvey Must Go" campaign of 1922–1923. The incident mentioned in the January 1923 letter to the attorney general took place at an African Methodist Episcopal church convention in Toronto in September 1922. Pickens was on his way into a church where he was to appear as a speaker when he was accosted by UNIA members "fingering their hip-pockets" and warning him not to make trouble for Garvey (*BA,* 29 September 1922). A southerner by birth, Pickens worked on the Scottsboro "Boys" case in the thirties and on the issue of Ku Klux Klan interference with black voting rights in the South. He came into conflict with W. E. B. DU BOIS, who lobbied for his dismissal from the organization in the early 1930s. Pickens remained with the NAACP until 1942, when he resigned to become director of the Interracial Section of the Savings Bond Division of the U.S. Treasury Department (William Pickens, "Africa for the Africans: The Garvey Movement," *Nation* 113, no. 2,947 [December 1921]: 750–751; idem, *The New Negro: His Political, Civil, and Mental Status and Related Essays* [1916; reprint, New York: AMS Press, 1969]; Minnie Finch, *The NAACP: Its Fight for Justice* [Metuchen, N.J.: Scarecrow Press, 1981], pp. 30, 65, 78; B. Joyce Ross, *J. E. Spingarn and the Rise of the NAACP* [New York: Atheneum, 1972], pp. 34, 210; Langston Hughes, *Fight for Freedom: The Story of the NAACP* [New York: Berkley, 1962]; Charles Flint Kellogg, *NAACP: A History of the National Association for the Advancement of Colored People* [Baltimore: Johns Hopkins

University Press, 1967], pp. 48 n. 7, 133, 185–186; *Garvey Papers* 1, 3–5).

PIED PIPER of Hamelin is a legendary figure preserved in German folklore and in nineteenth-century versions of the legend recorded by the English poet Robert Browning, the German folklorists Wilhelm and Jakob Grimm, and the German poet Johann Wolfgang von Goethe. According to the legend, which stems from ca. 1284, the Pied Piper charmed the rodents of Hamelin, Germany, out of the town by playing upon his flute. When the town fathers refused to pay him for this service, he sought his revenge by charming away their children. In her memoirs, AMY ASHWOOD Garvey recalled that the Pied Piper of Hamelin was one of Garvey's favorite stories as a youth. "Before long," she wrote, the young "Marcus produced his own plan to rid the parish of St. Ann of its rats." According to her account, he became a leader of a gang of lower-class children who challenged the authority of "the village elders by stoning the windows of the church and school" in protest against the St. Ann's parish council's failure to keep their promises to provide better facilities (Amy Ashwood Garvey, "Portrait of a Liberator" [unpub. ms., 1969], Amy Ashwood Garvey papers, New York, Lionel Yard, executor).

PITT, WILLIAM (first earl of Chatham, also known as the "Elder Pitt" or the "Great Commoner") (1708–1778), was a leader of the Seven Years' War (1756–1763). He was a proponent of moderation in Britain's policies toward the United States in the years prior to and during the American Revolution, favoring actions that would maintain a political alliance between the two countries by granting full rights and liberties to Americans as British subjects. Pitt's "On Affairs in America" (1777) was one of Garvey's favorite orations. Pitt's son and namesake, William Pitt (1759–1806) was prime minister of England (1783–1801 and 1804–1805).

PLATO (428–347 B.C.), Athenian philosopher and aristocrat, was a pupil of SOCRATES. His philosophical work took the form of dialogues and epistles, including the early Socratic dialogues, which explore the nature of virtue. His middle work includes the *Republic*, in which he presented his theory of the ideal state, and the poetic *Symposium*.

PLUMMER, HENRY VINTON (b. 1876), a real estate salesperson in Washington, D.C., and Maryland, became the head of the BLACK STAR LINE Bureau of Publicity and Propaganda and the chief of Garvey's secret service staff. Plummer was born in Hyattsville, Md. His father, Henry Vinton Plummer, Sr., was the first black chaplain to serve in the U. S. Army after the Civil War. The junior Plummer excelled in school; in 1889 he was valedictorian of his otherwise all-white high school class in Wyoming. He attended the University of Nebraska in 1897–1900 and was admitted to the bar in Omaha. He ran unsuccessfully as a Republican candidate for the Nebraska state legislature and later moved to Washington, D.C., where he established a real estate business in 1910. He was the assistant sergeant at arms at the Progressive party's national convention in 1912. He became involved in the UNIA African Legion (see AFRICAN GUARDS) in Newport News, Va., and in 1920 helped drill recruits and rewrite the U.S. Army drill regulations for use by the legions. Plummer relocated to New York, where he was a member of the UNIA delegation that greeted Liberian president C. D. B. King in March 1921. He participated in the 1920, 1922, and 1924 UNIA conventions as a delegate from New York (*NW*, 12 March and 27 August 1921; *WWCR; Garvey Papers* 2–5).

PORO COLLEGE. See ANNIE MALONE.

POWELL, ADAM CLAYTON, SR. (1865–1953), religious leader and author, was pastor of the Abyssinian Baptist Church in New York City from 1908 to 1931. Born in Virginia and ordained as a Baptist minister in 1892, he was a popular minister and community leader, and the Abyssinian Baptist Church grew quickly under his directorship. Until the early 1920s it met on West 40th Street, and in the summers it met in temporary outdoor quarters under a tent on a lot next door to LIBERTY HALL. In 1923 the church moved into new facilities built on that site on West 138th Street in Harlem. Powell was a member of the NAACP and the Urban League and president of the International League of Darker Peoples, a coalition group organized at MME C. J. WALKER's villa in January 1919 to compose a platform for black delegates to the Paris Peace Conference. He participated in Republican party politics but switched support to Franklin D. Roosevelt in the 1930s. He was a leader in Harlem activism against the ITALO-ETHIOPIAN WAR. He was the father of the Harlem politician and pastor Adam Clayton Powell, Jr. (*NYT*, 13 June 1953; Adam Clayton Powell, Sr., *Against the Tide* [New York: Richard R. Smith, 1938]; *Garvey Papers* 1, 2, 5).

PREMPEY (Prempe) (ca. 1871–1931), ruler of the Asante (Ashanti) nation, which encompassed much of the area of modern-day Ghana, reunited the Asante empire and opposed the British protectorate. In 1896 he was deported by the British to Sierra Leone; he returned home in 1924. Upon his death in 1931 his nephew, Prempe II (1892–1970), succeeded him as the British-sanctioned ruler of the Kumasi division and the unofficial ruler of Asante (Thomas J. Lewin, *Asante Before the British: The Prempean Years, 1875–1900* [Lawrence, Kans.: Regents Press of Kansas, 1978]; *DAHB*, pp. 193–194).

RAINES, FRANK O., one of the signers of the 1920 UNIA Declaration of Rights, was a member of the Chicago division of the UNIA (*NW*, 25 June 1921; *Garvey Papers* 2).

RALEIGH, SIR WALTER (1554?–1618), English courtier, poet, and adventurer, was a favorite of Elizabeth I and patron of Edmund Spenser. Raleigh organized a series of privateering expeditions, including one into the interior of Guiana in search of the fabled city of El Dorado. In the early 1600s he was imprisoned in the tower of London by James I and later executed on charges of treason.

RICKETTS, FREDERICK SAMUEL, of Colón, Panama, was president of the Colón Independent Mutual Benefit Cooperative Society. He had been involved in the UNIA in Colón since 1918. He addressed the 1920 UNIA convention delegates on affairs in Panama. Stating that most of the black population in the Panama Canal Zone was West Indian, Ricketts went on to describe efforts on the part of black laborers to organize and the violent means used by white officials to quell the strike called by the United Brotherhood of Maintenance of Way Employees and Railroad Shop Laborers in February 1920. Ricketts was a signer of the UNIA Declaration of Rights (*Garvey Papers* 2).

RILEY, RICHARD EDWARD, one of the signers of the 1920 UNIA Declaration of Rights, was deputy head of the Universal African Legion (AFRICAN GUARDS) in New Aberdeen, Nova Scotia (*NW,* 4 June 1921; *Garvey Papers* 2).

ROBESON, PAUL (1898–1976), a world-acclaimed dramatic actor, singer, recording artist, and political activist, was born the son of a minister and former slave in Princeton, N.J. He graduated from Rutgers University (1919), New Brunswick, N.J., where he excelled academically and became a national athletic hero, and then studied law at Columbia University Law School (1923). He began his theatrical career in New York in the early twenties, received notice for his role in the Provincetown Players' *All God's Chillun Got Wings* (1924), and gained stardom in the New York production of Eugene O'Neill's *Emperor Jones* (1925). He played title roles in other productions before traveling to London to appear in Jerome Kern's *Showboat.* During the same period he began performing as a concert singer, and his interpretation of spirituals and songs by black composers filled concert halls in New York, London, Paris, and Vienna. In the 1930s he became acclaimed as a Shakespearean actor for his leading role in *Othello.* He acted in the London production of *Stevedore* (the play Garvey criticizes in "Smiles for the Thoughtful"), which opened at the Embassy Theatre in May 1935. The pro-union script depicts a militant dock worker; Robeson apparently accepted the part "because it showed a black laborer with a strong racial feeling for his people but an equally strong feeling for his class" (Virginia Hamilton, *Paul Robeson: The Life and Times of a Free Black Man* [New York: Harper & Row, 1974], p. 66). He made a series of commercially successful but racially stereotypical films, including *Saunders of the River* (1935) and *King Solomon's Mines* (1937). Robeson was an active advocate of labor and civil rights and an admirer of the Soviet Union. His support for civil liberties and anti-Fascist and leftist causes subjected him to political and artistic blacklisting in the 1950s, when he was called to testify before the House Committee on Un-American Activities and forced into virtual exile through the revocation of his American passport (*NW,* 27 December 1924, 24 January and 7 February 1931; *BM* 1, no. 7 [June 1935]: 8–9; Thomas Cripps, "Paul Robeson and Black Identity in American Movies," *Massachusetts Review* 11, no. 3 [summer 1970]: 468–485; Roberta Yancy Dent, ed. and comp., *Paul Robeson: Tributes and Selected Writings* [New York: Paul Robeson Archives, 1976]; Shirley Graham, *Paul Robeson, Citizen of the World* [New York: Julian Messner, 1946]; Dorothy Butler Gilliam, *Paul Robeson: All-American* [Washington, D.C.: New Republic Book Co., 1976]).

ROCKEFELLER, JOHN D. (1839–1937), a wealthy industrialist, philanthropist, and financier, was cofounder of the Standard Oil Co. and a director of the U.S. Steel Corp. An example of success frequently cited by Garvey, Rockefeller rose from the modest job of bookkeeper to become a founder of Standard Oil and by the 1880s held a virtual monopoly over the oil-refining industry in the United States, controlling diverse holdings in railroads, pipeline distribution, and banking institutions. He was reputed to be the richest man in the world in the 1920s. At his death, the *New York Times* emphasized his rags-to-riches reputation and his "hard work" philosophy.

Rogers, Henry H. (1840–1909), was one of John D. Rockefeller's principal executives; like Rockefeller, he was a director of the U.S. Steel Corp. and of the Union Pacific and Santa Fe railroads. Though known for his ruthlessness in business dealings, Rogers was also a philanthropist. He gave generous financial backing to the Tuskegee Institute. Like Rockefeller, Rogers was heralded by Garvey as a model of individual capitalistic success. He was also the original owner of the Black Star Line steam yacht *Kanawha*.

Roosevelt, Theodore (1858–1919), author, conservationist, soldier, and Progressive reformer, succeeded to the presidency of the United States upon the death of William McKinley in 1901 and was elected to that office in 1904. Cultivating the philosophy of manly vigor associated with his name, he organized a volunteer cavalry regiment known as the Rough Riders to serve in Cuba in 1898. Booker T. Washington served as an informal political adviser during his presidency.

Rosenwald, Julius (1862–1932), was a multimillionaire businessman who became president of Sears, Roebuck & Co. in 1910. He used portions of his great fortune to aid black education in the United States and to provide relief to Jews abroad, as well as to construct Chicago's Museum of Science and Industry and many YMCAs in black neighborhoods.

Saint Ann's Bay, Marcus Garvey's birthplace, is a harbor town on the northern coast of Jamaica in the parish of St. Ann, twenty miles west of Port Maria. Garvey's parents, Malcus Mosiah Garvey and Sarah Jane Richards Garvey, were married there in 1889; he worked there as a mason and she as a domestic servant (*Garvey Papers* 1).

Santo Domingo and Saint Domingue are Spanish and French forms of the early name for the Dominican Republic, sometimes applied to the entire island of Hispaniola (including both the Dominican Republic and Haiti). Santo Domingo is also the name of the capital city of the Dominican Republic.

Sarah. See Abraham.

Saxon, Samuel T., a resident of New York, held a public meeting to denounce the Garvey movement at the Sterling Hotel in Cincinnati in October 1922. Saxon was in the midst of an anti-Garvey lecture when he was reportedly attacked by William Ware, the president of the Cincinnati division of the UNIA, whereupon general fighting broke out among members of the audience. Ware was convicted of assault and battery, and other UNIA members were fined for disorderly conduct in connection with the incident (*Chicago Whip*, 21 October 1922; *Garvey Papers* 5).

Schoen, Julian A., of Georgia, became deputy warden of Atlanta Federal Penitentiary on 31 January 1925. Schoen cited Garvey for "insolence" in

May 1926, following an incident between Garvey and a guard regarding the conduct of prisoners on a cleaning crew. Garvey was described in the report as head of the cleaning crew (deputy warden's report, 11 May 1926, Atlanta Federal Records Center, records of Atlanta penitentiary; *Register of the Department of Justice and the Courts of the United States*, 31st ed. [Washington, D.C.: General Printing Office, 1926], p. 115).

SCOTT, EMMETT JAY (1873–1957), was private adviser to BOOKER T. WASHINGTON and secretary of the TUSKEGEE INSTITUTE. Scott started out as a journalist with the *Houston Post* and an editor of the black *Texas Freeman* in Houston before becoming affiliated with Washington, whose ideas he had long endorsed. He became Washington's private secretary in 1897, and over the next eighteen years the two worked together in developing what became known as the Tuskegee political machine. Scott and Washington organized the National Negro Business League in 1900, and Scott served as its secretary until 1922. He was a Taft-appointed U.S. commissioner to Liberia in 1909. After Washington died in 1915, Scott stayed on as secretary for the board of trustees of the institute until 1917, when he became a special adviser on issues regarding black troops and civilians to Secretary of War Newton D. Baker. He was secretary-treasurer (1919–1934) and secretary (1934–1939) of HOWARD UNIVERSITY. He was made assistant publicity director for the Republican National Committee in 1939–1942. Scott corresponded with Garvey regarding the latter's proposed trip to Tuskegee in 1916. He received postal censorship reports concerning AMY ASHWOOD's correspondence and the activities of Marcus Garvey as a war department official in 1918 (*NYT,* 14 December 1957; Bruce Kellner, ed., *The Harlem Renaissance: A Historical Dictionary for the Era* [Westport, Conn.: Greenwood Press, 1984], p. 319; Louis R. Harlan, *Booker T. Washington: The Making of a Black Leader, 1856–1901* [London and New York: Oxford University Press, 1972], pp. 260–261; *Garvey Papers* 1, 2).

SEARS, ROEBUCK & Co. See JULIUS ROSENWALD.

SELFRIDGE, GORDON (1856–1947), one of the self-made entrepreneurs that Garvey admired, went to work at the age of fourteen, worked his way up through MARSHALL FIELD's company until he became a partner in 1892, and then opened his own highly successful department store enterprise in London in 1909. Selfridge advertised his business with a series of moral and philosophical essays in the London *Times*.

SELKRIDGE, JOHN FREDERICK, was a bishop of the United Christian Church who became involved in the Garvey movement in the early twenties, first as a special adviser to Garvey and later as a stock salesperson and field agent for the Liberian Construction Loan and BLACK STAR LINE. He officiated as a pastor over several sessions at the 1920 UNIA convention and helped organize that convention's grand parade. In 1920 Selkridge reported that he had lost a suitcase, and the stock certificates and loan notes it contained, while traveling in Pennsylvania; he was dismissed from his UNIA position in February 1921 for carelessness. He joined the African Orthodox church and was ordained into its ministry in May 1926. He served as pastor at the Christ Church in Brooklyn (*NW,* 26 February and 10 September 1921; *Negro Churchman* 4, no. 4 [April 1926]: 8; *Garvey Papers* 2–4).

SETH was a son of ADAM and EVE (Gen. 5:25–26, 6:1–8).

SHAKESPEARE, WILLIAM (b. 1895), a Jamaican house painter and Garvey supporter who lived in New Orleans, was arrested with his neighbor, CONSTANTINE DYER, for the shooting death of former Garveyite J. W. H. EASON in 1923. Both men were eventually found innocent of the crime (*Garvey Papers* 5).

SHERRILL, WILLIAM LE VAN (b. 1894), was president of the BLACK CROSS NAVIGATION AND TRADING CO. and became acting president general of the UNIA when Garvey was imprisoned in 1925. Born in Arkansas, he attended Philander Smith College, Little Rock, Ark., and Northwestern University, Chicago, served in the U.S. Army in WORLD WAR I, and entered upon a business career in Chicago and Baltimore. He attracted Garvey's notice as an orator at a UNIA meeting in 1922, and he became a delegate to the 1922 UNIA convention, where he was elected assistant president general and leader of American Negroes, replacing Rev. J. W. H. EASON. He was one of the UNIA representatives who traveled to Geneva to petition the League of Nations in September 1922. He continued in the capacity of assistant president general until Garvey's imprisonment, when he became acting head of the organization. A major power struggle followed; Garvey warned officials not to deal with Sherrill and ordered that a special convention be held in Detroit in March 1926, where a new slate of officers loyal to Garvey's authority was elected, with FRED A. TOOTE as the acting president general. Sherrill was denounced at the convention, and Garvey published charges of maladministration and disloyalty against him in the pages of the *NEGRO WORLD.* Garvey's dissatisfaction with Sherrill stemmed in part from Sherrill's decision to honor adverse court judgments ordering payment of back salaries to former UNIA and BLACK STAR LINE employees rather than to retain the money for use in BLACK CROSS NAVIGATION AND TRADING CO. investments, a decision that countermanded Garvey's orders. Sherrill and his colleagues in the New York division refused to accept the Garvey-engineered change in leadership. They held their own convention in LIBERTY HALL in August 1926, and Sherrill was elected supreme deputy potentate of the anti-Garvey faction. The 1926 split set the stage for the continuing conflict of leadership that characterized the movement in the years following Garvey's deportation from the United States. Sherrill renewed his active participation in the UNIA after Garvey's death. He worked with Ethel Collins and James Stewart on UNIA business in the early 1940s. In the 1950s he alternated with William Harvey as president general of the Philadelphia-based UNIA (rival to the wing of the movement based in Cleveland) and served as editor of *Garvey's Voice,* the UNIA periodical. He also continued offering the School of African Philosophy as a correspondence course, advertising it in the pages of *Garvey's Voice.* In 1956 he officiated as president general at a ceremony unveiling a memorial bust of Garvey in

Kingston, Jamaica (*NW*, 26 August 1922, 7 November 1925, 20 March 1926; *NYT*, 2 August and 3 August 1926; *NYAN*, 4 August 1926; *BA*, 7 August 1926; *CD*, 4 September and 11 September 1926; *Garvey's Voice*, June–July 1951, July 1956, January 1958; *Stewart's Voice*, February 1956; *G&G*, pp. 280–283; *Garvey Papers* 5).

SILVERSTON, ANTHONY RUDOLPH, a white shipping agent, was the president of the New York Ship Exchange, a shipping brokerage company in New York. He represented the Black Star Steamship Co. of New Jersey (formed in October 1920 as a front organization for the BLACK STAR LINE) in its negotiations for the purchase of the S.S. *Hong Kheng* and the S.S. *Orion*. He made arrangements to purchase the ships from the U.S. SHIPPING BOARD and then to sell them on credit, and at a greatly inflated price, to the Black Star Line. $25,000 in down payments had been made to Silverston in March–June 1921 when negotiations for the *Hong Kheng* were suspended and the decision was made to buy the *Orion* instead; the purchase of the *Orion* (which the UNIA planned to rename the *Phyllis Wheatley*) was never completed, although the ship was advertised as part of the Black Star Line fleet in the pages of the *NEGRO WORLD*. In March 1922 a Bureau of Investigation agent reported that he was "convinced that Silverston has been dishonest in his dealings with the line and is responsible in some measure for the present difficulties" (*Garvey Papers* 4: 545). By early 1922 Silverston's brokerage company, which he operated for seven or eight years, was defunct (*Garvey Papers* 3, 4).

SIMON (of Cyrene) carried the cross used for the Crucifixion of Jesus to Calvary (Matt. 27:32; Mark 15:21; Luke 23:26).

SIMON, THOMAS H.N., was a delegate to the 1920 UNIA convention and one of the signers of the declaration of rights. He worked as a pastor (*Garvey Papers* 2).

SIMONS, JOHN C., a minister, attended the 1920 UNIA convention. He signed the UNIA Declaration of Rights and was a contributor to the African Redemption Fund in September 1921 (*Garvey Papers* 2, 3).

SIMPSON, GEORGE (1870–1951), city magistrate of New York from 1919 to 1931, served one term as a state senator before Major John F. Hylan appointed him to the bench, where he heard mainly cases of commerical fraud. Simpson resigned along with other Tammany Hall appointees during the Seabury investigation of 1931.

SMITH, FREDERICK EDWIN (1872–1930), the first earl of Birkenhead, was a conservative British statesman and orator, most famous for his opposition to Irish Home Rule. He was secretary of state for India in 1924–1928.

SMITH, F. F. (d. 1921), a Philadelphia pastor, was one of the signers of the 1920 UNIA Declaration of Rights and a delegate to the 1920 convention. His death was announced to the delegates of the 1921 UNIA convention by Secretary General JAMES B. YEARWOOD, who refered to Smith as one "of our very active and very influential members" (*Garvey Papers* 3: 642).

SMITH, RUDOLPH E. B., a member of the UNIA Field Corps, was elected third assistant president general at the 1922 UNIA convention. He was a leading speaker at LIBERTY HALL in the 1920s and was a delegate from New York to the 1920 UNIA convention. He was elected Leader of the Eastern Province of the West Indies at the 1921 UNIA convention. Smith often appeared as the speaker preceding Garvey at Liberty Hall in 1922. He signed the UNIA petition to the League of Nations in July 1922, and at the UNIA convention in August, he was nominated from the floor to be one of the UNIA delegates to travel to Geneva to present the petition. In a later session Clifford Bourne charged Smith and other West Indian leaders with incompetency, whereby Smith defended himself by stating that it had been under Garvey's orders that he had remained in the United States after his election to office in 1921. Garvey came to Smith's defense, describing him as a loyal and devoted member of the UNIA and explaining that he had had Smith stay in the United States because of his excellent organizing and fund-raising skills. Garvey endorsed Smith's candidacy as third assistant president general, and he was subsequently elected to that office. Smith's salary was suspended in June 1923, along with that of HENRIETTA VINTON DAVIS and others. He reported the result of his travels to divisions in Ohio, West Virginia, Illinois, and Cuba to the 1924 UNIA convention (*Garvey Papers* 2–5).

SMITH, WILFORD H. (b. 1863), counsel general of the UNIA and Garvey's personal attorney in 1920–1921, was born in Mississippi. Before moving to New York in 1901 he was a personal attorney to BOOKER T. WASHINGTON, working with Washington quietly to challenge the grandfather clause in Alabama voting laws. When AMY ASHWOOD Garvey filed an affidavit for annulment in August 1920, she described Smith as "the oldest member of his race at the Bar, and a most eminent and learned attorney" (*Garvey Papers* 2: 640). Smith was elected counsel general at the 1920 UNIA convention and was one of the five members of the commission of UNIA officials that met with Liberian president C. D. B. King at the Waldorf-Astoria Hotel in New York in March 1921. He represented the BLACK STAR LINE in a number of legal suits, including the libel case of *Black Star Line v. W. E. B. Du Bois and NAACP* (no. 1944), brought in the New York State Supreme Court in January 1921, and in the September and October 1921 cases brought by former crew members of the *KANAWHA* against the UNIA line for nonpayment of wages. He also handled Garvey's personal litigation, including his legal entanglements with Ashwood and his conflicts with CYRIL BRIGGS. Garvey made Smith his personal representative and granted him power of attorney over Black Star Line financial matters when he traveled outside the United States in 1921. Although a Bureau of Investigation agent reported that Smith resigned from his UNIA position in November 1921 because "he found THOMPSON, GARCIA, SILVERSTON, and Nolan crooked," Smith seems to have remained loyal to Garvey and continued to act as his attorney (*Garvey Papers* 3: 629). He approached the government with an offer for an out-of-court settlement of the mail fraud case in July 1922 (Louis R. Harlan, *Booker T. Washington: The Making of a Black*

Leader, 1856–1901 [London and New York: Oxford University Press, 1972], p. 302; *Garvey Papers* 2–5).

SMITH-GREEN, EDWARD DAVID (1888–1969), an amateur historian and general secretary of the UNIA in 1917–1918, was born in British Guiana, where he became a civil servant in the colonial customs service. He immigrated to the United States and was employed by the American Sugar Co. in Brooklyn and later by an ammunition factory in Trenton, N.J. He claimed to have known Garvey since 1916, and he accepted a job offer as secretary of the BLACK STAR LINE from the UNIA leader in 1919. He was shot in an apparent robbery attempt in December 1919 but was not seriously wounded. In January 1920 he traveled aboard the S.S. *YARMOUTH* on its second voyage to Cuba, and in the following spring he was a frequent speaker at UNIA meetings in New York. He served on the board of directors of the line until the summer of 1920, when he resigned from that position and from membership in the UNIA, accusing Garvey of dictatorial behavior and gross mismanagement of the affairs of the Black Star Line. Garvey responded by printing an announcement implying that Smith-Green had misappropriated funds while an officer of the Black Star Line and warning UNIA members not to believe his statements. Smith-Green became affiliated with the African Saw Mill Steamship Co. after leaving the UNIA in 1920. He was the author of several unpublished historical manuscripts, (*Garvey Papers* 1, 2).

SNOOK, JOHN WILSON (1876–1975), was warden of the Atlanta Federal Penitentiary from 1925 until his resignation in 1929. Born in Salmon, Idaho, Snook spent several years as a deputy sheriff in Alaska before returning to his home state, where he served as a representative to the state legislature. He was warden of the Idaho state penitentiary from 1909 to 1917 and again in 1924 before taking up the position in Atlanta. He spent most of his later life as a rancher (*Idaho Recorder* [Salmon], 9 January 1975; *WWW*).

SOCRATES (469–399 B.C.), an Athenian philosopher, taught that the ethical nature of a statement was demonstrated in its consequences and that virtue—closely associated with knowledge—could be learned. He came into conflict with the Sophists and political critics of his ideas and conduct. Tried for heresy and the corruption of youth in 399 B.C, he was convicted and given hemlock to drink. PLATO's *Apology* and other Socratic dialogues are accounts of the philosopher's trial and death.

SOLOMON, son of DAVID and Bathsheba, was successor to David as king of Israel and, according to biblical tradition, "wiser than all men" (1 Kings 4:31). The UNIA taught that Solomon was a black man and referred to the biblical passage "I am black, but comely, O ye daughters of Jerusalem" (Song of Sol. 1:5). In 1924 Garveyite Rev. James Morris Webb told readers of the *NEGRO WORLD* that "King Solomon was a Negro by blood" (*NW,* 6 September 1924; 1 Kings 3–4; *DB,* pp. 827–830; *Garvey Papers* 5).

SOMME, a region in northern France around the Somme River, was the scene of intense warfare during WORLD WAR I. A British offensive on the Somme diverted German attention from the VERDUN region in July 1916, enabling the French to regain territory. Black French West African soldiers fought with the French during the war; over fifty thousand went to France in 1916 alone.

SPHINX, a mythical figure, was represented in the sculpture of ancient Egypt, Greece, and the Middle East. It usually had the head of a man or woman (but sometimes of a hawk or animal) and the body of a lion. The most well-known sphinx is the Great Sphinx of Al Jizah, Egypt, whose head is modeled on that of a pharaoh. In viewing the Great Sphinx in the late 1700s, Count Constantine de Volney described it as "typically Negro in all its features" and concluded that "the ancient Egyptians were true Negroes of the same type as all native-born Africans" and that it was "this race of black men, today our slave . . . to which we owe our arts, sciences, and even the use of speech" (St. Clair Drake, "The Roles of Egypt and Ethiopia in Black History," *UCLA Center for Afro-American Studies Newsletter* 10, no. 1 [1987]:1, 8–10). This vision of history was common among blacks in the twentieth century. A writer for the Jamaican *Plain Talk* wrote in the 20 July 1935 issue that "the Ethiopians were the architects that laid the plans and measured the spaces and laid the foundations of the Pyramids of Egypt . . . and put the finishing touch on the face of the Sphinx" (Ken Post, *Arise Ye Starvelings: The Jamaica Labour Rebellion of 1938 and its Aftermath* [London: Marinus Nijhoff, 1978], p. 170]). An image of the sphinx was prominently featured in the center of the masthead of the *Negro World* (Frank M. Snowden, Jr., *Blacks in Antiquity: Ethiopians in the Greco-Roman Experience* [Cambridge, Mass.: Harvard University Press, 1970]; W. E. B. Du Bois, "Ethiopia and Egypt," in *The Negro* [1915; reprint, Millwood, N.Y.: Kraus-Thomason, 1975], pp. 30–46).

STEPHENSON, GEORGE (1781–1848), self-educated English inventor and railway engineer, built and patented the first locomotive with a steam blast in 1815.

STEVEDORE. See PAUL ROBESON.

STEWART, GABRIEL E., high chancellor of the UNIA in 1920–1922 and master of ceremonies at UNIA meetings in New York when Garvey was out of the country in 1921, was an adroit fund-raiser for the BLACK STAR LINE. He was a member of the UNIA delegation that met with President C. D. B. King of Liberia in New York in March 1921 and was a prominent presence at the UNIA convention in August 1921. He signed the UNIA petition to the League of Nations in July 1922 but had become privately disillusioned with Garvey and the UNIA by that time. He resigned gracefully after reading his report on UNIA finances to delegates in convention on 18 August 1922, restating his dedication to the ideals of the association but declining to hold further office. A Jamaican by birth, Stewart was a minister by profession before assuming his duties with the UNIA (*NW*, 12 March 1921; *Garvey Papers* 2–4).

SYRACUSE a seaport in Sicily, was founded in 734 B.C. by Greek colonists. Syracuse grew into a powerful city-state and cultural center. It thrived until the Second Punic War, when its capture became the object of campaigns by the Carthaginians and the Romans. It was besieged and sacked by the Romans in 212 B.C.

TEKEL is the English transcription of an Aramaic word included in the phrase "Mene, Mene, tekel upharsin," inscribed on the wall at the feast of BELSHAZZAR. It is literally a reference to a Babylonian unit of measure (a shekel, approximately 2.6 pounds). DANIEL interpreted the prophetic meaning of the term with a play on words, describing *tekel* as, "You have been weighed in the balances and found wanting" (Dan. 5:25–27; *DB*, pp. 564, 926).

TEMPLE OF APOLLO AT DELPHI was, according to legend, deemed the center of the earth by Zeus. Mottoes composed by seven wise men were carved in Greek on the walls of the temple's antechamber, including "Know thyself" and "Nothing in excess."

TERRY, WATT (1877–1961), a black business leader and philanthropist, worked as a Pullman porter in his early years before establishing a career in real estate. He was said to have arrived in Brockton, Mass., with fifteen cents, which he parlayed into over half a million dollars over the next ten years. He moved to Harlem in the 1920s and carried on a successful business there, financing scholarships for many students to attend TUSKEGEE INSTITUTE before suffering severe financial losses at the onset of the Depression (*NYT*, 26 April 1961; *WWCA*).

TEXTBOOKS, DEPICTION OF BLACKS IN. Authors of classroom texts used in the Progressive era tended to characterize blacks and immigrants as social problems, extending the racial stereotypes (slothfulness, infantilism, criminality) of their own era's Social Darwinism into paternalistic interpretations of the events of the past, especially to those of slavery and the politics of Reconstruction. Few 1920s textbooks mentioned the existence of blacks in American society following emancipation, and those that did often did so in a negative manner. It was not until the civil rights movement of the 1960s that black history was formally introduced into public school curricula. The depiction of blacks in school texts was an important issue to members of the Garvey movement and was raised at both the 1929 and 1934 UNIA conventions in Jamaica (*DG*, 15 August 1929; *BM* 1, no. 6 [November 1934]: 27; Walter White, *Anti-Negro Propaganda in School Textbooks* [New York: NAACP, 1939]; Frances Fitzgerald, *America Revisited: History Schoolbooks in the Twentieth Century* [Boston: Little, Brown & Co., 1979]; *Garvey Papers* 6).

THERMOPYLAE, a pass between the cliffs of Mount Oeta and the shoreline of Malic Gulf, was used strategically as an entrance into Greece by invaders in ancient times and was the scene of major battles against the Persians (480 B.C.) and the Gauls (279 B.C.).

THOMAS, one of the Twelve Apostles, is best known for his desire to see the risen Jesus before accepting the Resurrection (John 20: 24–29).

THOMAS, A. BENJAMIN, one of the signers of the 1920 UNIA Declaration of Rights, was an optometrist and leader of the Toronto division of the UNIA (*NW*, 7 May 1921; *Garvey Papers* 2).

THOMPSON, NOAH DAVIS (b. 1877), was a journalist, businessperson, and president of the Los Angeles division of the UNIA in 1920–

1921. Born in Baltimore and educated at Greggs Business College in Chicago, he was associated with BOOKER T. WASHINGTON at TUSKEGEE INSTITUTE before moving to California in 1911. He became a community leader in Los Angeles, where he was chairperson of the black Soldiers' and Sailors' Welfare Committee during WORLD WAR I, a leading contender for the first black seat on the city council in 1919, and a nominee of California governor Hiram Johnson for U.S. minister to Liberia. Thompson was the publisher of the *Liberator* (1912–1913), a contributor to the *Los Angeles Times*, and a writer and editor for the white-owned *Los Angeles Evening Express*. He was also much in demand as an eloquent speaker on race issues. He was elected president of the Los Angeles UNIA division soon after its organization in 1920–1921 and was its delegate to the 1921 UNIA convention in New York. He was a notable presence at the convention, where he spoke frequently from the floor and openly questioned Garvey and the BLACK STAR LINE's financial dealings. He lobbied for greater accountability to the local divisions on the part of the parent body and for greater decentralization of power within the movement. His outspokenness earned him a nomination for the office of assistant president general during the convention election proceedings. Thompson returned to Los Angeles after the convention and reported his negative view of the national leadership. A major schism in the local division ensued, including some heated exchanges between the faction allied with Thompson and the one following G. M. Smith, a local teacher loyal to Garvey, who demanded Thompson's resignation. In October 1921 Garvey dispatched E. L. Gaines to Los Angeles. Gaines supported Smith's minority faction, and summarily dismissed the pro-Thompson group from the division leadership. The charter of the Los Angeles division was then revoked by the parent body. Thompson's supporters denounced Gaines's visit and what they termed a malicious attack upon Thompson that appeared under Garvey's name in the 21 October 1921 edition of the *New Age* (Los Angeles). In the second week of November they established the rival Pacific Coast Negro Improvement Association (PCNIA), with Thompson as its president. Many PCNIA members were drawn back into a revived UNIA by Garvey's visit to Los Angeles in June 1922, when Garvey pointedly praised Thompson during one of his speeches. The PCNIA became closely affiliated with a local chapter of the FRIENDS OF NEGRO FREEDOM, and merged with the California Development Co., a black business venture headed by CHANDLER OWEN, in September 1923 (Emory J. Tolbert, *The UNIA and Black Los Angeles* [Los Angeles: Center for Afro-American Studies, University of California, Los Angeles, 1980], pp. 54, 58–59, 62–68; *Garvey Papers* 3).

THOMPSON, ORLANDO M. (b. 1879), was vice president of the BLACK STAR LINE in 1920–1922. Thompson was born in Barbados and immigrated to the United States in 1907, where he worked as an accountant. He was a bookkeeper for the Black Star Line before his election to the board of directors in July 1920, and he took charge of negotiations for the purchase of ships that could be used to make the passage between the United States and Africa. When negotiations for the S.S. *Hong Kheng* and the S.S. *Orion* were unsuccessful, Thompson was widely accused of fraud. In February 1922 he was indicted along with Garvey, ELIE GARCIA, and GEORGE TOBIAS on mail fraud charges in connection with the premature sale of stock for the yet-unpurchased *Orion*, which the UNIA had planned to rename the *Phyllis Wheatley* and use for its first transatlantic run. Thompson was acquitted in June 1923 (*MG* v. *U.S.*; *Garvey Papers* 2, 3).

TIMBUCTU, a city in Mali (formerly the French Sudan), West Africa, near the Niger River, was a major stop on the trans-Saharan trade route and a center of commerce and Muslim culture between the eleventh and sixteenth centuries.

TNT (trinitrotoluene), an explosive, first began to be used in artillery ammunition in WORLD WAR I and has since been employed in bombs, shells, mines, grenades, and torpedoes.

TOBIAS, GEORGE W. (b. 1888), was second vice president of the UNIA in 1918–1919 and treasurer of the UNIA, BLACK STAR LINE, and NEGRO FACTORIES CORP. in 1919–1922. He was born in Grenada and worked in the Panama Canal Zone as a clerk before immigrating to the United States in 1913. In 1918, the year he met Garvey, Tobias was employed in the shipping department of the Pennsylvania Railroad in New York. He was an editorial assistant with the *NEGRO WORLD* before being elected to UNIA office. He became one of the first directors of the Black Star Line in June 1919 and remained on the board of directors until he was indicted with Garvey, ORLANDO THOMPSON, and ELIE GARCIA on charges of mail fraud in February 1922. He was acquitted on the charges in June 1923 (*MG* v. *U.S.*; *Garvey Papers* 1, 2, 4).

TOBITT, RICHARD HILTON (b. 1873), an African Methodist Episcopal minister, was a delegate from Bermuda to the 1920 UNIA convention. He was born in Antigua, BWI. After graduating from Mico College in Jamaica, he went to Bermuda, where he became principal of St. George's High School and pastor of St. David's African Methodist Episcopal Church. He became a leader of the UNIA in Bermuda and subsequently suffered from political pressures as his UNIA affiliations brought him under surveillance by the British colonial police and forced his resignation as pastor. At the 1920 convention in New York he reported on repressive conditions in Bermuda, the lack of representative government, unjust treatment of blacks before the courts, the monopolization of industry and trade by whites, and his support for a black-owned shipping line that could handle the produce grown by unorganized black farmers. He also described his teaching methods, advocating the teaching of black history to young black students. He helped officiate at UNIA religious services and was elected leader of the Eastern Division of West Indian Negroes. Tobitt visited British Guiana (Guyana) in June 1921, at the same time Garvey was on his fund-raising tour of the Caribbean, and helped to organize new divisions there and sell stock in the BLACK STAR LINE. He also traveled to Trinidad but was prevented from landing by government officials. He immigrated to the United States and became a pastor at an African Methodist Episcopal church in New York City. At the 1921 convention he was convicted of duality of service and was reduced to a desk position in the office of the parent body. His office as West Indian leader was declared vacant, and he was soon replaced by RUDOLPH SMITH. Despite this setback, he stayed on in the UNIA and became high commissioner to British Guiana and South America and represented Barbados and Dominica, BWI, at the 1922 convention. He was made a knight commander of the Sublime Order of the Nile by Garvey in January 1924. He acted in the dual capacity of high commissioner and UNIA ambassador to England in February 1924, when Garvey sent him to London to seek interviews with British officials, including the colonial secretary and the prime minister. The British government declined to see Tobitt, but the London UNIA division greeted him enthusiastically. In the 1940s he became chaplain of the Pioneer Negroes of the World, a pro-Garvey group based in New York (*NW*, 5 April 1924; *Garvey Papers* 2–5).

TOOTE, FREDERICK AUGUSTUS (1895–1951?), was president of the Philadelphia UNIA division and a director of the BLACK STAR LINE. He was born in Nassau, Bahamas, and educated in Nassau and at the City College of New York and Philadelphia Divinity School. He was ordained by GEORGE ALEXANDER MCGUIRE as an African Orthodox church priest in April 1923. He rose within the UNIA in the early twenties, leading one of the largest local divisions. His theological career was also marked by early success. He became the editor of the African Orthodox church's organ, the *Negro Churchman*, in 1923, and dean of the Bishop Holly Theological School. His fortunes dipped in both fields, however, when he was removed from his African Orthodox church positions by September 1924 and also fell out of favor with Garvey. He reemerged as a leading figure in the UNIA after Garvey's imprisonment in 1925, when he revived the flagging membership of the Philadelphia division and reestablished his reputation with the UNIA president general. He was Garvey's choice as first assistant president general at the emergency convention called under Garvey's orders in March 1926, which elected a slate of officers loyal to Garvey and opposed to the leadership of WILLIAM SHERRILL, George Weston, and others in New York. Toote spoke at the convention and communicated its proceedings to Garvey by telegram. He continued to administer the affairs of the organization under Garvey's direction, organizing local conventions in August 1926 and handling the financial dealings, legal cases, and properties of the UNIA, including Liberty University. The leadership-by-proxy arrangement was not without its frictions, however. Toote offered his resignation to Garvey on several occasions, and his stormy tenure in office ended in 1926, when he resigned from his positions both in the New York division and the parent body of the UNIA. E. B. Knox was appointed as Toote's successor. Toote reemerged yet again as a central figure after Garvey's death in 1940. He delivered the eulogy at the main UNIA memorial service held in New York City at St. Mark's Methodist Episcopal Church on 21 July 1940 and was widely backed to succeed Garvey as president general, a post that eventually went to James Stewart (*NW,* 21 August 1920, 7 March 1925, 27 March, 31 July, 7 August, 14 August 1926, 6 August 1927; correspondence, Fred A. Toote and Marcus Garvey, 1926, Atlanta Federal Records Center, records of Atlanta penitentiary; memorial service announcement on Frederick A. Toote letterhead, 21 July 1940, Schomburg Center for Research in Black Culture, UNIA Central Division records, box 14, file 28; Ethel Collins to Amy Jacques Garvey, 30 July 1940, Fisk University, Amy Jacques Garvey papers, box 1, file 5; *Garvey Papers* 2).

TOURS is a town on the Loire River in central France, where the Moorish advance into French territory was stopped by the armies of Charles Martel at the battle of Tours in 732.

TRUTH, SOJOURNER (Isabella Baumfree) (1797–1883), a black American abolitionist and feminist, was born in New York and freed from slavery by the New York State Emancipation Act of 1827. Six feet tall, she was a powerful orator who drew huge crowds to antislavery and woman's rights meetings. During the Civil War she worked in Washington, D.C., hospitals and aided blacks fleeing from slavery to find employment and lodging (Victoria Ortiz, *Sojourner Truth: A Self-made Woman* [Philadelphia and New York: J. B. Lippincott, 1974; *Narrative of Sojourner Truth,* comp. by Olive Gilbert [1878; reprint, New York: Arno, 1968]).

TUSKEGEE INSTITUTE was founded by BOOKER T. WASHINGTON in Tuskegee, Ala. Based on the Hampton model of industrial education, the school was opened in temporary quarters in the African Methodist Episcopal Zion Church on 4 July 1881. The majority of the first students who enrolled were already teachers in public schools. The school was soon moved to a farm on the outskirts of Tuskegee, where Washington began his pragmatic program of combining academic training with manual labor and the learning of trades. Graduates of Hampton Institute, Hampton, Va., and Fisk University, Nashville, were invited to form the faculty of the school, and Olivia A. Davidson became its first assistant principal and a driving force in securing funding from northern philanthropists. Washington married Davidson after the death of his first wife, Hampton graduate Fanny Smith, in 1884; when Davidson died in 1889, her post as lady principal was given to former Fisk teacher Margaret Murray. Murray in turn became Washington's wife in 1892. By 1900 Tuskegee had become a recognized model for black education (Louis R. Harlan, *Booker T. Washington: The Making of a Black Leader, 1856–1901* [London and New York: Oxford University Press, 1972]; Booker T. Washington, *Up from Slavery* [1901; reprint, Garden City, N.Y.: Doubleday, 1963]; *Garvey Papers* 1).

TUTANKUMEN (Tutankhamen) was a young king of Egypt's eighteenth dynasty, ca. 1350 B.C. In 1922 his tomb, which contained a wealth of magnificent artifacts, was discovered in the Valley of the Tombs near Luxor by a British archaeological team headed by Howard Carter and largely funded by GEORGE EDWARD STANHOPE MOLYNEUX, the earl of Carnarvon. Garvey often referred to Tutankhamen as black, and a 1924 advertisement in the *NEGRO WORLD* advanced the idea that "King

Tut was a Negro by blood." The subject of whether King Tut was black formed the basis of several articles in the *Negro World* in the early twenties. Scenes from wall paintings in the tomb of Kemsit, a princess of the eighteenth dynasty, depict other members of Egyptian royalty of the period as black (*Times* [London], 20 November and 1 December 1922; *NW,* 24 March and 6 September 1924; *BM* 1, no. 10 [late October 1935]: 14; St. Clair Drake, "The Roles of Egypt and Ethiopia in Black History," *UCLA Center for Afro-American Studies Newsletter* 10, no. 1 [1987]: 1, 8–10; Howard Carter, *The Tomb of Tutankhamen,* 3 vols. [1923–1933; reprint, New York: Cooper Square Publishers, 1963]).

UNIA. See UNIVERSAL NEGRO IMPROVEMENT ASSOCIATION.

UNITED FRUIT CO., an American-owned company founded in 1899, wielded great economic and political power in the Caribbean and banana-growing areas of Central America.   United Fruit officials were concerned with blocking UNIA efforts to organize among black laborers who worked in areas controlled by their company. In May 1929 the United Fruit Co. was the focus of a longshoremen's strike in Jamaica, a precursor to the more massive general strike of 1938. Garvey played a conciliatory role in the 1929 protest. He urged the laborers to return to work but encouraged them to organize a union for greater effectiveness in placing demands upon the company. He also met with J. G. Keifer, the company's top manager in Jamaica. While he criticized the company's dealings with its black work force, he nonetheless assured Keifer of his own faith in its operations (*Bm,* 10 May, 28 May, and 29 May 1929; *DW,* 27 September 1929; *NW,* 7 June 1930; *Garvey Papers* 2).

UNITED STATES SHIPPING BOARD (USSB), a federal regulatory and quasi-judicial body, was established by the Shipping Act of 7 September 1916, in order to facilitate the development of a merchant marine and a naval reserve to meet the needs of U.S. commercial ventures, and to lease and regulate U.S. ships engaged in international and interstate commerce. After WORLD WAR I, the board was also responsible for the disposition of German ships interned by the British and U.S. governments during the war. The BLACK STAR LINE had extensive dealings regularly with the USSB during its many negotiations regarding the purchase, registration, and payment for ships (*Garvey Papers* 2–4).

UNITED STATES v. MARCUS GARVEY. Garvey was indicted by a federal grand jury of the U.S. District Court for the Southern District of New York on 15 February 1922 for violation of U.S. Criminal Code Section 215 (using the mails to defraud). ELIE GARCIA, GEORGE TOBIAS, and ORLANDO THOMPSON were named as codefendants in the case. After a series of postponements, the trial began on 18 May 1923, with Judge JULIAN MACK presiding and Assistant U.S. District Attorney MAXWELL S. MATTUCK as the government's prosecutor. Early in the trial Garvey dismissed his lawyer, Cornelius McDougald, and acted as his own defense attorney, with some support late in the trial from Armin Kohn. The trial ended on 21 June 1923, with Garvey found guilty on one of four counts and sentenced to a $1,000 fine and five years' imprisonment. Garvey was removed to the Tombs Prison in

New York until 10 September 1923, when bail was paid for his release pending an appeal. On 2 February 1925 Garvey's conviction was upheld by the U.S. Circuit Court of Appeals, with Judge Charles M. Hough presiding. Garvey was arrested by federal marshals in New York City on 5 February 1925 and removed to the federal penitentiary at Atlanta on 7–8 February 1925. He remained incarcerated there until President CALVIN COOLIDGE commuted his sentence on 18 November 1927. On 2 December 1927 he was deported from the United States under a 1917 immigration statute mandating the deportation of alien residents convicted of crimes involving moral turpitude. Efforts to win an official pardon for Garvey continued throughout his lifetime and to the present day (*MG* v. *U.S.*; *Garvey Papers* 4–6).

UNIVERSAL NEGRO IMPROVEMENT ASSOCIATION (UNIA) was founded by Marcus Garvey in Kingston, Jamaica, 20 July 1914 (see also AFRICAN COMMUNITIES LEAGUE). It was originally conceived as a benevolent or fraternal reform association dedicated to racial uplift and the establishment of educational and industrial opportunities for blacks. A chapter of the membership organization was founded in Harlem in 1917 and soon became the headquarters of the movement. The UNIA, Inc., was officially incorporated in New York on 17 June 1918. By the mid-1920s nearly a thousand local divisions had been established in the United States, the Caribbean, Central America, Canada, and abroad. Membership in the organization declined after Garvey's incarceration, and his deportation in 1925–1927 increased the factionalization within the movement. A new UNIA and ACL (August 1929) of the World, over which Garvey presided, was incorporated at the 1929 UNIA convention in Kingston. It was distinguished from the rival UNIA, Inc., in New York, headed by FRED A. TOOTE in 1929, and by LIONEL FRANCIS in 1931. Part of the American-based movement remained loyal to Garvey, notably the Garvey Club and the Tiger Division of New York. In 1935 Garvey moved his headquarters to London. After his death in 1940, Garveyite loyalists elected a new slate of officers in New York, and the headquarters of the parent body was moved to Cleveland under the direction of the new president general, James Stewart, who eventually relocated to Monrovia, Liberia. While the movement waned in the 1940s and 1950s, remnants of the UNIA still exist, split between two rival groups, both claiming authority as the true UNIA. Thomas Harvey, WILLIAM SHERRILL, and others led one wing, centered in Philadelphia, in the 1950s; it is headed today by School of African Philosophy graduate Charles L. James. The other wing of the movement, an outgrowth of Stewart's administration in Cleveland, is headed by Mason Hargrave (*Garvey's Voice,* January 1956; *Garvey's Voice Bulletin,* June 1965; UNIA collection, Western Reserve Historical Society, Cleveland; Mason Hargrave collection, Cleveland; *Garvey Papers* 1).

UNIA, CONSTITUTION AND BYLAWS OF, were written in July 1918 and revised in convention in August 1920, 1921, and 1922. The preamble of the constitution defined the UNIA as "a social, friendly, humanitarian, charitable, educational, institutional, constructive, and expansive society" founded to "work for the general uplift of the Negro peoples of the world." The constitution went on to define the titles and duties of UNIA officers, the jurisdiction of the parent body over local divisions, rules regarding salaries and revenues, and the definition of "all persons of Negro blood and African descent" as "ordinary members" in the organization, with "those who pay the monthly dues" designated as "active members." The general laws of the UNIA covered such subjects as the rules for conventions, the granting of charters to local divisions and the functions of local officers, the payment of death grants, the official colors (red, black, and green), and the handling of stocks, ending with the designation of music and prayers to be used in the opening of each UNIA meeting. Article 5, section 3, of the original 1918 constitution read: "No one shall be received by the Potentate and his Consort who has been convicted of crime or felony." In 1920 the article was amended to read, ". . . except such crime or felony was committed in the interests of the UNIA" (*Garvey Papers* 1–4).

UNIA, FIRST EXECUTIVE COUNCIL OF, in the United States. The members of the UNIA executive council in November 1917 were: ISSAC B. ALLEN, president Marcus Garvey, international organizer; WALTER CONWAY, first vice president; C. C. Seifert, second vice president; SAMUEL A. DUNCAN, third vice president; EDWARD D. SMITH-GREEN, general secretary; BEN BURRELL, associate secretary; Serena Danridge, secretary; Isaac Samuel Bright, treasurer; IRENA MOORMAN-BLACKSTON, ladies' president; Eva Curtis, ladies' first vice president; Lizzie Sims, ladies' second vice president; Ethel Oughton-Clarke, general secretary of Ladies' Division; CARRIE MERO LEADETT, associate secretary of Ladies' Division; and John E. Bruce, chairman of the advisory board. The council was reorganized in February 1918 (*Garvey Papers* 1).

UNIA, FIRST INTERNATIONAL CONVENTION OF, opened in LIBERTY HALL, New York, on 1 August 1920. The convention met in regular sessions throughout the month and closed with ceremonies and festivities on 31 August 1920. Huge parades were held through Harlem, including one on 3 August that featured UNIA officers in full regalia, the BLACK STAR LINE band and choir, the African Legion (see AFRICAN GUARDS), the UNIA band, the BLACK CROSS NURSES, contingents of delegates from the United States, Canada, the Caribbean, Central America, and West Africa, various divisional bands, and the UNIA MOTOR CORPS. The parade was followed by an exuberant mass meeting at MADISON SQUARE GARDEN, which was filled to capacity. Garvey estimated the attendence at twenty-five thousand (*Garvey Papers* 2).

VANITY FAIR is a satirical novel (1848) by William Makepeace Thackeray (1811–1863), English novelist, poet, illustrator, and journalist. It was first published in twenty-four installments beginning in 1846 and ending in 1848. The title is also a reference to the allegorical town in John Bunyan's *Pilgrim's Progress* (1678). In Bunyan's work Christian and Faithful, travelers to the Celestial City, are waylaid by the merchants of Vanity Fair. After suffering imprisonment, the two men are tried and Faithful is tortured to death, whereupon his mutilated body is swept up into heaven by a horse-drawn chariot. Christian escapes and continues on his pilgrimage, accompanied by Hopeful, who rises out of Faithful's ashes (William Makepeace Thackeray, *Vanity Fair* [New York: Dodd, Mead & Co., 1943], p. 7; John Bunyan, *Pilgrim's Progress: From This World to That Which Is to Come* [London: James Nisbet & Co., 1860]).

VANN, ROBERT L. (1879–1940), prominent black journalist and publisher, was editor of the influential *Pittsburgh Courier* for nearly thirty years. Vann graduated from the University of Pittsburgh and was one of five blacks practicing law in Pittsburgh before he became the editor of the *Courier* in 1914. The newspaper was the best-selling black weekly in the United States by the late 1920s. George Schuyler, Joel Rogers, Julia Bumbrey Jones, and others were featured writers for the paper in the mid-twenties. Vann also produced a monthly, the *Competitor*, in 1920–1922. His wife, Jesse Matthews Vann, continued to operate the *Courier* after his death. It reached the peak of its circulation in 1947 (Andrew Buni, *Robert L. Vann of the Pittsburgh Courier: Politics and Black Journalism* [Pittsburgh: University of Pittsburgh Press, 1974]).

VAN PUTTEN, PHILIP, of SANTO DOMINGO, was a delegate to the 1920 UNIA convention. He reported on the foreign control of capital in his country, the low rates of pay for black labor, and the reduction of an attitude of "Anglomania" among blacks (*Garvey Papers* 2: 531–532). He signed the UNIA Declaration of Rights. Van Putten participated at a conference at LIBERTY HALL in April 1921 and was a delegate to the 1921 and 1922 UNIA conventions (*Garvey Papers* 2–4).

VERDUN, a commercial center on the Meuse River in northeastern France, was the site of the longest battle of WORLD WAR I, fought there from February to December 1916. A major German offensive was repelled by American and French troops (including French West African and black American soldiers) in the Verdun sector in 1918.

WALKER, MME C. J. (1869–1919), a multimillionaire cosmetics entrepreneur and patron of black schools and the arts, was born Sarah Breedlove in Louisiana. In the 1890s she began to sell a hair-straightening preparation, which she manufactured herself, door-to-door in Denver. She expanded the business in the early 1900s, trained other women to open franchises in her name, and eventually opened Walker schools and Walker beauty parlors across the country. In 1910 she moved her headquarters to Indianapolis and added a complete line of cosmetics to her products, including a skin-lightening cream called Tan-Off. Although the *NEGRO WORLD* carried advertisements for Walker's products, their emphasis on a Caucasian standard of beauty caused a rift between Walker and Garvey (*NYAN*, 6 July 1940). There were strong ties between Walker's company and the Garvey movement. The *Amsterdam News* reported that Walker "gave Garvey frequent donations" and "contributed the funds with which he started the Negro World and acquired what was later to be known as Liberty Hall" (6 July 1940). The fact that Walker was a UNIA supporter and made "donations to our cause" was confirmed by AMY ASHWOOD Garvey in her memoirs. When the purchase of the Liberty University property was announced at a New York meeting of the UNIA, F. B. Ransom, the manager and attorney of the Mme Walker Co., delivered the address on the viability of black-owned and black-supported enterprises (*NW,* 24 July 1926). In 1929 the Walker company convention was held in Jamaica at the same time as the UNIA convention, and a Walker representative, Marjorie Stewart Joyner, performed a recitation at Garvey's birthday celebration at Edelweiss Park (*NW,* 24 August and 7 September 1929). By 1938 Joyner had become the president of the Walker company and was also active as a speaker for the ladies' auxiliary of the New York Garvey Club (*NYT,* 26 May 1919; *PC,* 6 December 1924; *NW,* 13 December 1924, 21 February 1925, 6 January 1926; *Norfolk Journal and Guide,* 8 August 1925; Garvey Club announcement, 17 April 1938, Schomburg Center for the Study of Black Culture, New York, Records of the UNIA Central Division; James Weldon Johnson, *Black Manhattan* [1930; reprint, New York: Atheneum, 1969], p. 283; Claude McKay, *Home to Harlem* [New York: Harper and Brothers, 1928], p. 273).

WALKER, MAGGIE LENA (1867–1934), became executive secretary of the Independent Order of St. Luke in 1889 and secretary treasurer in 1899. Under her leadership the order moved beyond its initial purpose as a benefit society (to which members paid small dues to provide against disability and funeral expenses) to a full-scale financial and social institution with self-help goals similar to those of the UNIA. Walker offered members investment counseling and opened the St. Luke Bank and Trust Co., a savings institution that helped administer utility and tax payments and granted loans, encouraging black people "to own their homes, and to win their way to independence" (Benjamin Brawley, "Maggie L. Walker and Her Enterprise," in *Negro Builders and Heroes* [Chapel Hill: University of North Carolina Press, 1937], pp. 267–272). Like the UNIA, Walker's order held annual conventions, had over one hundred field workers and organizers, a newspaper, the *St. Luke Herald,* a women's division, and some 15,000 youths enrolled in local thrift clubs. In 1925 Walker's organization had some 103,000 dues-paying members and assets of over $2 million, including a $100,000 headquarters in Virginia. Walker was president of the National Association of Colored Women and organizer of the Council for Women, an interracial organization that raised grant money for women involved in community service and funded homes for black working women and delinquent girls. She also served on the board of directors of the NAACP and the Urban League (*Norfolk Journal and Guide,* 29 August 1925; Harry A. Ploski and Roscoe C. Brown, Jr., comps. and eds., *Negro Almanac* [New York: Bellwether Publishing Co., 1967], p. 770; *DANB*).

WALLACE, WILLIAM A. (1867–1946), was president of the Chicago division in the twenties and secretary general of the UNIA in 1926. Wallace was born in Port Deposit, Md., and attended Lincoln University in Pennsylvania. He operated a bakery in Chicago from 1904 to 1924. He represented Chicago at the 1920, 1921, and 1922 UNIA conventions

and the UNIA conference at LIBERTY HALL in April 1921. He was
nominated for the position of secretary general during the August 1921
election proceedings. He participated at the emergency conference
called in Detroit in March 1926 and was elected secretary general of
the national body after being recommended for the post by FRED
A. TOOTE. Garvey appointed Wallace UNIA high commissioner for
the states of Missouri, Kansas, and Illinois in January 1928. In the
early thirties he began a career as a county worker, beginning at
the Cook County Recorder's Office and holding a series of positions
in the ensuing years. He was elected to the state senate from the
Third District of Illinois in 1938 (*NW*, 27 March 1926, 21 January 1928;
Fred A. Toote to Marcus Garvey, 16 March 1926, Atlanta Federal
Records Center, records of Atlanta penitentiary; *Who's Who in
Chicago and Illinois* [Chicago: A. N. Marquis Co., 1945], p. 867; *Garvey
Papers* 3–6).

WANAMAKER, JOHN (1838–1922), one of the "self-made" men Garvey
admired, was a Philadelphia entrepreneur who built a small dry goods
shop into a lucrative department store conglomerate with branches in
Philadelphia and New York. Wanamaker was president of the Young
Men's Christian Association (1870–1883) and U.S. postmaster general
in the Harrison administration (1889–1893).

WARE, WILLIAM (b. 1872), was president of the Cincinnati division of
the UNIA. He was born in Lexington, Ky., and had organized
the Welfare Association for Colored People (WACP) in Cincinnati
before he attended the 1920 UNIA convention. He returned to
Cincinnati after the convention and reorganized the WACP as a
division of the UNIA, reportedly building its membership to nearly
eight thousand in the following years. He was a delegate to the
1921, 1922, and 1924 UNIA conventions and a member of the UNIA
Committee of Presidents in 1925. He was a candidate for speaker
at the pro-Garvey emergency convention called in Detroit in March
1926. Garvey appointed him UNIA high commissioner for Ohio,
Indiana, and Kentucky in January 1928. After the split between the
American-based and Jamaican-based wings of the movement at the 1929
UNIA convention in Kingston, Ware refused to affiliate the Cincinnati
division with the pro-Garvey UNIA (August 1929) of the World. While
praising Garvey as an individual, Ware unsuccessfully pressed charges
against seventeen people who started a new Cincinnati division in
affiliation with Garvey's Jamaica-based group. Garvey responded by
disavowing Ware in the pages of the *NEGRO WORLD* and endorsing the
rival division headed by R. H. Bachelor. In 1931 Ware wrote a series
of letters reporting alleged fraudulent activities of Garvey to the U.S.
attorney general's office, the U.S. State Department, and the Office
of the Postmaster General (*NW*, 27 March 1926, 21 January 1928, 21
June, 8 November, and 6 December 1930, 14 April 1931; William Ware
to U.S. Attorney General's Office, 2 February 1931, National Archives,
Washington, D.C., record group 59, Department of State; Wendell P.
Dabney, *Cincinnati's Colored Citizens* [Cincinnati: Dabney Publishing,
1926], pp. 213–214; *WWCA*; *Garvey Papers* 2, 3, 5, 6).

WARNER, RICHARD E. (b. 1883), was one of the initial directors of the BLACK STAR LINE and a signer of the certificate of incorporation. A professional journalist, he was the managing editor of the *New York News* before he was introduced to Garvey by EDGAR M. GREY in the summer of 1919, when he joined the UNIA. He was elected executive secretary of the UNIA the same night he became a member and a few weeks later became secretary for the shipping line. He served in that capacity for one month before resigning, accusing Garvey of misappropriating funds raised through the sale of Black Star Line stock. Garvey accused Warner and Grey of colluding with Assistant District Attorney EDWIN P. KILROE to "frame up Mr. Garvey" (*NW*, 2 August 1919). Warner became a Prohibition agent for the Internal Revenue Service in 1921. He was dismissed from that position in 1927 after being indicted for fraud in connection with collecting money from prohibition violators (*MG* v. *U.S.*, pp. 144–184; *Garvey Papers* 1).

WASHINGTON, BOOKER T. (1856–1915), was one of the most powerful black men of turn-of-the-century America, a leader in black education and a strong influence as a racial representative in national politics. He was born a slave in Hale's Ford, Va., the son of a white man who did not acknowledge him and a slave woman named Jane (Burroughs), who later married a fellow slave named Washington (Ferguson). He learned to read and write in the late 1860s at a primary school overseen by the Freedmen's Bureau and in 1872 became a student at the Hampton Institute, Hampton, Va., where he excelled. He was teaching at Hampton in 1881 when he was invited to become the first principal of the newly founded TUSKEGEE INSTITUTE in Tuskegee, Ala. Washington built a political machine through Tuskegee based on the financial backing of a coalition of northern financiers, members of the white southern elite, and conservatives attracted by his accommodationist rhetoric and his championing of the principle of self-help. His admirers included THEODORE ROOSEVELT, who invited him to dine at the White House in 1901 and consulted him as an advisor on racial issues and southern political patronage. The self-made man image created in Washington's 1901 autobiography and the philosophies of economic self-sufficiency and social segregation epitomized in the Tuskegee curriculum and in Washington's famous 1895 Atlanta address were inspirations to Garvey. Garvey contacted Washington in 1914–1915 and planned to meet with him to discuss the formation of a school in Jamaica based on the Tuskegee model; however, Washington died in November 1915, four months before Garvey arrived in the United States (Louis R. Harlan, *Booker T. Washington: The Making of a Black Leader, 1856–1901* [London, Oxford, and New York: Oxford University Press, 1972]; Louis R. Harlan and Raymond W. Smock, eds., *The Booker T. Washington Papers,* 13 vols. [Urbana: University of Illinois Press, 1972–1984]; Booker T. Washington, *Up from Slavery: An Autobiography* [1901; reprint, Garden City, N.Y.: Doubleday & Co., 1963]; *Garvey Papers* 1).

WATKIS, HARRY R. (often incorrectly referred to as Harry "Watkins"), was a BLACK STAR LINE stock salesman and traveling secretary of the UNIA from February through October 1920. Watkis was born in

Jamaica and was a young schoolmate of Garvey. He immigrated to the United States in 1902 and passed the bar examination in Missouri. He was a delegate to the August 1920 UNIA convention and signed the UNIA Declaration of Rights. A few months later, while selling stock, he was arrested in Youngstown, Ohio and charged with fraud. After spending the night in jail, he used UNIA money to deposit bond and did not return for prosecution. He resigned from the UNIA soon after this experience, and quarreled with AMY JACQUES Garvey. He subsequently sued the UNIA for back salary, claiming that no salary had been paid him in Youngstown or elsewhere. Watkis appeared as a prosecution witness at Garvey's 1923 mail fraud trial (*MG* v. *U.S.*, pp. 783–833; *Garvey Papers* 2).

WHITE, ELINOR ROBINSON, of Robbins, Ill., a suburb of Chicago, was a Garvey loyalist and a member of the first graduating class of the School of African Philosophy. She was a leader in gathering money for a Garvey defense fund in Chicago in 1925 and was the secretary of the Chicago division of the Garvey Club in the late 1920s and early 1930s. White was a delegate to the 1929 and 1934 UNIA conventions in Kingston, Jamaica. At the 1934 meeting she introduced a measure from the convention floor opposing birth control, and Garvey spoke in support of the resolution. She also attended the 1937 and 1938 conferences in Toronto and was among those personally chosen and instructed by Garvey in the School of African Philosophy in September 1937. White was appointed UNIA commissioner for the state of Illinois at the end of the month-long course. She remained active in the movement for more than twenty years after Garvey's death. She was a delegate to the UNIA national conference held at Liberty Farm, Oregonia, Ohio, in 1947 and was still organizing for the Chicago division in 1961. White served as an unofficial archivist of Garvey's writings, saving and transcribing old copies of the *NEGRO WORLD* and the *BLACK MAN*. She edited pamphlets of his writings, including *Excerpts of the Late Marcus Garvey* (Robbins, Ill., n.d.), *My People: History-Making Speeches by Marcus Garvey* (Robbins, Ill., 1958), and *A Dialogue: What's the Difference?* (n.d.), which she edited with William Davis. She corresponded with AMY JACQUES Garvey, who sent her African newspapers and copies of the *BLACKMAN*. White worked with N. H. Grissom as comanager of a dry goods business at 620 East 43rd Street in Chicago and was involved in community affairs. A devout Christian, she also compiled collections of conduct-of-life and biblical quotations, *A Book of Wisdom and Knowledge* (1956), and *The Book of Knowledge and Character Education* (1962). She also collected folktales, allegorical stories, and jokes. A prolific speaker for UNIA programs, she kept notebooks of proverbs and notes for topics of speeches on such themes as "Success," "Character," and the status of women (*NW,* 21 February 1931; *DG,* 9 August and 31 August 1934; *BM* 2, no. 8 [December 1937], pp. 4–5; Alex Nixon, El[i]nor White, and Bettie Lambert to Marcus Garvey, 23 December 1925, Atlanta Federal Records Center, records of Atlanta Penitentiary; printed pamphlets, n.d.; dry goods sale announcement, n.d.; Amy Jacques Garvey to

Elinor White, 24 June 1950, Elinor Robins[...]
Garvey Papers 6).

WHITING, NELLIE GRANT, of Newport N[...]
the 1920 UNIA convention. She r[...]
residential segregation in Newport N[...]
commercial establishments in black neigh[...]
the conciliatory attitudes of black small-bus[...]
and the assistance of preachers in the suppressio[...]
of the UNIA. Whiting signed the UNIA Declaration [...]
Papers 2).

WILCOX, ELLA WHEELER (1850–1919), was a prolific sentime[...]
whose poems exemplify the pious influences of romantic and Vic[...]
thought. Garvey was fond of her work. Her favorite themes include[...]
motherhood, purity, the primacy of the heart, unrequited love, illness
and death, and the innocence of childhood. She also captured some
of the spirit of modern progressivism and reform in her later poems,
which addressed the issues of temperance, women's roles, capital
punishment, and disarmament, as well as two of Garvey's favorite
themes, the ethic of success and the evolution of the black race out of
bondage. Wilcox wrote a daily poem for a syndicate of newspapers
and published over twenty collections of verse. Like Garvey, she
viewed the issue of race within the context of a cyclical "course of
empire" vision of history and professed a faith in progress away from
victimization toward a state of knowledge and self-reliance. Her poem
"The Problem" exhibits these themes as well as a nineteenth-century
brand of paternalism. The poem begins: "Out of the wilderness, out of
the night / Has the black man crawled to the dawn of light / Beaten by
lashes and bound by chains / A beast of burden, with soul and brains; /
He has come thro' sorrow and need and woe, / And the cry of his
heart is to know, to know" (Alonzo Potter Burgess Holly, *God and the
Negro: Synopsis of God and the Negro; or, The Biblical Record of the Race
of Man* [Nashville: National Baptist Publishing Board, 1937], p. 14;
Ada Patterson, "Ella Wheeler Wilcox as I Knew Her," *The New Success*
3, no. 8 [August 1919]: 25–26, 49–53; Virginia Woolf, "Wilcoxiana,"
in *Women and Writing,* ed. Michele Barrett, [New York: Harcourt
Brace Jovanovich, 1979], pp. 173–179; Ella Wheeler Wilcox, *Poems of
Pleasure* [Chicago: W. B. Conkey Co., 1897]; Wilcox, *Poems of Progress*
[Chicago: W. B. Conkey Co., 1909]).

WILKINS, JOHN THOMAS, a pastor, was executive secretary of the UNIA in
New York in 1918–1919. He attended the 1920 UNIA convention and
signed the UNIA Declaration of Rights (*NW,* 1 February and 5 April
1919; *Garvey Papers* 1).

WILLIAM THE CONQUEROR (William I) (1027–1087), of Normandy, was
king of England from 1066 until his death.

WILLIAMS, ARTHUR (b. 1881), a chiropractor, was active in the UNIA in
Seattle. He was born in Magnolia, Miss., and attended the Columbia
Institute of Chiropodists in New York. He moved to Seattle in 1908.
He was a delegate to the 1920 UNIA convention and signed the
declaration of rights (*Who's Who in Religious, Fraternal, Social, Civic,*

WINCHESTER RIFLE was a breech-loadin[...]
Winchester Repeating Arms Co[...]
shot breechloaders and muzzle-[...]
the Civil War. The point [...]
Philosophy was supporte[...]
advocating the repeate[...]
troops. Winchester [...]
his invention. He[...]
science of wa[...]
unknown e[...]
Winchest[...]
pp. 9[...]
WOLFE[...]

Jamaica and was a young schoolmate of Garvey. He immigrated to
the United States in 1902 and passed the bar examination in Missouri.
He was a delegate to the August 1920 UNIA convention and signed
the UNIA Declaration of Rights. A few months later, while selling
stock, he was arrested in Youngstown, Ohio and charged with fraud.
After spending the night in jail, he used UNIA money to deposit bond
and did not return for prosecution. He resigned from the UNIA soon
after this experience, and quarreled with AMY JACQUES Garvey. He
subsequently sued the UNIA for back salary, claiming that no salary
had been paid him in Youngstown or elsewhere. Watkis appeared as a
prosecution witness at Garvey's 1923 mail fraud trial (*MG* v. *U.S.*, pp.
783–833; *Garvey Papers* 2).

WHITE, ELINOR ROBINSON, of Robbins, Ill., a suburb of Chicago, was
a Garvey loyalist and a member of the first graduating class of the
School of African Philosophy. She was a leader in gathering money
for a Garvey defense fund in Chicago in 1925 and was the secretary of
the Chicago division of the Garvey Club in the late 1920s and early
1930s. White was a delegate to the 1929 and 1934 UNIA conventions
in Kingston, Jamaica. At the 1934 meeting she introduced a measure
from the convention floor opposing birth control, and Garvey spoke
in support of the resolution. She also attended the 1937 and 1938
conferences in Toronto and was among those personally chosen and
instructed by Garvey in the School of African Philosophy in September
1937. White was appointed UNIA commissioner for the state of Illinois
at the end of the month-long course. She remained active in the
movement for more than twenty years after Garvey's death. She was
a delegate to the UNIA national conference held at Liberty Farm,
Oregonia, Ohio, in 1947 and was still organizing for the Chicago
division in 1961. White served as an unofficial archivist of Garvey's
writings, saving and transcribing old copies of the *NEGRO WORLD*
and the *BLACK MAN*. She edited pamphlets of his writings, including
Excerpts of the Late Marcus Garvey (Robbins, Ill., n.d.), *My People:
History-Making Speeches by Marcus Garvey* (Robbins, Ill., 1958), and *A
Dialogue: What's the Difference?* (n.d.), which she edited with William
Davis. She corresponded with AMY JACQUES Garvey, who sent her
African newspapers and copies of the *BLACKMAN*. White worked with
N. H. Grissom as comanager of a dry goods business at 620 East 43rd
Street in Chicago and was involved in community affairs. A devout
Christian, she also compiled collections of conduct-of-life and biblical
quotations, *A Book of Wisdom and Knowledge* (1956), and *The Book of
Knowledge and Character Education* (1962). She also collected folktales,
allegorical stories, and jokes. A prolific speaker for UNIA programs,
she kept notebooks of proverbs and notes for topics of speeches on
such themes as "Success," "Character," and the status of women
(*NW*, 21 February 1931; *DG*, 9 August and 31 August 1934; *BM* 2,
no. 8 [December 1937], pp. 4–5; Alex Nixon, El[i]nor White, and
Bettie Lambert to Marcus Garvey, 23 December 1925, Atlanta Federal
Records Center, records of Atlanta Penitentiary; printed pamphlets,
n.d.; dry goods sale announcement, n.d.; Amy Jacques Garvey to

Elinor White, 24 June 1950, Elinor Robinson White papers, Chicago; *Garvey Papers* 6).

WHITING, NELLIE GRANT, of Newport News, Va., was a delegate to the 1920 UNIA convention. She reported to the convention on residential segregation in Newport News and the white ownership of commercial establishments in black neighborhoods. She also addressed the conciliatory attitudes of black small-business people and preachers and the assistance of preachers in the suppression of the local division of the UNIA. Whiting signed the UNIA Declaration of Rights (*Garvey Papers* 2).

WILCOX, ELLA WHEELER (1850–1919), was a prolific sentimental poet whose poems exemplify the pious influences of romantic and Victorian thought. Garvey was fond of her work. Her favorite themes included motherhood, purity, the primacy of the heart, unrequited love, illness and death, and the innocence of childhood. She also captured some of the spirit of modern progressivism and reform in her later poems, which addressed the issues of temperance, women's roles, capital punishment, and disarmament, as well as two of Garvey's favorite themes, the ethic of success and the evolution of the black race out of bondage. Wilcox wrote a daily poem for a syndicate of newspapers and published over twenty collections of verse. Like Garvey, she viewed the issue of race within the context of a cyclical "course of empire" vision of history and professed a faith in progress away from victimization toward a state of knowledge and self-reliance. Her poem "The Problem" exhibits these themes as well as a nineteenth-century brand of paternalism. The poem begins: "Out of the wilderness, out of the night / Has the black man crawled to the dawn of light / Beaten by lashes and bound by chains / A beast of burden, with soul and brains; / He has come thro' sorrow and need and woe, / And the cry of his heart is to know, to know" (Alonzo Potter Burgess Holly, *God and the Negro: Synopsis of God and the Negro; or, The Biblical Record of the Race of Man* [Nashville: National Baptist Publishing Board, 1937], p. 14; Ada Patterson, "Ella Wheeler Wilcox as I Knew Her," *The New Success* 3, no. 8 [August 1919]: 25–26, 49–53; Virginia Woolf, "Wilcoxiana," in *Women and Writing*, ed. Michele Barrett, [New York: Harcourt Brace Jovanovich, 1979], pp. 173–179; Ella Wheeler Wilcox, *Poems of Pleasure* [Chicago: W. B. Conkey Co., 1897]; Wilcox, *Poems of Progress* [Chicago: W. B. Conkey Co., 1909]).

WILKINS, JOHN THOMAS, a pastor, was executive secretary of the UNIA in New York in 1918–1919. He attended the 1920 UNIA convention and signed the UNIA Declaration of Rights (*NW*, 1 February and 5 April 1919; *Garvey Papers* 1).

WILLIAM THE CONQUEROR (William I) (1027–1087), of Normandy, was king of England from 1066 until his death.

WILLIAMS, ARTHUR (b. 1881), a chiropractor, was active in the UNIA in Seattle. He was born in Magnolia, Miss., and attended the Columbia Institute of Chiropodists in New York. He moved to Seattle in 1908. He was a delegate to the 1920 UNIA convention and signed the declaration of rights (*Who's Who in Religious, Fraternal, Social, Civic, and Commercial Life on the Pacific Coast, 1926–1927* [Seattle: Searchlight Publishing Co., 1927], p. 211; *Garvey Papers* 2).

WILLIAMS, SHEDRICK, was president of the Cleveland division in 1921. He was a delegate to the 1920 UNIA convention, and he addressed the issue of Jewish-black relations in his report, stating that he had found Jews in Cleveland supportive of blacks in the area of employment. He signed the UNIA Declaration of Rights. Garvey praised Williams's work in Cleveland at a February 1921 meeting, saying that Williams had increased the membership by some twenty-five hundred members and had purchased a LIBERTY HALL for use by the division. Williams was a delegate to the 1921 and 1922 UNIA conventions (*NW,* 19 February 1921; *Garvey Papers* 2, 3).

WILLIAMS, VERNAL J. (1896–1952), an attorney, was a UNIA field-worker in Washington, D.C., who accompanied Garvey on an organizational tour in Pennsylvania in 1920. He was appointed assistant counsel general for the UNIA in 1921–1923 and represented Garvey in private cases. Williams was born in Brown's Town, St. Anns, Jamaica, and moved to the United States in 1905. He worked in the settlement house movement prior to WORLD WAR I, graduated from New York University Law School, and practiced law in New York. In 1921 he married Doris Collins, who may have been related to Garvey loyalist Ethel Collins. He was nominated for the position of UNIA secretary general at the 1921 UNIA convention and was one of the signers of the UNIA petition to the League of Nations in July 1922. Williams resigned from the UNIA in a bitter disagreement with Garvey in August 1923. He formed the Consolidated Tenants League in New York in the 1930s and wrote several articles in defense of tenants' rights. He was also active in the Jamaica Progressive League (*NW,* 11 September 1920; *NYT,* 9 February 1952; *UNIA* v. *Vernal J. Williams,* no. 32717, New York Supreme Court, 1923, records on appeal; *WWCA; Garvey Papers* 2–6).

WILLIS, ANDREW N., of Bocas del Toro, Panama, was president of the Guabito, Panama, division of the UNIA, which served members in Panama and Costa Rica. He was a delegate to the 1920 UNIA convention and reported on the efforts of the UNITED FRUIT CO. to suppress the movement in Central America. He told the other delegates present that local ministers were on the salary of the American-based company and that they assisted the company in its repressive policies, urging their congregations to resist the appeals of UNIA organizers. Willis, a pastor himself by profession, signed the UNIA Declaration of Rights (*NW,* 17 July 1920; *Garvey Papers* 2).

WILSON, G. W., of Hartford, Conn., attended the 1920 UNIA convention and signed the UNIA Declaration of Rights. He represented Connecticut at a UNIA conference on the purchase of the S.S. *Phyllis Wheatley* at LIBERTY HALL in April 1921. The conference was attended by almost forty presidents of various branches from the West Indies and the United States (*Garvey Papers* 2, 3).

WILSON, WOODROW (1856–1924), lawyer, academician, and politician, was president of the United States during WORLD WAR I.

WINCHESTER RIFLE was a breech-loading repeating rifle marketed by the Winchester Repeating Arms Co. in the 1860s. It replaced single-shot breechloaders and muzzle-loading muskets, both widely used in the Civil War. The point Garvey makes in the School of African Philosophy was supported by Oliver Winchester himself. While advocating the repeater as the new standard-issue firearm for U.S. troops, Winchester voiced his worry over the possible ramifications of his invention. He warned that the change "may revolutionize the whole science of war," granting governments the capability of previously unknown efficiency in destruction (Duncan Barnes et al., *The History of Winchester Firearms, 1866–1980* [Tulsa, Okla.: Winchester Press, 1980], pp. 9–10).

WOLFE, JAMES (1727–1759), a British war hero, was second in command in the French and Indian Wars. He died in battle and became a favorite subject of romantic poets and painters.

WORLD WAR I (1914–1918) began after the assassination of Archduke Francis Ferdinand at Sarajevo in June 1914, when Austria-Hungary, supported by Germany, declared war on Serbia, Russia, and France, attacking France through Belgium and Luxembourg. Britain entered the war after Germany's violation of Belgian neutrality. Over the next three years Japan, Italy, Portugal, Romania, Greece, Australia, New Zealand, and the United States joined with the Western Allies in opposing the Central powers, which were backed by the Ottoman Empire. Fighting took place in the Middle East, Africa, and the Pacific, as well as on the western and eastern European fronts. The war was characterized by brutal trench warfare and the first widespread use of modern air raids, poison gas, submarines, and mechanized weapons. Over ten million people died in the fighting, with many more millions maimed and wounded or dead from starvation and disease (L. C. F. Turner, *Origins of the First World War* [1970; reprint, London: Edward Arnold, 1972]; Sidney Bradshaw Fay, *The Origins of the World War,* 2d rev. ed. [New York: Macmillan, 1930]; Robert Graves, *Goodbye to All That,* rev. ed. [London: Cassell & Co., 1957]).

WORLD WAR I, BLACKS IN. Blacks made up 13 percent of all Americans drafted for service in the First World War. With notable exceptions—such as the members of the decorated 369th U.S. Infantry (formerly the 15th New York Infantry, National Guard, of Harlem), the 370th U.S. Infantry (formerly the 8th Illinois Infantry), and the 371st and 372d regiments that served in France—the majority served in noncombat labor or stevedore batallions. Blacks were segregated in the armed services, directed mainly by white officers, relegated to low-status assignments, and subjected to severe discrimination while training or stationed in the United States. Black leaders like W. E. B. DU BOIS heralded the participation of blacks, hoping that their role as soldiers abroad would lead to greater civil rights at home; others, including A. Philip Randolph and CHANDLER OWEN, dissented from this view, stating that blacks should not fight to defend freedoms not extended to them within their own society. African soldiers took part in the war in Europe as well as in Africa; hundreds of thousands went to

Europe, and more than thirty thousand died there (A. D. Roberts, ed., *The Cambridge History of Africa*, vol. 7, *From 1905 to 1940* [London and Cambridge: Cambridge University Press, 1986], pp. 351–360; Morris J. MacGregor and Bernald C. Nalty, eds., *Blacks in the U.S. Armed Forces: Basic Documents* 4 [1917–1940] [Wilmington, Del.: Scholarly Resources, 1977]; Emmett J. Scott, *The American Negro in the World War* [n.p., 1919]; Arthur Barbeau and Florette Henri, *The Unknown Soldiers: Black American Troops in World War I* [Philadelphia: Temple University Press, 1974]; Jack D. Foner, "World War I and Black Servicemen," in *Blacks and the Military in American History* [New York: Prager, 1974], pp. 109–132).

WRIGHT, R. R. (1855–1947), educator, Republican politician, and a strong advocate of Negro rights, was the founder of the Citizens and Southern Bank and Trust Co. of Philadelphia and the first president of the National Bankers Association, a federation of black banks begun in 1926 (*Garvey Papers* 1–4).

S.S. *YARMOUTH,* the flag-ship of the BLACK STAR LINE, was purchased from the North American Steamship Co. in September 1919. JOSHUA COCKBURN, who was soon appointed as the first captain of the ship, participated as a broker in the negotiations, which resulted in agreement on a $165,000 purchase price to be paid in ten monthly installments. The *Yarmouth*—a small cargo ship formerly used for transatlantic shipping during WORLD WAR I and on a coal-hauling route between Nova Scotia and Boston—was thirty-two years old and in need of extensive repairs when it was acquired by the Black Star Line. Unofficially rechristened the S.S. *Frederick Douglass*, the ship made its maiden voyage for the Black Star Line in November 1919. It sailed to the West Indies and Central America and returned in January 1920. The voyage, which began with a glorious send-off from the 135th Street pier, was plagued by repair problems, controversies between officers, and disgruntlement on the part of crew members who were denied full wages. The *Yarmouth* was contracted to carry a cargo of whiskey to Cuba on its next trip; it left New York hurriedly after the passage of Prohibition in January 1920, listing badly as it departed. Two days later it was found sailing erratically and slowly sinking 101 miles outside of the harbor, manned by a drunken crew. It was towed back to port with assistance from the U.S. Coast Guard. Government agents temporarily seized its multimillion-dollar cargo. After further repairs, the *Yarmouth* was allowed to proceed with what cargo remained. It returned to the East Coast in May 1920, ran aground off Boston, and made one more trip to the West Indies under the direction of a different captain. In the autumn of 1920 it began to sink following a collision while at anchor in New York and had to be towed to dock for repairs. The Black Star Line was forced to defer its payments on the vessel; as of June 1920 the $44,779.71 income from the operation of the ship was overshadowed by $138,469.55 in operating losses, not including the costs incurred in the selling of stock and the payment of salaries, legal fees, and office expenses. In December 1921 the *Yarmouth* was sold (for $1,625) by court order at public auction to provide partial payment in settlement of a suit brought against the Black Star Line by the National Dry Dock and Repair Co. (*Black Moses,* pp. 53–56, 81–85; *Garvey Papers* 2–4).

YEARWOOD, JAMES BENJAMIN, was assistant secretary general of the UNIA in 1920–1925. Yearwood was born in Barbados and worked as a laborer on the Panama Canal before becoming a labor organizer and teacher in Panama. He opened a school in Panama City in 1915 and was active in organizing the West Indian community to provide school textbooks and supplies for the city's poor. He organized the Universal Loyal Negro Association (ULNA) in Panama and Costa Rica during WORLD WAR I. The organization supported the British cause in the war but also lobbied for better protection of black rights in British colonial regions. Yearwood attended the 1920 UNIA convention as a delegate from the ULNA and was elected a UNIA officer near the end of the proceedings. He subsequently encouraged ULNA members to support the UNIA. He was a member of the five-person UNIA delegation that met with Liberian president C. D. B. King at the Waldorf-Astoria Hotel in New York in March 1921. He attended the 1920, 1921, 1922, and 1924 UNIA conventions but resigned his post in 1925 (*Garvey Papers* 2–5).

YOUNG, JAMES, of Pittsburgh was a delegate to the 1920 UNIA convention and one of the signers of the UNIA Declaration of Rights. Young organized a series of meetings in Pittsburgh when Garvey and his entourage made an organizational tour of the city in September–October 1920. A Bureau of Investigation agent reported in October 1920 that Young was planning to organize the movement throughout Allegheny County, particularly among mill workers in Homestead and other mill towns (*Garvey Papers* 2, 3).

YOUNG MEN'S CHRISTIAN ASSOCIATION (YMCA), a nondenominational benevolent volunteer organization, began in London in 1844 and spread to North America in the 1850s. Several hundred black YMCA secretaries served as noncombatants at military camps in the United States and overseas under the direction of the Negro Men's Department of the International Committee in WORLD WAR I. The YMCA Commission on Interracial Co-operation was established in Atlanta in 1919, and in 1920 it recommended integration at staff and international committee levels. In 1922 the international YMCA convention approved a statement that the association should make greater outreach to black members and foster a closer working relationship between black and white leaders. The trend was not toward integration, however, but toward the creation of separate facilities for blacks. A 1936 study showed that a separate and unequal policy was indicative of the norm of operation in local areas, where black branches served a larger constituency than white and had a greater number of volunteers yet received less than half the amount of funding per constituent that white branches received (J. Howell Atwood, *The Racial Factor in YMCAs: A Report on Negro-White Relationships in Twenty-four Cities* [New York: Association Press, 1946], pp. v–vi, 113; Mayer N. Zald, *Organizational Change: The Political Economy of the YMCA* [Chicago: University of Chicago Press, 1970], pp. 146–152; C.

Howard Hopkins, "YMCA Race Relations Between the World Wars," in *History of the YMCA in North America* [New York: Association Press, 1951], pp. 540–543; W. Allison Sweeney, *History of the American Negro in the Great World War* [1919; reprint, New York: Negro Universities Press, 1969], pp. 248–253).

YOUNG WOMEN'S CHRISTIAN ASSOCIATION (YWCA), a federation of women's organizations that grew out of the prayer union–boardinghouse movement of mid-nineteenth-century Britain, was dedicated to promoting the religious training and social welfare of young working girls. The local Ladies' Christian Union of New York (1858) and the Young Women's Christian Association of Boston (1866) were forerunners of the movement in the United States. The national Young Women's Christian Associations of the United States was formed in 1906, and national headquarters were established in New York City in 1912. Unlike the YMCA, the YWCA became actively involved in controversial social reform issues, including temperance, labor reform, unionization, and pacificism. Like the YMCA, the YWCA had an official policy of racial integration (instituted in 1946), which was infrequently reflected in local practice. A black YWCA was organized in Dayton, Ohio, in 1893, and other black branches affiliated with the national YWCA movement before it was formalized in 1906. Although some black leaders served on boards of directors and as representatives to national conventions in the 1920s and 1930s, segregation still characterized racial relations within the organization (J. Howell Atwood, *The Racial Factor in YMCAs: A Report on Negro-White Relationships in Twenty-four Cities* [New York: Association Press, 1946], pp. 147, 154; Alice Dunbar Nelson, "Negro Women in War Work," in *The American Negro in the World War*, ed. Emmett J. Scott, [n.p., 1919], pp. 374–397; Mary S. Sims, *The Natural History of a Social Institution* [New York: Woman's Press, 1936]; idem, *The YWCA—An Unfolding Purpose* [New York: Woman's Press, 1950], pp. 34–35, 71–72).

ZULU are people of the historic region of Zululand, now part of Natal Province, Republic of South Africa. The Zulu actively resisted white settlement. Thousands were killed in the Battle of Blood River in 1838, when they encountered the disciplined musket and cannon fire of the Voortrekker forces while armed mainly with spears. The British invaded Zululand in 1879, suffering a major defeat at the hands of the Zulu at Isandhlwana before occupying Ulundi and driving the Zulu ruler Cetshwayo into temporary exile. Zululand was partitioned and its army disbanded. It was annexed by the British in 1887 and made part of Natal Province in 1897 (Monica Wilson and Leonard Thompson, eds., *The Oxford History of South Africa*, 2 vols. [London: Oxford University Press, 1969, 1971], 1: 336–364, 2: 261–267, 464–465; Brian Roberts, *The Zulu Kings* [New York: Charles Scribner's Sons, 1974]).

BIBLIOGRAPHY
AND ACKNOWLEDGMENTS

There are many available sources on the thought of Marcus Garvey and the history of the Garvey movement. Amy Jacques Garvey's compilation of Garvey's speeches and writings, *Philosophy and Opinions of Marcus Garvey,* was originally issued as two separate volumes, *Philosophy and Opinions of Marcus Garvey* (New York: Universal Publishing House, 1923; reprint, San Francisco: Julian Richardson, Associates, 1967) and *Philosophy and Opinions of Marcus Garvey; or, Africa for the Africans* (New York: Universal Publishing House, 1925). Reprint editions of the combined volumes include those issued by London's Frank Cass and Company in 1967 and New York's Atheneum Press in 1969. *Philosophy and Opinions* remains a classic, as does Jacques Garvey's memoir, *Garvey and Garveyism* (Kingston: private printing, 1963; reprint, New York: Collier, 1976). Len Nembhard's memorial edition of *Trials and Triumphs of Marcus Garvey* (Kingston: Gleaner Co., 1940) is the first, though little known, book-length essay on the life and thought of Garvey. The first major scholarly study of Garvey's career, E. David Cronon's *Black Moses: The Story of Marcus Garvey* (Madison: University of Wisconsin Press, 1955), is still a popular source on the UNIA leader's life and the business affairs of his organization. Newer additions to the biographical study of Garvey and the significance of the Garvey movement include Theodore Vincent's *Black Power and the Garvey Movement* (Berkeley, Calif.: Ramparts Press, 1971); John Henrik Clarke's anthology, compiled with the assistance of Amy Jacques Garvey, *Marcus Garvey and the Vision of Africa* (New York: Random House, 1974); Tony Martin's *Race First* (Westport, Conn.: Greenwood Press, 1976); W. F. Elkins's *Black Power in the Caribbean: The Beginnings of the Modern Nationalist Movement* (Brooklyn: Revisionist Press, 1977); Randall K. Burkett's *Black Redemption: Churchmen Speak for the Garvey Movement* (Philadelphia: Temple University Press, 1978) and *Garveyism as a Religious Movement: The Institutionalization of a Black Civil Religion* (Metuchen, N.J.: Scarecrow Press, 1978); Judith Stein's *The World of Marcus Garvey: Race and Class in Modern Society* (Baton Rouge: Louisiana State University Press, 1986); and Rupert Lewis's *Marcus Garvey: Anti-Colonial Champion* (London: Karia Press, 1987). Emory J. Tolbert's monograph, *The UNIA and Black Los Angeles* (Los Angeles: Center of Afro-American Studies, University of California, Los Angeles, 1980), is a contribution to the study of the UNIA on the local divisional level, and Lenwood G. Davis's and Janet Sims's *Marcus Garvey: An Annotated Bibliography* (Westport, Conn.: Greenwood Press, 1980) is a compilation of sources on the UNIA leader's career. Papers originally presented at the International Seminar on Marcus Garvey sponsored by the African Studies Association of the West Indies at Mona, Jamaica, in January 1973, have recently been reprinted as *Garvey, Africa, Europe, and the Americas,* edited by Rupert Lewis and Maureen Warner-Lewis (Kingston: Institute of Social and Economic Research, University of the West Indies, 1986).

The Schomburg Center for Research in Black Culture, New York Public Library, New York, holds important primary materials on the history of the UNIA in New York in its archives, including the surviving records of the UNIA Central Division. Fisk University, Nashville, houses the Amy Jacques Garvey and Marcus Garvey Memorial collections. The National Archives and Records Service, Washington, D.C., is also an important repository of materials about the Garvey movement.

Documentary compilations of the work of Marcus Garvey include *The Black Man: A Monthly Magazine of Negro Thought and Opinion,* edited by Robert A. Hill (Millwood, N.Y.: Kraus-Thomson, 1975) and *More Philosophy and Opinions of Marcus Garvey,* edited by E.U. Essien-Udom and Amy Jacques Garvey (London: Frank Cass and Co., 1977). Tony Martin has compiled *The Poetical Works of Marcus Garvey* (Dover, Mass.: Majority Press, 1983); *Literary Garveyism: Garvey, Black Arts, and the Harlem Renaissance* (Dover, Mass.: Majority Press, 1983); and *Message to the People: The Course of African Philosophy* (Dover, Mass.: Majority Press, 1986). The most comprehensive documentary edition of primary documents on Garvey and the Garvey movement is the *Marcus Garvey and Universal Negro Improvement Papers,* published by the University of California Press and produced by the Marcus Garvey and UNIA Papers project, African Studies Center, University of California, Los Angeles. It will eventually include volumes dealing with the impact of Garvey and the UNIA in North America, Latin America, the Caribbean, Europe, and Africa.

The Marcus Garvey and UNIA Papers project wishes to thank Bernard Stanley Hoyes for use of the original watercolor portrait of Marcus Garvey featured on the cover. Linda Robertson designed the volume, and Sylvia Tidwell copy edited the manuscript. The project acknowledges with special gratitude the support and assistance of James Kubeck of the University of California Press, the sponsoring editor of the Marcus Garvey Papers edition from its inception, who retired in 1986. Thanks are also extended to Stanley Holwitz, assistant director, Richard Lucas, director of marketing, and the entire staff of the University of California Press for their ongoing support of the project's work.

The exemplary staff members of the Marcus Garvey and UNIA Papers project all contributed to the preparation of this volume. Research assistance was provided by Allison Shutt. Editorial and production assistance was rendered by R. Kent Rasmussen and Edith Johnson. The text was transcribed and computer-coded by Diane L. Hill and Tracy Chriss. The manuscript was typeset by Stephen Gil de Montes using the TYXSET computer typesetting system. Technical assistance was graciously provided by the staff of the TYX Corporation, Reston, Virginia, and by Khanh Ha of Macrotype, Incorporated, Silver Spring, Maryland.

Goldie Stewart, widow of James Stewart, president general of the UNIA following the death of Marcus Garvey, and Elinor Robinson White, UNIA commissioner of Illinois and one of the original graduates of the School of African Philosophy in 1937, provided the project with original copies of Garvey's lessons from the School of African Philosophy. Mason Hargrave, current president general of the UNIA in Cleveland, provided additional documentation. The photograph appearing as the frontispiece, an official UNIA portrait of Garvey taken around 1923–1924 and autographed by the UNIA leader, appeared on the 1925 poster version of "African Fundamentalism," sold by the UNIA through advertisements in the *Negro World*.

The Marcus Garvey and UNIA Papers project is sponsored by the National Historical Publications and Records Commission, the National Endowment for the Humanities, and the University of California, Los Angeles. It is also supported by grants from the Ford Foundation and the Rockefeller Foundation.

We would like to express our appreciation to the New York African American Institute, which has cosponsored this centennial companion to the *The Marcus Garvey and UNIA Papers*. We extend special thanks to A. J. Williams-Meyers, acting director of the New York African American Institute, and Kenneth O. Hall, assistant vice chancellor for academic programs for the State University of New York and member of the advisory council and policy committee of the institute. The New York African American Institute was established in 1986 as a policy and research center for the study of black history and society in New York. It was created largely through the initiative of Arthur O. Eve, deputy speaker of the New York State Assembly.

Let us cheer the weary traveler,
    cheer the weary traveler;
Let us cheer the weary traveler,
    along the heavenly way.

AMERICAN NEGRO SPIRITUAL